Managing Airports

Managing Airports presents a comprehensive and cutting-edge insight into today's international airport industry.

Approaching management topics from a strategic and commercial perspective, rather than from an operational and technical viewpoint, the book provides an innovative insight into the processes behind running a successful airport. This fourth edition has been fully revised and updated to reflect the many important developments in the management of airports and issues facing the aviation industry since the third edition. This edition features:

- New content on: coping with an increasingly volatile and uncertain operating environment, social media and other trends in technology, the evolving airport–airline relationship, responding to sustainability pressures and new security policies.
- New chapter focusing on service quality and the passenger experience, reflecting the increasing need for airports to offer wide-ranging high-quality services to their diverse customer base to remain competitive and to achieve high satisfaction levels.
- Updated and new international case studies to show recent issues and theory in practice. New case studies on emerging economies including China, India and Brazil.

Accessible and up to date, *Managing Airports* is ideal for students, lecturers and researchers of transport and tourism, and practitioners within the air transport industry.

Anne Graham is a Reader in Air Transport and Tourism at the University of Westminster, UK.

Managing Airports

An international perspective

Fourth edition

Anne Graham

Routledge
Taylor & Francis Group

LONDON AND NEW YORK

First edition published 2001 by Elsevier
Third edition published 2008 by Elsevier
Fourth edition published 2014
by Routledge
2 Park Square, Milton Park, Abingdon, Oxon OX14 4RN

and by Routledge
270 Madison Ave, New York, NY 10016

Routledge is an imprint of the Taylor & Francis Group, an informa business

British Library Cataloguing in Publication Data
A catalogue record for this book is available from the British Library

Library of Congress Cataloging in Publication Data
A catalogue record for this book is available from the British Library
    Graham, Anne.
    Managing airports: an international perspective / Anne Graham.—4th edition.
      pages cm
    "Simultaneously published in the USA and Canada" —Title page verso.
    Previous edition: 2008.
    Includes bibliographical references and index.
    1. Airports—Management.   I. Title.
    TL725.3.M2G73 2013
    387.7'36068—dc23

                                                                    2013005290

ISBN: 978-0-415-52941-9 (pbk)
ISBN: 978-0-415-52940-2 (hbk)
ISBN: 978-0-203-11789-2 (ebk)

Typeset in Times New Roman
by RefineCatch Limited, Bungay, Suffolk

Printed in Great Britain by Bell & Bain Ltd, Glasgow

Contents

Figures

Tables

Case studies

Preface

When the first edition of this book was published in 2001, the airport industry had received relatively little attention in the printed literature and had been very much overshadowed by the airline sector. Hence the motivation for writing the book. Shortly after publication, the airport sector had to cope with the unparalleled consequences of the events of 9/11, the Iraq War, the outbreak of SARS and the continuing threat of terrorism. These issues were considered in the book's second edition, published in 2003. At the time of writing that edition, it was unclear what the longer-term impacts of these events would be. Five years on, the third edition in 2008 concluded that 9/11 had been a significant turning point for the industry and that since then it had been operating in a much more unstable environment. This was not just due to security concerns, but also because of changing airline structures and increased environmental pressures. Another five years have passed, and the world has experienced a severe global economic crisis, political unrest and a number of natural disasters. Hence an uncertain environment remains, and arguably is even more volatile.

While considerably more has now been written about the airport industry, there is still a comparative dearth of literature focusing on the up-to-date managerial and business aspects of running an airport. The aim of this book, as of previous editions, is to provide a comprehensive appreciation of the key management issues facing modern-day airport operators. As well as providing an up-to date review of the latest developments and trends, the discussion concerning the airport–airline relationship has been developed further to cover issues such as long-term contracts and the differentiation of airport services and facilities. Similarly, more attention is paid to the passenger experience and the factors that affect it. Numerous other new and diverse topics are covered, including the use of body security scanners; near-field communication technology; airport sister agreements; impacts of passenger taxes; airport carbon accreditation schemes; and social media applications.

Airports are now complex businesses requiring a range of competencies and skills. The emphasis here is on the economic, commercial and planning areas at a strategic level. The approach adopted reflects the international nature of most of the industry. The book uses material from a wide range of airports and has a very practical focus. New case studies cover recent topics and reflect the shift of economic power and corresponding traffic growth to Asia and other emerging economies. The book provides an overview of the key management challenges facing airports, so by necessity the scope is far-reaching. The book will enable the reader to acquire a broad, up-to-date insight into the workings of the industry that will meet the needs of anyone who wishes to work, or is already working, in the airport sector.

Acknowledgements

I am extremely grateful to all my colleagues, students, family and friends who have helped me in pursuing my passion to write about airports. I am also very appreciative of the enormous support from the team at Routledge, particularly Emma Travis, Philippa Mullins, and Peter Lloyd.

A very special thanks goes to Ian, Lorna, Callum and Ewan.

Abbreviations

AAHK	Airport Authority Hong Kong
AAI	Airport Authority of India
ACCC	Australian Competition and Consumer Commission
A-CDM	airport collaborative decision-making
ACI	Airports Council International
ACSA	Airports Company South Africa
AdP	Aéroports de Paris
AENA	Aeropuertos Espanoles y Navegacion Aerea
AGI	Airports Group International
AIP	Airport Improvement Program
APD	Air Passenger Duty
API	Advanced Passenger Information
ARI	Aer Rianta International
ASAS	Airport Surface Access Strategy
ASQ	Airport Service Quality
ATC	Air Traffic Control
ATF	Airport Transport Forum
ATM	air transport movement
ATU	Airport Throughput Unit
BA	British Airways
BAA	British Airports Authority (prior to 1987; from 1987 the company was known only as BAA; in 2012 it changed its name to Heathrow Airport Holdings)
BCBP	bar-coded boarding pass
BCIA	Beijing Capital International Airport
BOT	build, operate, transfer
BRIC	Brazil, Russia, India and China
BSCA	Brussels South Charleroi Airport
BSP	Billing and Settlement Plan
CAA	Civil Aviation Authority
CAAC	Civil Aviation Administration of China
CAEP	Committee on Aviation Environmental Protection

CAPEX	capital expenditure
CDA	continuous descent approach
CDG	Charles de Gaulle
CO_2	carbon dioxide
CPH	Copenhagen Airport A/S
CUSS	common-use self-service check-in
CUTE	common-use terminal equipment
DAA	Dublin Airport Authority
DDF	Dubai Duty Free
DEA	data envelopment analysis
DMU	decision-making unit
EBIT	earnings before interest and tax
EBITDA	earnings before interest, tax, depreciation and amortisation
ECAC	European Civil Aviation Conference
EDS	explosive detective system
EEA	European Economic Area
EMAS	Eco Management and Audit Scheme
ETS	Emissions Trading Scheme
EU	European Union
EV	enterprise value
F&B	food and beverage
FAA	Federal Aviation Administration
FAC	Federal Airports Corporation
GA	general aviation
GAO	General Accounting Office (US)
GDP	gross domestic product
GIP	global infrastructure partners
GRI	Global Reporting Initiative
HNA	Hainan Airline Group
HTA	Hochtief Airport
IATA	International Air Transport Association
ICAO	International Civil Aviation Organization
IPO	initial public offering
ISO	International Organization for Standardization
KPI	key performance indicator
LAGs	liquids, aerosols, gels
LCC	low-cost carrier
LCT	low-cost terminal
LOS	level of service
LTO	landing and take-off
MAP	Macquarie Airports
MAW	maximum authorised weight
MBMs	market-based measures
MCT	minimum connect time
MIDT	market information data tapes

MII	majority in interest
MLIT	Ministry of Land, Infrastructure, Transport and Tourism
MPPA	million passengers per annum
MRTD	machine-readable travel document
MTOW	maximum take-off weight
NFC	near-field communication
NRI	non-resident Indian
NOX	nitrogen oxide
OAG	official airline guide
OFT	Office of Fair Trading
PFC	passenger facility charge
PIATCO	Philippine International Air Terminals Co.
PNR	passenger name records; preferred noise route
POS	point of sale
PRM	people with reduced mobility
PSO	public service obligation
PPA	passengers per annum
PPP	public–private partnership
PSC	passenger service charge
QSI	quality service index
QSM	Quality of Survey Monitor
RAB	regulated asset base
RDF	Route Development Fund
RFID	radio frequency identification
RLT	rehabilitate, lease or rent and transfer
ROCE	return on capital employed
ROR	rate of return
ROT	rehabilitate, operate and transfer
SARS	severe acute respiratory syndrome
SDR	special drawing right
SLA	service-level agreement
SPT	simplifying passenger travel
STEBS	standard tamper-evident bags
TFP	total factor productivity
TSA	transport security administration
WACC	weighted average cost of capital
WLU	work load unit
UNWTO	United Nations World Tourism Organization
VFR	visiting friends and relatives
YVRAS	Vancouver Airport Services

1 Introduction

Airports are an essential part of the air transport system. They provide all the infrastructure needed to enable passengers and freight to transfer from surface to air modes of transport and to allow airlines to take off and land. The basic airport infrastructure consists of runways, taxiways, apron space, gates, passenger and freight terminals, and ground transport interchanges. Airports bring together a wide range of facilities and services in order to fulfil their role within the air transport industry. These services include air traffic control, security, and fire and rescue in the airfield. Handling facilities are provided so that passengers, their baggage and freight can be transferred successfully between aircraft and terminals, and processed within the terminal. Airports also offer a wide variety of commercial facilities ranging from shops and restaurants to hotels, conference services and business parks.

As well as playing a crucial role within the air transport sector, airports have a strategic importance to the regions they serve. In a number of countries they are increasingly becoming integrated within the overall transport system by establishing links to high-speed rail and key road networks. Airports can bring greater wealth, provide substantial employment opportunities and encourage economic development – and can be a lifeline to isolated communities. However, they do have a very significant effect, both on the environment in which they are located and on the quality of life of residents living nearby. Growing awareness of general environmental issues has heightened environmental concerns about airports.

The focus of this book is on management issues facing airport operators. These operators vary considerably in their ownership, management structure and style, degree of autonomy, and funding. Typically, airport operators themselves provide only a small proportion of an airport's facilities and services. The rest of these activities are undertaken by airlines, handling agents, government agencies, concessionaires and other specialist organisations. The way in which operators choose to provide the diverse range of airport facilities can have a major impact on their economic and operational performance and on their relationship with their customers.

Each airport operator will thus have a unique identity, but all have to assume overall control and responsibility at the airport. Each will be faced with the challenging task of coordinating all the services to enable the airport system to work efficiently. The providers of services are just some of the airport stakeholders that operators need to consider. Others include shareholders, airport users, employees, local residents, environmental lobbyists and government bodies. A complex situation exists, with many of these groups having different interests and possibly holding conflicting views about the strategic role of the airport. All the stakeholder relationships are important, but the development of a good relationship with the airlines is critical as ultimately this will largely determine the air services on offer at the airport.

Globally the airport industry is dominated by the regions of Europe, Asia/Pacific and North America in terms of passenger numbers (Figure 1.1) and Asia/Pacific and North America in terms of cargo tonnes (Figure 1.2). In total, Airports Council International (ACI) airports handled 5,400 million passengers, 93 million cargo tonnes and 77 million aircraft movements in 2011.

The importance of these three global regions is reflected in the individual traffic figures of the various airports (Figures 1.3–1.5). Out of the 20 largest global airports, seven are US airports, seven are Asia/Pacific airports and five are European (Figure 1.3). Not all the major cargo airports coincide with the major passenger airports. Memphis is the world's second largest cargo airport because FedEx is based there. Similarly, UPS has its base at Louisville. In terms of aircraft movements, North American airports tend to have comparatively high numbers because the average size of aircraft is smaller due to competitive pressures and the dominance of domestic traffic. The larger-than-average aircraft size in Asia means that none of the busiest airports in terms of movements is situated in this region, except for Beijing.

The aviation industry has been growing virtually continuously since the Second World War, with periodic fluctuations due to economic recessions or other external factors such as the Gulf War in 1991. However, this growth was dramatically halted due to the events of 9/11 in 2001 combined with a global economic downturn. Since then, the airport industry has experienced a number of volatile years, with further incidents including the outbreaks of SARS (2003) and swine flu (2009), the Eyjafjallajökull ash cloud (2010), the Japanese earthquake (2011) and the

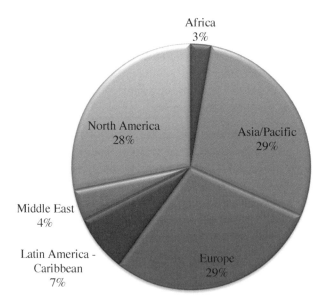

Figure 1.1 *Airport passengers by world region, 2011*
Source: ACI

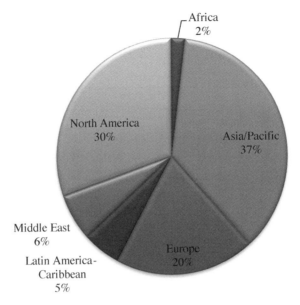

Figure 1.2 *Airport cargo tonnes by world region, 2011*
Source: ACI

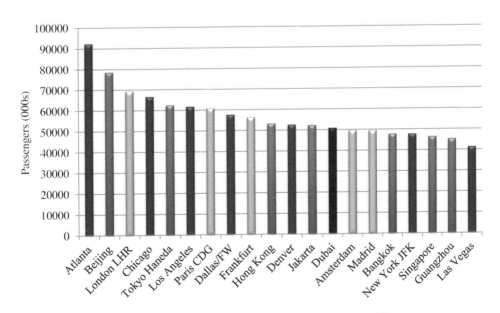

Figure 1.3 *The world's 20 largest airports by total passengers, 2011*
Source: ACI

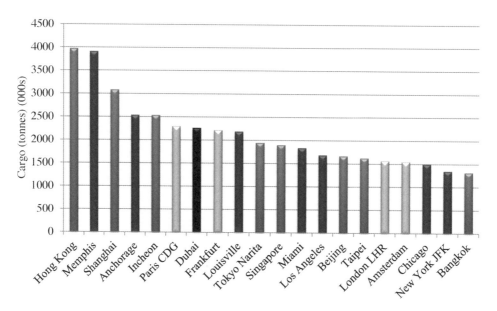

Figure 1.4 *The world's 20 largest airports by cargo tonnes, 2011*
Source: ACI

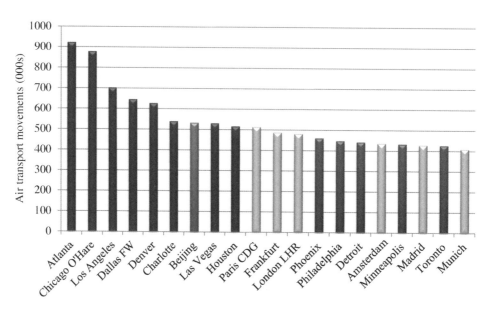

Figure 1.5 *The world's 20 largest airports by aircraft movements, 2011*
Source: ACI

Arab Spring uprisings (2010–12). These events have had various impacts in different world regions, as illustrated by Figure 1.6. For example, the influence of SARS in the Asia/Pacific region in 2003 can be seen clearly, as can the effect of the social and political unrest due to the Arab Spring uprisings in the African region in 2011. Of major significance almost everywhere was the global credit crunch and economic recession, which had a devastating impact on traffic in 2008 and 2009. Traffic growth returned for all regions in 2010 and 2011 (except Africa), but slowed down towards the second half of 2012 (full year figures are not yet available), particularly in Europe because of the continuing economic uncertainties due to the Eurozone crisis.

In 1999, North America had 47 per cent of the global market share of passenger numbers, followed by Europe with 30 per cent. Traffic in Asia/Pacific accounted for just 15 per cent of the total. Since then the share of traffic in this region has increased dramatically, particularly in China, where Beijing was the second largest airport in the world in 2011 with nearly 80 million passengers – having been in only ninth position with around 50 million passengers five years earlier. All the so-called BRIC countries (Brazil, Russia, India and China) have experienced higher-than-average growth in recent years. In addition, the Middle East area has seen very significant increases in traffic volumes, particular at Dubai airport, which handled over 50 million passengers in 2011 compared with fewer than 30 million in 2006.

The growth in demand for air transport has had very significant economic and environmental consequences for both the airline and airport industries. Moreover, since the 1970s there have been major regulatory and structural developments, which have profoundly affected the way in which the two industries operate. Initially most change was experienced within the airline sector as a consequence of airline deregulation, privatisation and globalisation trends. The pace of change was slower in the airport industry, but now this sector, too, has developed into a

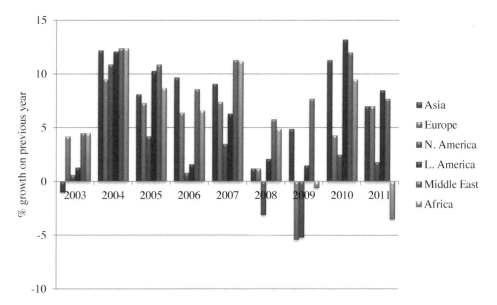

Figure 1.6 *Airport passenger growth by main region, 2003–11*
Source: ACI

fundamentally different business. The trend towards airline deregulation began in 1978 with the deregulation of the US domestic market. Many more markets were subsequently liberalised or deregulated, initially as the result of the adoption of more liberal bilateral air service agreements. In the European Union (EU), deregulation was achieved with a multilateral policy that evolved over a number of years with the introduction of the three deregulation packages in 1987, 1990 and 1993. The 1993 package, which did not become fully operational until 1997, was the most significant and had the most far-reaching impact. This European deregulation allowed a large low-cost carrier (LCC) industry to develop, which has had major consequences for many airports. This deregulation trend has continued in other parts of the world, a very significant milestone being the introduction of the EU–US open aviation area in 2008.

At the same time as the airline industry was being deregulated, airline ownership patterns changed. Most carriers, with the notable exception of those in the United States, traditionally were state owned and often were subsidised by their government owners. However, this situation has changed substantially as an increasing number of governments have opted for partially or totally private sector airline ownership, primarily to reduce the burden on public sector expenditure and to encourage greater operating efficiency. The other most significant development within the airline industry, partly due to deregulation and privatisation trends, has been the globalisation of the industry and the emergence of transnational airlines. Three major alliance groupings – Star, oneworld and Sky Team – have emerged with global networks. They dominate the airline business, accounting for over half of all traffic. Airline joint ventures and mergers have followed and are becoming increasingly popular, for example with Delta/Northwest and United/Continental in the United States, and Air France/KLM and British Airways/Iberia in Europe.

The airports found themselves caught up in this environment of change. Radical restructuring occurred, which in many ways mirrored that which had fundamentally changed the airline industry. Three key developments have been witnessed within the airport sector, as follows.

1. **Airport commercialisation**. The transformation of an airport from a public utility to a commercial enterprise and the adoption of a more business-like management philosophy.
2. **Airport privatisation**. The transfer of the management of an airport, and in many cases the ownership as well, to the private sector by a variety of methods. These include share flotations, the adoption of strategic partnerships and the introduction of private management contracts.
3. **Airport ownership diversification**. The emergence of a number of different types of new investors and operators of airports, such as financial investors and infrastructure companies, some of which have interests in a number of airports around the world.

This book discusses the implications of the development of the airport sector, which has moved from an industry characterised by public sector ownership and national requirements, into a new era of airport management where the private sector and international airport companies play a major role. Airports are now complex enterprises that require a wide range of business competencies and skills – just as any other industry. Airports no longer see their purpose simply as providers of infrastructure, but rather as providing facilities to meet the needs of their users.

Chapter 2 describes the changes in ownership and management models that have taken place, and reviews the current structure of the airport industry. These developments have had a major impact on airport economics and have significantly increased the need to benchmark performance, which is considered in Chapter 3. These airport industry trends, occurring at the same time as deregulation within the airline industry, have also meant that the traditional airline–airport relationship has been changed irreversibly. Chapter 4 looks at this, focusing primarily on airport charging, regulation and slots issues.

As the airport sector evolves, it has begun to focus on serving the needs of different types of customer rather than offering a more generic product that appeals to all. This is discussed in Chapter 5, as are regulatory and technological developments that are occurring in essential passenger processes such as security, border control and check-in. The consequences of these developments are assessed in Chapter 6, which considers the 'passenger experience' and the challenges in achieving overall passenger satisfaction, which has become a major concern for many airports.

A key consequence of airport commercialisation and privatisation trends is that airport operators are devoting much more time and effort to building up the non-aeronautical or commercial areas of the business. Chapter 7 looks in detail at this area of operation. Airport competition, hardly considered a relevant issue by many airports just one or two decades ago, is also becoming increasingly important. Marketing, which for so long has been a basic business competence in most other industries, but largely ignored in the past by many airports, is now a firmly accepted management practice at airports.

The remaining chapters take a broader view of the airport business and consider the role airports play in the environment and surrounding communities. This needs to be clearly understood if future growth in the airport industry is to continue. Chapter 8 discusses the economic impacts of airports and how they can act as catalysts for business and tourism development. Chapter 9 goes on to consider the environmental impacts and ways in which airports are attempting to minimise the adverse effects. Finally, Chapter 10 brings together the key issues in order to make predictions for the coming years and to assess the future prospects for the industry.

2 The structure of the airport industry

TRADITIONAL AIRPORT OWNERSHIP AND MANAGEMENT

The aim of this chapter is to discuss the structure of the airport industry, particularly in terms of the ownership and governance models that are used. It traces the development of the airport sector as it has moved from an industry characterised by public sector ownership and national requirements into a changed era of airport management, where the private sector and international companies play a significant role.

Virtually all airports were traditionally owned by the public sector. European airports serving major cities such as Paris, London, Dublin, Stockholm, Copenhagen, Madrid and Geneva were all owned by national governments, as were many other airports outside Europe, such as those in Tokyo, Singapore, Bangkok, Sydney and Johannesburg. Elsewhere, local governments, either at a regional or municipal level, were the airport owners. This was the situation with most US airports. Regional airports in the United Kingdom also followed this pattern. Manchester airport, for example, was owned by a consortium of local authorities, with 55 per cent ownership resting with Manchester City Council and the remaining 45 per cent split evenly among eight councils of other nearby towns. In Germany, Dusseldorf airport was jointly owned by the governments of North Rhine, Westphalia state and the city of Dusseldorf, while the joint owners of Hanover airport were the governments of the state of Lower Saxony and the city of Hanover.

With a number of airports, there may have been both local and national government interest. For example, Frankfurt airport was jointly owned by the state of Hesse (45 per cent), the city of Frankfurt (29 per cent) and the federal government (26 per cent). Similarly, Amsterdam was owned by the national government (76 per cent) and the municipalities of Amsterdam (22 per cent) and Rotterdam (2 per cent). Vienna airport was another example, owned by the Republic of Austria (50 per cent), the Province of Lower Austria (25 per cent) and the city of Vienna (25 per cent). Basel–Mulhouse or EuroAirport, situated on the border between Switzerland and France, was a unique airport being jointly owned by the national governments of both Switzerland and France.

It was only in the 1990s that there started to be a significant presence of privately (or partially privately) owned airports. Before this, the only privately owned airports were small general aviation (GA) or aeroclub airports, and so the influence of the private sector on the airport industry was very limited. Thus public ownership – either at a local and/ or national level – used to be the norm. However, the way in which the government owners chose to operate or manage the airports varied quite significantly and had a major impact on the airport's degree of independence and autonomy. The strictest form of control existed when the airport was operated directly by a government department, typically the Civil Aviation Authority (CAA), Ministry of Transport or, in a few cases, the military. This was the common practice for airports in areas such as Asia, the Middle East, Africa and South America. In Canada, the National Department of Transport directly operated the 150 commercial Canadian airports. Within Europe, Greece was a good example of a country where airports were effectively run by the CAA.

In other cases, semi-autonomous bodies or companies, but still under public ownership, operated the airports. In some instances these organisations managed more than one airport, as was the situation in Europe with the British Airports Authority (BAA) and Aer Rianta Irish Airports. There were also airport authorities or companies that operated just one major airport. This was the case at Amsterdam airport and many of the German airports. In the United States, airport authorities also existed for some airports, such as the Minneapolis–Saint Paul Metropolitan Airports Commission. In a few cases there were multipurpose transport authorities, such as the Port Authority of New York and New Jersey or Massport in Boston, which operated other transport facilities as well as airports.

There were also a few examples of airports being operated on a concession basis for the central government. At the larger Italian airports (e.g. Venice, Milan), companies with public (usually local) shareholdings and perhaps some minority private shareholdings as well held the operating concession for a long-term period, such as 60 years at Milan airport. The concession could cover management of the total airport and handling services (e.g. Milan, Turin) or just some of the services such as terminal management and handling (e.g. Palermo). At French regional airports, the concessions were given to the local chambers of commerce with the national government retaining some control over the airfield facilities. At Zurich airport, the Zurich Airport Authority, which was owned by the Canton of Zurich, was responsible for the planning and overall operation of the airport and the airfield infrastructure, while a mixed public–private company, FIG, managed and constructed the terminal infrastructure.

MOVES TOWARDS COMMERCIALISATION

These publicly owned and often strictly controlled airports were historically regarded as public utilities with public service obligations (Doganis, 1992). Consequently commercial and financial management practices were not given top priority. In the 1970s and 1980s, however, as the air transport industry grew and matured, and as the first steps towards airline privatisation and deregulation took place, views about airport management began to change. Many airports gradually started to be considered much more as commercial enterprises and a more business-like management philosophy was adopted. Thus 'commercialisation' of the airport industry began to take place. The pace of change varied considerably in different parts of the world, with Europe generally leading the way. By contrast, airports in areas such as Africa and South America generally held on to more traditional attitudes towards airports and experienced less change.

Moves towards commercialisation were reflected in a number of different, interrelated developments. First, various airports loosened their links with their government owners. This was achieved with the establishment of more independent airport authorities or, in some cases, by corporatisation, which involved setting up an airport company with public sector shareholders. Such developments generally gave the airports more commercial and operational freedom, and sometimes opened the door to private sector investment and partnerships.

There had always been a number of airports, such as Amsterdam and Frankfurt, that had been run by airport corporations or companies. However, changing attitudes led to many more airport authorities and companies being established. For example, in 1972 the International Airports Authority of India was established to manage the country's four international airports, while in 1986 the domestic airports came under the control of the National Airports Authority. These two authorities merged in 1995. In Indonesia, two organisations – Angkasa Pura I and II, in charge of the airports in the east and west of the country, respectively – became public enterprises in 1987 and limited liability companies in 1993. Other examples included the Polish Airport State Enterprise established in 1987; the Federal Airport Corporation of Australia set up in 1988; Aeropuertos Espanoles y Navegacion Aerea (AENA) in Spain and the Kenya Airports Authority, both formed in 1991; and Avinor in Norway in 2003.

In some cases, such as Copenhagen airport (1991), the South African airports (1994), and more recently Narita airport (2004), the establishment of an airport corporation was undertaken primarily as an interim step towards airport privatisation. Likewise in 2005, with the larger 12 French regional airports (eight in France – Nice, Lyon, Toulouse, Marseille, Bordeaux, Nantes, Strasbourg and Montpelier; four overseas – Pointe-à-Pitre, Fort de France, Saint Denis-Réunion and Cayenne) a new ownership and management structure was agreed, with the ultimate aim of leading to some privatisation. The new legislation stated that the French government would remain the landowner but companies would be created and granted a long-term airport concession of a maximum of 40 years. Initially these companies would have only public shareholders, namely the French state (60 per cent), local authorities, and the chamber of commerce and industry, but there could be private investors later on (Villard, 2011). The companies have been created but there has been no private involvement as yet, partly as the result of the recent poor economic climate.

Canada is an interesting example where the management of many of the country's major airports, previously under the direct central control of Transport Canada, was passed over by way of long-term leases to individual non-profit-making authorities in the 1990s. The aim behind this was to improve efficiency and integrate each airport more closely with the local economy. The first airport authorities were set up for Montreal's two airports, Vancouver, Calgary and Edmonton in 1992. By 2000, control of over 100 Canadian airports had been transferred to local organisations (Caves and Gosling, 1999). In China too, the central government began a process of handing over airports to local government control in 1988 with Xiamen airport, and by 2004 all airports, with the exception of Beijing and those in Tibet, were operated by local government airport corporations (Zhang and Yuen, 2008).

Greater attention began to be paid to the commercial aspects of running an airport, such as financial management, non-aeronautical revenue generation and airport marketing. The operational aspects of the airport had traditionally overshadowed other areas, and most airport directors and senior management were operational specialists. However, the commercial functions of an airport were gradually recognised as being equally important and, as a result, the resources and staff numbers employed in these areas were expanded. Relatively underused practices, such as benchmarking financial performance and quality management techniques, also began to be accepted – albeit rather slowly at the start – by a growing number of airports as essential management tools. In some airports, the typical functional organisation structure, with different departments for finance, operations, administration and so on, was replaced with departments or business units focused more on customers' needs, such as airline or passenger services.

One of the most visible indications of moves towards commercialisation and an increased focus on treating the airport as a business was greater reliance being placed on non-aeronautical or commercial revenues. Aeronautical revenues, such as landing and passenger fees from the airlines, traditionally had been by far the most important source. For a number of airports, notably in Europe, non-aeronautical sources overtook aeronautical sources as being the most important revenue. For instance, this occurred at Amsterdam airport in 1984. This development was primarily the result of greater space being allocated to retail and other non-aeronautical facilities, the quality being improved and the range of commercial activities being expanded.

The airport industry historically had played a rather passive role towards marketing and responded to customer needs only when necessary. A more business-like approach to airport management, coupled with a more commercially driven and competitive airline industry, encouraged airports to play a much more active and proactive role. In the United Kingdom, for example, many airports set up marketing departments, started to use pricing tactics and promotional campaigns to attract new customers, and began to undertake market research (Humphreys, 1999).

In the past, because of government controls, it was sometimes very difficult to obtain financial accounts that gave a true indication of an airport's financial and economic performance. Often an airport would adopt public accounting practices specific to the country and would use public sector rather than more standard commercial procedures. This meant that comparisons with other organisations could not easily be made. Moreover, some airports were not considered as separate accounting units. This meant that the airport's costs and revenues were treated as just one item within the government department's overall financial accounts, and rarely were matched together to assess the profitability of the airport. In certain cases no separate balance sheet existed for the airport.

However, an increasing number of airports started adopting more commercial accounting practices in the 1970s and 1980s. This was often a direct result of the loosening of government links with the establishment of an airport authority or corporation. For instance, in the United Kingdom in 1987, all the major regional airports became public limited companies. This meant that the airports adopted commercial private sector accounting procedures. One example of this was that for the first time they showed depreciation as a measure of cost of capital. Similarly, when Geneva airport became an independent authority in 1994, it began to show a balance sheet and asset values in its annual accounts, which had previously been omitted.

WHY PRIVATISATION?

While the 1970s and 1980s were dominated by airport commercialisation, the 1990s was the decade when airport privatisation became a reality. But what is meant by 'airport privatisation'? It is a vague term that can have various meanings. In its broadest sense, it is usually associated with the transfer of economic activity or control from the public to the private sector. This involves the transfer of management to private hands, but not always ownership.

The theoretical arguments for and against privatisation of publicly owned organisations are well known. They have been fiercely debated over the years and are well documented (e.g. Beesley, 1997; Parker and Saal, 2003). Supporters of privatisation argue that it will reduce the need for public sector investment and provide access to the commercial markets. It will limit government control and interference and may increase an organisation's ability to diversify. It may bring about improved efficiency, greater competition and wider share ownership, and provide greater incentives for management and employees to perform well and be commercially focused. Moreover, governments may gain financially from converting fixed public assets into cash and subjecting the privatised firms to paying company taxes. On the other hand, opponents argue that privatisation may create a private monopoly that overcharges, delivers poor standards of service, invests inadequately and gives insufficient consideration to externalities such as controlling environmental impacts and maintaining social justice. Less favourable employment conditions may be adopted, with redundancies occurring, and compromises may be made with health and safety.

A number of developments within the air transport industry in the 1980s and 1990s specifically strengthened the case for airport privatisation in some countries (Freathy and O'Connell, 1998). First, the demand for air transport continued to grow and was predicted to do so well into the future. In some markets, notably Europe and North America, deregulation encouraged growth and meant that the existing airport capacity could not cope with this growth. Airport privatisation was seen as a way of injecting additional finance into the airport system to pay for the needed future investment. Moreover, one of the major traditional sources of airport financing, namely public sector funds, became increasingly scarce in the modern-day global economic climate as governments strove to reduce their public sector spending or to shift their focus onto non-revenue-earning activities that appeared to be more worthy, such as health and education.

From one viewpoint, airport privatisation can be seen as just an evolutionary stage of airport development. Airports have evolved from public sector utilities to commercial enterprises, and privatisation can be considered as commercialisation taken to its limits. Increased commercialisation has brought about healthy profits and market-oriented management. Airports have shown that they have the proven ability to meet private sector requirements. At the same time, the changes within the airline industry have inevitably had a major impact on the airport sector. The transformation from a predominantly publicly owned and state-controlled airline industry to a global competitive business with much more commercial freedom has forced many airports to have a much more customer-focused outlook when coping with their airline customers.

The increasing number of airport privatisations that are taking place throughout the world demonstrate the growing acceptance of this process as a method of tackling some of the challenges that many airports face in the twenty-first century. However, airport ownership and control is always likely to be a controversial area. For many countries, transferring airports, which are considered to be vital national or regional assets, to the private sector remains a politically sensitive policy. The inherently monopolistic position of some airports will also continue to be of concern to politicians and airport users. The fear is that priority will be given to shareholders or investors, and that user and community needs will be neglected. To some opponents, the privatisation of airports, which is in effect the air transport 'infrastructure', does not make sense. It can be argued that, unlike the situation with the airlines (air transport 'operators', competition among which can more easily be encouraged), airports have a greater tendency to be natural monopolies that cannot be duplicated. Views about privatisation vary considerably in different regions of the world, in different countries and even between local and central government bodies in individual countries. As a result, commercialisation has by no means always led to privatisation, and there are a number of examples of airports (such as Amsterdam in the Netherlands and Changi Singapore airport) that are run on a very commercial basis but remain controlled by the public sector.

THE PRIVATISATION TIMETABLE

The first major airport privatisation took place in the United Kingdom in 1987. This was the total flotation of shares of BAA, which at that time owned three London airports (Heathrow, Gatwick and Stansted) and four Scottish airports (Aberdeen, Edinburgh, Glasgow and Prestwick). This successful privatisation opened up the debate at many other airports as to whether they too should be privatised. However, in the next few years only a handful of airports were actually privatised. In the United Kingdom, this included Liverpool airport, which was partially privatised in 1990; East Midlands, totally privatised in 1993; and Belfast International, which was subject to a management buyout in 1994. Elsewhere in Europe and in other continents there was little evidence of definite moves towards privatisation, with the notable exceptions of Vienna and Copenhagen airports. In 1992, 27 per cent of shares in Vienna airport were floated, followed by a secondary offering of a further 21 per cent in 1996. Similarly, at Copenhagen airport there were share flotations of 25 per cent in 1994 and a further 24 per cent in 1995.

The year 1996 appeared to be a turning point for the airport industry, and the following few years saw airport privatisation becoming a much more popular option in many areas of the world. In that year, for instance, Bournemouth and Cardiff airports were privatised in the United Kingdom, and private involvement in the new Athens airport at Spata was agreed. Airports as diverse as Dusseldorf, Sanford Orlando, Naples, Rome, Birmingham, Bristol, Melbourne, Brisbane and Perth were partially or totally privatised in 1997. Further privatisations took place in 1998 in Australia as well as in South Africa, Argentina, and other destinations such as Luton, Stockholm Skavsta, Auckland, Wellington and Hanover. In 1999 and 2000, a number of airports in central and southern American countries, such as Mexico, the Dominican Republic, Chile, Costa Rica and Cuba, were privatised. There were also share flotations for Malaysian Airports, Beijing Capital International Airport (BCIA) and Zurich Airport. The first partially private financed Indian airport was opened in Cochin, Kerala in southern India, having been financed 26 per cent from the state of Kerala and the rest from non-resident Indians (NRIs), financial institutions, and airport service providers.

In 2001, privatisation occurred at airports as varied as Frankfurt, Newcastle, Seeb and Salahah in Oman, and Sharm El Sheikh in Egypt. However, by the end of the year the events of 9/11, coupled with an economic downturn and airline failures in some regions, meant that airport privatisation temporarily became a less attractive option, and various privatisations at airports such as Milan, Brussels and Sydney were postponed or cancelled. As the air transport industry continued to be affected by external events such as the Iraq War and SARS, very few new privatisations took place in 2002 and 2003 – with the notable exceptions of Sydney and Malta. But by 2004 there were signs that airport privatisation was back on the agenda for a number of airports, for example with the successful privatisation of Brussels, and with agreements being reached to develop two greenfield airport sites in India, namely Bengaluru and Hyderabad, partially through private investment. Further privatisations followed in 2005, for instance in Cyprus (Larnaca and Paphos), Budapest and Venice. In 2006 a number of other airports, such as Paris, Kosice in Slovakia, Varna and Burgas in Bulgaria, and the regional airports in Peru, were partially or fully privatised. In the same year, private involvement at the main Indian airports of Delhi and Mumbai was agreed. In 2007–08, airport privatisation activity took place at Xi'an airport in China, in Pisa, Leeds-Bradford, the Macedonian airports of Skopje and Ohrid (although with a start date postponed until 2010), Antalya and Amman.

However, in 2009 this second burst of privatisation activity was again virtually brought to a halt primarily because of the onset of the credit crunch and the global economic recession. Active privatisation projects for airports such as Prague and Chicago Midway were postponed or cancelled. A very quiet period followed in the next couple of years, with only a handful of airport privatisations, for example at St Petersburg, Pristina, Male and Brussels Charleroi airports, and also with a few secondary sales, such as at the airports of Gatwick and Bristol. Prices for airports fell considerably in these years, but so did the availability of investment funds.

There are currently a number of airport privatisations in the pipeline. Edinburgh has just been sold and this has been followed by Stansted. Elsewhere in Europe, governments may be viewing privatisation as a way to restore some health to struggling public sector finances. This was the case with the planned privatisations of Madrid and Barcelona, which have now been postponed due to a change in government. There is also considerable uncertainty as to the future partial government shareholding of Athens airport. In Italy in December 2011, it was agreed that 30 per cent of SEA, the Milan airport company, would be sold to the Italian investment fund F2i (the same fund that bought a major shareholding in Naples in 2010), and Genoa airport is also planning to sell 60 per cent of its shares. In December 2012 in Portugal, ANA (which runs Lisbon, Porto, Faro, Santa Maria, Ponta Delgada, Horta and Flores airports) was sold to Vinci. There may also be privatisation of French regional airports, which has not happened as quickly as was planned. Privatisation has been discussed for the Dublin Airport Authority (DAA) or perhaps just its subsidiary Aer Rianta International. There have been a number of privatisations in South East and Eastern Europe as well as Central Asia (Zagreb being the latest privatisation in 2012), and it is likely that there will be more activity in these areas as investment funds and expertise are being sought to modernise a number of these airports, particularly in areas such as Russia, the Balkans, Poland and Bulgaria.

There seems to be relatively little activity in the USA or Canada, although Puerto Rico's Luis Muñoz Marín airport (San Juan) is in the process of being privatised. However, there appears to be increased privatisation in Latin America to prepare for high forecast growth rates. This is likely to include a 30-year concession at Cuzco's new Chinchero airport in Peru and Asuncion's Silvio Pettirossi airport in Paraguay. Brazil is another BRIC (Brazil, Russia, India and China) country where airport privatisation has been agreed, and more airport privatisation seems likely in India. There may also be opportunities in Japan, particularly Osaka, Seoul Incheon in Korea, Indonesia, Vietnam, the Philippines and China. Currently there is little private involvement in Africa, with just a few North African airports and South Africa, but the strong economic growth being predicted for certain countries in this continent may open up more privatisation options, and there has been strong interest in the private development of the international terminal at Nairobi airport in Kenya (CAPA Centre for Aviation, 2011a; Bentley, 2012).

CASE STUDY 2.1: THE EVOLUTION OF THE AIRPORT BUSINESS AT VIENNA AIRPORT

Vienna airport authority was created in 1954, when the airport handled just 64,000 passengers annually. The shareholders were the Federal Republic of Austria (50 per cent), the city of Vienna (25 per cent) and Province of Lower Austria (25 per cent). In the following two decades the airport embarked on major expansion projects of the runway, passenger terminal and cargo facilities, and by 1978 it was handling 2.8 million passengers. During this time, the authority was being run very much as a public utility, making losses and receiving subsidies from the public sector owners.

Between 1978 and 1985 the airport authority went through a major organisational restructuring, which meant that the airport began to be considered much more as a business enterprise. A new functional organisation structure was set up, with main departments for airport traffic operation, financial/accounting, planning and construction, maintenance and infrastructure services, and administration. New planning and management procedures were introduced and the airport began to market itself proactively to airlines. As a result, the airport made a profit for the first time in 1979. By 1985, the airport was handling 3.9 million passengers and had begun to pay dividends to its three public sector shareholders.

In the late 1980s, further commercialisation took place with the replacement of the functional organisation structure with a new system that allowed the airport authority to respond more effectively to its customers. It set up business units or customer divisions separately for airlines and passengers, and supported these with service divisions (construction, maintenance and technical service, safety and security, finance and accounting) and central offices (legal affairs, communications and environment, human resources). The business units were required to make profits, while the service units were there to provide services in the most cost-effective manner. Management practices, with greater emphasis on private sector practices in the areas of business and strategic planning and cost control, were introduced. A comprehensive management information system was launched, and training programmes focusing on customer orientation and effective business practices were set up. Attention was also given to developing the non-aeronautical side of the business, such as retail and catering, marketing and service quality provision (Gangl, 1998).

In 1990 it became apparent that a major capital expenditure programme was needed to extend the airport's annual capacity from 6 million to 12 million passengers. Eighty per cent of this capital was available through cash flow and retained profits, but other sources were needed for the remaining 20 per cent. Budget constraints meant that increasing the equity of the public shareholders was out of the question. The realistic options were either raising the money through loans/bonds, or raising equity on the capital markets. At that time, Austrian interest rates for medium- and long-term loans as well as bonds were high. On the other hand, the Vienna stock market, like most others throughout the world, was in a poor trading situation. Eventually, the airport decided on a share flotation for 1992. This was primarily because it did not want the large loan servicing costs right through until the next capacity expansion, which was planned in 2000, and then further debt requirements.

In order to be floated on the stock exchange, the airport authority had to implement a number of very significant changes. This included changing the corporate status from a limited liability company to a joint stock company, and increasing the share capital by 50 per cent. Business appraisals for valuing the company were undertaken and consultations were held with capital market analysts. Employee share-acquisition programmes and investor relations programmes were set up, and sales support was undertaken through marketing, advertising and road shows in areas such as Austria, the United Kingdom, Germany, Switzerland, Japan and Taiwan. The airport also had to ensure that it developed a private sector and market-oriented management approach with an appropriate corporate culture and image – a process that had begun in the 1980s and was further developed during the privatisation process. The organisational structure was further refined to be more customer focused, with aviation units (airside services, airline and terminal services, handling services) and non-aviation units (consumer services, technical services, land development, real estate) both being supported by central services.

In spite of the poor stock market conditions, the flotation or initial public offering (IPO) took place in June 1992 and was oversubscribed three times in Austria and five times internationally. The sale was used by the airport company to partly finance its expansion plans. The success of the flotation meant that the Austrian government opted to sell half of its remaining 36.5 per cent stake in the airport in a secondary offering in 1995. This gave private shareholders 47 per cent of the airport. In 2001, the public shareholding in the company was reduced to 40 per cent, which followed a share buy-back in 2000 that resulted in 10 per cent of shares being placed in an employee foundation. In 1995, Amsterdam airport also bought 1 per cent of the airport with the aim of establishing a strategic alliance to encourage commercial and technical cooperation. However, this arrangement was terminated in 1998 (Figures 2.1–2.4).

Like a number of major airports in Europe, the airport was keen to become involved in international projects. For example, it was partly responsible, with other investors, for a new international terminal and car park at Istanbul airport that was opened in 2000. In 2002 a consortium led by Vienna airport bought a 40 per cent stake in Malta airport. Most recently it was a member of the TwoOne consortium which acquired a 66 per cent share of Kosice airport in Slovakia in 2006, and it bought 25 per cent of Friedrichshafen airport in Germany in 2007.

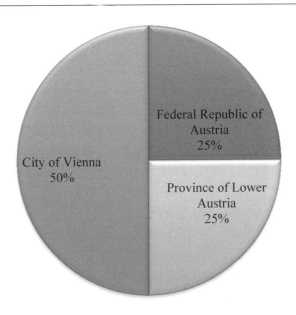

Figure 2.1 *Ownership of Vienna airport up until 1992*
Source: Vienna airport annual report

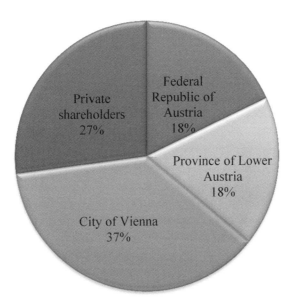

Figure 2.2 *Ownership of Vienna airport after IPO in 1992*
Source: Vienna airport annual report

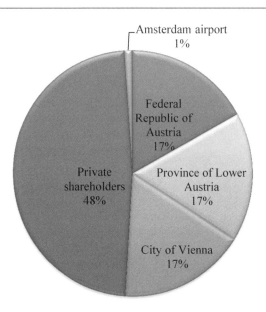

Figure 2.3 *Ownership of Vienna airport after secondary offering in 1995*
Source: Vienna airport annual report

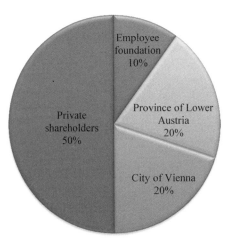

Figure 2.4 *Ownership of Vienna airport in 2012*
Source: Vienna airport annual report

CASE STUDY 2.2: THE CHANGING STRUCTURE OF THE CHINESE AIRPORT INDUSTRY

Chinese airports have had to cope with a rapidly growing number of Chinese residents who can now afford to fly, coupled with increasing numbers of inbound international leisure and business travellers. In 1994 there were 79 million passengers and by 2006 this had risen to 332 million – representing an average growth of rate of 14 per cent. Major improvements had to be made during this time and the government invested US$17 billion on rebuilding over 90 airports and constructing and upgrading 45 more (Yang *et al.*, 2008). There are now 180 airports for scheduled traffic and in 2010 passenger throughput reached 564 million passengers.

China's airports were historically owned and run by the Civil Aviation Administration of China (CAAC), which also operated all airline and air traffic control services. Then, in the late 1980s, liberalisation of the aviation industry began with the setting up of six operationally and financially independent airlines spun off from the old CAAC, the encouragement of non-CAAC airlines and the separation of airline and airport operations.

At this time, the huge traffic growth that was being experienced started to put pressure on the airport infrastructure. As a consequence the CAAC agreed to use Xiamen airport as a test case to transfer to local government control in 1988 to encourage local investment in airports. This decentralisation policy continued with a number of airports, such as China's third airport, Shanghai Hongqiao, being transferred to local control. In addition all new airports had to be managed at a local level. This localisation programme was completed in 2004 when all airports, with the exception of Beijing and those in politically sensitive Tibet, had been transferred to local ownership. Moreover, from the late 1990s the government encouraged the floating of state-owned airlines and airports on stock markets with the primary objective of encouraging improvements in corporate governance that would improve performance. Six airports were subsequently listed on the domestic or international Hong Kong stock market but with the public sector still having majority control (Fung *et al.*, 2008; Zhang and Yuen, 2008) (Table 2.1).

During the same period a number of mergers and acquisitions of airport operators took place. As a result, Beijing Capital International Airport Group (BCIA) now controls over 30 Chinese airports in nine provinces. Elsewhere the Shaaxi Airport Management Group merged with the Ningxia Airport Company in 2004 and the Qinghai Airport Company in 2006 to become the China West Airport Group. This group now manages 12 airports in four provinces. This diversification of airport ownership was accompanied by other airport reforms that enabled the airports to develop the non-aeronautical side of operations. For example, the revenue from non-aeronautical sources increased between 2001 and 2006 from 35 to 54 per cent at Xiamen International Airport and from 19 to 29 per cent at Shanghai International Airport (Yang *et al.*, 2008).

Table 2.1 China's listed airports

Airport	Year of listing	Stock exchange	Government share at time of listing in 2003 (per cent)	Passenger traffic in 2003 (million)
Xiamen International Airport	1996	Shanghai	75	4.3
Shenzhen International Airport	1998	Shenzhen	64	10.8
Shanghai Hongqiao International Airport	1998	Shanghai	63	9.7
Beijing Capital International Airport	2000	Hong Kong	65	24.3
Haikou Meilan International Airport	2002	Hong Kong	52	6.0
Guangzhou Baiyun International Airport	2003	Shanghai	60	15.0

Sources: Yang *et al.* (2008); Civil Aviation Administration of China (CAAC)

This localisation programme meant that the central government started to phase out its subsidisation of these airports. This made it financially difficult for many of these airports particularly because of the country's relatively undeveloped capital markets. Therefore some airports began to look for foreign investment, especially as from 2002 up to 49 per cent of this had been allowed at Chinese airports. This resulted, for instance, in Copenhagen taking a share of Haikou Meilan airport in 2002 (sold in 2007). The Airport Authority Hong Kong (AAHK) took a 35 per cent share of Hangzhou Xiaoshan airport in 2005, and in 2006 it was agreed that AAHK would jointly manage Zhuhai airport. There have been discussions about AAHK itself being privatised but there are no current plans for this. Another major player is the Hainan Airline Group (HNA), which is the majority (68 per cent) shareholder in Haikou Meilan airport. This is a large company with interests not only in the air transport sector but also in the hotel, logistics, real estate and tourism industries. It also manages 12 other Chinese airports.

The result of these developments is that airport management has become more commercially focused and ownership in China has become more much more diversified. A few airports remain under central government ownership but the majority of airports are now owned by municipalities or provincial governments. Some are operated by airport groups with cross-region ownership and a few airports also have minority domestic and foreign private ownership, even though some foreign investors, such as Aéroports de Paris (AdP) and Copenhagen, have subsequently decided to exit the Chinese market. A real challenge remains in efficiently providing

> sufficient infrastructure for the growing market (Wang and Seiden, 2007). While most airports are no longer maintained by subsidies from central government, there remains a lack of detailed, transparent information that hampers an assessment of the impact of these developments on airport efficiency.

TYPES OF PRIVATISATION

While it is accepted that privatisation is a trend with the airport industry, it is very difficult to define precisely because, as discussed above, it is a vague term that describes a range of different alternatives. To some it is the transfer of ownership to private organisations; to others it may be simply the transfer of management. The latter situation may be defined as private participation or private involvement, rather than privatisation, but in this discussion the term privatisation is used. This means there have been a number of different approaches to classifying privatisation models and the broader governance options that are now available to airports (e.g. Carney and Mew, 2003; Gillen, 2011; World Bank, 2011). Here privatisation models are divided into five types:

- share flotation
- trade sale
- concession
- project finance privatisation
- management contract.

The selection of the most appropriate type of privatisation involves a complex decision-making process that ultimately will depend on the government's objectives in seeking privatisation. For example, is the type of privatisation required to lessen the burden on public sector finances, generate funds from the airport sale, increase share ownership or encourage greater efficiency, competition or management expertise within the airport sector? In reaching a decision, factors such as the extent of control which the government wishes to maintain; the quality and expertise of the current airport operators; further investment requirements; and the financial robustness of the airports under consideration all have to be taken into account. In 2012 the International Civil Aviation Organization (ICAO) produced a manual on privatisation for the first time to help with the privatisation process (ICAO, 2012).

The extent of government control and whether ownership is handed over to the private sector is always a controversial decision. There is also the choice of partial privatisation, which has tended to be the more popular option for example in Europe, where 13 per cent of airports are owned by mixed public–private shareholders compared with just 9 per cent that are fully privatised (ACI Europe, 2010). The reason for this is clear. Many governments feel pressure to retain at least some stake in their airports, as these are generally considered to be strategic and vital national or regional assets that have both economic benefits and environmental costs to the communities they serve, as well as perhaps playing an important military role. This issue can become particularly sensitive if foreign private management is involved. Thus the size of the public stake in the airport will be dependent on weighing up the required influence over strategic planning decisions balanced against the obligations and risks of ownership and the benefits to be gained by devolving operational and financial responsibilities to the private sector. The private and public sectors are likely to have different objectives, and conflicts with government policy and its role as a regulator may also have to be considered. In general, when there is a model with both public and private sector involvement, it is typically defined as a public–private partnership (PPP) – although narrower, more specific definitions of PPPs also exist.

Share flotation

The first option is a share flotation or an initial public offering (IPO) with the airport company's share capital being issued and subsequently traded on the stock market. Management will usually be given options to acquire shares. To date, the only 100 per cent share flotation that has taken place was with BAA in 1987 (now de-listed). Other partially floated airport companies include Vienna airport (Flughafen Wien AG), Copenhagen Airports A/S (now de-listed), Zurich, Auckland Airport, Malaysia Airports (an organisation owning 37 airports in the country), Airports Authority of Thailand (AOT) (owning six Thai airports), Fraport (owning Frankfurt and other airports), Aéroports de Paris (AdP), Rome (now de-listed), Florence, Venice, Pisa, Hainan Meilan and Beijing Capital International Airport (BCIA). The BCIA flotation was interesting as it was the first airport where a share flotation came after an initial trade sale to a strategic partner, namely AdP. With this 'cornerstone' approach, AdP originally bought 10 per cent of the airport, ABN Amro Ventures bought another 8 per cent and institutional and retail investors a further 17 per cent – leaving the Chinese government with a 65 per cent share. As discussed above, a number of other Chinese airports (Shanghai, Shenzhen, Xiamen and Guangzhou) were also listed on the domestic stock exchanges. Table 2.2 shows that while share flotations were relatively popular in the early days of privatisation, in more recent years there have been very few.

With a share flotation, the government owner will give up total or partial ownership, while transferring the economic risks and effective control to the new shareholders. The stock markets have traditionally viewed purchases of shares in airport companies in a favourable light, with positive factors such as strong growth prospects, limited competition because of high barriers to entry and minimal threats of substitutes, and potential commercial opportunities influencing their views. However, opinions can be less positive in times of economic uncertainty and stock market volatility as the recent global economic problems have demonstrated.

Total or partial privatisation of this type will eliminate, or certainly reduce, the need for state involvement in the financing of airport investment. The proceeds from such a privatisation could be used for funding future investment at the airport, as with the IPO of 27 per cent at Vienna airport, or can go directly to the government, as with BAA. Even when total privatisation takes place, a degree of government influence can theoretically be maintained by issuing a golden share to the government so that in extreme cases national interests can be protected. To prevent domination by any individual shareholder, limits can be placed on the maximum shareholding. For instance, the UK government had a golden share in BAA which gave it the right of veto over undesirable takeovers deemed to be against national interests, and capped the amount of shares that any one shareholder could hold at 15 per cent. However, in 2003 the European Court of Justice declared this type of shareholding to be illegal because it prevents capital movements

Table 2.2 Examples of airport privatisation through share flotations

Airport	Date	Share of airport sold (per cent)
UK: BAA	1987	100
Austria: Vienna	1992	27
Denmark: Copenhagen	1994	25
Italy: Rome	1997	46
Slovenia: Ljubljana	1997	37
New Zealand: Auckland	1998	52
Malaysia: Malaysia Airports	1999	18
China: BCIA	2000	35
Switzerland: Zürich	2000	22
Italy: Florence	2000	39
Germany: Fraport	2001	29
China: Hainan Meilan	2002	20
Thailand: AOT	2004	30
Italy: Venice	2004	30
France: AdP	2005	28
Italy: Pisa	2006	33

The table shows only the first sale made; there may have been further sales. A number of other Chinese airports (Shanghai, Shenzhen, Xiamen, Guangzhou) have been listed on the domestic Chinese stock exchanges.
Source: Compiled by author from various sources

within the EU. This consequently meant that BAA was subject to a takeover by the Spanish company Ferrovial. There was a similar situation with Copenhagen, which resulted in a major shareholding being acquired in 2005 by the Australian company Macquarie Airports.

In order to be floated on the stock market, the airport company will be required to have a track record of minimum profits to make the airport attractive enough to investors. Airports not performing well would clearly find it hard to be successfully privatised in this way. Fully developed capital markets also need to be in existence, which may not be the situation in certain regions, for example in Africa. The airport company will have to get used to daily scrutiny of its financial performance by its shareholders and other investors and, as a consequence, may find it hard not to become preoccupied with the share price. The existing management will usually be able to remain in control of the company as the investors will tend to have a relatively passive role. Moreover, issuing shares to employees may give them an incentive and make them feel more involved in the affairs of the airport company.

Trade sale

With this option, some parts of the airport or the entire airport will be sold to a trade partner or consortium of investors, usually through a public tender. The winning operator, as well as being capable of bringing additional investment at the airport, will possess the construction, operations, financial and commercial development expertise to deal with all the complexities of the airport business. Typically it will be a consortium that comprises airport management specialists; domestic and foreign banks; and engineering or construction firms whose combined expertise will be attractive enough to draw in private capital. Restrictions can be imposed on the maximum stake held by each individual owner, or by overseas interests, or by owners of competing airports.

The first significant trade sale was in 1990 when 76 per cent of Liverpool airport in the UK, previously owned by local government, was sold to British Aerospace (Table 2.3). Subsequently

Table 2.3 *Examples of airport privatisation through trade sales*

Airport	Date	Share of airport sold (per cent)	Main buyer
UK: Liverpool	1990	76	British Aerospace
UK: Prestwick	1992	100	British Aerospace
UK: East Midlands	1993	100	National Express
UK: Southend	1994	100	Regional Airports Ltd
UK: Cardiff	1995	100	TBI
UK: Bournemouth	1995	100	National Express
UK: Belfast International	1996	100	TBI
UK: Birmingham	1997	51	Aer Rianta/Natwest Ventures (40 per cent)/other investors (11 per cent)
UK: Bristol	1997	51	Firstbus
UK: Liverpool	1997	76	Peel Holdings
UK: Kent International	1997	100	Wiggins
Italy: Naples	1997	65	BAA
Australia: Brisbane, Melbourne, Perth	1997	100	Various
US: Sanford Orlando	1997	100	TBI
Germany: Dusseldorf	1998	50	Hochtief and Aer Rianta
Sweden: Skavsta	1998	90	TBI
South Africa: ACSA	1998	20	ADRI South Africa consortium (Aeroporti di Roma had 69 per cent share)
Germany: Hanover	1998	30	Fraport
New Zealand: Wellington	1998	66	Infratil
Australia: 15 remaining major Australian airports (except Sydney)	1998	100	Various
UK: Humberside	1999	83	Manchester airport

Continued

Table 2.3 *Continued*

Airport	Date	Share of airport sold (per cent)	Main buyer
US: Stewart International	1999	100	National Express
Belgium: Liege	1999	25	AdP
Italy: Rome	2000	51	Leonardo consortium
Italy: Turin	2000	41	Benetton Group consortium
Germany: Hamburg	2000	36	Hochtief and Aer Rianta
UK: Newcastle	2001	49	Copenhagen airport
Australia: Sydney	2002	100	Macquarie/Hochtief consortium
Malta	2002	40	Vienna airport consortium
Belgium: Brussels	2004	70	Macquarie Airports consortium
Hungary: Budapest	2005	75	BAA
Germany: Luebeck	2005	75	Infratil
UK: Exeter and Devon	2006	100	Balfour Beatty consortium
Slovakia: Kosice	2006	66	TwoOne Vienna consortium
UK: Leeds Bradford	2007	100	Bridgepoint
China: Xi'an	2007	25	Fraport
Belgium: Charleroi	2009	28	SAVE (Venice airport) consortium

The table shows only the first sale made. In some case there are now different owners.
Source: Compiled by author from various sources

a number of other UK airports, including East Midlands, Cardiff, Bournemouth, Leeds-Bradford and Exeter/Devon and Southend, have been sold off totally to a trade partner. In the case of Birmingham, Newcastle and Humberside airports, a strategic partner was brought in through a partial sale. Elsewhere in Europe, Brussels, Hanover, Dusseldorf, Hamburg, Kosice, Charleroi and Naples airports have also been partially privatised through a trade sale. AdP has a 25 per cent share of Liege airport in Belgium, which it has developed as an alternative venue for freight activities. Outside Europe, 20 per cent of the Airports Company South Africa (ACSA) was sold to a strategic partner. The ACSA owns and manages nine South African airports including the three major international airports of Johannesburg, Durban and Cape Town. Two-thirds of Wellington airport in New Zealand has also been sold through a trade sale, as has a quarter of Xi'an airport in China. Airports which have been leased on long-term arrangements to strategic partners or consortia can also be included in this category – as effectively all control will be transferred from the publicly owned airport to the trade partner. The most notable example here is the Australian airports, the majority of which have been sold on long-term leases (50 years with a further possible option of 49 years) to different consortia. The privatisations at Budapest, Naples and Malta are other examples.

In many of these cases, the strategic partner is an established airport operator, or the purchasing consortium will contain a member with airport management experience. A number of governments insist on having an airport operator in the consortium. For example, BAA was the strategic partner in the Naples airport sale, and Vienna airport belongs to the consortium that bought part of Malta airport. With most of the Australian airport sales there was an airport interest within the successful consortia. Many of the airports participating in these airport privatisations were not actually privatised themselves, which leads to further complications in the definition of a 'private' airport. For example, the former Aer Rianta Irish Airports, which was a public corporation (now Dublin Airport Authority), was successfully involved in the partial privatisation of Birmingham, Hamburg and Dusseldorf airports. Similarly, the government-owned Schiphol group, which owns Amsterdam airports, has a few interests in other airports around the world. Privatisation has been discussed for both these airport operators but has not yet occurred.

Trade sales usually enable the airport to be sold at a higher price than with an IPO. This is because with this type of privatisation there can be more confidence in the airport performing well in the future, as a new management team can be brought in, whereas with an IPO operations will be more reliant on existing management and hence more uncertain. Financial and operational structures can be changed with a trade sale, which is more difficult with an IPO. Moreover, trade buyers will undertake detailed due diligence of the airport and so the risks associated with the purchase will be lower, which again may increase the pre-sale price.

Concession

With this type of arrangement, an airport management company or consortium will purchase a concession or lease to operate the 'privatised' airport for a defined period, commonly between 20 and 30 years, again usually through a tendering process. As with the trade sale, restrictions can be placed on the maximum involvement of certain organisations in the consortium. A concession approach tends to be quite complex, having high transactions costs (including legal and investment advice) and needing to be carefully designed and implemented to ensure the private contracts achieve the government policy objectives. This in turn may limit the airport operator's flexibility. A number of concession models exist; some of the most popular ones are rehabilitate, operate and transfer (ROT) or rehabilitate, lease or rent and transfer (RLT).

Financial terms will vary, but typically there may be an initial payment based on the assessed stream of cash flow from the business and/or payment of an annual fee throughout the term of the agreement and/or a revenue or profit-sharing mechanism. In addition, the agreement may set standards of service and may also identify required expansion work or a demand upper limit that will trigger capacity expansion. Unlike the share flotation and trade sale models, the government maintains ownership of the airport. Therefore these types of agreement are popular with governments that recognise they need the finance, expertise and know-how of the private operators but do not want to hand over permanent ownership.

A key feature of the concession agreement will be the allocation of risk between the airport operator and the government. The risks associated with operating and financing the airport and traffic will be handed over to the airport operator, who will generally be best able to assess and manage these risks, while other risks, such as those arising from planning delays, terrorism, *force majeure*, or changes in externally imposed safety or security regulations, may be retained by the government. The precise details related to such risks will vary. For example, the airport operator will tend to take the risks associated with traffic developing out of competing airports, although in some cases, as with the new second airport at Mumbai in India, the concessionaire of the current Mumbai airport has the right of first refusal to operate the new airport as long as it matches the top bid. Elsewhere, if a national carrier fails, the government may bear the risk and pay the concessionaire compensation payments due to the decline in revenues. The contract will also contain details about the regulatory regime and personnel issues. In addition, as it is never feasible to foresee all future developments, there will normally be some form of adjustment mechanism to balance the requirements of the stakeholders and also default/termination conditions and associated compensation payments (World Bank, 2008; Stiller, 2010; Cruz and Marques, 2011).

One of the earliest concession arrangements was agreed in 1997 for the three main airports of Bolivia: La Paz, Santa Cruz and Cochabamba. Airports Group International, the former airport management company (acquired by TBI and then later by Abertis), was awarded the 30-year concession, during which time it agreed to pay an annual fee of 21 per cent of gross revenues. The agreement did not specify a set level of investment, but called for continuous maintenance of the airports up to a certain standard, which ensured there was a progressive investment programme adapted to the traffic growth.

A further example is the 30-year concession for the 33 Argentinian airports, which was awarded to the consortium Aéroportuertos Argentinas 2000 (AA2000), which had among its partners SEA (the Milan airport company) and Ogden (the airport services company). The consortium agreed to pay an annual US$171 million a year for the first 5 years of the agreement and to invest US$2 billion. However, this concession amount was considered by many to be totally unrealistic, and it proved impossible for AA2000 to pay it all, especially because of the severe political and economic crisis the country went through after this privatisation occurred. Eventually, in 2007 it was agreed that the fee would be changed to 15 per cent of revenues (Lipovich, 2008).

Another concession agreement was signed between the Peruvian government and the Lima Airport Partners in 2001 (a consortium formed by Fraport and Alterra) when 47 per cent of revenues had to be paid to the government, and also there were a number of investment obligations in the first 3 years of operation, including US$1.3 million in the first 180 days (US$3.5 million was actually invested) and US$110 million by 2005 (US$135 million was invested) (Arbulu, 2007).

Since the privatised airport will be handed over only for a fixed period, the government owner will have a greater degree of control than with an outright sale, and will benefit financially from either an upfront payment, an annual revenue stream, or both. The fixed-term arrangement may also give the operators an incentive to improve their performance if they want to be given the concession again, and may ensure that investment in the airport is carried out in a speedier manner. For the government there will be an opportunity to introduce fresh management and new ideas when the concession term expires. However, a shortcoming of the fixed-term nature of the concession is that it may well provide weaker incentives for the operator to invest and to innovate, especially during the later stages of the concession, as there will be no guarantee that the concession will be extended and that the operator will make an adequate return on their investment. Costs may have to be inflated by the operator if it has to depreciate the assets over the period of the concession; or alternatively, if there are residual values of the assets, this may result in uncertainty and perhaps higher cost of capital and less favourable financial offers made by potential operators when bidding for the airport.

At Luton airport in the United Kingdom, a consortium originally consisting of Barclays Investment, Bechtel Enterprises and Airport Groups International (AGI, subsequently bought in 1999 by TBI, which is now part of Abertis) was given the 30-year concession to run the airport in 1998. A concessionaire-type arrangement was chosen, rather than a flotation or trade sale, since the local government owners had promised not to relinquish total control of this publicly owned asset to private hands. This arrangement involved paying an initial annual concession fee of US$19 million, which would increase as passenger traffic grows. Barclays and Bechtel have subsequently sold off their interest in this airport. In recent years a key obstacle to further investment at the airport has been the limited period left for the airport concession arrangement.

The situation was rather different in Mexico, where the country's 58 airports were divided into four groups: the North-Central Group (GACN – known as OMA from 2007), the Pacific Group (GAP), the Southeast Group (ASUR), and the Mexico City Group (AICM) (Rico, 2008). Each of these groups had at least one large airport (e.g. Mexico City, Cancun, Acapulco) which would make it desirable to private investors, but they also had some smaller airports as well. The very small airports were not allocated to any of these groups as, although they were seen as essential for public need, they were not considered to be attractive investments. Concession contracts were awarded for 15 per cent for three of these four groups for an initial 15-year period with an underlying 50-year agreement. There had to be local involvement and there had to be at least one airport operator from another country within each successful consortium to bring international expertise, but only 49 per cent could be under foreign ownership. It was also planned that there would be a subsequent flotation of remaining government shares. An upfront fee for buying the concession and an annual percentage of revenue had to be paid to the government by the consortia. The concession for ASUR was the first to be awarded in 1998 to a consortium formed by Copenhagen airport, and consequently the rest of the shares (except 0.01 per cent which was kept by the government) were sold through flotations in 2000 and 2005. In 1999, 15 per cent of the GAP Group of 12 airports was sold to a consortium with AENA, the Spanish airport group, as a key partner, and then in 2006 the rest of the shares were floated. In 2000, the 15 per cent share of the GACN group was sold to an AdP consortium again with a further flotation of shares in 2006. The Mexico City group has yet to be privatised because of uncertainty related to a new airport for the capital and other political and social issues.

Other countries that have had concession agreements for their airports include the Dominican Republic, Chile, Kosova, Macedonia, Uruguay, Costa Rica, Peru, Russia, Tanzania, the Maldives and India (Table 2.4). One of the most recent agreements was for Pulkovo airport in St Petersburg in 2010 for 30 years with a consortium that includes Fraport and the Russian bank VTB. There is a fixed annual lease payment of around €2 million and a variable concession fee of 11.5 per cent of gross revenues. Up until 2013 there was mandatory investment phase of around €775, after which additional investment will be driven by traffic growth (Pal, 2010).

Table 2.4 *Examples of airport privatisation through concession agreements*

Airport	Date	Length of concession (years)	Concessionaire
Columbia: Barranquilla	1997	15	AENA consortium
Columbia: Cartagena	1998	15	AENA consortium
Bolivia: La Paz, Santa Cruz, Cochabamba	1997	25	AGI*
UK: Luton	1998	30	AGI* Bechtel/Barclays consortium
Mexico: South East Group	1998	15†	Copenhagen airport consortium
Mexico: Pacific Group	1999	15†	AENA consortium
Argentinean Airport System	1998	33	Aeropuertos Argentina 2000 consortium (including SEA Milan and Ogden)
Tanzania: Kilimanjaro International Airport	1998	25	Mott Macdonald consortium
Dominican Republic: 6 airports including Santo Domingo	1999	20	YVRAS‡/Odgen consortium
Chile: Terminal at Santiago International Airport	1999	15	YVRAS‡ consortium
Uruguay: Montevideo	1999	25	YVRAS‡ consortium
Costa Rica: San Jose	1999	20	TBI*
Columbia: Cali	2000	20	AENA consortium
Mexico: North Central Group	2000	15b	AdP consortium
Peru: Lima	2001	30	Fraport/Alterra consortium
Jamaica: Montego Bay	2003	30	YVRAS‡ consortium
Peru: 12 regional airports	2006	25	Ferrovial consortium
India: Delhi	2006	30	GMR/Fraport/Malaysia Airports consortium
India: Mumbai	2006	30	GVK/ACSA consortium
Turkey: Antalya	2007	17	Fraport/IC Holding consortium
Turkey: Antalya Gazipasa	2009	25	TAV Airports
Maldives: Male	2010	25	GMR/MAHB
Kosovo: Pristina	2010	20	Limak/Aéroports de Lyon consortium
Russia: St Petersburg	2010	30	Fraport/VTB consortium
Croatia: Zagreb	2012	30	AdP consortium

The table shows only the first new operator. In some cases there are now different operators.
*AGI was bought by TBI in 1999; Abertis now owns TBI.
†Fifteen-year contract but underlying 50-year concession.
‡YVRAS changed its named to the Vantage Group in 2011.
Source: Compiled by author from various sources

Project finance

With this option, a company will usually build or redevelop and then operate an airport or specific facility, such as a terminal, for a certain length of time, typically 20–30 years. This company may be totally private or may be a public–private partnership. At the end of this period, control will revert to the government owners. Thus this approach can be viewed as a particular type of concession agreement. Generally such an arrangement will not usually require a large upfront payment, but the operating company will bear all the costs of building or redeveloping the facility. When it is built, the company will have to cover the operating costs but will also retain most revenues (often after paying an annual fee to the government) until the facility is handed back. Thus the airport company will take full economic risk for investment and operations but it will not have to go through the normal public sector procurement processes. There are a number of project finance privatisation methods that allocate different amounts of risk to the private sector. The most popular model is build, operate, transfer (BOT) when, as the name suggests, the company will build the facility, operate it for a certain length of time and then transfer management back to the government. Related models include build, lease, transfer (BLT) and build, own, operate, transfer (BOOT), but often all methods are referred to by the generic term BOT.

This type of arrangement is commonly used when relatively large investments are needed for totally new airports or perhaps for new passenger terminals or other major facilities. One of the first major projects of this type was terminal 3 at Toronto's Lester B. Pearson International Airport, which was developed as a BOT project by Huang and Danczkay and Lockheed Air Terminals (Ashford and Moore, 1999). The former Eurohub at Birmingham airport was built under a BOT-type arrangement by a company comprising Birmingham airport (25 per cent), British Airways (BA) (21.4 per cent), local authorities (14.3 per cent), National Car Parks (21.4 per cent), Forte (6 per cent) and John Laing Holdings (11.9 per cent). This terminal is now a fully owned and managed facility of Birmingham airport that is integrated with the rest of the facilities.

The Athens airport at Spata Eleftherios Venizelos was built under a 30-year BOT arrangement. The Greek government holds 55 per cent of the shares in the company Athens International Airport SA (AIA). The remaining share of 45 per cent share belongs to an international consortium, led by Hochtief. Another example of a BOT project was the international passenger terminal 3 at Ninoy Aquino International Airport in Manila. This was the first project finance model of its kind in the Asia-Pacific region, but proved unsuccessful after a few years because of a major dispute between the government and the private consortium Philippine International Air Terminals Co. (PIATCO), which was led by Fraport. A more recent example is a 25-year BOT project which was agreed in 2007 to develop a new terminal at Queen Alia International airport in Amman in Jordan. Like many of these types of project, this required an international airport operator to have a share in the winning consortium; in this case, AdP. The consortium AIG PSC agreed to pay 54 per cent of gross revenues to the government. There are also BOT projects at a number of other airports including Hyderabad, Bengaluru, Tirana, Larnaca, Varna, Burgas and Antalya (Table 2.5).

Management contract

The least radical privatisation option is a management contract where ownership remains with the government and the contractors take responsibility for the day-to-day operation of the airport,

Table 2.5 Examples of airport privatisation through project finance

Airport	Date	Length of agreement (years)	Contractor
Canada: Toronto Terminal 3	1987	Terminated	Lockheed consortium
UK: Birmingham Eurohub	1989	Terminated	Various including Birmingham airport, British Airways, National Car Parks
Greece: Athens	1996	30	Hochtief consortium
Philippines: Manila international terminal	1999	Terminated	Fraport consortium
US: New York JFK international arrivals terminal	1997	20	Schiphol consortium
Turkey: Ankara	2003	20	TAV Airports
India: Hyderabad	2004	30	Siemens/Zurich airport consortium
India: Bengaluru	2004	30	GMR/Malaysia Airports consortium
Albania: Tirana	2005	20	Hochtief consortium
Cyprus: Larnaca and Paphos	2005	25	YVRAS* consortium
Bulgaria: Varna and Burgas	2006	35	Fraport consortium
Jordan: Amman	2007	25	AdP consortium
Georgia: Tbilisi and Batumi	2007	20	TAV consortium
Tunisia: Monastir and Enfidha	2007	40	TAV consortium
Turkey: Izmir	2012	20	TAV
Saudi Arabia: Medina	2012	25	TAV consortium

*YVRAS changed its named to the Vantage Group in 2011.
Source: Compiled by author from various sources

usually for a period of 5–10 years. Either the government pays an annual management fee to the contractor, usually related to the performance of the airport, or the contractor will pay the government a share of its revenues. Normally investment will remain the responsibility of the government owner and so the overall economic risk is shared between the owner and the management company. For the government owner this may be politically more acceptable, whereas for the contractor such an arrangement may be attractive in countries where greater financial exposure, through a trade sale, for example, may be seen as too great a risk.

An early example within Europe was Brussels, where the terminal was under a management contract to a private company, the Brussels Airport Terminal Company, from 1987. In 1998, however, this company merged with the public company operating the rest of the airport to become the Brussels International Airport Company. More common is for airport operators to have management contracts in other areas of the world. For example, the Spanish airport company AENA has a management contract for Cayo Coco airport in Cuba, while the Vantage Airport Group (formerly Vancouver Airport Services, YVRAS) has a number of contracts including in the Bahamas, Dominican Republic and Turks and Caicos Islands. AdP has similar involvement in Algeria, Egypt, Guinea, Madagascar, Saudi Arabia and Cambodia; Schiphol in Aruba; and Fraport in Saudi Arabia and Egypt. Such arrangements can cover all airport operations or just one aspect, such as retail. BAA, for instance, had retail contracts at Pittsburgh, Baltimore, Cleveland and Boston until these were terminated in 2010 as a result of its strategy to focus on core assets. Dublin Airport Authority, through its subsidiary Aer Rianta International, has retail contracts at various airports including in Canada, Russia, Bahrain, Beirut, Muscat, Egypt, India, Cyprus and China.

REGULATION, COMPETITION AND EFFICIENCY ISSUES

The amount of influence that a government can exert over a private airport clearly depends on the type of privatisation model chosen. A government may hold on to a considerable amount of control if a management or private finance contract is chosen, while very little state influence may remain after an airport company has been floated on the stock market or sold to a strategic partner. In these latter cases, if the airport has substantial market power it is often feared that the privatised airport will act like a private monopoly, and may not always operate with the best interests of the airport users in mind, by raising charges, reducing the quality of service and under-investing in facilities. Therefore economic regulation has been introduced at a number of airports when the privatisation process has taken place. Chapter 4 explains in detail the types of regulation introduced and the rationale behind this.

There is also another competition issue that has to be taken into account if a group of airports, rather than a single individual airport, is being considered for privatisation: should the airports be sold off together as a group or should they be split up into different companies? This is particularly an issue when the airport group or system may contain a few large international airports that are profitable and a number of smaller regional or local airports that are loss-makers. This was the case with the Australian airports and also in a number of South American countries prior to privatisation. If the airport group is sold as a single entity, and if generally this group as a whole has a good financial track record, a higher sale price may be achieved primarily because of the lack of perceived competition from other airport operators. Moreover, there will be lower administration and transaction costs related to the process of privatisation. In addition, any unprofitable parts of the airport system (usually the smaller airports) will not have to remain under public ownership if the whole group is sold, and raising capital on the commercial money markets for future investments may be easier for a larger company. However, if the group does contain a number of loss-making airports this may make it less attractive to investors and the sale price may suffer accordingly. Furthermore, there may have to be special conditions built into the privatisation arrangements to ensure the new private owner does not neglect the management of the smaller airports. On the other hand, if only the profitable airports are privatised, for example with a concession arrangement, another option would be to use the concession fees to subsidise the smaller airports.

Selling off airports in a group may inhibit competition, although the extent of competition that exists between airports in a group can vary significantly depending on the local circumstances (see Chapter 8). It is a different situation when the airports have overlapping catchment areas (such as the former BAA airports in London) compared with serving totally different markets. Airlines inherently tend to be suspicious of airport groups, fearing that they will be paying charges at one airport which will finance the development of another airport, typically in some remote area which they do not use. However, in response airports often argue that they achieve economies of scale and are making the best use of resources and expertise by operating as an airport group, and that such management enables a strategic and coordinated approach to airport development. Airports can also be developed to focus on certain types of traffic, for example in London with LCCs at Stansted and network carriers' traffic at Heathrow. Many airport groups exist, and this is a common issue that needs to be addressed irrespective of whether privatisation is occurring. For example, in Europe: in Finland Finavia operates 24 airports, in Norway Avinor operates 46 airports, in Spain AENA operates 47 airports, and in Sweden LFV operates 16 airports (ACI Europe, 2010).

In Australia, the government decided on individual privatisations for the major international airports but with packages of some of the smaller ones. Restrictions were imposed to stop the same operator from having overall control at a number of airports. As regards privatisation in South America, all 33 Argentinian airports were covered under the same concession agreements, while in Mexico the airports were divided into four different groups with a mixture of small and large airports in each group. In the United Kingdom, after much debate, BAA, which was an airport group of seven airports, was privatised in 1987 as a single entity, but this remained a controversial issue and eventually led to a requirement for the group to be split up in 2009. It continues to be a subject of debate in countries that are likely to experience privatisation in the near future, and indeed was considered in Portugal prior to the recent privatisation which maintained the group structure of the main airports (Marques, 2011).

As well as affecting competition between airports, it is often argued that privatisation will lead to greater efficiency and improved financial performance. To date, there has been only fairly limited research in this area with somewhat contradictory findings – although this may partly be to do with the adoption of different methodologies to assess the situation (Graham, 2011). (See Chapter 3 for a discussion concerning performance measurement at airports.) For example, Parker (1999) investigated BAA before and after its privatisation and found no significant variation in performance, as did Holvad and Graham (2004) when they considered the whole of the UK airport industry. For Australian and New Zealand airports, Domney *et al.* (2005) concluded that privatisation was actually negatively associated with profitability and that there was no statistically significant association with efficiency. Vasigh and Gorjidooz (2006) did not find a significant relationship between efficiency and airport ownership when a sample of 22, both public and private US/European airports were examined. Moreover, when Oum *et al.* (2003) looked at a large sample of major Asia-Pacific, European and North American airports, they again found that ownership had no significant impact.

In a study of 35 European airports, Vogel (2006) found that partially and fully privatised airports operated more efficiently than public ones. Similarly, Barros and Dieke (2007) found that private Italian airports were more efficient than public Italian airports, while both Fung *et al.* (2008) and Yuen and Zhang (2009) observed that airports that had been publicly listed in China were more efficient than non-listed ones. However, Zhang and Yuen (2008) questioned whether this was more to do with the specific inherent characteristics of the listed airports. In a further global study, Oum *et al.* (2006) concluded that airports with government majority ownership were significantly less efficient than airports with a private majority ownership, although there was still no statistically significant evidence that fully state-owned airports were less efficient. Likewise, Oum *et al.* (2008) concluded that there was a high probability that airports owned/operated by a majority private firm achieved higher efficiency than those owned/operated by a mixed enterprise with government majority ownership. Therefore both these latter studies suggested that minority private sector participation should be avoided in favour of even 100 per cent state ownership – maybe due to the conflicting objectives that may occur with such public–private partnerships.

Understandably, the airlines tend to assess the success of airport privatisation in terms of service levels and cost-effectiveness rather than by financial gains. Within this context a study of 12 airport privatisations in Europe, Asia and Latin America was undertaken a few years ago, and from the airlines' viewpoint some disappointing results were observed (IATA, 2005). Key problems identified were the lack of independent or effective economic regulation in some cases (e.g. at Vienna, Zurich and Auckland airports), and too-high concession fees being paid to the government (e.g. in Argentina, at Lima airport in Peru and at Juan Santamaria airport in Costa Rica). The view of the Director General of IATA, who wrote the Foreword to the study, was that it did not matter who owned the airport as long as it performed appropriately in terms of cost efficiency and service quality.

PRIVATISATION EXAMPLES

United Kingdom

The United Kingdom is worthy of special attention when privatisation is being considered, not only because the first major airport privatisation took place in this country, but also because subsequent privatisations have been quite varied in nature. Airport privatisation came about because of a major piece of legislation, the Airports Act introduced in 1986. The first part of the Act was concerned with the then government-owned BAA, which operated seven UK airports: London Heathrow, London Gatwick, London Stansted, and the four Scottish airports of Aberdeen, Edinburgh, Glasgow and Prestwick. The Act made provision for BAA to become a private company through a subsequent 100 per cent share flotation in 1997. This reflected the overall aim of the conservative Thatcher government of the time to privatise nationalised industries such as utilities and communications, and to increase share ownership among the UK population (Graham, 2008).

The second part of the Act required all airports with a turnover of more than £1 million in two of the previous three years to become companies. Prior to this Act, these airports had been run directly by their local government owners. Sixteen airports were covered by this part of the Act, ranging from Manchester airport, owned by a consortium of local authorities which at that time had a throughput of 9 million passengers, to Southend airport, owned by Southend Borough Council and handling just over 100,000 passengers. The shareholders of these airport companies were initially to be the local government owners, but the shares could then be sold off to private investors if desired by the public sector owners. This was the Conservative government's ultimate aim. The Act also introduced economic regulation at these airports (discussed in Chapter 4).

BAA was floated in 1987 with £1.2 billion going to the government. This gave BAA the freedom to borrow from commercial markets and diversify into areas of operations such as hotels, property management and hospital shops, which it did in its first few years of operation (Doganis, 1992). BAA subsequently dramatically expanded the retail part of its business and became a global player in airport management through interests in airports in as diverse areas as Australia, Italy, the United States, Mauritius and Oman, although these links no longer exist as the company has focused back on its core activities in the UK. Meanwhile, the new situation at the regional airports gave them considerably more opportunity to commercialise their activities. As a result the share of non-aeronautical revenue increased at the majority of these airports and more resources were devoted to commercial activities such as marketing (Humphreys, 1999).

The most significant impact of the Airports Act was the change in ownership patterns that emerged (Table 2.6). By the early 1990s, the regional airports were finding it increasingly difficult to obtain permission to borrow funds for investment, and in 1993 the government announced that there would be no further spending allocation for airports. The only alternative for airports

Table 2.6 Ownership patterns at main* UK airports, 2012

Airport	Ownership in 2012	Private interest (per cent)	Privatisation date	Passenger numbers 2011 (000s)
Aberdeen	BAA†	100	1987	3,082
Belfast City	Eiser Infrastructure Fund	100	n/a	2,397
Belfast International	Abertis	100	1994	4,104
Birmingham	Local authorities/Ontario Teachers' Pension Plan/Victorian Funds Management Corporation/Employee Share Trust	51	1997	8,616
Bournemouth	Manchester airport	†	1995	614
Bristol	Macquarie European Infrastructure Fund 1/ Sydney Airport/Ontario Teachers' Pension Plan	100	1997	5,781
Cardiff	Abertis	100	1995	1,223
Doncaster (Robin Hood)	Peels Airports	100	n/a	823
Durham Tees Valley	Local authorities/Peel Investments	75	2003	
East Midlands	Manchester airport	†	1993	4,215
Edinburgh	BAA†	100	1987	9,385
Exeter	Regional and City Airports/Galaxy Fund	100	2007	717

Continued

Table 2.6 Continued

Airport	Ownership in 2012	Private interest (per cent)	Privatisation date	Passenger numbers 2011 (000s)
Glasgow	BAA†	100	1987	6,880
Highlands and Islands Airports	Scottish Office	0	n/a	§
Leeds Bradford	Bridgepoint	100	2007	2,977
Liverpool	Peel Airports	100	1990	5,251
London City	Global Infrastructure Partners (GIP)/Highstar Capital	100	n/a	2,992
London Gatwick	GIP/Abu Dhabi Investment Authority (ADIA), National Pension Service of Korea (NPS), California Public Employees' Retirement System (CalPERS) and the Future Fund of Australia	100	1987	33,674
London Heathrow	BAA†	100	1987	69,433
London Luton	Abertis	100¶	1998	9,513
London Stansted	BAA†	100	1987	18,052
Manchester	Local authorities	0	n/a	18,893
Newcastle	Local authorities/ Copenhagen airport	49	2001	4,346
Norwich	Local Authorities/ Omniport	80	2004	414
Prestwick	Infratil	100	1987	1,297
Southampton	BAA†	100	1961	1,762

n/a, not applicable; the table shows the most recent owner, not necessarily the first private sector owner.

*Largest 25 airports by annual passengers in 2011 (excluding Highlands and Islands).

†BAA is owned by Ferrovial, Caisse de dépôt et placement du Québec, GIC Special Investments and Alinda Capital Partners. In November 2012 it was announced that the China Investment Corporation would take a 10 per cent shareholding. In 2012 the BAA name was dropped and just the individual airport names are used.

‡Eighty-three per cent share is held by Manchester airport, which is under local authority ownership.

§Ten airports including Inverness with over 582,000 passengers.

¶The private investors have a 30-year concession contract. Ownership remains with the local authorities.

Source: Compiled by author from various sources

that wished to invest was privatisation, which an increasing number of airports had no choice but to adopt. Political pressures from a Conservative central government, which was very much ideologically attracted to the transfer of public service to the private sector whenever possible, undoubtedly played a major role.

Various airports, such as East Midlands, Cardiff and Bournemouth, chose full privatisation through a trade sale to a strategic partner. Southend airport was also totally privatised, but in this case the sale was undertaken to ensure the survival of the airport rather than to give access to finance for expansion as with many of the other airports (Humphreys, 1999). Some airports, such as Newcastle and Norwich, opted for a partially privatised approach that gave them access to finance but also enabled some local public control to be maintained. Birmingham airport is an interesting example which initially overcame funding difficulties by establishing a joint venture company to build the additional Eurohub terminal with a BOT project without a change in overall ownership. This solved the short-term problem of funding, but subsequent traffic growth meant that there was once again pressure for additional investment, and this time the airport opted for a partial privatisation.

A few local authority airport owners remained strongly opposed to privatisation moves – arguing that the airport should remain in public sector hands to maintain its role as a regional public asset. Manchester was one such airport and financed the whole of its second runway project from retained profits. Its public sector status, however, meant that it was not free to expand inter- nationally on equal terms with competing private airports. It was involved with the successful consortium in the sale of Adelaide/Parafield and Coolangatta airports in Australia, but because of its status could only act on a consultancy basis with no equity share involved. From 1999, however, this situation changed with legislation introduced to allow for the larger profitable regional airports which were still in local government hands (Manchester, Newcastle, Leeds- Bradford and Norwich) to be able to borrow money on the open market. This enabled Manchester to purchase 83 per cent of the nearby Humberside airport soon afterwards, and it has subse- quently also bought Bournemouth and East Midlands airports. Manchester Airport Group was partially privatised in 2013.

There are also a few other airports in the United Kingdom which have had a different history. The relatively newly developed London City airport and Belfast City airport have always been in private hands. Belfast International was privatised by means of a management buyout in 1994 and was subsequently sold to TBI in 1996. Most of the very small regional airports in the United Kingdom remain under public sector ownership. Highlands and Islands Airports Ltd, a state- owned company, operates ten airports in Scotland with the help of a government subsidy.

Looking back to 1986 before the Airports Act, a number of the main regional airports, such as Exeter, Humberside, Liverpool, London Stansted, Norwich and Prestwick, recorded a loss. By 2005–06, all airports were in a profitable situation with the exception of Durham Tees Valley and the Highland and Islands airports. However, the poor economic situation as the result of the credit crunch and economic recession forced a few airports (such as Leeds Bradford and Humber- side) into a loss-making situation, and Coventry and Plymouth airports closed (although Coventry airport has now reopened for cargo and GA flights). It also contributed to some secondary sales. For example, 65 per cent of Peel Airports was sold to Vantage Airport Group in Holdings in 2011, and in 2012 Peel Airport's 75 per cent shareholding of Durham Tees Valley was sold to Peel Investments. Humberside airport was also sold by Manchester airport in 2012.

There are now a number of airport groups that manage more than one airport in the UK, including Heathrow Airport Holdings, Abertis, Peel Airports, GIP, Manchester Airports Group, GIP, Stobbart Holdings, Regional and City airports and Highlands and Islands (Ison *et al.*, 2011) (Table 2.7). However, there have also been cases where group ownership has not gone ahead as it was viewed as anti-competitive, for example with Bristol and Exeter airports and with Belfast City and Belfast International airports. Moreover, at the time of the privatisation of BAA there were extensive debates as to whether the airports of BAA should be privatised as a group or separately (see Chapter 8). In the end there was group privatisation, but since then the airline regulatory environment has become progressively more liberal, providing more opportunities for airport competition. Consequently there have been various reviews investigating whether BAA should be split up, the most comprehensive being undertaken by the UK's competition authority, the Competition Commission in 2007–09. This resulted in BAA being required to sell Gatwick, Stansted and Glasgow or Edinburgh (Competition Commission, 2009).

Australia and New Zealand

Between 1988 and 1997, most of Australia's airports were operated by the state-owned Federal Airports Corporation (FAC). At the beginning of 1997, the FAC operated 22 airports and handled over 60 million passengers annually. The FAC corporate office undertook various central services and imposed a common charging policy on its airports. Discussions relating to the privatisation of the FAC began in the early 1990s, and a firm decision to privatise them was made in 1996. Considerable attention was given to whether the airports should be sold off as a system (as had happened with BAA, which was the only other airport group at that time that had been privatised) or whether they should be sold off individually. Issues relating to the national interest, efficiency and competition were fiercely debated. Political factors played a key role, particularly because government forecasts had shown that separate sales would generate more income.

Table 2.7 Group ownership of UK airports, 2012

Owner	Airport
Abertis	Belfast International, Cardiff, Luton
BAA	Heathrow, Stansted, Southampton, Aberdeen, Glasgow, Edinburgh
GIP	Gatwick, London City Airport
Infratil	Prestwick, Manston
Ontario Teachers Pensions Plan	Birmingham, Bristol
Peel Investments/Peel Airports	Liverpool, Doncaster Robin Hood, Durham Tees Valley
Regional and City Airports	Exeter, Blackpool
Stobart Group	Southend, Carlisle
Manchester Airports Group	Humberside, East Midlands and Bournemouth
Scottish government	Highlands and Islands Airports

Source: Compiled by author from various sources

Eventually, it was decided that the airports would be leased off individually on long-term 50-year leases, with a further option for 49 years.

In phase 1 of the privatisation process, three airports – Melbourne, Brisbane and Perth – were sold in 1997. After Sydney, these three airports were the most profitable airports in the FAC system and they handled most of the traffic. It was the government's intention to bring competition and diversity into the airport system and so there were strict cross-ownership limits associated with the airport sales. Potential buyers had to have a majority Australian interest and airport management experience. As in the United Kingdom, the privatised airports were initially price-regulated. In addition, they were required to undertake quality-of-service monitoring and to provide evidence of this to the regulator. They also had to provide development guarantees by preparing 5-yearly master plans and pledging a certain sum for investment.

A number of airport companies were interested in operating the Australian airports, including BAA, Manchester, Vienna, Amsterdam, Aer Rianta, National Express and AGI. In the end BAA, Amsterdam and AGI were each partners in winning consortia (Table 2.8). The price paid for the Australian airports was particularly high, not only due to the fact that there were a large number of bidders, but also because high growth was being forecast and the infrastructure needs were relatively small.

It was decided that a further group of airports would be privatised in 1998. These 'phase-2' airports included Adelaide, which was the largest airport with just under 4 million passengers, and GA airports such as Archerfield, Parafield and Jandakot. Whereas the phase-1 airports had been relatively independent profitable entities, over half of these smaller airports were making losses and were much more reliant on the services of the FAC corporate office. Considerable preparation was therefore involved in getting the airports ready to be stand-alone entities. In spite of the fact that these airports were smaller and not in such a healthy position, again there was considerable interest in the sales, and relatively high purchase prices were paid. Some airport companies involved with the phase-1 airports, such as BAA and AGI, gained further airports under this phase-2 privatisation. Former FAC employees also gained interest in a number of airports such as Jandakot, Moorabbin, Townsville and Mount Isa. Cross-ownership restrictions prevented certain neighbouring airports coming under single ownership. Airlines were also not allowed to have greater than a 5 per cent share in any airport. Since the initial phase-1 and phase-2 privatisations, a number of these airports have also been subject to secondary sales with different investors.

Sydney Kingsford airport and the GA airports in the Sydney basin (Bankstown, Camden and Hoxton Park) were excluded from these two phases of privatisation because of unresolved issues related to noise control at Sydney Kingsford airport and continuing controversy over if, when and where a second Sydney airport would be built. In 1998, a separate state-owned entity, Sydney Airports Corporation, was established to run the four Sydney airports and Elldeson, the GA airport in Victoria which had been withdrawn from the privatisation process. In 2000, plans to develop a second Sydney airport were shelved for at least a decade, clearing the way for privatisation in 2001. However, the collapse of the Australian carrier Ansett and the events of 9/11 meant that the privatisation of Sydney airport was postponed until 2002, when it was bought by a consortium led by the two companies Macquarie Airports and Hochtief Airport.

Table 2.8 *Privatisation details of Australian airports*

Airport	Ownership	Privatisation date	Sale price (million A$)
Brisbane	Brisbane Airport Corporation Ltd (Schiphol Group, Commonwealth Investments, Port of Brisbane and others)	July 1997	1,397
Melbourne	Australia Pacific Airports Pty Ltd (BAA, AMP, Deutsche Asset Management and Hastings Fund)	July 1997	1,307
Perth	Westralia Airports Corporation Ltd (AGI, Hastings Fund, Infratil)	July 1997	639
Adelaide/Parafield	Adelaide Airport Ltd, Parafield Airport Ltd (Unisuper, Macquarie Airport Group, John Laing, Serco, and others)	May 1998	365
Alice Springs/Darwin/ Tennant Creek	Northern Territories Airports Ltd (AGI/Infratil)	May 1998	110
Archerfield	Archerfield Airport Corporation Ltd (Miengrove Pty)	May 1998	3
Canberra	Capital Airports Group (local company)	May 1998	66
Coolangatta	Gold Coast Airport Ltd (Unisuper, Macquarie Airport Group, Serco and others)	May 1998	104
Hobart	Hobart International Airport Corporation (AGI, Hobart Ports, Hambros)	May 1998	36
Jandakot	Jandakot Airport Holdings (property investors and former FAC employees)	June 1998	7
Launceston	Australia Pacific Airports Pty Ltd (BAA, AMP, Deutsche Asset Management and Hastings Fund)	May 1998	17
Moorabbin	Metropolitan Airport Consortium (property investors and former FAC employees)	May 1998	8
Townsville/Mount Isa	Australian Airports Ltd (former FAC CEO and financial investors)	May 1998	16
Sydney	Southern Cross Airports Consortium (Macquarie Airport Group, Hochtief, and others)	June 2002	5,588

Source: Compiled by author from individual airport regulation reports and other sources.

Unlike in Australia, the airports in New Zealand had always been operated individually, not as a group. The road to airport privatisation began in 1985 when the government decided that the airports would become public companies owned by the government and local authorities. This happened at the three largest airports, Auckland, Wellington and Christchurch, in the late 1990s, and since then all the other major airports have moved to such a structure. The first airport to be privatised was Auckland in 1998, when the government sold its 52 per cent shareholders through an IPO. This was the first airport in the Asia-Pacific region to be floated on the stock exchange. This is still the current ownership structure of the airport, although in 2007 the airport was the subject of an attempted takeover bid by Dubai Aerospace Enterprise and the Canada Pension Plan. It is now an investor itself, having involvement in New Zealand with Queenstown airport and in Australia with Cairns and Mackay airports. Also in 1998, 66 per cent of Wellington's shares were acquired by the utility company Infratil through a trade sale. By contrast, Christchurch airport remains in public ownership, with Christchurch City having 75 per cent of the shares and the central government owning the rest. There is also some partial private ownership at some of the smaller airports, but most airports still maintain some local government ownership (Lyon and Francis, 2006).

Both Australia and New Zealand are very reliant on air transport with large distances and poor surface transport, and both countries are politically, culturally and economically fairly similar. They were relatively early in privatising their airports compared with elsewhere, and they did this at a time when other public enterprises in the two countries were being privatised. However, the nature of the airport privatisation was in some ways quite different. Moreover, different approaches to airport regulation were adopted (which will be explored in Chapter 4).

United States

Since the United States has always possessed a private airline industry, it is often assumed that the airport industry must be driven primarily by private sector considerations. This is not the case. Nearly all US airports remain under local public ownership – with the pace towards privatisation being much slower than in many other parts of the world.

There are two key factors that make US airports unique when possible privatisation is being considered. First, US airports enter into legally binding contracts with their airline customers, known as airport use agreements, which detail the charging and conditions for the use of both airfield and terminal facilities. The airports, in reality, operate very closely with the airlines, and the airlines have a considerable amount of influence as regards future developments at the airports. Airline approval would be needed, therefore, if privatisation were to take place. Second, the airports are funded through a mixture of private and public funds. Most airports, and all the major ones, already have access to private financing through the commercial bond markets, where the airports have tax-exempt status due to their public ownership. Funding is also available from passenger facility charges (PFCs), which are generated by the passengers at individual airports and from grants from the Airport Improvement Program (AIP), which comes from the federal government's Aviation Trust Fund (which also funds air traffic control), financed primarily by a national passenger tax. At major airports tax-exempt commercial bonds and PFCs make up the bulk of the investment funds, whereas at smaller airports the AIP funds are proportionally more important (GAO, 2007). For example, for funding sources for committed projects in 2011 to 2015, it is estimated that overall 39 per cent will come from bonds, 24 per cent from PFCs and 16 per cent from the AIP. For large airports the split will be 46, 26 and 9 per cent, whereas by contrast for small airports it will be 24, 23 and 35 per cent (ACI North America, 2011) (Figures 2.5 and 2.6).

For some time there has been a concern that these funds will not be adequate, or are not the most appropriate, to meet future airport (and air traffic control) investment needs. Inevitably as

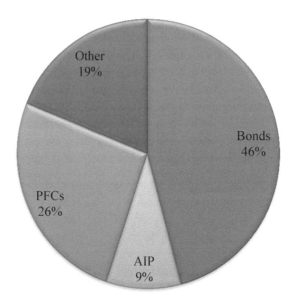

Figure 2.5 *Funding sources for committed projects at US large hubs, 2011–15*
Source: ACI North America (2011)

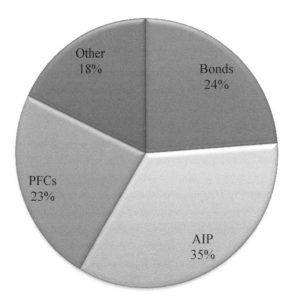

Figure 2.6 *Funding sources for committed projects at US small hubs, 2011–15*
Source: ACI North America (2011)

elsewhere where airport funding has become an issue, privatisation has also been considered as an option. In the United States, though, it is not an easy process. Way back in 1995, the privatisation of John Wayne Airport in California's Orange County was discussed as part of the solution to the county's bankruptcy. However, the likelihood of litigation by the airlines – who argued that federal law prohibited the use of airport revenues (including sale proceeds) for non-airport purposes (so-called 'revenue diversion') – led to the conclusion that airport privatisation was not feasible. This key issue, namely the inability of airport owners to reap the financial benefits from the airports, is seen as one of the key obstacles to airport privatisation in the United States. Many argue that if airport revenues were diverted to other municipal purposes, costs at the airports would rise for both passengers and airlines. Also, many local politicians who hold very powerful positions do not wish to give up control of their airports. Various other issues would have to be resolved if such privatisation were to take place. For example, would private airports survive if they could not use trust fund, PFC or tax-exempt debt financing? Would they have to pay back the federal grants? At many of the airports, the use agreements with the airlines could mean that the airports could be privatised only as the agreements expire, or that privatisation would have to be limited within the bounds of the agreement.

There have been some, albeit rather limited, moves towards airport privatisation with the introduction of the airport privatisation pilot programme in October 1996. This makes provision for five airports to be exempted from some of the legal requirements that impede their sale to private entities. For example, the restrictions on prohibiting revenues to be used for non-aeronautical reasons (i.e. general municipal purposes) have been waived. Such privatisations need approval of the 65 per cent of airlines using the airport if the revenues are to be used for other purposes. Under the scheme, there must be a GA airport and only one large hub airport. GA airports may be leased or sold, but larger airports can only be leased (FAA, 2012).

There has been only limited interest in this scheme particularly because of slow and rather complex approval procedures and the majority airline consensus rule. The only airport privatised under the scheme to date is Stewart International Airport in New York, which was given a 99-year lease to the British company National Express. The airport transferred management in April 2000. However, the airport never received the approval of the required majority of airlines and so the lease payments still had to be used for airport purposes. Then in 2006 the airport lease was sold back to a public body, the Port Authority of New York and New Jersey, as National Express no longer has an interest in operating airports. Other airports such as Brown Field (a GA facility in San Diego) and New Orleans Lakefront have also been looked at under the scheme, but none has actually been privatised.

In 2009, it appeared that Chicago Midway was to become the first large hub to be privatised under this scheme. However, the winning consortium, which included the Vancouver airport operator (YVRAS, called the Vantage Group since December 2011) failed to be able to raise sufficient funding in the tough economic conditions of 2009 and so the privatisation was postponed and seems unlikely to go ahead now. Louis Armstrong New Orleans airport was also given preliminary approval under the scheme in 2009 but withdrew in 2010. The other active projects are the small airports of Gwinnett County Briscoe and Hendry County Airglades, and the more significant Luis Muñoz Marin San Juan airport in Puerto Rico, which could be the first privately run concession in a US-controlled Territory.

In spite of these developments, more radical privatisation still seems fairly remote, although interest in this area remains (Enrico *et al.*, 2012). Some private participation has been achieved through the adoption of management contracts and project finance schemes, but this has been very limited. The former company Airports Group International had some management contracts before the 1990s, but mostly at small airports with the exception of the international terminal at Atlanta airport. However, in 1995 BAA won the 10-year management contract for Indianapolis airport, which was an airport of considerable size at that time with a throughput of 6.7 million passengers. Under the scheme, BAA was not to receive any fixed management fee but would share in the savings it generated. The company guaranteed average annual savings of more than US$3 million (US$32 million over a 10-year agreement) and would not be paid any fees until it produced average annual savings of nearly US$6 million (US$58 million over a 10-year agreement). BAA expected to save the airport $100 million during the 10-year contract by increasing non-aviation revenue and reducing expenditure from energy supply, equipment and payroll costs. The airport board would continue to set policy, enforce agreements and control rates and charges (Ott, 1998). In 1998 an amended new 10-year contract was signed. BAA also had retail management contracts at Boston and Pittsburgh, but has subsequently given these up to focus on its core activities in the UK.

In another development in 1997, the financing, construction and operation of the international arrivals building at New York JFK airport was handed over to a private consortium (which included Amsterdam Schiphol airport) for 20 years. There have also been some plans to develop a new airport in Illinois (Abraham Lincoln National Airport) through a public–private partnership where the government would own the land and the private contractor would own and operate the facilities. Generally, however, the fiscal and political constraints that exist at US airports have meant that private sector involvement has in some cases been difficult to maintain successfully. The notable example here is the airport of Harrisburg, where BAA lost a management contract after managing the airport for only 3 years of the 10-year agreement primarily because the airport's administration changed. The former Wiggins (Planestation) group also withdrew its interest at Smyrna airport near Nashville, Tennessee because of administrative constraints.

More recently, however, there has been the development of the Branson airport in Missouri which is privately owned and managed. It opened in 2009 to appeal to LCCs at a total project cost of $140 million, being funded $26.5 million by private equity and $114 million in bonds (Branson airport, 2012). Privatisation continues to be discussed at some airports, for example Ontario airport, which is currently operated by Los Angeles World Airports. Capital funding, as always, remains an issue (ACI North America, 2011). This is not only because of the fact the AIP grants are currently frozen as the US Congress failed to re-enact the FAA reauthorisation legislation which authorises federal grant funding, but also, as in many other countries throughout the world, there is a shortfall in general public sector funding.

India

The recent development of India's economy, together with a rapidly expanding middle class and a more liberal domestic and international regulatory aviation environment, has resulted in a huge growth in air travel over the past few years. Annual passenger growth has exceeded 10 per cent in all but one of the past nine years (Table 2.9). There are many more airlines now serving

Table 2.9 *Total airport traffic at Indian airports, 2002–11*

Period (Apr–Mar)	02–03	03–04	04–05	05–06	06–07	07–08	08–09	09–10	10–11
Passengers (million)	44.0	48.7	59.3	73.4	96.4	116.9	108.9	123.7	143.4
Freight (000 tonnes)	982.4	1,068.2	1,280.6	1,404.0	1,553.5	1,714.0	1,697.2	1,957.1	2,348.4
Aircraft movements (000)	560.6	638.6	719.1	838.4	1,075.5	1,307.6	1,305.9	1,330.6	1,393.4
Growth rates (per cent):									
Passengers	10.0	10.7	12.8	23.8	31.3	21.2	−6.9	13.6	15.9
Freight	15.1	8.7	19.9	9.6	10.6	10.5	−1.0	15.0	19.8
Aircraft movements	9.9	13.9	12.6	16.6	28.2	21.3	−0.1	1.8	4.7

Source: Airports Authority of India

domestic and international routes and there is a growing Indian LCC industry. All of this has meant that many of the airports have inadequate and ageing infrastructure and that there is a lack of internationally accepted standards to cope with this increased demand.

There are 449 airports and airfields in India. Up until recently all major commercial airports in India were managed by a state organisation, the Airport Authority of India (AAI), which was formed in 1995 with the merging of the National Airports Authority and the International Airports Authority of India. AAI manages 92 airports directly and is also responsible for 28 civil passenger enclaves at defence airfields as well as providing all the air traffic control services. Even before the recent traffic boom of the past few years, privatisation was being discussed in the late 1990s for the four main international airports (Delhi, Mumbai, Chennai and Kolkata) but this came to nothing – particularly because no foreign investment was allowed in airports at that time. The first actual privatisation project did not occur with these airports, but at Cochin, Kerala in southern India, where a new airport opened in 1999 having been financed 26 per cent from the state of Kerala and the rest from NRIs, financial institutions and airport service providers.

After many bureaucratic, legal and political delays, two 30-year (with another 30-year option) BOT greenfield airport projects were set up in 2004. This was after it was agreed that the AAI could enter into joint ventures with private and foreign investors as long as 26 per cent public ownership was retained. These two airports are in the IT centres of Bengaluru and Hyderabad (Brunner, 2007). At Bengaluru the private consortium consisted of Siemens, Zurich Airport and the Indian engineering and construction company Larsen and Toubro (L&T), while at Hyderabad the private investors were GMR, a large Indian infrastructure company, and Malaysia Airports Holdings Berhad. Both airports opened in 2008.

Then again, after many delays and a very lengthy bidding process, public–private joint venture partnerships were eventually agreed for India's two largest airports (accounting for nearly half of total Indian traffic), namely Delhi and Mumbai in 2006 (Jain *et al.*, 2007). These are 30-year concession agreements – again with a possibility of a further 30 years – which aim to upgrade and modernise the two airports. In both cases the AAI has a 26 per cent share in the new airport companies, Delhi International Airport Private Limited (DIAL) and Mumbai International Airport Private Limited (MIAL). The international airport operators Fraport and Malaysia Airports Holdings BhD both have a share in DIAL as well as GMR. The South African airport company ACSA has a stake in MIAL together with a large Indian infrastructure company GVK. DIAL agreed to pay 46 per cent of revenues to the government and to invest around US$2 billion on the first stage of development, which involved upgrading the existing terminal and constructing a new domestic terminal and runway. MIAL agreed to pay 39 per cent of revenues and to invest US$1.6 billion to develop the city of the airport from its current 18 million passengers to 40 million (CAPA Centre for Aviation, 2007) (Table 2.10).

Further privatisation is likely to occur to develop and modernise many of the other Indian airports, and there have also been discussions of a number of new greenfield sites being funded through BOT arrangements (Raghunath, 2010). For example, a new airport is being built at Durgapur with Singapore Changi airport having a major interest with this development. Also there is a new second Mumbai airport (Navi Mumbai International airport) where again a BOT project with 74 per cent private involvement is planned

Table 2.10 Major privatisation projects at Indian airports

Airport	Privatisation date	Airport partners	Passengers 2006–07 (million)	Percentage share of AAI traffic
Cochin	1999	26 per cent State of Kerala; 74 per cent non-resident Indians, financial institutions and airport service providers.	2.6	2.7
Bengaluru	2004	26 per cent AAI/State of Karnataka; 74 per cent Siemens/Zurich Airport/L&T	8.1	8.4
Hyderabad	2004	26 per cent AAI/State of Andhra Pradesh; 74 per cent GMR/Malaysia Airports	5.8	6.0
Delhi	2006	26 per cent AAI; 74 per cent GMR/Fraport/Malaysia Airports/other private investors	20.4	21.1
Mumbai	2006	26 per cent AAI; 74 per cent GVK/ACSA/other private investors	22.2	23.0

Source: Compiled by the author from various sources

Brazil

After many years of economic and political problems relating to inflation and economic stagna-tion, Brazil's economy began to stabilise in the 1990s and foreign investments grew rapidly. It is now one of the four BRIC countries which are experiencing major economic growth that is expected to continue into the future. It has a population of over 200 million people, making it the fifth largest country in the world and the largest in South America; in 2012 it became the world's sixth largest economy. This has meant that there are approximately 90 million Brazilian middle-class citizens compared with just 50 million in 2003 (Lunsford, 2012; LeighFisher, 2011). All these developments have meant there has been a huge increase in domestic and international traffic. Between 1997 and 2003 the annual average growth in passengers was 4 per cent, but between 2003 and 2010 this increased to just under 12 per cent per annum (Figure 2.7). The sheer size and geography of the country means that air transport is essential for the development of trade, communications and tourism.

Brazil has in excess of 2,000 airfields. The main 67 airports that handle over 95 per cent of the traffic have traditionally been managed by the state-owned Brazilian Airport Infrastructure Enter-prise (Infraero), which was established in 1972. In 1987 this was divided into seven regional areas, each containing at least one major airport and having a separate head office. In 2010 Infraero handled 155 million passengers, 2,648 thousand aircraft movements and 1,324 thousand tonnes of freight. The speed of air transport growth has put very significant pressure on the existing airport

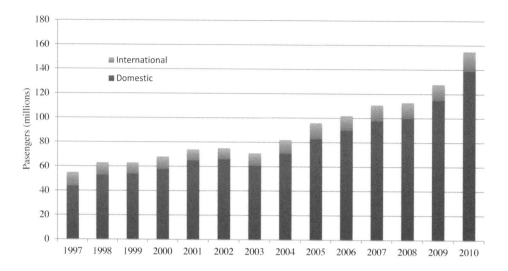

Figure 2.7 *Passengers at Infraero Airports in Brazil, 1997–2010*
Source: Infraero

capacity, resulting in delays and poor service levels. Of the 20 largest domestic airports, 10 had saturated passenger terminals in 2009 with a further four joining this status by 2014 as a result of traffic being predicted to increase by over 5 per cent per year. The choice of Brazil to host the football World Cup in 2014 and then the summer Olympic Games in 2016 has increased the urgency to provide modernised and expanded infrastructure to cope with these events. In the long term it is estimated that the airport capacity needs to increase by nearly two and half times by 2030 from the current 130 million to 310 million (McKinsey and Company, 2010).

Traditionally, Brazil has been one of few countries in South America where it was not considered politically acceptable to view airport privatisation as a way to finance investment. Infraero was viewed as a branch of the military and the airports were run with very little consideration of commercial goals. However, there was an ideological shift in 2010 when the government announced that it would seek concessions contracts from private sector companies to expand and modernise some of the country's airports. This was in spite of the concern expressed by the airport workers' unions and some airlines, who feared a hike in prices as occurred in Argentina and Mexico. In order to focus on the provision of adequate airport facilities, a new Ministry of Civil Aviation, separate for the first time from the Ministry of Defence, was also created.

The next significant development was a BOT privatisation that was agreed in 2011 to develop a greenfield airport in the city of Natal, in the north-east of Brazil. The winning bidder was the consortium Infra America, consisting of the Brazilian engineering firm Engevix teamed up with Argentina's Corporacion America, which is the majority owner of AA 2000, and also has interests in Montevideo Uruguay, Guayaquil Ecuador, Italy and Armenia. The new airport is to be built within three years and then operated for 25 years (with a possible one-off five-year extension) with an excess of $US400 million investment funds. The Brazilian government, via

Infraero, is responsible for the construction of the airfield facilities but has no actual involvement in the concession agreement (CAPA Centre for Aviation, 2011b)

The success of this private project, using an approach previously untested by the government and raising much more money than the government had planned (US$106 million compared with the set minimum amount of $US33 million), encouraged the further offering as concessions of the three major international airports – São Paulo Guarulhos (the main international gateway to Brazil and the largest airport in Latin America), Sao Paulo Viracopos Campinas (Sao Paulo's third airport and a major cargo hub), and Brasília (serving the capital). These three airports handle around a third of all the passenger traffic. A different concessionaire had to be chosen for each airport although each consortium could bid for more than one airport. By relieving Infraero of the burden of investment in these major airports, it is hoped that it will be free to focus on others where work is needed to prepare for the World Cup and the Olympics. The detailed terms of the concession vary, but for all three airports the government, through Infraero, is maintaining a 49 per cent share in each concession and in addition has a power of veto over strategic issues, which undoubtedly has increased the risks for investors. Airlines cannot have more than 1 per cent involvement in any consortium. The bid price has to be paid back in inflation-linked equal instalments, and in addition a certain share of revenues has to be given to the government.

The winning bidders were selected in February 2012 and each had a mixture of foreign and Brazilian consortium partners (Table 2.11). Interestingly, one of the winning bidding companies was the South African airport company ACSA which had experience of handling Olympic traffic. There were a larger number of initial bids, particularly for Guarulhos and Brasília (ten and eight respectively compared to four at Viracopos) (Lunsford, 2012) and at all three airports the winning bid was well in excess of the minimum bid raising concerns again from the airlines that this will result in high fees. One-third of the investment has to be spent before the World Cup which will undoubtedly prove very challenging for the consortia. Subsequently three further privatisations were announced for Rio de Janeiro Galeao International Airport, Rio de Janeiro Santos Dumont Airport and Confins Belo Horizonte Airport in 2012.

Japan

The geography of Japan has meant that aviation plays a key role in its economic development and in the generation of outbound and inbound tourism. There are a large number of airports for public use, in total around 100. Historically the Ministry of Land, Infrastructure, Transport and Tourism (MLIT) classified Japan's airports according to their traffic characteristics. There were five Class 1 international airports (Toyko-Narita Airport, Toyko-Haneda Airport, Osaka-Kansai Airport, Osaka-Itami Airport, Chubu-Centrair Airport); 24 Class 2 airports serving major domestic routes (19 Class 2(A) airports being managed by MLIT and five Class 2(B) being managed by local government); 53 Class 3 airports serving regional and local traffic; and 15 other airports, some of which were jointly used by the Defence Agency or the US Air Force, or were private. The airports are now identified (in the 2008 New Airport Act) as 'International' or 'Other' airports, with further classifications related to who manages them. Three of the five Class 1 airports (Narita, Kansai and Centrair) are run by limited corporations and two (Haneda and Itami) directly by the MLIT. The Class 3 airports are managed by local government (Kato *et al.*, 2011).

Table 2.11 Major privatisation projects at Brazil airports

Airport	Passenger numbers in 2010 (000s)	Cargo tonnes in 2010 (000s)	Revenue R$ (million)	Concession conditions	Winning consortium
Sao Paulo Guarulhos	26,849	431	770	20 years Minimum bid: R$ 3.4 billion (US$1.97 billion) 10 per cent annual gross revenue per annum Investment required R$ 4.6 billion (US$2.7 billion)	South Africa's ACSA with Brazil's Invepar and OAS Bid: R$16.2 billion (US$9.4 billion)
Sao Paulo Viracopos Campinas	5,430	258	264	30 years Minimum bid: R$ 1.5 billion (US$871 billion) 5 per cent annual gross revenue per annum Investment required R$ 8.7 billion (US$5.05 billion)	France's Egis with Brazil's Triunfo Participacoes Bid R$3.8 billion (US$2.6 billion)
Brasilia	14,347	33	129	25 years Minimum bid: R$ 582 million (US$338 million) 2 per cent annual gross revenue per annum Investment required R$2.8 billion ($US$1.6 billion)	Argentina's Corporacion America with Brazil's Engevix (R$4.51 billion)

Sources: LeighFisher (2011); Infraero

In comparison with typical practice in other countries, the airports are unusual in that their scope of business is limited by law, which means that the non-aeronautical facilities (such as the passenger or cargo terminal buildings and car parking) are managed by different entities from the basic aeronautical facilities (such as runways, taxiways and aprons). These commercial assets are usually run by mixed public/private corporations, primarily as a result of the shortage of available government funding for terminals when the airport industry in Japan began to expand rapidly in the 1950s and 1960s. It is only at Narita, Kansai and Centrair where there is integrated management that has responsibility for both the airfield and terminal facilities.

The long period of high and stable economic development in Japan and population growth that followed the Second World War required huge investment in existing and new airports. In 1956 the Airport Development Act was passed, and this was linked to five-yearly development plans, which were first introduced in 1967 (Shibata, 1999). The Act defined who was responsible for the airports, with central government through the MLIT being fully responsible for providing and administering the Class 1 and 2A airports and covering the development costs. However, there was subsequent special legislation concerning the international airports of Narita, Kansai and Centrair which exempted them from this general legislation. The MLIT was also responsible for providing the Class 2(B) airports, which were administered by local governments, and 55 per cent of the financial burden of the aeronautical facilities. For Class 3 airports, the MLIT shared half of the development costs with the local government, which was responsible for providing and administrating the airports (Ohta, 1999).

The aeronautical revenues generated by Haneda, Itami and the Class 2A airports go to a national government fund for airport construction and maintenance, the Kuko Seibi Tokubetsu Kaikei or the Airport Special Account (ASA) (now known as the Airport Development Account). The MLIT then distributes this money (and additional funding from general national accounts) through capital grants to the individual airports. This account was set up in 1970 to ensure there were sufficient funds to finance improvement projects which were being identified in the five-yearly airport development plans. The fund does not finance the terminals or car park operations, and so revenues from these facilities do not go into the account. The aeronautical revenues from the Class 2B and 3 airports that are managed by local government are kept by the airport operator and not given to the account. The fund does, however, finance development at these airports, and so in effect the revenues from the Class 1 and Class 2A airports are used to subsidise these smaller airports. The Airport Development Act did not allow airports to be operated by independent corporations, which is why special legislation was established in order to allow for different governance models at Narita, Kansai and Centrair. This situation was primarily in response to a shortage of account funds to finance these airports, and it consequently means that these three airports do not contribute to the fund but neither are they supported by it.

The economic development of Japan has been predominantly concentrated in the three metropolitan regions of Tokyo, Osaka and Nagoya, which is where the international airports are located. In 1966 the state-controlled New Tokyo International Airport Authority was established to finance and run Tokyo's second airport, Narita, which opened in 1978 despite fierce and prolonged opposition by the local community. Then in 2004 a new 100 per cent public entity, the Narita International Airport Corporation, took over the responsibility of owning and managing Narita. Up until recently, the other Tokyo airport, Haneda, which is nearer to Tokyo city centre, has handled almost exclusively domestic traffic, with Narita taking the international traffic. In the Osaka region, Kansai International Airport, which is built on an artificial island of reclaimed land in the sea, was opened in 1994 to overcome capacity shortages at Itami airport. Itami, which is closer to the city centre of Osaka, now receives only domestic traffic. Kansai International Airport Company owns and operates both the airfield and terminal facilities of Kansai. This company is 67 per cent owned by the central government with the remaining shares belonging to 12 different local governments and 803 companies and individuals. In 2005, Centrair airport opened to serve the Chubu region of Japan which had previously relied on the congested Nagoya airport. Like Kansai airport, it is owned by a company that operates both the airfield and terminal buildings.

One of the major issues relates to this method of financing the Japanese airports, which has encouraged an unbalanced and inefficient system (Yoshida and Fujimoto, 2004; Barros *et al.*, 2010). The pooling and redistributing of funds means that the incentives for individual airports to strive for greater efficiency are weakened. Moreover, it has been argued that the allocation of the funds from the airport account has often been determined on a basis of political rather than economic need, and has led to significant overinvestment at a number of regional airports. There has been a belief that every prefecture has the right to have at least one airport, even if there is no actual need demonstrated. This has undoubtedly contributed to the poor financial health of the airports. Kato *et al.* (2011) concluded that only airports serving more than 5.2 million passengers are profitable. It is also the case that the Class 1/2A airports cross-subsidise the Class 2B/3 airports (with only the former group contributing to the fund but with both benefiting from it), and this in turn is a contributing factor to the overinvestment at the smaller airports and underinvestment at the larger airports. As a result of growing dissatisfaction with this policy, the Airport Development Act was revised in 2008 (now just called the Airport Act) to focus more on improving the utilisation and efficiency of existing airports rather than on development of the regional airports (Barros *et al.*, 2010).

Another key issue is the inability of most airports to benefit from commercial revenues due to the facilities associated with these activities being operated by different entities. This lack of an integrated management model hinders efficiency and means that airports miss out on this additional source of income, which can potentially be used to cross-subsidise aeronautical operations and lower airport charges. There is growing concern that these high charges, combined with capacity constraints particularly in the Tokyo area, make the international airports very uncompetitive compared with other East and South East Asian rivals. Japan has been moving progressively to a more deregulated airline environment in recent years, but the airport situation appears to be impeding this development. The capacity problems at the major airports are compounded by the fact there is very little available land and that land prices are high. There also tends to be strong opposition to any airport expansion from local residents and landowners, and there are high costs associated with noise-protection measures.

The airports serving Tokyo (Narita and Haneda) are particularly problematic as they both have been operating to capacity for many years, partly because of limited operating hours due to environmental pressures and partly because of fierce resistance to any expansion plans. This lack of capacity, and the dual airport system that historically inhibited international–domestic transfers (with Narita being the international airport and Haneda being the domestic one), increased demands on the government to re-internationalise Haneda (Feldhoff, 2003). As a result, a dedicated international terminal was opened in 2010 at the same time as the completion of a fourth runway. Another challenging airport is Kansai, where traffic has not been nearly as high as expected. Some domestic routes from Itami have been shifted to Kansai to try and improve the situation, but at the same time the competition from the *Shinkansen* (bullet train) has been strengthened. In addition, traffic is likely to have been deterred by the very expensive airport charges due to the high airport costs. In particular, the artificial island that the airport is built on is sinking at a far greater rate than was expected, and the airport has had to introduce costly measures to handle the effects of this and to cope with further sinking that may occur in the future. This, combined with the original high construction costs of the airport and the costs of a second runway that opened in 2007, means the airport company has huge debt and interest payments of 1.3 trillion yen and has had to rely heavily on injections of public money to survive. Meanwhile, the neighbouring domestic airport of Itami, which remains open although it was originally planned to be closed when Kansai was built, continues to be profitable (Kato *et al.*, 2011).

In general the management and finance of Japanese airports has changed very little over the years. However, in May 2011 the Diet of Japan passed legislation to allow for a new Kansai International Airport Corporation to be set up by April 2012 to integrate the management of the two airports in the Osaka area. This wholly government-owned airport company owns the runways of both airports, the land assets of Itami airport and the terminal facilities of Kansai, inheriting about 400 billion yen worth of Kansai's interest-bearing debts. However, it is also planned that the rights to operate the airports will be transferred to the private sector in terms of a concession agreement for at least 30 years by March 2016. It is expected that this will earn the government about the same amount as the total debts. In addition it is planned that a separate company will take over Kansai's land assets and the rest of the debt. This debt will be reduced by renting the land to the new airport company (*Japan Times Online*, 2011). It is hoped that these changes will allow the airport to compete more effectively with the congested Tokyo airports as an international hub and, through having greater pricing and management freedom, will be able to become a major international airport for Asian cargo operations and for LCC operators to attract inbound tourism.

As regards the other airports, the latest development was in 2012 when the MLIT drafted a bill that could lead to 94 regional airports being run by integrated companies (e.g. covering both airfield and terminal operations) who could have long-term concessions for 30–50 years. Again it is hoped that this will reduce the level of airport charges and make the airports more attractive. Meanwhile, Narita International Airport Corporation continues to be fully owned by the public sector, although originally it was envisaged when the corporation was established in 2004 that this would be followed by a sell-off of shares to the private sector.

The past few years have clearly been a very challenging time for the Japanese airport industry. Poor economic conditions in Japan, coupled with a declining population and the collapse in January 2010 of JAL and its subsequent reorganisation and shrinking of the network, have all resulted in a decline in traffic. These problems were compounded by the effects of the devastating earthquake of March 2011. However, it does appear that some of the inherent weaknesses of the Japanese airport system, namely the pooling of airport revenues and the lack of integrated management models, are now being addressed.

AIRPORT OPERATORS AND INVESTORS

Airport privatisation has attracted a variety of different investors and companies that have become interested in making airport purchases or managing airports. In the early stages of privatisation in the 1990s, many potential investors were well established airport companies that welcomed the opportunity to expand beyond previously well defined national barriers. Many of these companies, for example BAA, AdP, Aer Rianta (now the Dublin Airport Authority), Schiphol (owner of Amsterdam airport) and Fraport (owner of Frankfurt airport), had already been active in providing consultancy services and running management contracts at other airports, and it was a natural evolution of the business to become more heavily involved in other airports. AdP had built a reputation in the management of engineering and construction projects in countries such as China, Vietnam, Cyprus, the Philippines, Indonesia and the Lebanon. Fraport had been involved with ground-handling contracts and baggage systems in areas as diverse as Spain, the United States and Kenya. Aer Rianta had specialised mostly in retail contracts.

So privatisation increased the opportunities for international expansion for airport companies, particularly because in many cases the potential buyers had to provide evidence of airport management expertise. By 2000, BAA had airport interests in Italy, the United States, Australia and Mauritius. The Schiphol Group had involvement in other airports in the Netherlands, Australia and the United States. Other European airports or airport groups with international interests included Rome, Milan, Copenhagen, Vienna, Zurich and AENA. Some of the European airports, such as Rome, Milan, Schiphol and Fraport, also had involvement with other airports in their own country. Outside Europe, international airport companies were less involved, the notable exception being YVR Airport Services (YVRAS) (a subsidiary of Vancouver airport, now called Vantage), and had interests in a number of South and Central American airports and Sharm El Sheikh airport in Egypt (although the latter was subsequently cancelled by the Egyptian government).

Some airport operators, such as AdP, Fraport, Zurich and the Vantage Airport Group, have continued to expand their involvement in other airports and have been joined by more recent players such as Changi Singapore airport (corporatised in 2009), Incheon Seoul and Malaysia Airport Holdings Berhad. This reflects the growing importance of Asia within the global airport industry and the increased interest in privatisation in the area. Others have reduced their involvement, such as the Dublin Airport Authority which has sold its share in Hamburg and Birmingham airports, and BAA which disposed of all its international interests to focus on its core UK activities. Schiphol airport seems to be focusing on its existing investments at JFK, New York and Brisbane. Copenhagen sold its stake in China's Hainan Meilan Airport in 2007, the ASUR airports in Mexico in 2010 and Newcastle in 2012.

There were also a number of property, utility, infrastructure and construction organisations that saw some potential synergies with airport operations and took advantage of the early airport privatisations. One such property developer was TBI, which developed its involvement in the airport sector in the mid- to late 1990s by acquiring interests in the United Kingdom in Cardiff (1995) and Belfast International (1996), Orlando Sanford International airport in the United States (1997) and Stockholm Skavsta airport in Sweden (1998). In 1999 it took the decision to concentrate on its airport business and so disposed of all property interests except the Cardiff

Hilton Hotel. It subsequently took over AGI and acquired extra interests in Australia, Bolivia, USA, Canada and Luton (although a number of these have now been disposed of). In 2005 it was taken over by the Spanish infrastructure company Abertis, with the company expanding further in 2007 with the acquisition of Desarrollo de Concesiones Aéroportuarias (DCA), which had stakes in 15 airports in Mexico, Jamaica, Chile and Columbia. This means that the company now has interests in 30 airports in nine countries. Another UK property developer is Peel Holdings, which acquired Liverpool airport in 1997 and Durham Tees Valley in 2003, and subsequently went on to develop Robin Hood Doncaster airport which was previously a military base. However, it has experienced financial difficulties in recent years, and consequently 65 per cent of the company was bought by YVRAS in 2010. Then there is the New Zealand utility company Infratil, which became involved with airports when it purchased two-thirds of Wellington airport in 1998. More recently it went on to purchase Prestwick and London Manston airport in the United Kingdom, and acquired a shareholding in Perth and North Territory airports in Australia. Unlike many of the other investors, it has specialised in managing relatively small airports. It also used to own 90 per cent of Luebeck airport in Germany until 2009, when it sold its shares back to the City of Luebeck as a result of passenger growth not being as high as expected.

The Spanish infrastructure company Ferrovial emerged somewhat later as a major player within the airport industry. In the early 2000s it acquired interests in Bristol and Belfast City in the United Kingdom, Niagara Falls in the United States and Antofagasta in Chile. However, it was its purchase of BAA in 2006 which transformed Ferrovial into one of the world's largest airport operators (in terms of passenger numbers), although it has subsequently reduced its shareholding in the company to 34 per cent. In the past there has also been interest from transport companies, most notably National Express, which had stakes in East Midlands, Bournemouth (and Stewart International) until 2001 when it sold its UK airports to concentrate on other transport activities. UK transport operators Firstgroup and Stagecoach also owned one UK airport each in the late 1990s but have now sold these airports. This shows that perhaps the synergies from airport operations which these transport operators had hoped for were not as significant as was first thought.

Meanwhile, a number of construction companies have shown an interest in operating airports, partly because this can provide them with an opportunity for involvement in some major construction projects. In France the company Vinci, which has had a close partnership with AdP on international projects, has been involved in a number of privatisations. In Germany Hochtief was an international construction services company which for many years had been involved in the planning, constructing and financing of airports before being active in any privatisation developments. This changed in 1996 when it led the consortium that won the BOT project contract for the new Athens airport. Then in 1997, in response to the growing number of privatisation opportunities, Hochtief founded the fully owned subsidiary Hochtief AirPort (HTA). HTA's next airport involvement came in 1998, when it formed a consortium with the former Irish airport operator Aer Rianta to buy 50 per cent of Dusseldorf airport through a trade sale. This was followed by the purchase of another German airport, Hamburg airport in 2000, when again it teamed up with Aer Rianta to buy 49 per cent of the airport. In 2002 it was part of the successful Southern Cross Airports Consortium which bought Sydney airport, and in 2005 it led a consortium which won a BOT contract at Tirana airport in Albania. It has a 47 per cent share in the consortium and the project will last until 2025. Then in 2007 it bought a 37 per cent interest in the secondary sale of BAA's shareholdings in Budapest airport. HTA now has a portfolio of a number of airports, but Hochtief has been planning to sell these airport interests to concentrate more on the core activities of services and maintenance. The Spanish construction company ACS is now actually the largest shareholder of the parent company Hochtief.

Elsewhere, in India there are two large infrastructure companies that have become involved with airports. One is the GMR group, which has interests in energy, highways and urban infrastructure as well as airports. The other is GVK, which also has involvement in the hospitality, services and manufacturing sectors. GMR has participated in the privatisation projects at the Indian airports of Delhi and Hyderabad as well as in Turkey and the Maldives, while GVK has involvement with airports in Mumbai, Bengaluru and also Yogyakarta in Indonesia.

An area of considerable debate is whether airlines should buy and operate airports. In the United States airlines already partially or totally lease terminals, and in Australia some of the domestic terminals are leased to Qantas. This means the airlines get exclusive rights to parts of the terminal. Elsewhere, however, such practice is not very common. An unusual example was the Birmingham Eurohub, which was partially financed by BA. A more recent development was Lufthansa's joint venture partnership with Munich airport in developing its second terminal, which opened in 2003. The airport company has a 60 per cent shareholding while Lufthansa has a 40 per cent shareholding (Kerkloh, 2007). Also, Lufthansa now has a 10 per cent stake in the airport. The main reason given for this purchase was to enable Lufthansa to intensify its partnership with Fraport and to strengthen its position at Frankfurt, which is its major hub.

Thai Airways and Bangkok Airways have shown an interest in operating airports to achieve greater control, with Thai Airways having a 10-year management contract at Chittagong airport in Bangladesh, and Bangkok Airways building and operating three small Thai airports serving tourist destinations. In China, too, airlines such as Hainan Airlines, Sichuan Airlines and Shandong have all become involved with airports, primarily to ensure investment takes place at the airports that they serve. In Russia, Aeroflot owns 53 per cent of Moscow Sheremetyeveo, and additionally Moscow Domodedovo is managed by the East Line Group, which began life as an airline. In 2004 the travel company TUI took over the management of Coventry airport, which was one of its bases in the UK, to ensure there was adequate infrastructure, but then pulled out when it met obstacles to its expansion plans. In the future it is also planned that Air Baltic will build and operate the new terminal at Riga airport, and other airlines have expressed interest in becoming involved in airport management, for example Air New Zealand at Queensland airport and Iberia in Paraguay.

If an individual airline or alliance grouping wanted to buy a substantial share of an airport to obtain more control over the facilities and develop a stronger brand presence, there may be a number of regulatory and competition issues that need to be considered to ensure this does not lead to discriminatory practices. In some cases there may be limits to airline ownership when an airport is privatised. Low-cost carriers have expressed an interest in running their own facilities in order to keep the service simple and keep costs down. For example, Jazeera, a Kuwait-based

LCC, has plans for a dedicated terminal. easyJet, in its early years when it was developing services out of London Luton airport, unsuccessfully tried to buy the airport when it was up for sale. It also expressed interest in being involved with Gatwick's secondary sale (as did Virgin Atlantic). Ryanair has also been unsuccessful in gaining approval to build its own low-cost terminal at Dublin, which it had been demanding for many years. Elsewhere this airline has made substantial investment in facilities at Bremen and has expressed interest in running facilities at Stansted.

Finally there are the financial investors, such as investment banks, pension funds and private equity funds, who were relatively late in becoming directly involved with airport sales compared with other organisations (although they always participated in the financing of privatisation deals), but now play a major role by being able to raise substantial amounts of capital to purchase stakes, and often controlling interests, in airports. One such investor was the Macquarie Group, a very large Australian company offering a wide range of international banking, financial, advisory and investment services. In recent years it developed a very broad range of infrastructure, real estate and private equity investment funds in Australia and other countries. The group's first involvement with airport privatisation was in the United Kingdom when the private equity investment fund Macquarie Airports Group (MAG) acquired shares in Birmingham and Bristol airports. Then in 2002 the special purpose investment fund Macquarie Airports (MAp) was founded and listed on the stock exchange, and became independent from the Macquarie Group in 2009. The first major involvement of MAp was with Sydney airport in 2002, followed by Rome airport in 2003, Brussels airport in 2004 and Copenhagen airport in 2005.

MAp grew very quickly to become the second largest private owner–operator after BAA/Ferrovial, and the first major financial investor to have a major involvement in airport privatisation. However, in 2007 MAp chose to withdraw from its involvement in Birmingham airport to focus on other activities; and to withdraw from Rome airport primarily because of disagreement with the other main investor Leonardo about future investments at the airport. Then in 2007 MAp made a minority strategic investment in the Japan Airport Terminal (a private company that owns, manages and operates the three passenger terminals at Haneda airport and operates retail and catering businesses at Narita and Kansai airports), but this was subsequently sold back in 2009 primarily as a result of concern expressed by Japanese government regarding this foreign ownership. Consequently in 2011 MAp disposed of its interests in Brussels (39 per cent) and Copenhagen (31 per cent) with a share swap with Ontario Teachers Pension Plan and their 11 per cent stake in Sydney airport. MAp is now focusing entirely on its operation of Sydney airport and has subsequently changed its name to Sydney Airport Holdings.

As a result of this, Ontario Teachers Pension Plan is a major airport investor with interests not only at Brussels and Copenhagen but also Bristol and Birmingham. Another example is Hastings Funds Management, which is particularly active in Australia. Elsewhere the infrastructure fund investor Global Infrastructure Partners (GIP) was established in 2006 with the investment bank Credit Suisse and the US company General Electric acting as joint founding investors. In late 2006 GIP acquired 100 per cent of London City Airport jointly with AIG Financial Products (AIG-FP), and GIP now has a 75 per cent interest in the airport. In 2009 a GIP-led consortium bought Gatwick airport and in 2012 it acquired Edinburgh airport as well.

CASE STUDY 2.3: FRAPORT: A GLOBAL AIRPORT OPERATOR

Fraport operates Frankfurt airport, Europe's third largest airport, handling more than 56 million passengers in 2011. Formerly Flughafen Frankfurt/Main AG, Fraport was listed on the stock exchange in July 2001 when 29 per cent of the company was sold to private investors. Fraport has always been active in providing airport services, particularly ground handling, on a consultancy or management contract basis, but over the past decade or so has sought to build up its involvement in owning or managing other airports.

One of its first investments was in 1998 when it acquired a 30 per cent shareholding in nearby Hanover airport. It also had a 51 per cent share in Saarbrücken airport operating company, but it disposed of this in 2007. In addition it owned 65 per cent of the low-cost airport Frankfurt Hahn, but withdrew from its involvement in 2009 primarily because of the poor financial performance of the airport. Globally it has been expanding operations by becoming involved with airport privatisations in Lima, Delhi, Varna and Burgas, Antalya and St Petersburg. It addition it was the first foreign investor to get involved with an unlisted Chinese airport, namely Xi'an in 2007 (Table 2.12). It also had a 25 per cent share in the BOT project for the international terminal at Manila, which was cancelled in 2005 and has been the subject of a long dispute between Fraport and the Philippine government.

Table 2.12 Fraport's international activities

	Fraport's share of airport operator (per cent)	Date of initial involvement	Passenger numbers in 2011 (000s)
Delhi	10	2006	35,002
Hanover	30	1998	5,341
Antalya	51	2007	24,964
Varna and Burgas	60	2006	3,435
Lima	100	2001	11,796
Pulkova St Petersburg	35.5	2010	9,610
Xi'an	24.5	2007	21,163

Source: Fraport website

These airport operations, in addition to management contracts in countries such as Saudi (Jeddah and Riyadh), Egypt (Cairo) and Senegal (Dakar), are part of Fraport's External Activities and Services business segment, which also covers over 50 other subsidiaries, joint venture, associated companies and investments including the facility management and information and telecommunication service units. In 2011 Fraport generated €496 million from this business segment, with an earnings before interest, tax and amortisation (EBITDA) value of €255 million. Over recent years, earnings from this segment have grown in importance while the other business segments – aviation, retail, real estate and ground handling – have been declining (Figure 2.8).

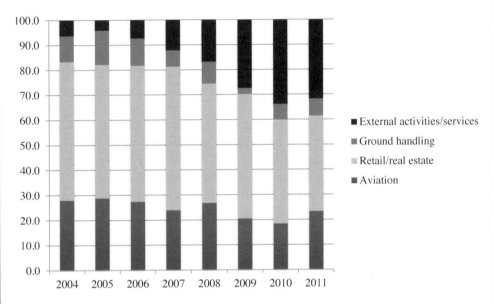

Figure 2.8 *EBITDA share of Fraport's business segments (%), 2004–11*
Source: Fraport annual report

CASE STUDY 2.4: TAV AIRPORTS: PROVIDING INTEGRATED AIRPORT SERVICES FOR EASTERN EUROPE, NORTH AFRICA AND CENTRAL ASIA

TAV Airports Holdings was founded in Turkey in 1997 as a joint venture between the two Tepe and Akfen Groups. Its first involvement in airports was the BOT project international terminal at Istanbul Atatürk Airport, which was completed in 2000. In 2006 the company was restructured into TAV Airports and TAV Construction, and in 2007 TAV Airports was floated on the Istanbul Stock Exchange. TAV Construction has consequently been involved a number of projects at airports in countries such as the United Arab Emirates, Oman, Egypt, Qatar, Libya and Bahrain, and with airports that are operated by TAV airports. In addition TAV Airports focuses on specific areas of airport operations with a number of different service companies that, for instance, cover duty-free sales (ATU), food and beverage services (BTA), ground handling (HAVAS), information technology (TAV IT) and security (TAV Security), and specialist operations (TAV O&M). TAV is therefore able to offer help with developing an integrated airport product, which is viewed as essential in many of the emerging markets.

Over the past decade TAV Airports has been steadily expanding its business. In 2004 it took control of the construction and operation of the domestic and inter-national terminals at Ankara Esenboğa airport, and in 2005 the international terminal at Izmir Adnan Menderes airport. In the same year it took responsibility for operating the domestic as well as the international terminal at Istanbul, and was awarded the tender for operations of Tbilisi and Batumi airports in Georgia. Then in 2007 it was awarded the tender for operations of Antalya's second airport Gazipasa in Turkey and Monastir Habib Bourguiba International airport and the Enfidha airport in Tunisia, followed by being the successful bidder for Skopje Alexander the Great airport and Ohrid St Paul the Apostle International airport in Macedonia in 2008. More recent developments include setting up a joint venture with Air Baltic to build and operate the new terminal building at Latvia's Riga airport, and being awarded the tender to operate the duty-free, food and beverage and other commercial spaces at this airport. In 2011 TAV Airports led a consortium that was selected for a 25-year BOT project at Medina airport in Saudi Arabia. This now means that TAV Airports operates a number of different airport concessions in Turkey, Eastern Europe, the Middle East and North Africa, which in total handled 53 million passengers in 2011 (Table 2.13).

Table 2.13 *TAV Airports: portfolio of airports*

	Istanbul	Ankara	Izmir	Antalya Gazipasa	Tunisia	Georgia	Macedonia
Passengers 2011 (million)	37.5	8.5	2.5	n/a	2.5	1.2	0.8
Revenues 2011 (million €)	344	42	35	0	35	25	17
EBITDA* 2011 (million €)	136	20	22	−1	6	13	2
TAV Airports' ownership of airport operator (per cent)	100	100	100	100	67	76	100
Termination date	2021	2023	2032	2034	2047	2027	2030

*Earnings before interest, tax, depreciation and amortisation.
†In 2011 TAV Airports also led a consortium that was selected for a 25-year build–operate–transfer (BOT) project at Medina airport in Saudi Arabia.
Source: TAV Airports Holding Financial Results, 2011

In 2012 AdP (through its wholly owned subsidiary Aéroports de Paris Management) announced that it will be buying a 38 per cent share of TAV Airports and a 49 per cent share of TAV Construction. In addition to the three major airports and 10 regional airfields, AdP also has involvements in Mexico, Cambodia, Mauritius and Amman, and in airports serving locations such as Conakry, Algiers, Liege and Jeddah. AdP has stated that the investment will fit in with its international strategy – to invest in international airports of more than 10 million passengers with strong EBITDA potential in OECD and BRIC countries. Together the group will manage, directly or indirectly, 180 million passengers in 37 countries, and it is claimed that it will have excellent growth potential, both organically and through further acquisitions. The stated benefits will be the leverage of respective skills and the geographic footprint to boost international developments, in particular outside Turkey; the sharing of best practice; the fostering of ambitious career paths for the two groups; and further growth of the assets base through a more systematic cross-selling between AdP and TAV (TAV Group, 2012).

CONSEQUENCES OF PRIVATISATION AND INTERNATIONALISATION OF THE AIRPORT INDUSTRY

Impacts of privatisation

It is evident that the structure of the airport industry has changed substantially over the past 25 years and that the private sector is now playing a very significant role in managing airports. In a global study of 459 airports in 2007, it was found that 24 per cent of airports had full or partial private ownership (ICAO, 2008). Specifically within Europe in 2008, 13 per cent of the airports were owned by public–private shareholders and nine were fully privatised. However, these partially or totally privately owned airports handled proportionally more European passenger traffic (48 per cent) as private operators are predominantly found at larger airports (ACI Europe, 2010). Globally, half of the remaining public airports are run as autonomous entities, whereas specifically in Europe three-quarters of all public airports are now run by corporatised airport operators. In developing countries, or low-/middle-income countries as defined by the World Bank, 48 countries were involved with private participation in their airports, amounting to more than US$32 billion investment commitment (World Bank, 2011).

The 2008 ICAO study showed that management with a concession or leasing agreement was a very popular option, with 28 per cent of all airports (both public and private) being operated with such an arrangement. According to the World Bank (2011), concessions were the most common form of airport privatisation in developing countries, accounting for 49 per cent of airport contracts and 62 per cent per cent of investment commitment between 1990 and 2010. These were mostly used in Latin American and sub-Saharan African airports in the 1990s, but also in East Europe and Central/South Asia as well (Andrew and Dochia, 2006; Hooper, 2002). Moreover, greenfield models such as BOTs were used for more than 23 per cent of privatisation in 1990–2010, mostly for construction of new terminals in Eastern Europe and East/Central Asia. Divestitures (both IPOs and trade sales) in the developing countries accounted for only 15 per cent of privatisations, and even globally there are only around 20 or so major airport companies listed on international or domestic stock exchanges. In terms of market capitalisation among private operators, the largest companies in 2011 were AdP, then Fraport, followed by MAp (before exiting Copenhagen and Brussels), Shanghai, Zurich, Copenhagen, GAP, BCIA, Auckland, Malaysia Airports, ASUR and the Airports of Thailand (CAPA Centre for Aviation, 2011c). However, public ownership is still prevalent – of the 30 largest airports by passengers in 2010, three are in private ownership, eight in public/private ownership and 19 in public ownership (Big Pond Aviation, 2010).

In a study of academic papers that considered privatisation over the past two decades, Graham (2011) found that the two most important drivers of privatisation were the aim to make improvements in efficiency and performance, coupled with a need for greater investment. Other popular objectives included improvements in quality, financial benefits to the government, less state interference, and the encouragement of better management or diversification. While in some developed countries, such as the UK, privatisation had been viewed in more ideological terms as reducing state control and inducing greater efficiency, in less developed countries practical considerations, such as the need for investment or management expertise, appeared to be more dominant. Overall there certainly seems to be a change in the way airport privatisation is viewed. With most recent privatisations that have taken place, the ideological justifications have tended to be downplayed or are non-existent, with the objectives focused entirely on the need for funding and, maybe in addition, the acquisition of management and operational expertise. This may be in part a result of the majority of recent privatisations taking place in emerging economies where there is a substantial need for new investment.

The number of airport privatisations has grown over the years as generally airports were seen as attractive organisations to investors for a number of reasons. First, it appeared that the airport industry had strong growth potential. Many of the airports, particularly the major ones, faced limited competition from other airports and from other modes of transport. There were very high barriers to entry within the industry due to the large capital investment needed and the difficulties in finding appropriate, convenient locations where airport development is allowed. In the mid-2000s the success of many past airport privatisations, coupled with high predicted growth patterns and the need for capital investment at many airports, resulted in more and more investors and companies being interested in becoming potential purchasers, and the competition intensified. Also, an active secondary market developed, and there were a number of examples of privatised airports (such as Rome, Copenhagen, BAA, Budapest, Bournemouth, Prestwick and Birmingham) where there were further changes in ownership. Inevitably this led to the purchase prices being pushed up, particularly where financial investors were involved who were able to accept a much more highly leveraged debt structure. Potential buyers typically will consider the price of the airport (enterprise value, EV) in relation to profit (EBITDA or earnings before interest and tax, EBIT) when deciding whether to invest. For earlier IPO privatisations such as BAA, Vienna, Copenhagen and Auckland, the EV/EBITDA multiples were in the region of five to ten. For the earlier trade sales of the Australian airports and some of the UK regional airports, such as Bristol and Cardiff, higher multiples in the region of 15 were achieved. However, the increased interest in airport privatisation in the mid-2000s and the emergence of the financial investor meant there were some very high values for trade sales. For example, in 2006 the values for trade sales were 28× at London City, 16× for BAA, 29× for Budapest (in 2005) and 23× for an aborted sale at Bratislava (Schrankler, 2006). As discussed above, prices for IPOs have tended to be lower than for trade sales, with the average for flotations (up to 2006) being 8.1× compared with the much higher figure of 16.9× for trade sales (Kalenda, 2007).

However, not all these privatisations have been successful. There are a number of different reasons, such as conflicts that have arisen between governments and the new private operator and the enforcement of the terms of privatisation agreements, problems related to the selection of the most suitable investor, or inappropriate/unrealistic estimations of passenger airline demand and the financial situation. For example, Fraport was involved with a privatisation project at Manila airport in the Philippines which led to a complex and extended dispute with the Philippine government. In Berlin, there were several separate attempts to use private investors to develop a new airport to serve the city until this approach was abandoned following a number of legal challenges between bidders and complaints from local residents. In Toronto, the privatisation of terminals 1 and 2 was cancelled after the contract had been awarded to a consortium, as it was criticised as not maximising the public interest and consequently large compensation payments had to be made. In Argentina, the new airport operator overestimated the profits that could be generated from the airports, which eventually meant the privatisation agreement had to be renegotiated.

The onset of the credit crunch in 2008 and the subsequent poor economic climate changed attitudes towards airport privatisation. Traffic fell at many airports and passenger growth was no longer seen as a guarantee. Capital funds were hard to obtain and overall investors became much more cautious. EBITDA multiples have now fallen to 10–13× compared with some values in excess of 20× a few years earlier – for example, Gatwick in 2009 had a multiple of around 12× (CAPA Centre for Aviation, 2011a). On the other hand, many governments, particularly in Europe, have started to look at privatisation as a way to improve the poor health of their public sector finances. Overall the pressure on public finance throughout the world means governments are going to be less able to provide direct funding for airports, but as yet this has not led to many privatisations.

Smaller airports particularly are being viewed as less attractive in this new economic climate. Traditionally privatisation of such assets has been more difficult as the transaction costs represent a substantial share of the transaction, and because of the perceived greater risk associated with the lower traffic volume and often the dependence on a few dominant airlines. However, the emergence of the LCC sector, and experience at airports where these airlines have either negotiated a hard deal or left and moved on to another airport, have made investors even more cautious in becoming involved with such airports. A few airports, such as Frankfurt Hahn and Luebeck in Germany and Cardiff in Wales, have even gone back to total public ownership.

Internationalisation of the airport industry

Taking a longer-term view of airport privatisation, undoubtedly the emergence of new international airport operators has major implications for the airport industry. In particular with the increased number of potential airport investors, there has been considerable debate as to which type of investor is likely to be the most successful and most appropriate for the long-term development of the airport industry. The traditional airport companies have core skills and competencies related to both the operational and business aspects of managing an airport, which they have already gained through airport management in the home country, and which have been used to grow their business. In the early stages of privatisation, purchasing other airports was viewed by some as a natural progression for airport companies that had gone through the processes of commercialisation and then privatisation. Once privatisation had proved successful, it seemed quite logical that the commercially minded airports might next seek to acquire other interests to expand and add value to their company. For such airport companies there may be distinct advantages in expanding internationally if their own core infrastructure (e.g. terminal or runway) is physically or environmentally constrained, or serves a relatively small catchment area, as with Zurich. Financial growth in the home market may be hindered by a regulatory system which may limit the amount of revenue generated from aeronautical sources. In addition, international expansion can provide the much needed finance for development in the home market and may safeguard the success of the core business.

However, it is not just the privatised or partially privatised airports (such as those of AdP, Fraport and Zurich) which sought to become international companies. There are also companies such as AENA and Changi that are not responsible to private shareholders, but are just as keen to acquire other airports. The motivation for such expansion is not always totally clear – although it is true that such airports, too, are increasingly under greater pressure to perform well. In the early stages of airport privatisation for some airports there was definitely an element of fear of being left behind in the race to become international airport operators.

Internationalisation strategies for airport companies have changed since these early 'gold rush' years in the late 1990s. In the early and mid-2000s, a more volatile aviation industry, coupled with more experience of international operations, meant that generally airports became more cautious in their approach, and a number of companies reassessed their international expansion ambitions. There began to be far more focus on considering whether the investment would make strategic sense or really add value. This resulted in a number of airports pulling out from some of their international projects. For example, Aéroporti de Roma sold its share in the Airports Company of South Africa in 2005, and AdP disposed of its share of BCIA in 2007. Similarly, Copenhagen airport sold its interest in Hainan Meilan in 2007.

The successful airport companies are the ones that have become competent in bid and project management, and in developing new skills in change management and business development to cope with the opportunities arising from the new investments. Some of the utility, property and construction companies that had a number of these skills began airport operations primarily because of the synergies which existed with their businesses. Koch and Budde (2005) argued that some of the most important success factors for international airport companies are likely to be the availability of capital resources, personnel resources and know-how (operational expertise, international know-how, an efficient organisational structure), a management approach with a focus on value creation, international experience and established credibility.

In most cases a consortium of different organisations will be involved with airport privatisations. These consortia need to bring together the appropriate mix of operational expertise, capital and local experience (Feldman, 2008). It may be difficult to get the different entities to work successful together, particularly if the government is still a major shareholder, which will usually add more complexity and may involve coping with conflicting objectives of private and public bodies. Having a local partner in the consortium may help it to understand the local language and culture, handle the local press and politicians, and be familiar, for example, with other local labour relations issues or environmental legislation. On the other hand, global partners are likely to bring knowledge of global customers (e.g. airlines alliances), international suppliers and the global financial markets. In turn, this may mean they will be able to obtain favourable long-term financing. As a consequence, it will often be stipulated during the privatisation process that there has to be both local and foreign interests within the consortium. Sometimes there may even be a mixture of local and central government involvement, as with the Indian airport privatisations.

For all airport privatisations, a number of important considerations need to be taken into account to minimise the risk to any specific project. As well as having the appropriate local partner, the financial structure related to the consortium partners and their exact roles need to be considered in detail, as do any cultural differences or communication problems between the consortium partners and local staff. All this means that the contractual framework and choice of consortium partners is very important. There will also be political risks over which the investor may have very limited control. For example, even if a government has relinquished all effective control of an airport to a private operator, a change in the air transport regulatory system or the introduction of more stringent environmental legislation or different planning regulations could have a funda-mental impact on how the airport operates. Also, the extent of any political instability and the general political and legal situation need to be considered, as well as the government's relation-ship with the other stakeholders such as the airlines and the border control and immigration agencies. These risks and others may be reduced, but not eliminated totally, by carrying out a comprehensive due-diligence assessment of all areas of the airport business, which is the usual procedure for privatisation models such as trade sales, concessions and project finance models.

Benefits of multi-airport companies

As with many other industries, growing the business through mergers and acquisitions can produce higher returns and increased shareholder value. Also, risks may be reduced by going global, thereby placing less relevance on any one national economy and lessening exposure to downturns in individual economies. There has been a significant trend towards consolidation in the airline industry, and on the surface it may appear as if this trend is simply being replicated in the airport industry. However, there do not seem to be such obvious synergies in controlling a global group of airports as there are with airlines, particularly when the airports are operating in different regulatory environments. While airline alliances are being driven primarily by a need to expand networks and increase market accessibility, most of the potential benefits of operating a group of airports appear to come from shared knowledge, expertise and financial resources rather than marketing opportunities. In other words, this trend appears to have been driven more by increased profit opportunities that investing in new airports can bring, rather than by strategic industry-specific considerations of investors.

Airport groups potentially can reduce costs through bulk buying and joint purchasing in some areas. For example, cost reductions could be achieved with joint purchasing of equipment such as ramp buses and fire engines, and through negotiation of more favourable insurance policies. Costs could also be saved by having a single head office and through centralising many functions such as accounting and information technology. Joint training programmes could be arranged, and there may be cost advantages through combined marketing. Standard commercial contracts could be agreed with core partners at the airports. In addition, the advantages of size could help the airport company keep up to date with technology developments and the latest airport management tools and techniques around the world. However, since the airport location is fixed and cannot be moved, a number of costs will remain influenced primarily by local conditions.

One of the major advantages of internationalisation or globalisation for airlines and other companies is that of being able to sell one common product or one global brand to the customer. For international airport companies, branding could involve the use of similar signposting, colour schemes and interior design for the entire airport. Examples of this have existed for many years with national airport groups. For example, BAA traditionally used a common and constant brand image for its UK airports. The merits of branding within the airport industry are, however, very questionable (see Chapter 8). Most passengers, particularly leisure passengers who travel infrequently, would probably not be aware of any common branding and would find it very difficult to define any distinguishing features of a certain airport brand.

For many airport groups, the individual airports will serve different markets and will not have any potential to compete with each other, for example Schiphol's involvement with Brisbane airport or Fraport's involvement with Lima. However, there are clearly many more advantages to multi-airport groups if the airports are sufficiently close to compete, as common group operation may reduce airport competition and enable the operator to gain market dominance (Forsyth *et al.*, 2011). This has meant that some privatisations of competing airports have not been allowed to go ahead – in the UK (as mentioned) but also elsewhere, as with Vienna airport operating Bratislava airport. Other advantages of general group operation in the same country, such as investment and traffic coordination, may also exist.

There could potentially be benefits for an individual airline or airline alliance in operating out of more than one airport which is owned by an international airport company. For example, standard contracts could be agreed for the whole airport network, quantity discounts on charging could be negotiated, and there could be common agreements on the use of gates and other facilities. This was the idea behind the Wiggins Group's expansion into airports: the company's overall objective was to develop a global network of over 20 regional airports under its so-called PlaneStation concept. Wiggins believed that the power of the PlaneStation brand would significantly benefit the airports within this network and would bring the resources needed to improve their performance, which had previously been unavailable under individual, public ownership. Wiggins therefore had a very different strategy from most of the other emerging global airport companies, which tended to buy up airports that already were successful or appeared to have great potential. Wiggins claimed that common standards and processes at all the network airports, along with a single administrative system, provided the potential for improving the quality and effectiveness of the facilities offered to the airline operators and logistic organisations that planned to operate from a number of airports in the network. There would also be scope for the building of close relationships with airlines and other operators with, for example, risk sharing, simplified negotiation and common tariffs (Lewin, 2002). However, Wiggins/Planestation went out of business in 2005 primarily because of the financial failure of its main airline at Manston airport, the low-cost carrier EUjet, in which the airport company had invested when the financial problems of the airline became evident.

Emergence of airport alliances

The main driving force behind the internationalisation of the airport industry has been airport privatisation, which has enabled a growing number of airports to be purchased outright or at least managed on a long-term basis by an external airport operator. However, this internationalisation could also occur as a result of greater cooperation between airport operators, or through the establishment of airport alliances (Forsyth *et al.*, 2011). Unlike airline cooperation, which is driven primarily by a need to expand networks and increase accessibility and market power, airport cooperation is likely to be encouraged by a desire to benefit from shared knowledge, expertise and financial resources. In the late 1990s there was considerable discussion about the possibility of the development of airport alliances, particularly in the light of increased competition in the airline industry and the emergence of their global alliances. This had meant that airports themselves faced increased competition and were under greater pressure to reduce costs, improve quality and add value to their organisations – all of which, theoretically, could have been helped by airport cooperation.

The first real development of airport alliances occurred in 1999 when Galaxy International Cargo Alliance was established by Washington Dulles International Airport and Chateauroux-Doels, with an overall aim of cooperating in joint marketing by establishing a common brand for member airports. By 2001 it had over 21 airports. Then in 2000 Aviation Handling Service (AHS) was established as a joint venture of three German airports and grew in numbers in the following years to provide common quality standards for ground-handling services. However, the establishment of both these alliances had only limited effects. Also in 2000, the Schiphol–Fraport 'Pantares' alliance was formed, which was potentially a more far-reaching alliance agreement. Schiphol and Fraport believed that there was scope for cooperation because the two airports were both European hubs but serving different airlines alliances; they had complementary competencies, they were at similar levels of globalisation and they shared the same strategic approach. They identified six key areas where cooperation seemed possible: aviation ground services; ground and cargo handling; retail and passengers; facility management; real estate; information technology; and international projects. As part of the alliance partnership, the airports agreed not to compete against each other on international contracts. As a result the two airports cooperated in a few minor areas, but overall very few benefits were achieved.

However, in 2008 Schiphol entered into a new strategic alliance, this time with AdP, which somewhat mirrored the earlier merger of the two Skyteam airlines KLM and Air France. This 'Hublink' alliance of initially 12 years involved the exchange of 8 per cent equity stakes and increased cooperation to enhance the functioning of the dual hub system of AF–KLM in the areas of aviation, non-aviation and international development, with eight steering committees covering: dual-hub and network attractiveness; airport operations; retail; international development; real estate; telecoms and IT; sustainable development; and purchasing. Combined revenue and cost synergies of around €71 million per annum were expected to be realised by 2013, combined with a reduction in capital expenditure of €18 million on average per annum from 2013 onwards (Aéroports de Paris, 2008). While there are clearly potential benefits here from knowledge transfer and cost savings which it is too early to measure, in this specific case there could also be less favourable consequences for users because of an increase of market power of the dual hub. The latest development here has been the signing of a memorandum of understanding in 2010 between Incheon airport (a base of another key SkyTeam member, Korean Airlines) and AdP and Schiphol, where it has been agreed that the airports will exchange best practices, benchmark and conduct joint projects focusing on passenger operations, retail, cargo and human resources.

Elsewhere in recent years there has been the development of 'sister' agreements which can potentially bring benefits, especially between airports of different global regions where there is no competition. This usually involves having the agreements formalised in the shape of a memorandum of understanding. The airports may agree to work jointly on developing or supporting new routes between the airports (e.g. Birmingham/Chicago; Delhi/Sydney) and/or sharing information and best practice, as in the case with Singapore and Narita airports. It may also involve providing consultancy services, as with Incheon and the Bangladesh airports. Many of these are multiple airport agreements, such as Airports of Thailand with Munich, Incheon, Narita and Beijing; Beijing with Singapore, Sydney, Narita, Thailand, Chicago and Hong Kong; Munich with Beijing, Denver, Nagoya, Bangkok and Singapore; Abu Dhabi with Chicago, Narita and Bangkok; and Chicago with Beijing, Shanghai, Hong Kong, Incheon, Abu Dhabi and Narita. It is uncertain whether this is a development that will become more widespread in the future.

REFERENCES

ACI Europe (2010) *The Ownership of Europe's Airports*, Brussels: ACI Europe.

ACI North America (2011) *Airport Capital Development Costs 2011–2015*. Washington, DC: ACI North America.

Aéroports de Paris (AdP) (2008) *Aéroports de Paris and Schiphol Group to create a leading global alliance in the airport industry*, press release, 21 October. Online. Available HTTP: <http://www.aeroportsdeparis.fr/Adp/Resources/b38cfe19-4de0-491d-a013-23c8b73649bf-cp21oct08en.pdf (accessed 28 September 2011).

Andrew, D. and Dochia, S. (2006) *The Growing and Evolving Business of Private Participation in Airports*, Public–Private Infrastructure Advisory Facility (PPIAF) Note, 15 September. Online. Available HTTP: <http://www.ppiaf.org/ppiaf/sites/ppiaf.org/files/publication/Gridlines-15-%20The%20Growing%20 Business%20of%20PPI%20in%20Airports%20-%20DAndrew%20SDochia.pdf> (accessed 16 October 2007).

Arbulu, J.D. (2007) 'From Peru to the world', *International Airport Review*, 2: 88–89.

Ashford, N. and Moore, C. (1999) *Airport Finance*, 2nd edn, Loughborough: Loughborough Airport Consultancy.

Barros, C., Managi, S. and Yoshida, Y. (2010) 'Productivity growth and biased technological change in Japanese airports', *Transport Policy*, 17(4): 259–65.

Barros, C. and Dieke, P. (2007) 'Performance evaluation of Italian airports with data envelopment analysis', *Journal of Air Transport Management*, 13(4): 184–91.

Beesley, M.E. (1997) *Privatisation, Regulation and Deregulation*, 2nd edn, London: Routledge.

Bentley, D. (2012) 'Global airport investment privatisation and market sentiment in 2012', in Airports Council International (ACI) (ed.), *ACI Airport Economics Survey*, ACI: Montreal.

Big Pond Aviation (2010) *Newsletter 3*, April/May 2010. Online. Available HTTP: <http://www.bigpondaviation.com/publications.html> (accessed 2 December 2011).

Branson airport (2012) 'Financing'. Online. Available HTTP: <http://flybranson.com/about.php#FIN> (accessed 30 January 2012).

Brunner, A. (2007) 'Bengaluru International Airport: India's largest private sector Greenfield airport', *Journal of Airport Management*, 1(3): 226–31.

CAPA Centre for Aviation (2007) 'Is airport privatisation running out of steam?', in ACI, *ACI Airport Economics Survey 2007*, Montreal: ACI.

—— (2011a) 'Review of the year – global airport privatisation still robust, but patchy'. Online. Available HTTP <http://centreforaviation.com/analysis/review-of-the-year---global-airport-privatisation-still-robust-but-patchy-64488> (accessed 15 December 2011).

—— (2011b) 'Time is running out on Brazil's bid to privatise its airports successfully', 10 November. Online. Available HTTP: <http://www.centreforaviation.com/analysis/time-is-running-out-on-brazils-bid-to-privatise-its-airports-successfully-62128> (accessed 1 December 2011).

—— (2011c) 'AdP tops airport capitalisation list'. Online. Available HTTP <http://www.centreforaviation.com/analysis/adp-tops-airport-capitalisation-list-47865> (accessed 1 November 2011).

Carney, M. and Mew, K. (2003) 'Airport governance reform: a strategic management perspective', *Journal of Air Transport Management*, 9(4): 221–32.

Caves, R. and Gosling, G. (1999) *Strategic Airport Planning*, Oxford: Elsevier.

Competition Commission (2009) *BAA Airports Market Investigation*, final report, London: Competition Commission.

Cruz, C. and Marques, R. (2011) 'Contribution to the study of PPP arrangements in airport development, management and operation', *Transport Policy*, 18(2): 392–400.

Doganis, R. (1992) *The Airport Business*, London: Routledge.

Domney, M., Wilson, H. and Chen, E. (2005) 'Natural monopoly privatisation under different regulatory regimes', *International Journal of Public Sector Management*, 18(3): 274–92.

Enrico, S., Boudreau, B., Reimer, D. and Van Beek., S. (2012) *ARCP Report 66: Considering and Evaluating Airport Privatisation*, Washington, DC: Transportation Research Board.

FAA (2012) *Fact Sheet – What is the Airport Privatisation Pilot Program?*, Federal Aviation Authority. Online. Available HTTP: <http://www.faa.gov/news/fact_sheets/news_story.cfm?newsId=13333&omniRss=fact_sheetsAoc&cid=103_F_S> (assessed 30 January 2012).

Feldhoff, T. (2003) 'Japan's capital Tokyo and its airports: problems and prospects from subnational and supranational perspectives', *Journal of Transport Geography*, 9(4): 241–54.

Feldman, D. (2008) 'Making airport privatisation consortia work', *Journal of Airport Management*, 3(1): 48–53.

Forsyth, P., Niemeier, H.-M. and Wolf, H. (2011) 'Airport alliances and mergers – structural change in the airport industry?', *Journal of Air Transport Management*, 17(1): 49–58.

Freathy, P. and O'Connell, F. (1998) *European Airport Retailing*, London: Macmillan.

Fung, M., Wan, K., Hui, Y. and Law, J. (2008) 'Productivity changes in Chinese airports 1995–2004', *Transportation Research Part E*, 44(3): 521–42.

Gangl, S. (1998) 'Experiences of privatisation', *University of Westminster/Cranfield University Airport Economics and Finance Symposium*, London, March.

GAO (2007) *Airport finance: Preliminary Analysis Indicates Proposed Changes in the Airport Improvement Program May Not Resolve Funding Needs for Smaller Airports*, Washington, DC: General Accounting Office.

Gillen, D. (2011) 'The evolution of airport ownership and governance', *Journal of Air Transport Management*, 17(1): 3–13.

Graham, A. (2008) 'Airport planning and regulation in the United Kingdom', in C. Winston and G. de Rus (eds), *Aviation Infrastructure Performance*, Washington, DC: Brookings Institution Press.

—— (2011) 'The objectives and outcomes of airport privatisation', *Research in Transportation Business and Management*, 1(1): 3–14.

Holvad, T. and Graham, A. (2004) 'Efficiency measurement for UK Airports: an application of data envelopment analysis', *Empirical Economics Letters*, 3(1): 31–39.

Hooper, P. (2002) 'Privatisation of airports in Asia', *Journal of Air Transport Management*, 8(5): 289–300.

Humphreys, I. (1999) 'Privatisation and commercialisation changes in UK airport ownership patterns', *Journal of Transport Geography*, 7(2): 121–34.

IATA (2005). *Airport Privatisation*, IATA economic briefing, Geneva: International Air Transport Association.

ICAO (2008) *Ownership, Organisation and Regulatory Practices of Airports and Air Navigation Services Providers 2007*, Montreal: International Civil Aviation Organization.

—— (2012) *Manual on Privatisation in the Provision of Airports and Air Navigation Services*, Montreal: International Civil Aviation Organization.

Ison, S., Francis, G., Humphreys, C. and Page, R. (2011) 'UK regional airport commercialisation and privatisation: 25 years on', *Journal of Transport Geography*, 19(6): 1341–49.

Jain, R., Raghuram, G. and Gangwar, R. (2007). 'Airport privatisation in India: lessons from the bidding process in Delhi and Mumbai', *Air Transport Research Society Conference*, Berkeley, July.

Japan Times Online (2011) 'Integration of Osaka airport targets huge debt', 18 May. Online. Available HTTP: <http://www.japantimes.co.jp/text/nn20110518a5.html> (accessed 12 August 2011).

Kalenda, R. (2007) What significance does the capital market attach to airports?, *10th Hamburg Aviation Conference*, Hamburg, February.

Kato, K., Uemura, T., Indo, Y., Okada, A., Tanabe, K., Saito, S., Oguma, H., Yamauchi, H., Shiomi, E., Saegusa, M. and Migita, K. (2011) 'Current accounts of Japanese airports', *Journal of Air Transport Management*, 17(2): 88–93.

Kerkloh, M. (2007) 'Munich airport's terminal 2: a successful airport–airline collaboration', *Journal of Airport Management*, 1(4): 330–37.

Koch, B. and Budde, S. (2005) 'Internationalisation strategies in airport companies', in W. Delfmann, H. Baum, S. Auerbach and S. Albers (eds), *Strategic Management in the Aviation Industry*, Aldershot: Ashgate.

LeighFisher (2011) 'Brazil: the waking giant seeks a private pilot', in *Finding the Opportunity in Change*. Online. Available HTTP: <http://www.leighfisher.com/new/publication/finding-opportunity-change-stories-around-world> (accessed 30 January 2012).

Lewin, R. (2002) 'Developing a global network of airports', *University of Westminster/Cranfield University Airport Economics and Finance Symposium*, London, March.

Lipovich, G. (2008) 'The privatisation of Argentine airports', *Journal of Air Transport Management*, 14(1): 8–15.

Lunsford, M. (2012) 'Waking giant seeks a private pilot', *ACI Economics and Finance Conference*, London, March

Lyon, D. and Francis, G. (2006) 'Managing New Zealand's airports in the face of commercial challenges', *Journal of Air Transport Management*, 12(5): 220–26.

McKinsey and Company (2010) *Study of the Air Transport Sector in Brazil*, Sao Paulo: McKinsey and Company.

Marques, R. (2011) 'Together or separately? The efficiency and market structure of Portuguese airports', *Journal of Air Transport Management*, 17(6): 136–39.

Ohta, K. (1999) 'International airports: financing methods in Japan', *Journal of Air Transport Management*, 5(4): 223–34.

Ott, J. (1998) 'Indianapolis serves as a privatisation testbed', *Aviation Week and Space Technology*, 14 December: 52.

Oum, T., Yu, C. and Fu, X. (2003) 'A comparative analysis of productivity performance of the world's major airports: summary report of the ATRS global airport benchmarking research report – 2002', *Journal of Air Transport Management*, 9(5): 285–97.

Oum, T., Adler, N. and Yu, C. (2006) 'Privatisation, corporatisation, ownership forms and their effects on the performance of the world's major airports', *Journal of Air Transport Management*, 12(3): 109–21.

Oum, T., Yan, J. and Yu, C. (2008) 'Ownership forms matter for airport efficiency: a stochastic frontier investigation of worldwide airports', *Journal of Urban Economics*, 64(2): 422–35.

Pal, A. (2010) 'Pulkovo Airport: creating a blueprint for Russian airport privatisation', *AEB North-Western Regional Committee: Infrastructure Development of St. Petersburg and the Leningrad region*. Online, Available HTTP: <http://www.aebrus.ru/application/views/aebrus/files/events_files/Pulkovo_airport_presentation_file_2010_12_07_17_36_22.pdf> (assessed 2 December 2011).

Parker, D. (1999) 'The performance of BAA before and after privatisation: a DEA study', *Journal of Transport Economics and Policy*, 33(2):133–46.

Parker, D. and Saal, D. (eds) (2003) *International Handbook on Privatisation*, Cheltenham: Edward Elgar.

Raghunath, S. (2010) 'Airport privatisation in India: investment opportunities in the next phase of development', *Journal of Airport Management*, 4(3): 235–51.

Rico, O. (2008) 'The privatisation of Mexican airports', *Journal of Air Transport Management*, 14(6): 320–23.

Schrankler, R. (2006) 'Current trends in equity finance and its consequences for project finance', *Global Airport Development Conference*, Rome, November.

Shibata, I. (1999) 'Japanese laws related to airport development and the need to revise them', *Journal of Air Law and Commerce*, 65(1): 125–36.

Stiller, D. (2010) 'Assessing the development of airport concession models and financing in times of a financial crisis', *Journal of Airport Management*, 4(3): 226–34.

TAV Group (2012) 'Aéroports de Paris to buy a stake in TAV: building a worldwide partnership in the airport industry', press release, 12 March. Online. Available HTTP: <http://www.tavyatirimciiliskileri.com/en-EN/Documents/ADPTAVEN.pdf> (assessed 17 March 2012).

Vasigh, B. and Gorjidooz, J. (2006) 'Productivity analysis of public and private airports: a causal investigation', *Journal of Air Transportation*, 11(3): 144–63.

Villard, P. (2011). 'Changing frames of reference and regulatory structures: French airport policy in transition', *Journal of Public Policy*, 31(1): 73–93.

Vogel, H.-A. (2006) 'Impact of privatisation on the financial and economic performance of European airports', *Aeronautical Journal*, 110(1106): 197–213.

Wang, X. and Seiden, E. (2007) 'Aviation infrastructure investment in China: great needs, great opportunities and great challenges', *Journal of Airport Management*, 1(3): 232–41.

World Bank (2008) *Airport Bots & Concessions of Legal and Regulatory Issues – Checklist*. Online. Available HTTP: <http://ppp.worldbank.org/public-private-partnership/ppp-overview/practical-tools/checklists-and-risk-matrices/airport-concession-checklist>

—— (2011) *Private Participation in Infrastructure Database*. Online. Available HTTP: <http://ppi.worldbank.org/explore/ppi_exploreSubSector.aspx?SubSectorID=5> (accessed 5 November 2011).

Yang, X., Tok, S. and Su, F. (2008) 'The privatisation and commercialisation of China's airports', *Journal of Air Transport Management*, 8(5): 243–51.

Yoshida, Y. and Fujimoto, H. (2004) 'Japanese-airport benchmarking with the DEA and endogenous-weight TFP methods: testing the criticism of overinvestment in Japanese regional airports', *Transportation Research Part E*, 40(6): 533–46.

Yuen, A. and Zhang, A. (2009) 'Effects of competition and policy changes on Chinese airport productivity: an empirical investigation,' *Journal of Air Transport Management*, 15(4): 166–74.

Zhang, A. and Yuen, A. (2008). 'Airport policy and performance in mainland China and Hong Kong', in C. Winston and G. de Rus (eds), *Aviation Infrastructure Performance*, Washington, DC: Brookings Institution Press.

3 Airport economics and performance benchmarking

INDUSTRY PROFIT LEVELS

This chapter considers the economics of the airport industry. The modern-day commercial and business pressures being placed on most airports mean that a thorough understanding of the economics of airports is now, more than ever before, a fundamental prerequisite for all airport managers. The chapter begins by looking at profit levels within the industry and describing the revenue and cost structures. It goes on to discuss some of the key factors that influence the economics of airports. This leads to a discussion of how economic performance can be measured and the alternative methods currently being used to benchmark airport performance.

Table 3.1 shows the profit levels for 50 of the largest airport operators in the world in 2010/11. Nearly all the airports produced an operating profit (profit before interest and tax) with the exception of AENA, Miami and Dallas Fort Worth. The operating profit margin for most airports was above 10 per cent and at a number of airports was substantially greater than this.

Figure 3.1 shows profits for both the 100 leading airport groups and the 150 major airlines. For the airports in 2011 an average operating margin of 19 per cent was recorded. In comparison, the 150 major airlines experienced a lower profit margin of 2 per cent in 2011. Similar differences in the level of profits were experienced in the previous years, and there are a number of reasons why this so-called 'profitability gap', which is frequently a bone of contention between the airlines and airports, exists. First, although airports increasingly face much greater competition than before, the airlines generally deal with much stiffer competition which particularly puts pressure on them to reduce their fares. In a number of countries there tends to be a shortage of airport capacity that can push up prices, while in many airline markets there is overcapacity which has the opposite effect. In many cases the airports have a more diverse customer base than airlines, which means that airports have less exposure to downturns in individual markets. Also, not all airport revenues (e.g. landing charges, rents) are directly related to passenger numbers, which means that fluctuations in passenger numbers generally have less impact on airports. Finally, on the cost side, airports have less dependence on fuel prices, a key input cost for airlines over which they have very little control.

However, these relatively healthy profit figures tend to relate only to major airports. If smaller ones are included, a different picture emerges. For example, in Europe in 2010, 48 per cent of all

Table 3.1 *Profitability for 50 major airport operators 2010/11*

Airport operator	Country	Total revenues (million US$)	Operating profit (million US$)	Operating margin (per cent)
1 Ferrovial	Spain	5,157	334	6.5
2 AENA	Spain	3,923	−191	−4.9
3 Aéroports de Paris	France	3,615	716	19.8
4 Fraport	Germany	2,897	569	19.6
5 Narita International Airport	Japan	2,209	n/a	11.9*
6 Port Authority of New York & New Jersey	USA	2,125	409	19.2
7 Infraero	Brazil	1,754	72	4.1
8 Schiphol Group	Netherlands	1,558	392	25.1
9 Flughafen München	Germany	1,503	374	24.9
10 Hong Kong International	China	1,361	902	66.3
11 Avinor	Norway	1,299	288	22.2
12 Seoul Incheon International	South Korea	1,110	460	41.5
13 Changi Airport Group	Singapore	1,097	n/a	n/a
14 Greater Toronto Airports Authority	Canada	1,079	418	38.7
15 Kansai International Airport Company	Japan	1,051	224	21.3
16 TAV Airports Holding	Turkey	1,036	n/a	n/a
17 State Airport Authority	Turkey	1,027	441	42.9
18 Airports Authority of India	India	880	165	18.7
19 Southern Cross Airports	Australia	865	709	82.0
20 Beijing Capital International Airport Group	China	855	223	26.0
21 City of Chicago Department of Aviation	USA	852	185	21.7
22 Flughafen Zurich	Switzerland	832	421	50.6
23 Aeroporti di Roma	Italy	797	195	24.5
24 SEA Aeroporti di Milano	Italy	776	204	26.3
25 Los Angeles World Airports	USA	752	27	3.5
26 Dublin Airport Authority	Ireland	737	96	13.0
27 Airports of Thailand	Thailand	733	114	15.6
28 Flughafen Wien	Austria	705	135	19.2
29 Swedavia	Sweden	675†	n/a	n/a
30 Flughafen Berlin-Schönefeld	Germany	668	13	1.9
31 Miami Dade County Aviation Dept	USA	657	−47	−7.2
32 Airports Company South Africa	South Africa	650	163	25.1
33 Shanghai Airport Authority	China	619	174	28.0
34 Metro Washington Airports Authority	USA	604	30	4.9
35 City and County of Denver Aviation Dept	USA	601	10	1.7
36 San Francisco International	USA	577	103	17.8
37 Copenhagen Airports	Denmark	574	261	45.4

Continued

Table 3.1 *(Continued)*

Airport operator	Country	Total revenues (million US$)	Operating profit (million US$)	Operating margin (per cent)
38 Guangzhou Balyun International	China	572	123	21.6
39 Malaysia Airports Holdings Berhad	Malaysia	565	170	30.0
40 Aeroportos de Portugal	Portugal	546	217	39.7
41 Manchester Airports Group	UK	545	80	14.6
42 Flughafen Dusseldorf	Germany	537	58	10.8
43 GMR Infrastructure	India	527	n/a	36.2*
44 Dallas/Fort Worth International	USA	501	−51	−10.2
45 Central Japan International	Japan	500	49	9.7
46 Brussels International Airport Company	Brussels	484	269	55.6
47 Athens International Airport	Greece	471	302	64.1
48 Australia Pacific Airports	Australia	457	342	74.8
49 Taiwan Taoyuan International Airport	Taiwan	450†	n/a	n/a
50 Massachusetts Port Authority	USA	448	197	43.9

*2009/10; †estimates.
Sources: Airline Business/Annual reports

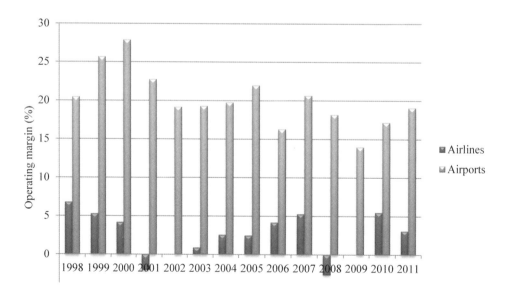

Figure 3.1 *Operating margin of world airlines (top 150) and airports (top 50/100 depending on year) 1998–2011*
Source: Airline Business

airports were loss-making, albeit that this was exaggerated by the poor economic conditions. Of the smallest airports (under 1 million passengers per year) over 75 per cent were not profitable if public subsidies and/or other non-operating income is not taken into account.

Organisations are interested not just in the level of profits, but also in how they use capital to generate profits by looking at return on capital employed figures. With these measures the differences between the major airports and airlines are less evident. For example, ACI Europe quotes an average figure of around 10 per cent for airports compared with 6 per cent for airlines (ACI Europe, 2005). IATA (2006) recorded a return of 5 per cent for airlines compared with 6 per cent for airports. In a study of European airports and airlines, Vogel and Graham (2011) found there were no statistically significant differences in profitability between the two sectors when measured in terms of returns on capital or assets. This can be explained primarily by the higher capital intensity of the airport industry, and by also the growing airline industry practice of placing aircraft off the balance sheet by leasing rather than buying them.

REVENUE AND COST STRUCTURES

Airport revenue is usually classified into two main categories: aeronautical (or aviation) and non-aeronautical (or commercial) revenues (Table 3.2).

Aeronautical revenues are those sources of income that arise directly from the operation of aircraft and the processing of passengers and freight. Non-aeronautical revenues are those generated by activities that are not directly related to the operation of aircraft, notably those from commercial activities within the terminal and rents for terminal space and airport land. Then there are a few categories that can be classified as either type of revenue. For example, handling revenues are usually treated as aeronautical revenues, unless handling is undertaken by handling agents or airlines when the associated revenue (rent or fee based on turnover) is included under rents or concession revenue items. In the USA there are terminal rental fees paid by the airlines that are classified as aviation revenue, while usually rents are considered as commercial items.

Table 3.2 *Airport operating revenue sources*

Aeronautical	Non-aeronautical
Landing fees	Retail*
Passenger fees	Food and beverage (F&B)*
Aircraft parking fees	Car hire*
Handling fees (if handling is provided by the airport operator)	Advertising*
Terminal rental fees (e.g. in USA)	Car park*
Other aeronautical fees (air traffic control, lighting, airbridges etc.)	Recharges (for gas, water, electricity etc.)
	Other non-aeronautical revenue (consultancy, visitor and business services, property development etc.)

* Usually shown as 'concession revenue' if provided by a third party.

Revenue received by the airport from aircraft fuel companies or from airlines as a fuel throughput fee could be regarded as directly related to aircraft operations and hence an aeronautical revenue. Alternatively, this could be considered as commercial revenue and hence a non-aeronautical item. Revenues, including interest received and income earned from subsidiary companies, are usually included under a different 'non-operating' revenue category.

Figure 3.2 presents the average operating revenue breakdown for 2010/11 from the ACI economics survey (excluding non-operating items). This is a survey undertaken every year that covers 604 airports representing 62 per cent of worldwide traffic (ACI, 2011). Overall aeronautical revenue accounted for just over half the revenues.

Unlike with revenues, there is no industry standard or unique way of reporting airport operating costs. ICAO (2006) recommends having operations and maintenance (personnel costs, supplies, contracted services), administrative overheads, capital costs and other costs. The ACI classification shows that personnel costs are the highest, followed by contracted services (outsourcing cost to third parties); communications, energy and waste; and maintenance (Figure 3.3). When these costs are differentiated by function, then terminal and landside operations are the most important, followed by administration, airside operations and security. It is important to note that these ACI figures do not include depreciation as an operating cost. However, by collecting financial data directly from the annual reports of a sample of European airports, it is apparent that depreciation in this region represents on average around 20 per cent of operating costs, with labour costs accounting for a further 31 per cent (Table 3.3). Over the years labour costs have decreased in significance. In part this is due to more outsourcing being undertaken by airport operators, particularly in the handling area, and in many cases the use of a more productive labour force as a result of a focus on greater efficiency. Various technological developments have also reduced the need for so many staff.

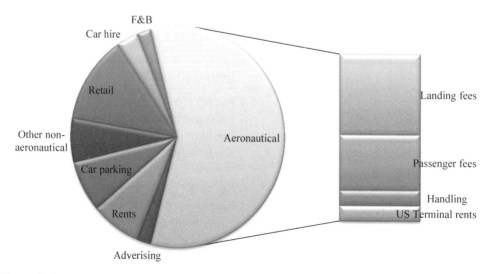

Figure 3.2 *Revenue structures at ACI airports, 2010 (excluding non-operating items)*
Source: adapted from ACI (2011)

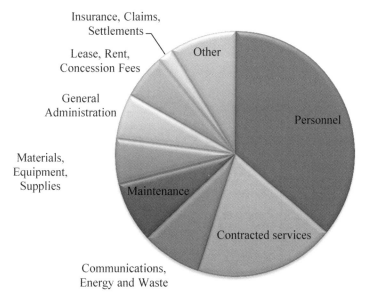

Figure 3.3 *Cost structures at ACI airports, 2010*
Source: ACI (2011)

However, airport operators tend to have less scope to reduce staff costs compared with some industries, including the airline sector, as the majority of staff functions tend to be related to the essential safety and security aspects of operating an airport. In general, airports are fixed-cost businesses, having longer planning horizons than airlines and requiring major investments in runways, terminals and equipment. As a result, airports have limited flexibility to adjust these costs when traffic fluctuates. For example, for a sample of 10 UK airports between 2000/01 and 2010/11, the operating-cost-to-passenger-demand elasticity was calculated as 0.44 (Steer Davies Gleave, 2012). This means that if passenger demand falls by 10 per cent, the operating cost will reduce by just 4.4 per cent.

Table 3.3 also gives a broad breakdown of revenues for the sample of European airports. The dominant trend up to 1998 was a decline in the importance of aeronautical revenues with a subsequent increase in reliance on non-aeronautical sources. This reflected not only pressures from airlines and regulatory bodies to keep airport charge increases to a minimum, but also the increased focus being placed on commercial activities. At some airports, the increase in the proportion of non-aeronautical revenue over the 15 years from 1983 to 1998 had been considerable – for example, at Copenhagen airport the share increased from 41 to 54 per cent and at Geneva airport it rose from 40 to 51 per cent. This trend was halted in 1999 because of the impact of the abolition of EU duty- and tax-free goods in that year, and since then the share of revenue from non-aeronautical sources has reduced slightly. There are a number of reasons for this, including increased retail competition from the internet and stricter security control, discussed in detail in Chapter 7.

These average values hide the variation between individual airports that in some cases is quite considerable. Table 3.4 shows the data for a number of European airports. The revenue figures reflect differences in strategy towards aeronautical and commercial activities, but also differences in the functions carried out by the airport operator itself. For example, many of the German, Italian and Austrian airports are involved in providing their own handling services. Overall, the

Table 3.3 *Average operating revenue and cost structures at European airports, 1983–2011*

	1983/84	1988/89	1993/94	1998/99	2003/04	2008/09	2009/10	2010/11
Revenue shares (per cent)								
Aeronautical	59	56	54	50	51	54	54	53
Non-aeronautical	41	44	46	50	49	46	46	47
Total	100	100	100	100	100	100	100	100
Cost shares (per cent)								
Labour	46	43	39	35	33	31	32	29
Depreciation	18	21	22	19	22	20	20	21
Other	36	36	39	46	45	49	48	50
Total	100	100	100	100	100	100	100	100

Sources: Annual reports

Table 3.4 Operating revenue and cost structures at a selection of European airports, 2010/11

Airport	Revenues (per cent)			Costs (per cent)			
	Aeronautical	Non-aeronautical	Total	Labour	Depreciation	Other	Total
Amsterdam	59	41	100	20	21	59	100
Basel-Mulhouse	46	54	100	23	29	47	100
Belfast Intl	47	53	100	27	7	67	100
Birmingham	49	51	100	26	26	48	100
Cologne	65	35	100	40	14	47	100
Copenhagen	52	48	100	46	24	30	100
Dusseldorf	67	33	100	32	18	50	100
East Midlands	47	53	100	27	18	55	100
Florence	59	41	100	35	7	58	100
Frankfurt	62	38	100	48	15	37	100
Gatwick	51	49	100	34	21	45	100
Geneva	50	50	100	43	21	37	100
Hamburg	71	29	100	35	16	49	100
Hanover	63	37	100	39	15	46	100
Heathrow	53	47	100	12	33	54	100
Ljubljana	69	31	100	41	24	35	100
Malta	64	36	100	27	15	58	100
Manchester	46	54	100	24	25	52	100
Munich	50	50	100	36	18	46	100
Oslo	42	58	100	16	21	63	100
Paris	56	44	100	36	17	47	100
Rome	51	49	100	26	26	48	100
Stansted	54	46	100	21	24	55	100
Venice	35	65	100	31	8	62	100
Vienna	80	20	100	53	15	32	100
Zurich	62	38	100	26	31	44	100

The data may include other airports when the airport operator owns more than one airport, but most are associated with the major airport shown.
Sources: Annual reports

total amount generated from commercial revenues tends to be high in Europe, reflecting in part the high proportion of international traffic, greater opportunities for landside as well as airside sales, and often high rents for surrounding land in many densely populated areas. The table also shows how labour costs vary quite considerably. At Vienna and Frankfurt they account for around half the total costs, again reflecting their heavy involvement in the labour-intensive handling activity. By contrast, airports such as Basel-Mulhouse, Amsterdam, London Heathrow and Oslo, which are not involved with so many activities, have much lower staff costs.

In the United States, airports tend to use a different breakdown of their activities and revenues, with aeronautical revenues including not only aircraft landing fees and fuel charges but also rents and lease revenues from land, terminal and other buildings or hangars used by airlines. The remaining non-aviation revenues are the same as commercial or non-aeronautical revenues. Generally the proportion of revenue from airport charges is low compared with elsewhere because the airports do not charge a passenger charge (although there is a passenger facility charge, but this is treated as non-operating revenue – see Chapter 4). They also do not get involved in providing services such as air traffic control or handling. The same situation applies in Canada. On the other hand, the revenue from rentals is higher because of the greater amount of space and facilities that are rented or leased to the airlines. The most important commercial revenues are associated with car activities, such as car parking and car hire, rather than retail, as is usually the situation elsewhere. In terms of costs, the share of staff costs are low by international standards – again because these airports tend to get involved in very few additional services. These characteristics are illustrated in Table 3.5, which shows the revenue and cost structures for a number of US and Canadian airports. For most of these airports the staff costs are less than 30 per cent of total costs. Elsewhere in the world (Table 3.6) the share of staff costs also tends to be quite low, reflecting lower local wages costs (e.g. in Mexico) or minimum involvement in additional activities (e.g. the Australian airports).

Table 3.5 *Operating revenue and cost structures at a selection of US and Canadian airports, 2010/11*

Airport	Revenues (per cent)			Costs (per cent)			
	Aeronautical	Non-aeronautical	Total	Labour	Depreciation	Other	Total
USA							
Atlanta	40	60	100	24	45	31	100
Charlotte	46	54	100	19	34	48	100
Chicago O'Hare	70	30	100	25	31	44	100
Denver	62	38	100	19	31	50	100
Detroit	55	45	100	21	42	36	100
Indianapolis	40	60	100	17	63	20	100
Kansas City	35	65	100	23	42	35	100
Las Vegas	52	48	100	30	37	33	100
Los Angeles	59	41	100	51	14	34	100
Memphis	73	27	100	22	52	27	100
Miami	67	33	100	33	31	37	100
Minneapolis– St Paul	39	61	100	25	48	27	100
Nashville	35	65	100	34	31	35	100
Orlando	36	64	100	17	43	39	100
Palm Beach	42	58	100	17	36	47	100
Salt Lake City	43	57	100	32	38	30	100

Continued

Table 3.5 Continued

Airport	Revenues (per cent)			Costs (per cent)			
	Aeronautical	Non-aeronautical	Total	Labour	Depreciation	Other	Total
Tampa	32	68	100	24	48	28	100
Canada							
Calgary	44	56	100	10	43	48	100
Edmonton	40	60	100	24	34	41	100
Halifax	53	47	100	30	26	44	100
Montreal	52	48	100	17	28	54	100
Ottawa	53	47	100	24	26	50	100
Toronto	67	33	100	16	29	55	100
Vancouver	44	56	100	15	38	47	100
Victoria	34	66	100	24	27	49	100
Winnipeg	53	47	100	33	14	53	100

Sources: FAA/Annual reports

Table 3.6 Operating revenue and cost structures at a selection of other airports, 2010/11

Airport	Revenues (per cent)			Costs (per cent)			
	Aeronautical	Non-aeronautical	Total	Labour	Depreciation	Other	Total
Australia							
Adelaide	56	44	100	15	24	61	100
Brisbane	43	57	100	15	31	53	100
Melbourne	42	58	100	15	29	56	100
Perth	36	64	100	22	17	61	100
Sydney	54	46	100	10	56	34	100
New Zealand							
Auckland	38	62	100	22	39	39	100
Christchurch	46	54	100	26	37	37	100
Wellington	58	42	100	12	25	63	100
Other							
Aeropuertos del Sureste, Mexico	54	46	100	10	15	75	100
Airports Company South Africa	41	59	100	25	40	35	100
Airports of Thailand	58	42	100	19	41	40	100
Beijing	61	39	100	8	37	55	100
Hainan Meilan	67	33	100	21	24	55	100

Continued

Table 3.6 Continued

Airport	Revenues (per cent)			Costs (per cent)			
	Aeronautical	Non-aeronautical	Total	Labour	Depreciation	Other	Total
Hong Kong	55	45	100	12	40	48	100
Malaysia Airports Holding Berhad	45	55	100	28	12	61	100
Operadora Mexicana de Aeropuertos	62	38	100	6	22	72	100

Sources: Annual reports

FACTORS INFLUENCING COSTS, REVENUES AND EFFICIENCY LEVELS

There are many factors that affect an airport's level and structure of costs and revenues, and in a broader sense its overall economic efficiency. Some of these are more easily influenced by airport management than others. First, the volume and nature of the traffic, over which the airport operator has only limited control, can have a major impact on the airport's economic performance. As airports increase their traffic throughput, the costs per unit of traffic, or unit costs, is thought to decline. Studies of British airports in the 1970s showed that unit costs, measured in costs per passenger handled or per work load unit (a WLU is equivalent to one passenger or 100 kg of freight), fell dramatically as total traffic increased to around 1 or 1.5 million passengers (or WLU). Then, at a traffic level of around 3 million passengers or WLU, the unit costs tended to flatten out and ceased to exhibit a strong relationship with airport size (Doganis and Thompson, 1973). For small airports there will be certain fixed costs associated with the provision of infrastructure and services which will be incurred at the airport, irrespective of the traffic levels, which will push up the unit costs. More complex studies of performance and efficiency also confirm that airports experience economies of scale. This evidence now exists for different countries including the USA (Gillen and Lall, 1997), Europe (Pels *et al.*, 2001), Argentina (Barros, 2008c), Brazil (Wanke, 2012), Italy (Barros and Dieke, 2007), Spain (Salazar de la Cruz, 1999) and Japan (Yoshida, 2004). Martin and Voltes-Dorta (2011c), in their study of Spanish airports, found that the scale economies were not exhausted at any level of traffic, tending to disagree with most of the other research which found, like Doganis and Thompson, that the airports ceased to benefit from these after reaching a certain size.

Some researchers (e.g. Murillo-Melchor, 1999) have advocated that as airports become large they start to experience diseconomies of scale. This suggests there might be an optimal size of airport in economic terms (Pels *et al.*, 2001). This may be because the airport system will become more complex, for example with a number of different terminals that involve more coordination and duplication of services and facilities. Surface access expenditure and costs to alleviate greater environmental damage will also grow significantly as airports become large. It has also been suggested by Kamp *et al.* (2007) that the costs might rise because of more expensive labour costs (due to higher unionisation and using staff from farther distances) and the scarcity of cheap land, but as yet the evidence regarding diseconomies of scale is far from conclusive.

However, as discussed in more detail in Chapter 7, larger airports are normally in a better position to provide a greater range of commercial facilities for passengers and other consumers, and therefore tend to have a greater reliance on non-aeronautical revenues. Often, but not always, larger airports have a higher share of international passengers. Costs associated with international passengers tend to rise as this type of traffic requires more space in the terminal for customs and immigration, and these passengers spend longer in the terminal. International passengers also tend to have more luggage and need larger baggage-handling facilities. However, as international passengers have more dwell time in the terminal, they spend more money on commercial facilities such as retail and food and beverage (F&B) that will push up unit revenues – particularly if they have access to duty- and tax-free shopping. A number of performance studies, including those undertaken by the Air Transport Research Society (ATRS), confirm that the proportion of international traffic does have a significant impact on airport performance (e.g. Oum *et al.*, 2003).

Low-cost and charter passengers will not usually need certain services, such as airline lounges and transfer facilities, which will influence the airport's cost and revenue levels. They also have different spending patterns from traditional scheduled terminal passengers, as do transfer passengers at hub airports (a more detailed description of different spending patterns is given in Chapter 7). Airports serving holiday destinations may have a problem with seasonality and uneven capacity utilisation which can push up costs and reduce efficiency, as observed by Tsekeris (2011) in Greece and Gitto and Mancuso (2012a) in Italy. Elsewhere hub airports, with a 'wave' pattern of flights with well defined peaks and troughs of traffic, will find it more costly to handle this type of traffic than a more evenly spread distribution of flights. In a broader sense, operating as a hub may increase an airport's overall attractiveness and thus improve its performance. This helps explain why the evidence related to hub traffic and airport performance is mixed, with Oum *et al.* (2004) observing that having a hub role lowered performance, while Sarkis (2000); Lin and Hong (2006); Barros and Dieke (2008); Perelman and Serebrisky (2010); and Assaf (2011) argue that hub airports achieve better performance.

Airport operators have greater choice over the physical and service standards they consider desirable to provide an acceptable level of service for their passengers. If an airport decides to offer a more exclusive and upmarket product, as with the business airport London City or Gimbo Seoul airport in Korea, this will clearly have resource implications. At the other extreme, there are a few airports, such as Singapore Changi, Kuala Lumpur, Marseille and Lyon, that offer a dedicated low-cost terminal which again has implications for the cost levels of the airport (see Chapter 5).

There is no 'typical' airport when it comes to looking at the services and facilities provided. Beyond the basic operational functions, different airports have little in common. The level of direct involvement will vary, with some airport operators providing activities such as security, air traffic control, handling, car parking, duty-free shops and cleaning, while others will contract these out. In the extreme case, terminals may also be leased, as is the situation in the United States. All this will have an impact on both cost and revenue levels. For example, Vienna airport generates over 30 per cent of gross revenues from handling. This is very different from airports, such as London Heathrow and Amsterdam Schiphol, that generate a relatively small amount of revenues from this activity in the form of rents and concession fees paid by the airlines and handling agents. Handling services may even be produced jointly, for example with the airport supplying the check-in desks and the airlines staffing the desks. In some cases the situation may be even more complicated – the government may pay for the provision of certain services, as is typically the case with the provision of policing, security or fire and rescue.

Economic comparisons in any industry must acknowledge the accounting policies adopted by individual operators. Within the airport industry, accounting procedures vary considerably, particularly as some airports adopt government or public authority accounting methods rather than commercial practices. With government-owned airports it is possible, for example, to find that the airport's land will not be considered to be an airport asset, and hence will not appear in any balance sheet. Views differ on how assets should be depreciated. For example, Zurich depreciates buildings for 40 years, Amsterdam for 20–40 years, Copenhagen 80 years. At Dublin, runways are depreciated for 10–50 years, at Amsterdam for 15–60 years, and at Copenhagen for 80 years. Airports are subject to different taxation regimes, with many public sector airports, for instance those in the United States, being exempt from most business taxes. This will have an impact on any comparative analysis of net profit levels.

Chapters 2 and 4 discuss whether privatisation and economic regulation, respectively, have had an impact on economic performance. Ownership patterns can influence factors such as funding arrangements and the cost of capital that may well affect an airport's finances. In addition, an airport's performance is likely to depend very much on where it is positioned in the investment life cycle, as investment at airports tends to be long-term, large and 'lumpy' rather than continuous and gradual. When major developments have taken place, capital costs are likely to be high and poor utilisation may push up the operating costs. Later in the cycle the capital costs will reduce and utilisation will hopefully improve. If an airport is congested, it may not be very attractive to its customers, but from an economic viewpoint it may perform relatively well. This leads to the expression 'sweating the assets'.

There are many other factors dependent on an airport's location and geographical situation that, to a large extent, will be beyond the airport operator's specific control. For instance, weather-related expenses, such as snow removal and de-icing facilities, will be incurred only at certain airports. Location and possible physical constraints are also likely to influence the layout and design of the airport and the positioning of both airfield and terminal facilities. For example, an airport may require two or more runways not to meet traffic needs, but because of wind conditions or some other particular climatic or geographical characteristic. Environmental limits, imposed to reduce noise or other adverse impacts of air transport, may also mean that the airport cannot make the most efficient use of all resources. An airport may be forced to close at night even if there is sufficient demand to make night flying feasible. There may also be differing national laws and regulations that will affect an airport's operating and business environment. In a more general sense, locational factors may also affect the cost and quality of labour and the availability of capital for investment.

Overall, it is very apparent that numerous factors influence an airport's performance, with different degrees of control existing for the airport operator. Typically, external factors mostly beyond management control are the volume and nature of traffic; ownership, governance and regulatory systems; environmental constraints; and location costs. Internal factors under management control include the degree of outsourcing; the quality of service; and the investment cycle. Reinhold *et al.* (2010) classify the factors that influence performance – in other words, heterogeneities – as external (exogenous) and internal (endogenous). Exogenous heterogeneities are caused by the environment (e.g. geographical constraints or social particularities) while endogenous heterogeneities may be due to national differences in the regulatory framework or managerial decisions.

MEASURING ECONOMIC PERFORMANCE AND EFFICIENCY

Growing interest in performance assessment and benchmarking

Until the 1980s, the systematic monitoring and comparing of airport economic performance was not a widely practised activity within the airport industry. This can be attributed largely to insufficient commercial and business pressures for airports, and the general lack of experience of benchmarking techniques within the public sector as a whole. The difficulties involved with producing meaningful comparisons, such as varying involvement in airport activities and different accounting policies, only further discouraged most airports from seriously attempting to analyse their comparative performance.

With airport commercialisation and privatisation has come a marked interest in performance comparisons and benchmarking. As airports have become more commercially oriented, they have been keen to identify the strong performers in the industry and adopt what are seen as best practices. Senior managers can use performance measures to help them define goals and targets. Comparative performance analysis can also give valuable insight into issues including whether privatised airports are more efficiently run than public sector airports; what is the best organisational framework for an airport; and whether airports operated as part of national networks or systems perform better than individual airports. There is thus a growing recognition of the value of continuous performance appraisal within the airport industry.

Many other organisations external to the airport sector are also showing a keen interest in using performance measures to compare achievements between airports. Such organisations will have a different ultimate objective for comparing performance and hence are likely to view the findings from a different perspective. Investors and bankers, traditionally much more used to using financial ratios and other benchmarking techniques, are anxious to identify possible business opportunities and to ensure their chosen airport investments continue to perform well. Airlines, now operating in a much more cost-conscious and competitive environment, have an interest in identifying that airports are being inefficiently managed – particularly to add substance to any lobbying against increases in user charges. Economic regulators of privatised or autonomously managed airports also have good reason to monitor airport performance to ensure users are being charged fairly and that the airports are run efficiently (see Chapter 4). Local communities may also be anxious to ensure the airport is being run in an efficient manner so that they can benefit fully from the economic benefits, such as tourism and inward investment, that the airport can bring.

Analysing an airport's economic performance has therefore become an important task for many of those involved, directly or indirectly, with the airport industry. Economic performance appraisal is only one aspect of airport performance that needs to be assessed (Graham, 2005). There are a wide range of operational activities that need to monitored by looking at measures relating to airside delays, baggage delivery, terminal processing times, equipment availability and so on. In addition, consumer satisfaction levels should be assessed, typically through passenger surveys. With growing concern for the environment, there is an increasing use of environmental indicators at airports. A recent study related to US airports (Infrastructure

Management Group *et al.*, 2010) identified seven broad areas for performance investigation (safety, security, customer services, environmental sustainability, people, customer relations and IT) while the ACI (2012) identified six (core, safety and security, service quality, productivity/ cost-effectiveness, financial/commercial and environmental). Some of these non-economic areas are considered in detail in other chapters, but the interrelationships between these different aspects of performance must be recognised. For example, any decision on service levels or operational procedures will greatly influence an airport's cost and manning levels, and *vice versa*.

With the growth of this emphasis on performance assessment of different aspects of airport management, a number of performance measurement frameworks have been adopted. In particular, a balanced scorecard system is used by a number of North American airports including Dayton, Salt Lake City, Dallas Fort Worth and Toronto, and elsewhere, for example at Dublin airport. This approach views an airport typically from four different perspectives, one of which relates to the financial area. The other three usually relate to the customer, internal processes, and learning and growth. For each of these four perspectives there are objectives, measures and targets. The scorecard shows how these measures are interrelated and affect one another. At Hartsfield Atlanta, the financial measures cover areas including revenue generation, overtime practices, debt coverage and overruns on budgets. The customers' measures range from responses to comment cards to measurement of passenger transit time. Processes consider issues such as payment of invoices, while within the learning and growth area measures look at training hours, employment satisfaction, existence of vacant positions and so on (Ricondo and Associates *et al.* 2009). At Dublin airport there are six perspectives: customer experience, optimum return to shareholder, strategic focus, organisation/people/processes, focused communication and flawless execution (Ryan, 2012). This balanced scorecard approach is just one example of the many different systems of performance measurement that are now used at airports.

Performance concepts

More consideration is now given to the performance concepts specifically related to economic performance and efficiency. In simple terms, performance measures analyse the relationship between inputs and outputs at an airport. This relationship can be expressed in both financial and physical terms. As with other businesses, labour and capital are the major inputs of the airport system. The simplest physical measure of the labour input is the total number of employees. Any part-time and temporary staff should be converted to full-time equivalents. To capture the effect of the cost of labour as well as productivity per head, the labour input can also be measured in financial terms: employee wages and salaries.

Determining a reliable measure of the capital input is much more difficult. In physical terms, capital input is measured by the production capability or capacity of the system. At an airport this cannot be assessed by one measure. The capacity of the runways, terminal, gates and so on all have to be considered. Capacity can be measured on an hourly, daily or annual basis. Depreciation or asset values can be used to measure the financial capital input. These will, however, reflect the accounting policies of the specific airport and may not always be closely related to its economic production capability.

The financial measurement of output is relatively straightforward and can be measured by considering the total revenues generated. Physically, the output of an airport can be assessed in three ways: in terms of quantities of aircraft, passengers or freight. These measures do not cover all aspects of an airport (e.g. its role as a retail facility), but they do capture the key outputs. The use of aircraft movements is not ideal as such measures will not differentiate between different sizes and different types of aircraft. Since most airports handle both passengers and freight, this suggests the use of an output measure that combines the two, such as the WLU. The WLU originated from the airline industry and uses a weight criteria for combining these two types of traffic (one WLU = one passenger or 100 kg of freight). Some argue, however, that the focus should be on passenger numbers, as freight handling at airports is very much an airline activity and has little impact on an airport's economic performance.

The WLU, although probably the most widely accepted aggregate measure, is a rather arbitrary method of linking the two outputs, as the same weight of passengers and freight does not involve using the same resources. Ideally, the WLU formula should therefore reflect the relative importance or value of the different outputs and perhaps should include an aircraft movement element. Costs or employee numbers associated with the different outputs theoretically could be used to determine the scaling factor, but there is the major problem of joint costs or joint tasks undertaken by the staff. An alternative scaling parameter could be the relative prices of the outputs, but this assumes a close relationship between price and cost which is not usually the case at airports because of market imperfections, regulation and government interference and, sometimes, cross-subsidies between different traffic. There is the additional problem that there are even different costs and revenues associated with different passenger types, the most notable examples being international and domestic passengers or terminal and transfer passengers.

LeighFisher produces annual global benchmarking and uses a different measure of output, the airport throughput unit (ATU) (LeighFisher, 2012). It is defined as:

$$ATU = (passengers + 10) \times (freight\ tonnes + 100) \times ATM$$

It thus keeps the WLU relationship of 1:10 between passengers and freight, but also includes an aircraft movement component. The value of 100 was derived by looking at past studies and determining that handling one air transport movement (ATM) required approximately the same effort as handling 100 WLU.

To summarise, performance measures or indicators are all about relating one or more of the outputs to one or more inputs. By using a number of these indicators, an airport can assess different aspects of its performance and identify where its strengths and weaknesses lie. These indicators can be grouped into certain categories, such as cost efficiency, labour and capital productivity, revenue generation, and commercial performance and profitability. In addition to these input:output ratios, a few other key measures (e.g. share of revenue from aeronautical sources; percentage of costs allocated to staff) can give further insights into comparative performance. Table 3.7 presents around 20 indicators that cover all airport operations typically used at a senior management level. These are often defined as key performance indicators (KPIs), each with an important target that links to the airport achieving its strategic and operational goals. Beneath these KPIs may be a hierarchical system of more specific indicators that cover various aspects of performance in greater detail. In their comprehensive study of all performance indicators at airports, Hazel et al. (2011) describe a three-level hierarchical system consisting of core, key/departmental and other indicators.

The industry body ACI and its regional organisations has shown increased interest in collaborative airport benchmarking studies in recent years, which involve voluntary participation of its members. For example, 36 members of ACI Europe, representing 106 airports, are involved in an annual benchmarking KPI project that began back in 2003. The KPIs cover six areas: revenues structures, revenue generation, staff, cost structure, cost efficiency and financial (Table 3.8). Also, since 2005 there has been an ACI North America annual benchmarking survey which in 2011 involved 96 airports, including seven from Canada. It covers about 75 operational and financial measures.

Table 3.7 *Performance indicators commonly used to assess economic performance**

Indicator	Area
Cost efficiency	Costs excluding depreciation per WLU†
	Costs including depreciation per WLU
	Depreciation costs per WLU
	Labour costs per WLU
	Depreciation share of operating costs
	Labour share of operating costs
Labour productivity	WLU per employee
	Revenues per employee
Capital productivity	WLU/total assets
	Revenues/total assets
	Total assets per employee
Revenue generation	Revenues per WLU
	Aeronautical revenues per WLU
	Non-aeronautical revenues per WLU
	Aeronautical share of total revenues
Commercial performance	Concession plus rental revenues per passenger
	Concession revenues per passenger
Profitability	Operating margin
	Operating profit excluding depreciation per WLU
	Operating profit including depreciation per WLU
	Operating profit including/excluding depreciation/total assets
	Net retained profit after interest and taxation per WLU

* Only operating revenues and cost are included (interest, extraordinary items, taxation and dividends are excluded) with the exception of the final indicator (net retained profit after interest and taxation per WLU).

† Some analysts use passenger numbers rather than work load units (WLU) and may include aircraft movements as an airport output measure.

Table 3.8 *Key performance indicators used by ACI Europe*

Indicator	Area
Revenue structure	Aeronautical revenues/turnover
	Non-aeronautical revenues/turnover
	Airport charges/turnover
	Security fees/turnover
	Commercial revenues/turnover
Revenue generation	Aeronautical revenues/PAX
	Aeronautical revenues/work load unit (WLU)
	Non-aeronautical revenues/PAX
	Airport charges/PAX
	Airport charges/WLU
	Retail revenues/departing/PAX
	Car parking revenues/PAX
	Advertising revenues/PAX
	Security revenues/departing PAX
Staff	Staff costs/employee
	Passenger/employee
	Turnover/employee
Cost structure	Staff costs/operating costs
	Depreciation and amortization/operating costs
	Other operating costs/operating costs
Cost efficiency	Staff costs/passengers
	Staff costs/WLU
	Utilities/passengers
	Utilities/WLU
	Security costs/departing passengers
	Maintenance external costs/passengers
	Maintenance external costs/WLU
Financial	EBITDA/passenger
	EBITDA/WLU
	EBITDA/employee
	Average capital employed/passenger
	Debt/equity
	Cash flow/average capex
	Average capex/passenger
	EBITDA margin
	Return on capital employed

Source: ACI Europe

While airport managers will be very keen to understand how efficiently the airport is using its infrastructure and how cost-effectively it is doing so, the financial sector will be focused more on ratios related to the business potential of the airport, including profit levels, liquidity ratios and capital expenditure levels. In the international financial markets, profit excluding depreciation is known as earnings before interest, tax, depreciation and amortisation (EBITDA) and profit including depreciation is known as earnings before interest and tax (EBIT) – the latter being very similar to the operating profit, except that it includes non-operating items. Another indicator is the EBITDA or EBIT margin: earnings expressed as a percentage of revenue. The ratio of operating profit to total assets is commonly referred to as return on capital employed (ROCE) or return on assets. Putting the traditional indicators in these financial terms enables comparisons to be made easily with other business sectors. Other standard financial ratios, including the interest cover (EBIT:interest), the dividend cover (post-tax profit/dividends), and gearing (debt as a share of shareholders funds), can be used to assess the financial wellbeing and capital structure of the airport company. Capital expenditure (capex) per WLU or passenger, employee or revenues can also give an indication as to the amount of investment that is taking place (Vogel and Graham, 2006).

For the publicly quoted airport companies, such as Fraport and Vienna, additional indicators associated with the value of the company can be used. A number of these ratios relate the enterprise value (EV), which shows the market value of the company's core businesses, to sales, earnings or throughput (e.g. EV:total revenues; EV:EBITDA; EV:EBIT; EV:WLU). Reference has already been made to these value ratios in Chapter 2, where privatisation trends are considered. The price earnings ratio (PER), which shows the relationship between the price of the share and earnings attributable to that share, can also be used.

Inter-airport performance

Airport benchmarking can be undertaken internally through time (self-benchmarking) and/or with different airports or peers when performance is measured against others with similar characteristics. Comparisons can be with an industry standard (e.g. an average) or best practice (e.g. the best performing airport). However, producing meaningful inter-airport performance indicators is fraught with difficulty because of serious problems of comparability – particularly due to the varying range of activities undertaken by airport operators themselves. Comparing indicators from the raw data can give misleading impressions, as airports involved with more activities would inevitably have higher cost and revenue levels and poorer labour productivity. The situation is also complicated by the fact that is not just the number of outsourcing activities that are a cost to the airport operator (e.g. cleaning) which varies, but also the range of services actually provided by airport operator, for which it has associated costs and revenues, will differ. For example, if an airport operator chooses to 'outsource' handling it will have very few costs and revenues associated with this, unlike the cleaning case where it still has to cover all the costs.

These problems can be addressed by standardising or normalising the airport data so that each airport's performance is presented as though it undertakes a uniform set of activities by taking into account the typical profit margins associated with each separate airport activity. For example, if an airport operator undertakes ground-handling activities itself, the assumed costs, revenues and staff numbers associated with this can be deducted to make the data more comparable with airports with no involvement with this activity. A hypothetical concession income from handling agents can then be added to the airport's revenues. Similar adjustments can be made for car parking and other commercial activities. This is the approach used by LeighFisher in its airport benchmarking work (LeighFisher 2012). In the USA there is also a comparability problem because in some cases the airlines have developed and operated the terminals. One option here that has been used in benchmarking studies is to add in the relevant airline data to ensure more 'like-with-like' assessments are being made (ACI, 2006).

However, there will obviously be an element of subjectivity in any assumptions that are used when making adjustments. Using such adjustments will inevitably mean there is a movement away from reality – which may be less helpful for the airports concerned – and the complementarity of the different activities or the reasons why the airport chooses to provide certain services may be ignored. Ideally, the accounts of each airport could also be adjusted to conform to a common treatment of depreciation, asset values and so on, but the problems associated with getting sufficient detail related to the capital input normally make this too difficult a task. Another way to lessen some of these comparability problems is to aim to choose a set of airports that are as similar as possible, but this is often a very difficult task given the multi-dimensional nature of airport operations and data limitations.

An additional issue to be faced in comparing airport performance is the difference in cost of living between countries. Official exchange rates may not be a close reflection of relative prices at different airports in different countries. This problem can be addressed by using purchasing power parity exchange rates rather than market exchange rates. Purchasing power parity exchange rates are calculated by dividing the cost of a given basket of goods in one currency by the cost of the same basket of goods in another country. So, effectively, they convert currencies on the basis of equalising buying power rather than on the basis of prevailing market conditions. They also overcome problems of currency fluctuations during the period under investigation. Alternatively, the special drawing right (SDR) – a basket of four currencies (the euro, the US dollar, pound sterling and the yen), weighted according to the relative importance of the currency in international trade and finance – can be used to overcome the currency fluctuation problem.

Figure 3.4 presents a sample indicator – total costs per passenger – from LeighFisher's benchmarking study that adjusts the data to produce a standardised airport. Forty-four airports from the study have been selected from North America, Europe and Asia-Pacific. The figure shows quite clearly how the Asia-Pacific airports (except Tokyo Narita) and North American airports have a cost advantage over European airports.

Overall performance measures

The performance measures in Table 3.7 are partial measures in that they give an indication of performance that relates specifically to the inputs and outputs that have been chosen. These measures usually require only limited data (unless the data are being adjusted), are relatively easy to compute, and are intuitively simple to understand. They can highlight strengths and weaknesses in certain areas and indicate where specific improvements can be made, but they cannot give an overall picture or identify the 'best in class'. By definition, they give only a partial and rather disjointed diagnosis of the situation, and can be misleading if only selected indicators are chosen. To cover all areas many measures are needed. These cannot take account of factor substitution, for example if one airport uses an employee to undertake a specific task while another may use a machine. It is also difficult to take account of differences in the prices of the inputs (e.g. labour) and, as discussed above, there are difficulties in choosing an output measure that covers a number of outputs (e.g. passengers and freight) if this is appropriate.

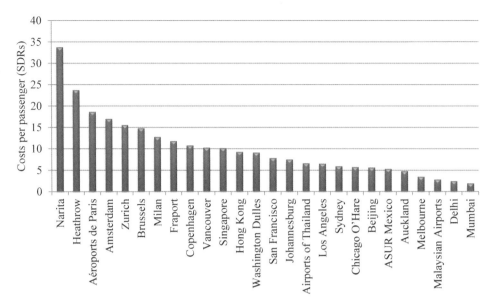

Figure 3.4 *Total costs per passenger for selected world airports, 2010*
Source: LeighFisher (2012)

These shortcomings can be overcome by investigating the relationship between the combined inputs and combined outputs to produce a single or overall efficiency measure. In contrast to other transport operations and public sector organisations, there was little exploration of the use of such methodologies until the 1990s, the airport sector preferring to concentrate mostly on partial measures (Lemaitre, 1998). Since then there has been growing interest in these alternative measures and a considerable number of efficiency studies have been undertaken for various countries and regions of the world (Merkert *et al.*, 2012), albeit that many of these have focused more on technical or operating efficiency and productivity analysis rather than purely financial or economic performance – primarily due to the data problems associated with the financial data (Vogel and Graham, 2006).

There are a number of different ways in which overall performance or efficiency can be assessed (Table 3.9) A parametric or statistical approach can be adopted by using a production or cost function that recognises several variables influencing performance. For example, the cost function expresses cost as a function of outputs, input prices and other factors, such as traffic characteristics, that may influence output or input. This function can be estimated by using regression analysis (ordinary or corrected least squares) or by the stochastic frontier method, which involves the estimation of a 'frontier' – the airport is efficient only if it operates on the frontier. These models can be used, for example, to investigate the impact of variations of input and output prices and to test for economies of scale. However, this approach has detailed data requirements.

Alternatively, a non-parametric index numbers method, such as the Tornqvist total factor productivity (TFP), can be used. This requires the aggregation of all outputs into a weighted outputs index and of all inputs into a weighted input index, with no assumptions or estimates of the parameters of the underlying production or cost functions having to be made. The outputs are weighted by revenue shares and the inputs are weighted by input cost shares. One of the most comprehensive studies of total factor productivity in the airport sector is contained in the Global

Table 3.9 Examples of airport performance and efficiency studies

Reference	Data sample (number of airports and nationality)	Period
Parametric cost/production		
Pels *et al.* (2001)	34 European	1995–97
Martin-Cejas (2002)	31 Spanish	1996–97
Pels *et al.* (2003)	34 European	1995–97
Barros (2008a)	27 UK	2000/01–2004/05
Barros (2008b)	13 Portuguese	1990–2000
Oum *et al.* (2008)	109 global	2001–4
Assaf (2009)	27 UK	2002/03–2006/07
Barros (2009)	27 UK	2000/01–2006/07
Martin *et al.* (2009)	37 Spanish	1991–97
Tovar and Martin-Cejas (2009)	26 Spanish	1993–99
Chow and Fung (2009)	46 Chinese	2000
Abrate and Erbetta (2010)	26 Italian	2000–05
Assaf (2010a)	13 Australian	2002–07
Tovar and Martin-Cejas (2010)	26 Spanish	1993–99
Martín and Voltes-Dorta (2011a)	161 global	1991–2008
Martín and Voltes-Dorta (2011b)	161 global	1991–2008
Martín and Voltes-Dorta (2011c)	36 Spanish	1991–97
Assaf and Gillen (2012)	73 Global	2003–08
Scotti *et al.* (2012)	38 Italian	2005–08
Non-parametric index number method		
Hooper and Hensher (1997)	6 Australian	1988/89–1991/92
Nyshadham and Rao (2000)	25 European	1995
Oum *et al.* (2003)	50 global	1999
Oum and Yu (2004)	76 global	2000–01
Oum *et al.* (2004)	60 global	1999
Yoshida (2004)	30 Japanese	2000
Yoshida and Fujimoto (2004)*	67 Japanese	2000
Oum *et al.* (2006)	116 global	2001–03
Vasigh and Gorjidooz (2006)	22 US and European	2000–04
Non-parametric frontier		
Gillen and Lall (1997)	21 US	1989–93
Murillo-Melchor (1999)	33 Spanish	1992–94
Parker (1999)	BAA; 22 UK	1979/80–1995/96; 1988/89–1996/97
Salazar de la Cruz (1999)	16 Spanish	1993–95
Sarkis (2000)	44 US	1990–94
Adler and Berechman (2001)	26 global	1996
Gillen and Lall (2001)	22 US	1989/90–1992/93
Martin and Roman (2001)	37 Spanish	1997

Continued

Table 3.9 *Continued*

Reference	Data sample (number of airports and nationality)	Period
Abbott and Wu (2002)	12 Australian	1989/90– 1999/2000
Fernandes and Pachero (2002)	35 Brazilian	1998
Bazargan and Vasigh (2003)	45 US	1996–2000
Pachero and Fernandes (2003)	35 Brazilian	1998
Barros and Sampaio (2004)	10 Portuguese	1990–2000
Holvad and Graham (2004)	21 UK	2000/01
Sarkis and Talluri (2004)	44 US	1990–94
Yu (2004)	14 Taiwanese	1994–2000
Lin and Hong (2006)	20 global	2003
Martin and Roman (2006)	34 Spanish	1997
Pachero *et al.* (2006)	58 Brazilian	1998–2001
Vogel (2006a)	35 European	1990–99
Vogel (2006b)	35 European	1990–99
Vogel and Graham (2006)	31 European	1990–99
Barros and Dieke (2007)	31 Italian	2001–03
Barros (2008c)	32 Argentine	2003–07
Barros and Dieke (2008)	31 Italian	2001–03
Fung *et al.* (2008)	25 Chinese	1995–2004
Martin and Roman (2008)	34 Spanish	1997
Pathomsiri *et al.* (2008)	56 US	2000–03
Yu *et al.* (2008)	4 Taiwanese	1995–99
Barros and Weber (2009)	27 UK	2000/01–2004/05
Chi-Lok and Zhang (2009)	25 Chinese	1995–2006
Lam *et al.* (2009)	11 Asia-Pacific	2001–05
Ablanedo-Rosas and Gemoets (2010)	37 Mexican	2009
Assaf (2010b)	27 UK	2007
Barros *et al.* (2010)	16 Japanese	1987–2005
Curi *et al.* (2010)	36 Italian	2001–03
Suzuki *et al.* (2010)	30 European	2003
Yu (2010)	15 Taiwanese	2006
Assaf (2011)	13 Australian	2002–07
Curi *et al.* (2011)	18 Italian	2000–04
Gitto and Mancuso (2012a)	28 Italian	2000–06
Kocak (2011)	40 Turkish	2008
Psaraki-Kalouptsidi and Kalakou (2011)	27 Greek	2004–07
Sharma *et al.* (2011)	29 Asia-Pacific	2001–05
Tsekeris (2011)	39 Greek	2007
Gitto and Mancuso (2012b)	28 Italian	2000–06
Wanke (2012)	65 Brazilian	2009

Airport Benchmarking Report, produced annually (since 2002) by the Air Transport Research Society. The 2012 report (ATRS, 2012) looked at 185 airports and 25 airport groups in Asia-Pacific, Europe and North America. It considered various partial measures of performance, but unlike LeighFisher's global study did not adjust the data to take account of different involvement in activities. The TFP method that was adopted was an index number approach using revenue shares as weights for the outputs (aircraft movements, passengers, cargo and other revenue) and cost shares as weights for the inputs (labour, other non-capital inputs, runways, terminals, gates). The capital input was excluded in most measures because of the difficulties in obtaining accurate, comparable data for this, and so an index called variable factor productivity (VFP) was considered. Two overall VFP measures were produced, the 'gross' value and the 'net' or 'residual' value. The net value had the effect of certain factors that were considered beyond management control removed, including airport size, the share of international and cargo traffic and capacity constraints, in order to leave a measure that was more likely to reflect managerial efficiency. As an illustration, Figure 3.5 shows the value for a selection of Asian airports – the higher the score, the better the performance. While Figures 3.4 and 3.5 measure different aspects of performance, it is interesting that Narita does not seem to perform very well with both measures, and Singapore and Hong Kong appear to have very similar performance with both measures.

The most popular methods are non-parametric frontier methods and, in particular, a linear programming technique called data envelopment analysis (DEA), which also produces a weighted output index relative to a weighted input index similar to the non-parametric TFP measure. The key advantages of this non-parametric method are that it does not involve the estimation of underlying production or cost functions, and the weights for the inputs and outputs are not predetermined but instead are the result of the programming procedure. DEA is therefore a more attractive technique than the index number TFP for dealing with multiple input and output activities because

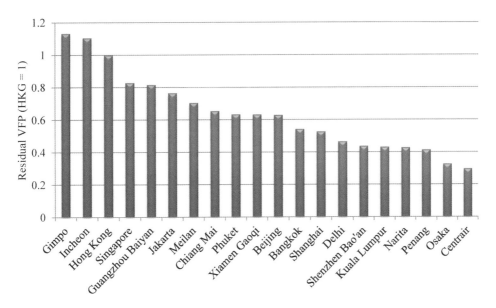

Figure 3.5 *Residual variable factor productivity at selected Asia-Pacific airports, 2010*
Source: ATRS (2012)

it has less demanding data requirements. It assesses the relative efficiency of a set of decision-making units (DMUs), in this case airports, that are engaged in performing the same function, with efficiency being measured not in absolute terms but in relation to the sample. The most efficient DMUs are located on the frontier with a relative index of 1. Another advantage of the DEA approach is that it can be used to measure scale effects on airports as there are both constant and variable returns to scale models. However, a key limitation of DEA is its sensitivity to outliers and parameter selection, and the results may be very different if the input and output selection is different. If the combined number of inputs/outputs is large relative to the DMUs, DEA tends to overstate performance and leads to many DMUs achieving a maximum efficiency value of 1. DEA produces relative rankings, but does not by itself explain the observations. This can be partially overcome with application of the Malmquist index which, when used with DEA, is a useful way of identifying the sources of productivity differences over a certain time period as this index allows productivity change to be decomposed into technical changes gained from adopting new technologies and efficiency changes. Regression analysis can be with DEA scores to investigate explanatory variables and, in recent years, techniques called bootstrapping procedures have been used to improve the reliability of this analysis.

In summary, over the past decade or so an increasing number of performance techniques have been applied to the airport industry, and this has helped to increase the understanding of comparative airport performance which was previously very limited. All these methods have their own advantages and disadvantages, cover various aspects of performance and require different data and assumptions. The majority of studies have been confined to one specific country because of the lack of central sources and problems of obtaining detailed and comparable data for a number of different countries, which does mean that the international context is lost. Also, in some cases only airport group data are available, without specific data for individual airports. The shortcomings of the partial performance measures suggest that it might also be useful to consider the relationship of the combined inputs with the combined output produced, when the difficult task of interpreting a varied set of partial indicators is spared and in some cases, influencing variables, such as economies of scale can be taken into account. However, with such an aggregate overall efficiency value it may not always be apparent what this is measuring, and thus may not be very informative for management action unless additional research to explore the observed differences is undertaken.

Hence it seems that airport benchmarking has now been generally accepted as a useful exercise to undertake. However, as Morrison (2009) argues, often the results of airport benchmarking tools appear to be very sensitive to the definitions of variables, model structure, underlying assumptions and the methodology employed. As a result, it remains very difficult to determine with any certainty whether variations are due to management policy, external factors or data inconsistencies. With continuing research, hopefully some of the shortcomings of the current approaches may be overcome.

REFERENCES

Abbott, M. and Wu, S. (2002) 'Total factor productivity and efficiency of Australian airports', *Australian Economic Review*, 35(3): 244–60.

Ablanedo-Rosas, J. and Gemoets, L. (2010) 'Measuring the efficiency of Mexican airports', *Journal of Air Transport Management*, 16(6): 343–45.

Abrate, G. and Erbetta, F. (2010) 'Efficiency and patterns of service mix in airport companies: an input distance function approach', *Transportation Research Part E*, 46(5): 693–708.

ACI (2006) *Airport Benchmarking to Maximize Efficiency*, Geneva: Airports Council International.

—— (2011) *Airport Economics Survey 2011*, Montreal: Airports Council International.

—— (2012) *Guide to Airport Performance Measures*, Montreal: Airports Council International.

ACI Europe (2005) *Building for the Future: Paying for the Airports of Tomorrow*, Brussels: ACI Europe.

Adler, N. and Berechman, J. (2001) 'Measuring airport quality from airlines' viewpoint: an application of data envelopment analysis', *Transport Policy*, 8(3): 171–81.

Assaf, A. (2009) 'Accounting for size in efficiency comparisons of airports', *Journal of Air Transport Management*, 15(5): 256–58.

—— (2010a) 'The cost efficiency of Australian airports post privatisation', *Tourism Management*, 31(2): 267–73.

—— (2010b) 'Bootstrapped scale efficiency measures of UK airports', *Journal of Air Transport Management*, 16(1): 42–44.

—— (2011) 'Bootstrapped Malmquist indices of Australian airports', *Service Industries Journal*, 31(5): 829–46.

ATRS (2012) *Global Airport Benchmarking Report*, Vancouver: ATRS.

Assaf, A. and Gillen, D. (2012) 'Measuring the joint impact of governance form and economic regulation on airport efficiency', *European Journal of Operational Research*, 220(1): 187–98.

Barros, C. (2008a) 'Technical efficiency of UK airports', *Journal of Air Transport Management*, 14(6): 175–78.

—— (2008b) 'Technical change and productivity growth in airports: a case study', *Transportation Research Part A*, 42(5), 818–32.

—— (2008c) 'Airports in Argentina: technical efficiency in the context of an economic crisis', *Journal of Air Transport Management*, 14(6): 315–19.

—— (2009) 'The measurement of efficiency of UK airports, using a stochastic latent class frontier model', *Transport Review*, 29(4): 479–98.

Barros, C. and Dieke, P. (2007) 'Performance evaluation of Italian airports: a data envelopment analysis', *Journal of Air Transport Management*, 13(4): 184–91.

Barros, C. and Dieke, P. (2008) 'Measuring the economic efficiency of airports: a Simar–Wilson methodology analysis', *Transportation Research Part E*, 44(6): 1039–51.

Barros, C., Managi, S. and Yoshida, Y. (2010) 'Productivity growth and biased technological change in Japanese airports', *Transport Policy*, 17(4): 259–65.

Barros, C. and Sampaio, A. (2004) 'Technical and allocative efficiency in airports', *International Journal of Transport Economics*, 31(3): 355–77.

Barros, C. and Weber, W. (2009) 'Productivity growth and biased technological change in UK airports', *Transportation Research Part E*, 45(4): 642–53.

Bazargan, M. and Vasigh, B. (2003) 'Size versus efficiency: a case study of US commercial airports', *Journal of Air Transport Management*, 9(3): 187–93.

Chi-Lok, A. and Zhang, A. (2009) 'Effects of competition and policy changes on Chinese airport productivity', *Journal of Air Transport Management*, 15(4): 166–74.

Chow, C.K.W. and Fung, M.K.Y (2009) 'Efficiencies and scope economies of Chinese airports in moving passengers and cargo', *Journal of Air Transport Management*, 15: 324–29.

Curi, C., Gitto, S. and Mancuso, P. (2010) 'The Italian airport industry in transition: a performance analysis', *Journal of Air Transport Management*, 16(4): 218–21.

Curi, C., Gitto, S. and Mancuso, P. (2011) 'New evidence of the efficiency of Italian airports: a bootstrapped DEA analysis', *Socio-Economic Planning Sciences*, 45(2): 84–93.

Doganis, R.S. and Thompson, G.F. (1973) *The Economics of British Airports*, Transport Studies Group Research Report 1, London: University of Westminster (formerly Polytechnic of Central London).

Fernandes, E. and Pachero, R. (2002) 'Efficient use of airport capacity', *Transportation Research Part A*, 36(3): 225–38.

Fung, M.K.Y., Wan, K.K.H., Hui, Y.V. and Law, J.S. (2008) 'Productivity changes in Chinese airports 1995–2004', *Transportation Research Part E*, 44(3), 521–42.

Graham, A. (2005) 'Airport benchmarking: a review of the current situation', *Benchmarking: An International Journal*, 12(2): 99–111.

Gillen, D. and Lall, A. (1997) 'Developing measures of airport productivity and performance: an application of data envelopment analysis', *Transportation Research E*, 33(4): 261–74.

—— (2001) 'Non-parametric measures of efficiency of US airports', *International Journal of Transport Economics*, 28(3): 283–306.

Gitto, S. and Mancuso, P. (2012a) 'Two faces of airport business: a non-parametric analysis of the Italian airport industry', *Journal of Air Transport Management*, 20: 39–42.

—— (2012b) 'Bootstrapping the Malmquist indexes for Italian airports', *International Journal of Production Economics*, 135(1): 403–11.

Hazel, R., Blais, J., Browne, T. and Benzon, D. (2011) *Resource Guide to Airport Performance indicators*, ACRP Report 19A, Washington, DC: Transportation Research Board.

Holvad, T. and Graham, A. (2004) 'Efficiency measurement for UK airports: an application of data envelopment analysis', *Empirical Economic Letters*, 3(1): 29–39.

Hooper, P. and Hensher, D. (1997) 'Measuring total factor productivity of airports – an index number approach', *Transportation Research E*, 33(4): 249–59.

IATA (2006) Value Chain Profitability, Economics Briefing No. 4, June. Geneva: International Air Transport Association.

ICAO (2006) *Airport Economics Manual*, 2nd edn, Doc. 9562. Montreal: International Civil Aviation Organization.

Infrastructure Management Group, Performance Institute and Counter Technology Incorporated (2010) *Developing an Airport Performance-Measurement System*, ACRP report 19, Washington, DC: Transportation Research Board.

Kamp, V., Niemeier H.-M. and Mueller, J. (2007) 'What can be learned from benchmarking studies? Examining the apparent poor performance of German airports', *Journal of Airport Management*, 1(3): 294–308.

Kocak, H. (2011) 'Efficiency examination of Turkish airports with DEA approach', *International Business Research*, 4(2): 204–12.

Lam, S., Low, J. and Tang, L. (2009), 'Operational efficiencies across Asia Pacific airports', *Transport Research Part E*, 45(4): 654–65.

LeighFisher (2012) *Airport Performance Indicators 2012*, London: LeighFisher.

Lemaitre, A. (1998) 'The development of performance indicators at airports', *Air Transport Research Group Conference*, Vancouver, July.

Lin, L. and Hong, C. (2006) 'Operational performance evaluation of international major airports: an application of data envelopment analysis', *Journal of Air Transport Management*, 12(6): 342–51.

Martin, J. and Roman, C. (2001) 'An application of DEA to measure the efficiency of Spanish airports prior to privatisation', *Journal of Air Transport Management*, 7(3): 149–57.

—— (2006) 'A benchmarking analysis of Spanish commercial airports. A comparison between SMOP and DEA ranking methods', *Networks and Spatial Economics*, 6(2): 111–34.

—— (2008) 'The relationship between size and efficiency: a benchmarking analysis of Spanish commercial airports', *Journal of Airport Management*, 2(2): 183–97.

Martin, J., Roman, C. and Voltes-Dorta, A. (2009) 'A stochastic frontier analysis to estimate the relative efficiency of Spanish airports', *Journal of Productivity Analysis*, 31(3): 163–76.

Martín, J. and Voltes-Dorta, A. (2011a) 'The econometric estimation of airports' cost function', *Transportation Research B*, 45(1): 112–27.

—— (2011b) 'The dilemma between capacity expansions and multi-airport systems: empirical evidence from the industry's cost function', *Transportation Research E*, 47(3): 382–89.

—— (2011c) 'Scale economies in marginal costs in Spanish airports', *Transportation Research E*, 47(2): 238–48.

Martin-Cejas, R. (2002) 'An approximation to the productive efficiency of the Spanish airports network through a deterministic cost frontier', *Journal of Air Transport Management*, 8(4): 233–38.

Merkert, R., Odeck, J., Brathen, S. and Pagliari, R. (2012) 'A review of different benchmarking methods in the context of regional airports', *Transport Reviews*, 32(3): 379–95.

Morrison, W. (2009) 'Understanding the complexities and challenges of airport performance benchmarking', *Journal of Airport Management*, 3(2): 145–58.

Murillo-Melchor, C. (1999) 'An analysis of the technical efficiency and productive change in Spanish airports using the Malmquist Index', *International Journal of Transport Economics*, 26(2): 271–91

Nyshadham, E. and Rao, V. (2000) 'Assessing efficiency of European airports', *Public Works Management and Policy*, 5(1): 106–14.

Oum, T., Adler, N. and Yu, C. (2006) 'Privatisation, corporatisation, ownership forms and their effects on the performance of the world's airports', *Journal of Air Transport Management*, 12(2): 109–21.

Oum, T. and Yu, C. (2004) 'Measuring airports' operating efficiency: a summary of the 2003 ATRS global airport benchmarking report', *Transportation Research Part E*, 40(6): 515–32.

Oum, T., Yu, C. and Fu, X. (2003) 'A comparative analysis of productivity performance of the world's major airports: summary report of the ATRS global airport benchmarking research report – 2002', *Journal of Air Transport Management*, 9(5): 285–97.

Oum, T., Zhang, A. and Zhang, Y. (2004) 'Alternative forms of economic regulation and their efficiency implications for airports', *Journal of Transport Economics and Policy*, 38(2): 217–46.

Oum, T., Yan, J. and Yu, C. (2008) 'Ownership forms matter for airport efficiency: a stochastic frontier investigation of worldwide airports', *Journal of Urban Economics*, 64(2): 422–35.

Pachero, R. and Fernandes, E. (2003) 'Managerial efficiency of Brazilian airports', *Transportation Research A*, 37(4): 667–80.

Pachero, R., Fernandes, E. and Santos, M. (2006) 'Management style and airport performance in Brazil', *Journal of Air Transport Management*, 12(6): 324–30.

Parker, D. (1999) 'The performance of BAA before and after privatisation: a DEA study', *Journal of Transport Economics and Policy*, 33(2), 133–46.

Pathomsiri, S., Haghani, A., Dresner, M. and Windle, R.J. (2008) 'Impact of undesirable outputs on the productivity of US airports', *Transportation Research Part E*, 44(2): 235–59.

Pels, E., Nijkamp, P. and Rietveld, P. (2001) 'Relative efficiency of European airports', *Transport Policy*, 8(3): 183–92.

—— (2003) 'Inefficiencies and scale economies of European airport operations', *Transportation Research Part E*, 39(5): 341–61.

Perelman, S. and Serebrisky, T. (2010) *Measuring the Technical Efficiency of Airports in Latin America*, World Bank Policy Research Working Paper 5339. Online. Available HTTP: < http://www-wds.worldbank. org/servlet/WDSContentServer/WDSP/IB/2010/06/15/000158349_20100615083006/Rendered/PDF/ WPS5339.pdf > (accessed 30 March 2012).

Psaraki-Kalouptsidi, V. and Kalakou, S. (2011) 'Assessment of efficiency of Greek airports', *Journal of Airport Management*, 5(2): 170–86.

Reinhold, A., Niemeier, H.-M., Kamp, V. and Mueller, J. (2010) 'An evaluation of yardstick regulation for European airports', *Journal of Air Transport Management*, 16(2): 74–80.

Ryan, M. (2012) 'Performance management in the Dublin Airport Authority', *ACI Airport Economics and Finance Conference*, London, March.

Sarkis, J. (2000) 'An analysis of the operational efficiency of major airports in the United States', *Journal of Operations Management*, 18(3): 335–51.

Sarkis, J. and Talluri, S. (2004) 'Performance based clustering for benchmarking of US airports', *Transportation Research A*, 38(5): 329–46.

Salazar de la Cruz, F. (1999) 'A DEA approach to the airport production function', *International Journal of Transport Economics*, 26(2): 255–70.

Scotti, D., Malighetti, P., Martini, G. and Volta, N. (2012) 'The impact of airport competition on technical efficiency: a stochastic frontier analysis applied to Italian airport', *Journal of Air Transport Management*, 22: 9–15.

Sharma, V., Dwivedi, P. and Seth, P. (2011) 'Airports and productivity', *International Journal of Aviation Management*, 1(1/2): 105–23.

Steer Davies Gleave (2012) *Review of Operating Expenditure and Investment.* Online. Available HTTP < http://www.caa.co.uk/docs/5/SDGStanstedReport.pdf> (accessed 15 June 2012).

Suzuki, A., Nijkamp, P., Rietveld, P. and Pels, E. (2010) 'A distance friction minimization approach in data envelopment analysis: a comparative study on airport efficiency', *European Journal of Operational Research*, 207(2): 1104–15

Ricondo and Associates, Booz Allen Hamilton, George Mason University and National Service Research (2009) *Strategic Planning in the Airport Industry*, ACRP Report 19. Washington, DC: Transportation Research Board

Tovar, B. and Martin-Cejas, R. (2009) 'Are outsourcing and non-aeronautical revenues important drivers in the efficiency of Spanish airports?', *Journal of Air Transport Management*, 15(5): 217–20.

—— (2010) 'Technical efficiency and productivity changes in Spanish airports: a parametric distance functions approach', *Transportation Research Part E*, 46(2): 249–60.

Tsekeris, T. (2011) 'Greek airports: efficiency measurement and analysis of determinants', *Journal of Air Transport Management*, 12(4): 182–90.

Vasigh, B. and Gorjidooz, J. (2006) 'Productivity analysis of public and private airports: a causal investigation', *Journal of Air Transportation*, 11(3): 144–63.

Vogel, H. (2006a) 'Airport privatisation: ownership structure and financial performance of European commercial airports', *Competition and Regulation in Network Industries*, 1(2): 139–62.

—— (2006b) 'Impact of privatisation on the financial and economic performance of European airports', *Aeronautical Journal*, April: 197–213.

Vogel, H. and Graham, A. (2006) 'A comparison of alternative airport performance measurement techniques: a European case study', *Journal of Airport Management*, 1(1): 59–74.

—— (2011) 'Profitability in the airline versus airport business: a long-term perspective', *Journal of Airport Management*, 5(3): 255–68.

Wanke, P. (2012) 'Efficiency of Brazil's airports: evidences from bootstrapped DEA and FDH estimates', *Journal of Air Transport Management*, 23: 47–53.

Yoshida, Y. (2004) 'Endogenous-weight TFP measurement: methodology and its application to Japanese-airport benchmarking', *Transportation Research E*, 40(2): 151–82.

Yoshida, Y. and Fujimoto, H. (2004) 'Japanese-airport benchmarking with the DEA and endogenous-weight TFP methods: testing the criticism of overinvestment in Japanese regional airports', *Transportation Research Part E*, 40(6): 533–46.

Yu, M.-M. (2004) 'Measuring physical efficiency of domestic airports in Taiwan with undesirable outputs and environmental factors', *Journal of Air Transport Management*, 10(5): 295–303.

—— (2010) 'Assessment of airport performance using the SBM–NDEA model', *Omega*, 38(6): 440–452.

Yu, M.-M., Hsu, S.-H., Chang, C.-C. and Lee, D.-H. (2008) 'Productivity growth of Taiwan's major domestic airports in the presence of aircraft noise', *Transportation Research Part E*, 44(3): 543–54.

4 | The airport–airline relationship

The relationship between the airport operator and airlines is clearly fundamental to the success of any airport business. The sweeping changes that have occurred within the airline industry mean that airlines, more than ever before, are trying to control their costs in order to improve their financial position in an ever-increasing competitive and deregulated environment. At the same time, most carriers have been facing major increases in the price of fuel, over which they have little control. This is having an impact on the aeronautical policies of airports and their regulation. In addition, an ongoing problem is that demand is outstripping capacity at a growing number of airports, even despite the recent downturn in traffic, so the traditional mechanism for allocating slots is having to be revisited. All these issues are considered in this chapter.

THE STRUCTURE OF AERONAUTICAL CHARGES

Aeronautical charging historically was relatively simple, with most revenue coming from a weight-based landing charge and a passenger fee dependent on passenger numbers. Many airports still generate their aeronautical revenue in this way. At other airports, charging practices have become more complex and more market based. This reflects the increasingly commercial and competitive airport environment and the contemporary challenges faced by airports, including the growing pressure on facilities, environmental concerns and rising security costs.

Landing or aircraft-based charges

Most airports have a weight-related landing charge based on maximum take-off weight (MTOW) or maximum authorized weight (MAW). The simplest method is to charge a fixed-amount unit rate (e.g. US$x per tonne) regardless of the size of the aircraft. A fixed unit rate will favour smaller aircraft types since tonnage tends to increase faster than aircraft capacity or payload. It will also benefit airlines that have high load factors or seating capacities. This simple method is used at many airports throughout the world, including those in the USA, many of the German airports and Copenhagen. Some airports have a unit landing charge that declines as the weight of the aircraft increases, such as Oslo. At other airports, for example at Delhi, the unit rate increases for larger aircraft.

This charging mechanism uses 'ability to pay' principles, as airlines using larger aircraft are in a better position to pay higher charges. Some costs, such as runway wear and tear, do increase with weight and also larger aircraft require vortex separations that can reduce the number of aircraft movements during a certain period. Overall, however, there is not a strong relationship between aircraft weight and airfield cost. A flat-rate landing charge for all aircraft types may be more appropriate, particularly at congested airports. This is because the cost of occupying the congested runway is movement-related and independent of aircraft size. Each aircraft movement will consume the same resource.

Very few airports have adopted a movement-related charge, which tends to be very unpopular with airlines flying small aircraft types. Notable exceptions are Heathrow, where there is a fixed runway charge for all aircraft above 16 tonnes. A similar charge exists at Gatwick, although in this case this is differentiated between peak and off-peak periods. Other airports have not gone this far, but have made an attempt to charge the smallest aircraft more to encourage general aviation traffic to move away from congested major airports. For example, Frankfurt airport has a minimum landing charge set at 35 tonnes. Some other airports have differential landing charges by time of day (such as Manchester) or time of year (such as Dublin) to reflect peaking of demand. At some airports, domestic or short-haul services traditionally have paid a reduced landing fee. This is not a cost-related charge since the cost to land an aircraft is independent of its origin. Instead, it tends to exist to support local and regional services, which tend to be comparatively expensive to operate. Occasionally such services will have a social role in linking together regional communities, so in effect this policy will act as an unofficial subsidy.

Sometimes charges for air-traffic control (ATC) or terminal navigational facilities will be incorporated in the landing charge. At other airports, the airport operator may levy a separate charge. Typically this charge will, like the landing charge, be related to the weight of the aircraft. There is no logical cost rationale for this as each aircraft movement, regardless of the size of the airport, imposes the same costs on the ATC infrastructure. Alternatively, the airline will pay the ATC agencies directly and the airport operator will not be involved in the financing of ATC services at all. In addition, a growing number of airports have noise- and emissions-related surcharges or discounts associated with their landing charges as a result of increasing concerns about the environment. These are covered in Chapter 10.

Passenger charges

Passenger charges or passenger service charges (PSC) are the other main source of aeronautical revenue. These charges are most commonly levied per departing passenger. At most airports there tends to be a lower charge for domestic passengers to reflect the lower costs associated with these types of passenger. At the Paris airports there are four types of charge: domestic, Schengen-EU, non-Schengen-EU and international; at Lisbon three (Schengen, non-Schengen and international), while London Heathrow just charges differently for European and other destinations. As with the landing charge, in some cases there may be political or social reasons for keeping down the cost of domestic travel. Historically, such policies were often maintained to subsidise the national carrier which had a large domestic operation. It can be argued, however, that domestic passengers have less potential for generating commercial revenues and hence do not justify the lower passenger charge. Some other airports also have differential charges to reflect peaking, such as East Midlands and Glasgow airports. An interesting development at some of the German airports, such as Dusseldorf and Frankfurt, is a fee cap related to passenger charges. This means that a refunded amount is provided for all passengers when the load factor exceeds 80 or 83 per cent, respectively. Low-cost carrier terminals, such as at Marseille and Lyon, also have lower passenger charges, as discussed in Chapter 5.

A number of airports charge a lower fee for transfer passengers, particularly in Europe (e.g. Amsterdam, Dublin, Frankfurt, Heathrow, Helsinki, Vienna, Paris, Zurich, Munich and Copenhagen). Elsewhere some airports waive the fee completely (e.g. Dubai and Incheon). A lower transfer charge can be justifiable on cost grounds, as such passengers will have no surface access requirements, will not have associated meeters and greeters, and very often will not need check-in, security and immigration facilities either. On the other hand, transfer passengers still require facilities such as baggage handling, and may require special facilities in order that a rapid transfer is achieved.

Security charges

The responsibility for the provision and financing of airport security varies considerably from country to country (see Chapter 5). Security services may be provided by the airport's own employees, or by a private company under contract to the airport, the airlines, or a government agency. In many cases responsibility may be shared between these different bodies. This results in different systems being in place to finance the security measures. They may be paid for by the government via general taxation or via a special government departure tax. In other countries, security costs may be financed directly by the airport operator, who will have a special security charge or include it in the passenger charge. In the United States there is a US$2.50 security tax per passenger to cover some of the security costs. Sometimes there is a security charge based on aircraft tonnes as well as passengers, as at Frankfurt. The security charge is normally collected, as with the other charges, when the ticket is sold by the airline. Exceptions exist, however, as at Riga airport, where Ryanair has not agreed to collect the tax and so the charge is €7 per Ryanair passenger compared with €6.50 for other passengers.

Other charges

There are also a number of other charges that tend to be fairly low compared with the landing and passenger fees. First, there is the parking charge which is usually based on the weight of the aircraft or, sometimes, on aircraft wingspan (e.g. Malta, Singapore and Boston Massport), size of parking stands (e.g. Frankfurt and Shannon airports), or as a percentage of the landing fee (e.g. Vienna airport). There is normally an hourly or daily charge with, perhaps, a rebate for using remote stands. Most airports have a free parking charge, typically ranging from 1 to 4 hours to allow the airline to turn around at the airport without incurring any charges. At some airports this may be for even longer, as at Charleroi airport where it is 12 hours. A few airports have no free parking charge (e.g. Frankfurt) or a short period (e.g. 30 minutes for narrow-bodied aircraft at Heathrow) to encourage the airlines to minimise turnaround time. For those airports that have a 24-hour charge, such as Amsterdam, Malta, Massport and Düsseldorf, there is clearly no incentive for airlines to make the most effective use of the apron space. Other airports, such as Paris and Frankfurt, differentiate between different areas of parking and between night and day.

A recent development, evident particularly at small regional UK and Irish airports that are not performing well financially, is the airport development or facility fee, which is paid directly by passengers in addition to the normal passenger fee. For example, Durham Tees Valley airport in the UK has a £6 fee that is levied from the passengers with the airport message 'Secure our future' directed at the local residents who fly. There have been similar charges at Blackpool airport (£10), Newquay (£5), Knock (€10) and Galway (€10) airports. There may be other charges for certain facilities or services that airports choose to price separately rather than including them in the landing or passenger charge. There may be a charge for handling passengers with reduced mobility (PRM). At some airports, such as Dublin, there may be an airbridge fee, typically charged per movement or based on the length of time that the airbridge is occupied. Sometimes, similar to the passenger charge, there are cargo charges based on the weight of loaded or unloaded cargo, as is the case at the Rome airports. There may be a lower fee for all-cargo aircraft, as at Amsterdam and Manchester airports, whereas at some airports, such as Belfast International, the landing charge for such aircraft is higher. There may be additional charges related to services such as fire-fighting, storage facilities, hangar use and other airport specific activities.

Ground handling and fuel charges

Airlines incur three types of charge when they use an airport. First, they pay landing and passenger and, sometimes, other airport fees, discussed above. Then there are ground handling fees, which the airport operator may levy if it chooses to provide some of these services itself rather than leaving them to handling agents or airlines. Finally, there are the fuel charges that are levied by the fuel companies which are normally independent of the airport operator. There a few notable exceptions, such as certain Middle Eastern airports, where the fuelling is provided by a government company. Hence all services at the airport can be offered to the airline in one overall package.

It is difficult to find published data relating to handling and fuel charges. These are usually negotiable and the agreed prices will depend on various factors, including the size of the airline, the scale of its operation at the airport in question, and whether other airports used by the airline are served by the same handling and fuel companies. Further complexities occur since there are a variety of ways of charging for activities, including ramp handling, passenger handling, apron buses, aircraft cleaning, ground power, pushback and so on. In some cases there may be just one or two charges that cover everything, whereas elsewhere there may be a multitude of individual fees.

Government taxes

Table 4.1 summarises the charges at an airport. There is one final charge that airlines or their passengers often experience at an airport: government taxes. This income does not go directly to the airport operator, but does impact on the overall cost of the 'turnaround' from an airline's point of view. For the passenger, it is very difficult to distinguish between these taxes which go to the government, and airport passenger charges that represent revenue for the airport, as both

Table 4.1 *Main aeronautical charges at airports*

Charge	Common basis for charging	Income to airport operator?
Landing	Weight of aircraft	Yes
Terminal navigation	Included in landing charge or based on weight of aircraft	Sometimes
Airbridge	Included in landing charge or based on aircraft movement	Yes
Passenger	Departing passenger	Yes
Security	Included in passenger charge or based on passenger numbers	Yes
Parking	Weight of aircraft per hour or 24 hours after free period	Yes
Ground handling	Different charges for different activities	Sometimes
Fuel	Volume of fuel	No
Government taxes	Departing passenger	No

are usually shown as 'airport taxes and charges' on the ticket. Sometimes these taxes may have a travel-related objective, as is the case with a number of taxes in the USA. In Greece there is a government airport development fund that was designed initially to contribute towards airport investment. The taxes may also cover the provision of some security services (e.g. Portugal) or noise-mitigation measures (e.g. Amsterdam). Elsewhere such taxation is used just as a means of supplementing general government taxation income from other sources. A number of other countries, including Mexico, Hong Kong and Mauritius, impose a tourist tax on international passengers.

In the United Kingdom, a departure tax called the Air Passenger Duty, which goes directly to the Treasury, was introduced in 1994. This was greeted with considerable opposition, especially from the new breed of low-cost carriers who complained that it was too large in proportion to the fares that were being offered. As a compromise, in 2001 a differential tax system with different amounts for economy and business-class passengers was used. Since then the tax has increased substantially. In France in 2006, a 'solidarity tax' of €1 (economy) and €10 (premium) for European passengers and €4/€40 for intercontinental passengers was introduced to fund development aid in poorer countries. In July 2008, the Dutch government introduced a passenger tax of €11 for European travel and €45 for long-haul travel (transfer passengers were exempt) which was bitterly opposed by the airlines and was subsequently abandoned a year later. Similar taxes have now been introduced in other countries, including Germany, Austria and Ireland. The impact of these taxes is investigated further in Chapter 9.

LEVEL OF AERONAUTICAL CHARGES

In general there has been a trend towards giving greater relative importance to the passenger fee as compared with the landing or aircraft-based fee. This is primarily because the aircraft-related fee represents a fixed charge for airlines, as it does not vary with load factor, while the passenger-based fee is a variable cost. Airlines will prefer the focus on the passenger fee as passenger numbers drive most of their revenues. In this case, more risk is also shared by the airport operator. In addition, as passenger charges are shown separately on the ticket under 'airport charges and taxes', this can also have a marketing advantage as it will have the effect of apparently reducing the overall fare (excluding charges and taxes) that the airline charges. As there is increased differentiation of airport services in the terminal (particularly for LCCs – see Chapter 5), this approach gives airlines more flexibility in that they pay only for passenger services they use, which can have a significant effect on the overall level of charges paid. Figure 4.1 shows that, on average, passenger-based charges now represent 61 per cent of all charges, and in almost every world region they account for over half the charges. The exception is North America, where the existence of high terminal rental fees and the passenger facility charge (discussed below) complicates the comparison. Some airports have gone further than this, particularly those serving LCC, such as Brussels South Charleroi airport (BSCA), by having a charge that is totally passenger related.

It is very difficult to compare the level of charges at different airports because of the varied nature of the charging structures. To overcome this problem, comparisons have to be made by examining the representative airport charges for an Airbus A319 on a regional cross-border service (Figure 4.2). A small sample of different airports has been chosen. The costs are divided between aircraft-related costs, which include landing charges as well as ATC and airbridge

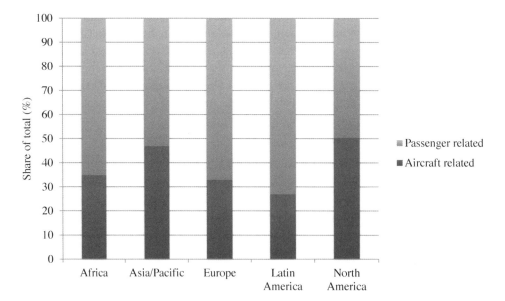

Figure 4.1 *Aeronautical charges by source at ACI airports, 2010*
Excludes terminal rental revenue in North America which represents 36 per cent of total revenue.
Source: ACI (2011)

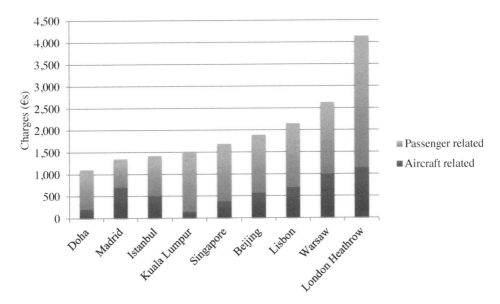

Figure 4.2 *Aeronautical charges and taxes for a regional cross-border A319 turnaround in 2011/12 at world airports*
Source: Cranfield University

charges, if these exist; passenger-related costs, which include passenger charges and any security charges; but not government taxes. The data were not sufficient to allow ground handling and fuel costs to be added. Only published charges were used, so the figures do not take account of any discounts that may be available.

There is a wide spread of charges (excluding taxes) ranging from around €1,000 in Doha to over €4,000 at London Heathrow. Every year LeighFisher undertakes a review of charges at over 50 airports, and in 2011 airports that had the highest charges included Toronto, Osaka, Newark, Athens, Sydney, Tokyo Narita and Vancouver, while the lowest charges were observed at Hong Kong, Kuala Lumpur, Dubai and Jeddah. As in Figure 4.2, the highest charges were as much as three or four times more than the lowest ones (LeighFisher, 2012).

IMPACT OF AERONAUTICAL CHARGES ON AIRLINE OPERATIONS

In recent years, airport charges have become subject to increased scrutiny from the airlines. A more competitive airline environment and falling yields have forced airlines to focus on major cost-saving initiatives, including outsourcing, reductions in staff numbers and pegging the level of wages. These are all internal costs over which the airlines have a considerable degree of control. However, airlines have also been looking at their external costs such as airport charges, and calling for airports to adopt more cost-cutting and efficiency-saving measures themselves, rather than raising their charges. The existence of a profitability gap (discussed in Chapter 3) as a result of airports generally achieving much higher operating profits than airlines has also contributed to the friction between airports and airlines that has been experienced at some airports.

On average, airport charges represent a relatively small part (typically around 4 per cent) of an airline's total operating costs, but this varies considerably for different types of airline. They are least important when long-haul operations are being considered, as the charges are levied relatively infrequently. Airport charges are the most significant for the charter and low-cost carriers as these airlines have minimised or completely avoided some of the other costs that more traditional scheduled airlines face. Most LCCs operate short sectors, which means that they pay airport charges more frequently. It is hardly surprising that this type of airline has been most active in attempting to bring down their airport costs by negotiating incentive deals at airports, or operating out of secondary or regional airports that have lower charges. However, accurate figures illustrating this are difficult to obtain because many airlines do not report the passenger fee as an airport charge, and very often the airport charges may be combined with some other cost item. However, some data do exist for UK airlines, and in 2010–11 landing and passenger fees together (excluding parking, handling and other charges) for British Airways, with a mix of long- and short-haul flights, represented around 3 per cent of total costs. For Virgin as well, which only had long-haul flights, airport charges were only 4 per cent. This share was much larger for the LCC easyJet (21 per cent) and the charter airline Thomson Airways (16 per cent) (CAA, 2012).

As discussed, peak charges have been introduced by a few airports to make the airlines that are generating the peak demand pay for the peak capacity infrastructure costs. They have also been used with the intent of shifting some peak operations into off-peak. This is unlikely to occur unless the differential between peak and off-peak pricing is very much higher than current practice. Airline scheduling is a complex task that has to take into account factors including passenger demand patterns, airport curfews and environmental restrictions, crew availability, and peak profiles at other airport. If the airline were to shift operations to outside the peak period, this could well mean that the peak is merely shifted to another time. In effect, these schedule constraints, coupled with the fact that charges make a relatively small contribution to airline total costs, mean that often demand can be fairly inelastic to changes in airport fees. Most peak pricing has very little impact on airline operations other than making it more expensive for airlines to operate in the peak. (The same is arguably true of noise and emission charges where maintenance costs and fuel burn considerations are generally likely to have a far greater impact on aircraft renewal strategies than increased airport charges.)

BAA was one of the few airport operators that developed a peak pricing charging system based on a detailed assessment of marginal costs. In theory, marginal cost pricing leads to the most efficient allocation of resources as only the users, who value a facility at least as much as the cost of providing it, will pay the price for using it. In practice such pricing policies are complex and very difficult to implement. In the 1970s, BAA introduced a peak surcharge on runway movements on certain summer days and a peak passenger and parking charge based on marginal cost principles at Heathrow and Gatwick airports. It proved to be ineffectual in shifting any demand largely because of the scheduling problems already described, but also because the charging system was so complex that it was very difficult for the airlines to react. The airport operator faced widespread opposition from the airlines, particularly the US carriers, to its peak charges, which were considered discriminatory. BAA and the US airlines finally resolved their differences through international arbitration which required BAA to phase out the peak passenger charges. Heathrow is now effectively full in most hours and so the concept in this case of the peak hour has become far less relevant.

An airport charging policy probably has its greatest impact on airline operations when new routes are being considered, particularly when there are incentive schemes or discounts. These are most likely to be offered at smaller airports that want to encourage growth and provide inducements to airlines that might otherwise not choose to use the airport. Such discounts have, in many cases, been a critical factor when low-cost carriers are selecting suitable airports for their operations (in addition to sufficient demand and fast turnaround facilities). This has been the case particularly when there have been a number of neighbouring or equally suitable airports from which to choose. These discount schemes are discussed in more detail in Chapter 8.

Of major concern to all airlines is what airport facilities and services are considered when the airport prices are being set. There are two alternative approaches: the single-till approach where all airport activities are included, and the dual-till approach where just the aeronautical aspects of the operation are taken into account (Lu and Pagliari, 2004; Czerny, 2006). With the single-till concept, growth in non-aeronautical revenue can be used to offset increases in aeronautical charges. Within the airport industry such single-till practices, when commercial activities are used to reduce aeronautical charges, used to be widespread and were accepted by ICAO in its charging recommendations. The rationale for the single till is that without the aeronautical activities, there would be no market for the commercial operations and hence it is appropriate to offset the level of airport charges with profits earned from non-aeronautical facilities. This is the key justification the airlines use in favouring such a system, which is clearly likely to bring the lowest level of actual charges for them.

As traffic increases, the single-till principle will tend to pull down airport charges. This may encourage growth and have the effect of increasing congestion and delays at the airport. The busiest, most congested airports are likely to be in the best position to significantly offset commercial revenues against airport charges. Yet it is these airports that need to manage their limited capacity the most. Bringing down the airport charges for such scarce resources makes no economic sense. In addition, it can be argued that using commercial revenues to offset aeronautical fees prevents these revenues from being used to help finance capital investment, or to aid the development of better commercial facilities. There is thus less incentive to develop commercial operations to their full potential.

By contrast, the dual-till concept treats the aeronautical and non-aeronautical areas as separate financial entities and focuses on the monopoly aeronautical airport services. This is a difficult task because of having to allocate many fixed and joint costs between the aeronautical and non-aeronautical areas. At the London airports it was calculated some time ago that the transfer from a single-till to a dual-till approach could mean that airport charges would have to be increased by 35 per cent (Monopolies and Mergers Commission, 1996). The method does, however, provide airports with incentives to develop the commercial side of their business which effectively is uncontrolled, unlike with the single-till approach, where any development in the commercial areas may well be accompanied by a reduction in aeronautical charges. There is a major logical argument in not including commercial activities within the regulatory framework as they cannot be considered as monopoly facilities. A further argument in favour of the dual till is that it can provide better incentives for aeronautical investment. This is because as well as gaining from additional aeronautical revenues if there is aeronautical investment, the airport can benefit from increased unregulated commercial revenues that will have been generated because of the additional passenger volumes. The counter argument here, however, is that with a dual till the incentives to invest on the aeronautical side might be worse, as in this case commercial investment might be favoured over aeronautical investment.

Another area of concern for airlines as regards charging policies is cross-subsidisation within an airport group under common ownership. This typically occurs when a large international airport provides financial support for a smaller airport, usually serving primarily domestic services. Operators of airport groups argue that the individual airports need to operate as a system to make the most efficient use of resources and to produce cost savings. The airlines tend to be strongly opposed to such cross-subsidising and often argue that if the smaller airports really need financial help for social or economic reasons, they should be supported by government funds instead. There can be a similar issue when a system approach to pricing is used to fund investment at one particular airport in the system. The airport operator may justify this by arguing that such investment will bring benefits to the whole system, not just the individual airport.

A further important airport–airline issue is the pre-financing of future airport infrastructure through airport charges. Pre-financing has traditionally not been an acceptable principle, for a number of reasons. First, there is no guarantee that the airlines paying the charges will actually be the airlines that will benefit from the new infrastructure. Also, there may be no certainty that the airport charges will be spent efficiently to provide new facilities. The airlines tend to be fearful that they will pay twice for the infrastructure, both before it is built and once it is operational. However, in spite of these airline concerns, some airports have fees for pre-financing purposes. The most notable example is the United States, where passenger facility charges (PFCs) go towards future development projects. A somewhat similar situation exists at Canadian airports. Elsewhere, for example in the United Kingdom, the regulator takes into account the fact that some pre-financing will take place when setting the appropriate level of charges. Airports tend to argue that pre-financing in certain circumstances can provide a useful, cheaper source for funding investment in addition to loans and equity which can also be used as security for raising extra finance. Airports claim that pre-financing also avoids large increases in airport charges when the infrastructure comes on stream, as was experienced at Narita and Kansai airports in Japan. As regards the ICAO view of this, a long established cost-recovery policy in the ICAO guidelines on airport charges was that charges should not be levied for any facilities until they become operational. However, in recent years ICAO has acknowledged that, with the growing commercialisation within the industry and diminishing dependence on government sources for financing, pre-funding could perhaps be considered, but only in specific safeguarded circumstances.

THE AIRPORT REGULATORY ENVIRONMENT

Airports are subject to a number of different regulations at both international and national levels. Many of these are technical regulations related to the operational, safety and security aspects of managing an airport. Airports are also becoming increasingly subject to environmental regulations that may, for example, restrict aircraft movements due to noise considerations or limit airport infrastructure development. These environmental issues are discussed in Chapter 10. Then there is economic regulation, with the main focus being on charge or tariff control. Other economic aspects of operation, including handling activities and slot allocation, are also regulated in some areas of the world. Overall, economic regulatory interest in airports seems to be increasing at a time when, ironically, the airlines business is being progressively deregulated.

On a worldwide basis, the 1944 Chicago Convention, which established an international regulatory air transport system, provides a basis for airport charging. Article 15 gives international authority for the levying of charges by ICAO member states and specifies that there shall be no discrimination between users, particularly from different countries. ICAO produces more detailed guidelines that have an overriding principle that charges should be cost-related. They also recommend that the charging system should be transparent and that consultation should take place between airport operators and their customers if changes are proposed (ICAO, 2012). They are only guidelines and are open to different interpretations, but nevertheless have generally led to fairly similar overall pricing regimes being adopted by most airports, being broadly related to average cost pricing combined with some market or ability-to-pay pricing. Airport charges can also be subject to the international obligations of bilateral agreements – although this is becoming much less common now. For example, the old UK–US bilateral air service Bermuda 2 (replaced in 2008 by the EU–US Open Skies agreement) stated that airport charges must be related to costs and should allow only reasonable profits. This resulted in a lengthy dispute over Heathrow charges in the 1980s and 1990s between the US and UK governments.

Within Europe, the first proposal for any EU-wide regulation appeared in 1985, and subsequently there were several other attempts to seek approval for such legislation. Eventually the European Union adopted a directive in March 2009, which had to be implemented in all Member States by March 2011 at the latest (EC, 2009). This covers all airports handling 5 million or more passengers. It builds on, and is complementary to, the ICAO policies. Key features include greater transparency regarding the costs that charges are to cover, with airports being obliged to provide a detailed breakdown of costs for the airlines. The ICAO principle of non-discrimination is maintained, although airports can differentiate their services as long as the criteria for doing so are clear and transparent. They can also vary charges on environmental grounds. Consultation on charges between airports and airlines is compulsory, and there has to be an independent supervisory authority whose job is to help settle disputes over charges between airports and airlines (Table 4.2).

Regulation of individual airports

At a national or individual airport level, the degree of government control varies considerably. Many airports under public sector ownership usually need to seek government approval before changing their charging level or structure. In some cases this may be just a formality. At the other extreme, it may be the government's responsibility to set charges – perhaps after receiving recommendations from the airports. In some countries, particularly where there has been privatisation, there may be a more formal economic regulation system. In a study of 50 major European airports in 2005, it was found that only 5 per cent needed no government approval and 10 per cent had automatic approval. A further 52 per cent had approval (often against transparent

Table 4.2 Main features of the 2009 EU airport charges directive

Policy	Details
Non-discrimination	Charges must not discriminate between users but can be modulated for issues of general/public and environmental interest
Airport network	Airport operators may decide to introduce a charging system that covers the whole network in a transparent manner
Common charging systems	Airport operators are authorised to apply a common and transparent charging system for airports serving the same urban community or conurbation
Consultation and remedy	Users will be consulted regularly (at least once a year) concerning the level of charges and quality of service
Transparency requirements	Users will be informed about components serving as a basis for determining the level of charges covering the services and infrastructure provided, the methodology used, the revenue generated, any financing from public authorities and forecasts. Users will submit traffic/fleet forecasts and development plans to the airport operators
New infrastructure	Airport operators will consult with users before plans for new infrastructure are finalised
Differentiation of services	The difference in quality and scope of services may result in a variation in airport charges
Independent supervisory authority	Countries are required to have an independent supervisory authority to ensure compliance with the directive

Source: EC (2009)

criteria) following negotiation and 31 per cent had their charges set more formally with an agreed formula (SH&E, 2006).

Often a more formal regulatory system is established when there are serious concerns that airports with considerable market power will abuse this situation. This is particularly relevant when airports are privatised, and a number of new regulatory frameworks have been set up in countries where privatisation has occurred. This has involved using regulatory authorities that are already in existence (as in the UK) or creating new bodies specifically for this purpose (as in Ireland). Although the regulatory systems at different airports vary, their common purpose is usually to allow the regulated airports a reasonable rate of return (ROR) on capital while providing the correct incentives for an efficient operation and an appropriate investment policy. In choosing the most suitable regulatory system, consideration has to be given to the best incentives to encourage appropriate investment, the treatment of commercial revenues and the maintenance of standards of service. A suitable review process also has to be established.

In general, there are three key ways in which organisations can be regulated:

- ROR or cost-based regulation
- price cap regulation
- reserve regulation.

The ROR mechanism, or so-called cost-based or profit control regulation, is the traditional mechanism that has been used extensively, for example in the United States and Australia, to regulate natural monopolies. The aim is to prevent regulated companies from setting prices that bear no relation to costs. A certain ROR is established and price increases can be justified only when an increase in costs is incurred. While such a system can ensure the prices are related to costs, it provides no incentives to reduce costs. The operator will be guaranteed a certain ROR irrespective of efficiency. Cost inefficiencies can be built into the cost structure which can be passed on to consumers through increased prices. Such a system can also encourage over investment. To ensure this does not occur, the regulator has to scrutinise carefully the financial operations and development plans of the regulated companies.

To overcome these shortcomings, alternative regulatory systems were sought. In the 1980s, price cap regulation began to be used – for example in the United Kingdom, where a number of the state utilities, including gas and electricity, were privatised. This type of regulation, often called incentive regulation, was considered to be more favourable as it can provide the regulated company with incentives to reduce costs while simultaneously controlling price increases. It works by establishing a formula that provides a maximum price that can be set. Typically, the formula will be adjusted for inflation and an efficiency factor:

price cap $CPI - X$ or $RPI - X$

where CPI is the consumer price index, RPI the retail price index and X the efficiency gain target. Costs that are beyond the control of the company (e.g. security costs) can be excluded from the regulation:

price cap $CPI - X + Y$

where Y is the external costs.

Since there is no cap on the profit levels, unlike the ROR method, any efficiency gains that the regulated company can make in excess of the required X will directly benefit the company. Such a method tends to be simpler to administer, as companies can change their level or structure of prices as long as they still conform to the price cap without any justification from the regulator, which would be the situation with the ROR system. However, there is an issue that the price cap may give inadequate incentives to investment because of the focus on short-term operational efficiency gains within each relatively small price control period combined with the lumpiness and long lead time of investments.

On the other hand, it has also been argued that price cap regulation is not an effective alternative to cost-based regulation as the regulator will take into account the ROR of the company, as well as other factors including operational efficiency, planned investment and the competitive situation, when setting the price cap. For example, in order to calculate the total revenue required, a regulated asset base (RAB) is usually defined and valued at the beginning of the price control period and then consequently enlarged to take account of projected capital expenditure. A weighted average cost of capital (WACC) and depreciation allowance based on this RAB is then added to the projected level of operating expenditure (which will have taken account of any feasible improvements in efficiency) to arrive at the total revenue requirement. The RAB valuation and WACC assumptions are therefore key in determining the maximum level of prices allowed. Thus the regulated company may still have an incentive to overstate the capital expenditure needed, which will be discouraged only by careful scrutiny of the regulator. In spite of these shortcomings, price cap regulation has been the most popular approach adopted for privatised airports.

A further type of regulation is the 'light-handed' approach or 'trigger', 'reserve', 'shadow' or 'conduct' regulation. While the technical definitions of these vary somewhat, the general principle is that the regulator will become involved in the price-setting process only if the airport's market power is actually abused or if the company and its customers cannot reach agreement. In this case it is the threat of regulation, rather than actual regulation, that is used to provide an effective safeguard against anti-competitive behaviour. Sometimes, with reserve regulation for example, there may be a predetermined regulatory model that will become effective at this stage.

With regulated airports, decisions have to be made as to which airport facilities and services are to be considered under the pricing regime, that is, whether a single or dual till should be used. In addition, if a price cap is used the regulator must also decide how the 'price' element of the formula is to be set. The main choice is whether to use a revenue yield or tariff basket methodology. The revenue yield formula means that the predicted revenue per unit (usually passengers in the case of airports) in the forthcoming year will be allowed to increase by the CPI − X or RPI − X percentage. With the tariff basket definition, the weighted average price of a specified 'basket' of tariffs or charges will be allowed to be raised by CPI − X. Both methods have their drawbacks, and their relative strengths have been fiercely debated by regulators and the industry. The tariff basket approach tends to be simpler as it operates directly on charges and is independent of any forecasts. Companies might, however, be encouraged to put the largest increases on the faster-growing traffic as the weights used in the tariff basket are from a previous period. With the revenue yield methodology, an artificial incentive may be created to increase passengers to inflate the denominator in the definition. This could lead to the setting of some charges below the marginal costs of the corresponding services. In general the tariff basket approach is usually considered to give airports greater incentives to move to a more efficient pricing structure. Within Europe over half (59 per cent) of airports with a price cap use the tariff basket approach, as opposed to 41 per cent who use the revenue yield method (SH&E, 2006).

It is common practice to set the price cap in relation to the average costs, which will include consideration of any proposed investment programme, additional costs related to improvements in the quality of service and a reasonable ROR. There has been some debate, however, as to whether industry benchmarking could have a much more active role in this process. Industry best practice could, in theory, replace an assessment of accounting costs as the basis for setting the price cap. This has already been used by the utility regulators for both England and the Netherlands. This would mean that the regulatory control would be independent of any company action inappropriately influencing the key variables used in the regulatory formula, including inflating the asset base. Alternatively, benchmarking could be used much more as a cross-check to internal methods of setting the price, estimating investment costs or assessing the scope for efficiency and service quality improvements.

However, the adoption of such regulatory benchmarking or 'yardstick' regulation is fraught with difficulties because of the extensive problems of comparability associated with such an exercise, the subjective nature of how some of the associated problems are overcome, and the lack of general consensus as to the optimal method of benchmarking (see Chapter 3). There is also the fundamental issue that such an approach assumes high costs are in fact the result of inefficiency, whereas in reality they may be due to a number of other factors. Only a very detailed assessment of the benchmarking data may be able to identify these factors.

A few countries (e.g. the UK, Ireland, Belgium, Austria, Italy) have used benchmarking to informally help the regulatory decisions. For example in the UK, for the pricing period 2008–13, the Civil Aviation Authority (CAA) benchmarked a number of processes that accounted for around 20–30 per cent of operating costs using a sample of 14 UK and other European and international airports. The Irish regulator also tried to use benchmarking techniques, but came under criticism for failing to take full account of outsourcing and the nature of traffic and choosing an inappropriate selection of comparator airports. For the next price period beginning in 2014, the UK CAA has ruled out both yardstick regulation and pegging prices to a comparator, primarily because they have stated that the airport market is too heterogeneous, although again as before benchmarking is being used to help inform specific decisions in certain areas. More generally, Reinhold *et al.* (2009) also argued that although benchmarking methods are not totally robust, they can nevertheless serve as an effective decision aid tool in airport regulation as long as the limitations are recognised.

Another area of major concern within any regulatory framework is often the quality of service. When the regulation does not formally establish service standards or require an appropriate quality-monitoring system, there may be little incentive for the airport operator to optimise quality. In reducing the service standards at the airport, the operator could be able to soften the blow of the price control. This could be overcome, in theory, by ensuring there are measures of congestion and delays to assess the adequacy of the airport facilities, and by assessing passenger and airline feedback to determine the operational efficiency of the airport. In Australia, the initial regulatory framework that was set up when the airports were privatised included some formal service quality monitoring and reporting. At BAA airports, service quality came under close scrutiny during the review process, although there were no explicit regulations until 2003. Further detail is provided in Chapter 6.

Regulation examples

Overall, the study of 50 major airports in Europe in 2005 found that 51 per cent used a price cap formula while only 14 per cent used an ROR formula – with the single till being the most popular approach (SH&E, 2006). Table 4.3 provides a more up-to-date overview of the situation and compares the key features of economic regulation systems that currently exist at major European airports.

Table 4.3 *Examples of economic regulation at selected European airports**

Airport	Type of regulation	Single or dual till
Amsterdam	Cost-based	Dual till
Brussels	Cost-based	Single till
Budapest	Price cap	Dual till
Copenhagen	Price cap	Dual till
Dublin	Price cap	Single till
Frankfurt	Cost-based	Dual till
Hamburg	Price cap	Dual till
Malta	Price cap	Dual till
London Gatwick	Price cap	Single till
London Heathrow	Price cap	Single till
Lisbon	Price cap	Single till
Madrid	Cost-based	Single till
Munich	Cost-based	Single till
Oslo	Cost-based	Single till
Paris	Price cap	Single till
Rome	Cost-based	Dual till
Vienna	Price cap	Dual till

*To provide an overview just two options for each feature are shown, but in practice there are considerable differences in the detailed regulation of the airports.
Sources: Compiled by the author from various sources

In the United Kingdom, both BAA London and Manchester airports became subject to single-till price cap regulation in 1987. The other smaller regional airports did not have direct price control as they were not considered to have sufficient market power to warrant this. The price cap was reviewed every 5 years after an extensive assessment of the airport's operations, financial performance and future plans has been undertaken (Graham, 2008). Over the years, the approach has tended to drift much more closely to an ROR method, with very detailed consideration of the RAB and cost of capital – which, as discussed, tends to be one of the shortcomings of the price cap approach. The revenue yield method was adopted at these airports.

Initially the price cap was the same at all airports, being RPI–1 (Table 4.4). During the second 5-year review period in the early 1990s, the price cap was far more restrictive, particularly for the London airports. For 1997–2002, the London airport formula did not take account of the loss of EU duty- and tax-free sales in 1999. Instead, a compensatory 15 per cent increase in charges over 2 years following abolition of sales was allowed. At Manchester, the abolition was considered when setting the value of X. These airports could allow most increases in security costs to be passed straight through to the airline. Initially 75 per cent of costs were permitted to be passed through, with this percentage rising to 95 per cent after the first 5-yearly review. A major impact of the single-till regulation at the London airports in the earlier years was that the commercial aspects of the business expanded considerably, which simultaneously led to a substantial reduction in real charges to airline users. This was until 2003–08 at Heathrow airport, when the price

Table 4.4 The X value used for the UK airport price caps

Airport	1987–91	1992–93	1994	1995–96	1997–2002*	2003–08	2008–13†
Heathrow	−1	−8	−4	−1	−3	+6.5	+7.5
Gatwick	−1	−8	−4	−1	−3	0	+2.0
Stansted	−1	−8	−4	−1	+1	0	+1.6
	1988–92	1993–94	1995	1996–97	1998–2002	2003–08	2008–13
Manchester	−1	−3	3	−3	−5	−5	N/A

*The normal 5-year charging period was extended to 6 years because of the timing of decisions related to the development of Terminal 5 at Heathrow.
†The 2008–13 charging period has been extended to 2014, when the new regulation is due to be introduced.

cap was set at RPI + 6.5 per cent to take account of £7.4 billion investment needs (particularly terminal 5). It was also decided at this time that there should be rebates for users if certain service quality standards were not achieved (see Chapter 6 for details) (CAA, 2003).

The regulation process is somewhat complex because there are two regulators involved (Graham, 2008). There is the sector regulator with detailed knowledge of the aviation industry: the CAA and the Competition Commission (previously known as the Monopolies and Mergers Commission) which is a very experienced more general trading regulator. It is the Competition Commission that undertakes the detailed review of the airports' operations every 5 years and then offers advice to the CAA concerning the most appropriate level of price control. The CAA makes the final decision on the price cap after consultation with the industry and other interested parties. While the skills of these two regulators should be complementary, the two bodies have not always been in agreement. For example, in the 1991 review of BAA they had very different views on assumptions concerning the cost of capital that led to substantially different values of X in the pricing formula being suggested until a compromise was eventually reached (Toms, 2004). Also, in the review for the years 2003–08, the CAA favoured a shift to the dual till while the Competition Commission wanted retention of the single till. In the end the single till was kept. In the review for 2008–13, a price cap of +23.5 and +21.0 per cent has been applied for Heathrow and Gatwick, respectively, for 2008–09, followed by +7.5 per cent and +2.0 per cent for the other 4 years (CAA, 2008). These positive values of X are to take account of the increases in costs of security and recent and new investments – particularly at Heathrow with terminal 5 and Heathrow East – but the scale of increases was very unpopular with the airline industry. Manchester airport is no longer price regulated as, after a review by the government, it was decided that the airport did not have enough market power to warrant this (Department for Transport, 2008a). Stansted was also investigated, but in this case the price cap was kept (Department for Transport, 2008b).

After being in force for 20 years, the UK government undertook an extensive review of the airport regulatory system in 2009, and a new system will be introduced in 2014 (Department for Transport, 2009). This will give the CAA a single overriding duty to further the interests of passengers and owners of cargo in the provision of airport operation services with a more flexible licensing regime. The CAA will be allowed, where appropriate, to replace fixed price caps on airports with lighter-touch forms of regulation. This will replace the previous one-size-fits-all policy for all designated airports for price control regulation. The CAA will also be empowered to carry out a market power test to determine whether an airport operator should or should not be subject to economic regulation. This replaces the designation of airports for price control regulation directly by the government; moreover there will be no automatic referral to the Competition Commission.

Other countries, such as South Africa, have adopted a similar single-till price cap regulatory mechanism when the major airports were privatised. In Ireland, too, single-till price cap regulation, with different limits related to off-peak periods and cargo, was introduced in 2001. These airports are owned by the public sector Dublin Airport Authority company which has considerable market power and handles over 95 per cent of all passenger traffic in Ireland. Two airports privatised more recently, Malta and Budapest, also have price cap regulation, but in these cases linked to a dual till. In India in 2008, an independent regulatory agency called the Airports Economic Authority of India (AERA) was established. After a lengthy consultation process, in 2011 AERA announced that it would be adopting an approach broadly based on single-till principles. At Vienna airport, a slightly different model has been adopted taking into account both inflation rates and traffic growth patterns. The regulation is applied directly to the charges. There is a sliding scale that protects revenues when there is slow growth, while requiring productivity gains to be made when traffic growth is high. Amsterdam airport uses a ROR/cost-based dual-till method.

The regulation of the Australian airports has received considerable attention (e.g. Schuster, 2008; Littlechild, 2012). The initial regulatory framework for the privatised Australian airports was fairly similar to that adopted by the UK airports, in that there was a CPI – X formula, although there was a dual rather than a single till. The Australian airports used the basket tariff rather than the revenue yield approach. As in the United Kingdom, the price cap was set for an initial 5 years, but the Australian regulatory framework had more formal conditions relating to airport access and quality of service monitoring that did not apply to the UK airports. The problems of inadequate investment under such regulation were also recognised and so provision was made for an upward adjustment to the price cap if approved investment was undertaken. The only major airport that was not controlled in this way was Sydney airport, which was not privatised when this regulation was introduced and was subject to a ROR-type regulation that just involved the surveillance or monitoring of prices rather than more restrictive price control (Forsyth, 2008).

This price regulation of Australian airports was identified as causing a number of problems (particularly the requirement of detailed and cumbersome regulatory intervention if investment was planned) and overall profit volatility. These problems became acute with the events of 9/11 and the collapse of Ansett, Australia's second largest domestic airline. As a consequence, in October 2001 the Australian government suspended the price regulation at all but the four largest airports. Price surveillance was maintained at Sydney airport; at Melbourne, Perth and Brisbane the price caps were adjusted upwards, which allowed the airports to increase their charges substantially. Under the regulatory system, the Australian Productivity Commission was required to undertake a review after it had been in force for 5 years. It was recommended that price regulation should be replaced by a much more light-handed price monitoring or surveillance approach, although the price control could be reintroduced if the airports abused their pricing freedom. Among some of the arguments used to support this change in regulatory approach (i.e. reserve regulation) was the fact that the price cap system had been costly to administer, had produced poor financial results for the airports, and was unnecessary as commercial pressures would ensure the airports would not abuse their market power. The temporary relaxation of the pricing controls was subsequently made permanent and the airports moved to this reserve regulation system. In 2006 a further review undertaken by the Productivity Commission recommended a continuation of the current system for a further 6 years, and the government accepted this recommendation (Forsyth, 2008). The Productivity Commission subsequently reviewed the system again in 2011 and recommended that the system should continue to operate, although with some enhancements. Subsequently, in 2012, the government accepted their overall decision.

Related to this is the case of New Zealand, where the two main airports of New Zealand, Auckland and Wellington, were partially privatised in 1998. The privatisation legislation allowed for these airports and Christchurch airport to review their charges every 3 years, but they were not subject to any formal price regulation. The legislation also called for the regulator to conduct periodic reviews to assess whether price controls were necessary. However, this light-handed approach led to much conflict between the airport operators and users regarding the level of charges, particularly at Auckland airport, and in 2002 it was recommended by the Commerce Commission that price control should be introduced at Auckland airport. This was not recommended for Christchurch and Wellington, however, where the abuse of market power was not considered to be a major issue. In spite of this, in 2003 the Commerce Minster decided that there would be no controls on any of the three airports (Mackenzie-Williams, 2004). However, since 2011 the airports have been required to disclose more information and to comply with more auditing, certification and verification standards.

Long-term contracts between airports and airlines

Another alternative to formal economic regulation can be some kind of negotiated agreement between the airlines and airports. Historically the normal contract between an airline and an airport is the published airport conditions of use, which describe the services provided in exchange for the aeronautical fees. Traditionally this has not been a formalised relationship as it did not identify the rights and obligations of both parties. For example, there was no agreement as regards the standard of services to expect, and no process was identified should disputes between the airlines and airports arise. The only country that has always tended to have the rights and obligations clearly defined and incorporated into a legally binding contract is the United States. These use-and-lease agreements concentrate on the fees and rentals to be paid, the method by which these are calculated, and the conditions of use of the facilities. Service standards are not usually incorporated into these agreements.

However, in recent years there has been some evidence of a more formalised airline–airport relationship emerging. For example, at airports with light-handed regulation, airports usually have voluntarily agreed charge levels directly with their airline customers rather than having to go through a regulator. For example, at Copenhagen airport the airport operator Danish airlines and IATA (representing foreign airlines) have established agreements concerning airport charges. Most recently, it was agreed that charges would not increase between 2009 and 2011 and then by CPI + 1 per cent between 2011–15. The government regulates the airport only if the airport and airlines cannot reach an agreement. Likewise in Australia, the movement from price regulation to price monitoring encouraged the airports and airlines to reach 5-year agreements that cover charges and service.

Perhaps of greater significance, going beyond the focus of regulation, has been the development of long-term contracts between LCCs and airports within Europe. Starkie (2012) and Graham (2013) have argued that this has been a result of a fundamental change in the airline–airport relationship here. Deregulation has meant that the airlines have considerable freedom, especially with the cost of the internet reducing the cost of entry for airlines into the local markets. This has resulted in the LCC business models operating on a pan-European basis and in airlines having increased buying power. In turn, this has given more business risk to the airports and therefore long-term contracts seem to be a way in which airports can attempt to introduce more stability into this increasingly unstable situation.

Details about the contracts are difficult to obtain because of their confidential nature, but generally they range from 5 to 20 years, where the airport operator will offer discounted charges in return for long-term commitment from the airlines. The charges will tend to be simple, usually on a departing passenger basis linked to a price inflation index since, as discussed earlier, it is passenger numbers that drive the revenues of the LCCs. There may also be volume discounts available. There will be a number of other obligations on the airport operator, including the quality of service to be supplied regarding minimum turnaround times and the requirement to undertake marketing on behalf of the airline. If the contract covers a long period there might be commitments by the airport operator to undertake staged investment. In return, the airline will typically be obliged to guarantee to base a certain number of aircraft initially at the airport and to provide a roll-out programme for adding additional aircraft. Sometimes the airline will also have to guarantee a minimum number of passengers. One of the earliest contracts was agreed between easyJet and Liverpool airport in 1998. Another example includes a 10-year contract signed between Durham Tees Valley airport in the UK and bmibaby (a subsidiary of BMI) in 2003. Initially it was agreed that bmibaby would operate a minimum of two B737s exclusively from the airport in return for discounted charges and other financial support from both the airport and local government. It could well be that that this long-term contract approach is how the industry will evolve to cope with this new airline–airport relationship, especially where LCCs are concerned. However, if public airports are involved it can raise issues related to state aid (discussed in Chapter 8).

Overall, in recent years there has been considerable debate within the airport sector as to what, if any, is the optimal method of economic regulation to use (e.g. Marques and Brochado, 2008; Starkie, 2008; Niemeier, 2010). Some argue that, given that airports are operating in an increasingly competitive environment, they should no longer be considered as monopoly providers and consequently in the future more governments should move towards a more reserved or light-handed approach, perhaps with airline contracts. It has also been contended that many of the current regulatory systems are time-consuming, bureaucratic and costly, and that in most cases litigation or national competition law could cope with any abuses of market power.

SLOT ALLOCATION

Traditional system and recent changes

The rise in air traffic in recent years has put increasing pressure on airport capacity, particularly runway capacity, throughout the world. Theoretically, while timely capacity addition might provide a solution to this problem, in many cases environmental, physical or financial constraints have meant that in practice this has not been a feasible or desirable option. Instead, attention has been focused on more short-term solutions to provide some relief for the shortage of capacity, both by consideration of capacity or supply-side approaches and by the assessment of demand management options. In a climate of growing environmental opposition to new developments, such solutions may be politically more acceptable. Supply-side options aim to make more efficient use of existing capacity by improving ATC services and ground-side facilities, and thus provide for incremental increases in traffic. Demand management techniques consider the most appropriate mechanisms for allocating airport slots. Airport slots are usually defined as an arrival or departure time at an airport – typically within a 15- or 30-minute period. They are different from ATC slots, which are operational take-off and landing times assigned to the airline by ATC authorities.

Alternative slot allocation procedures have to be considered at airports because the pricing mechanism fails to balance demand with the available supply. As already discussed, the current level of charges at airports and peak/off-peak differentials when in existence have a relatively limited impact on airline demand. Peak charges would have to be considerably higher to ration demand or to be the equivalent of the market-clearing price needed to match supply and demand or 'clear the market'. This is obviously not helped by the acceptance at many airports of the single-till concept which can pull down the level of charges to below that of the cost of supply.

Currently, in all parts of the world except the United States, the mechanism for allocating slots is industry self-regulation by using the administrative system that involves IATA Schedule Co-ordination Conferences and Committees. These voluntary conferences of both IATA and non-IATA airlines are held twice a year for the summer and winter seasons, with the aim of reaching consensus on how schedules can be coordinated at designated capacity-constrained airports. These airports are designated at two levels.

Schedules-facilitated airports: demand is approaching capacity, but slot allocation can be resolved through voluntary cooperation. These are known as level 2 airports.

Fully coordinated airports: demand exceeds capacity and formal procedures are used to allocate slots. These are known as level 3 airports. The most important of these procedures is 'grandfather rights'. This means that any airline that has operated a slot in the previous similar season has the right to operate it again. This is as long as the airline operates 80 per cent of the flights – the so-called slot-retention requirement or 'use-it-or-lose-it' rule. The airline does not, however, have to use its slots for the same services each year and can switch them, for example, between domestic and international routes. Preference is also given to airlines that plan to use a slot more intensively to make the most effective use of the capacity. For example, priority would be given to an airline that plans a daily service rather than one that is less than daily, or a service that operates throughout the season rather than only in the peak.

There are also level 1 airports that are non-coordinated airports, where supply exceeds demand and slot allocations can be decided through simple discussions between the airline, handling agent (if relevant) and airport.

Between 1990 and 1999 the number of fully coordinated (level 3) airports increased by 18 per cent, while for the schedules-facilitated (level 2) airports there was a higher growth of 63 per cent. In 1999 there were 120 fully coordinated airports with more than ten others being fully coordinated in the summer months only. Around 80 airports were schedules facilitated. According to IATA (2012), there are now currently 159 fully coordinated airports in the world and 121 schedules-facilitated. Europe has most fully coordinated airports, followed by the Asia-Pacific area. Many US airports are also capacity constrained, but do not come under the IATA Scheduling Committee mechanism. Within Europe there are 89 fully coordinated airports (62 are co-ordinated year-round and 27 are coordinated seasonally) with 18 countries having at least one coordinated airport. Sometimes demand substantially exceeds capacity at all times (e.g. at London Heathrow and Paris Orly) whereas elsewhere capacity is scarce only during certain peak periods (Steer Davies Gleave, 2010).

Within the EU, slot allocation comes under regulation EU/95/93, which was introduced in 1993 (EC, 1993). While the IATA coordination system is voluntary, the EU rules are a legal requirement. The IATA system developed primarily as a process to coordinate schedules and to avoid unnecessary congestion, whereas the EU regulation had other key objectives, including making the most efficient use of capacity and encouraging competition. Nevertheless many of the IATA features were just incorporated into the European law (Table 4.5). However, an important difference with the European regulation when it was introduced was that the slot coordinator had to be independent of all airlines at the airport. This enabled the process to be more transparent and impartial, as traditionally the coordinator tended to be the national carrier at the airport. In order for an airport to become coordinated, the legislation required that a thorough capacity analysis and consultation process should take place.

The European legislation aimed to encourage new entrants, who were clearly disadvantaged by the grandfather rights system, by giving them preference of up to 50 per cent of any new or unused slots. New entrants were defined as airlines with less than 4 per cent of daily slots at an airport or less than 3 per cent of slots in an airport system, such as the London airports. They were also airlines that had requested slots for a non-stop intra-EU service where two incumbent airlines already operated. Under certain conditions, slots could be reserved for domestic regional services or routes with public service requirements – so-called 'ring-fencing'. The grandfather rights system was adopted with an 80 per cent slot retention requirement, although this use-it-or-lose-it rule was temporarily suspended after 9/11 and in the summer of 2009. In these cases, airlines dropped routes because of the sudden drop in traffic, but did not want to lose their historical slots. This was permitted as the result of an amendment in 2002 which stated that in certain exceptional circumstances air carriers will not lose their grandfather rights to slots.

Table 4.5 *Key features of the 1993 EU slot-allocation regulation*

Slots are allocated on basis of historical precedence or 'grandfather rights'
Airlines must use slots of 80 per cent of the time – 'use it or lose it' rule
There is a slot pool for new or returned slots
50 per cent of slots in the pool are allocated to new entrants
Certain slots can be ringfenced if they are vital for social or economic reasons
Airports are non-coordinated, coordinated (schedules facilitated) or fully coordinated
Coordination status is defined after capacity review and consultation
An independent coordinator supervises the allocation of slots

Source: EC (1993)

The EC undertook a review of this slot allocation process and found little evidence that it had encouraged competition or lessened the influence of the major network carriers at the airports. This is hardly surprising given that the European regime largely maintained the grandfather rights system. At the same time, delays and congestion at many European airports had increased. After a long period of further review and consultation, the EC put forward some new proposals in 2001. The proposals were divided into two parts: first, some immediate technical amendments to the existing regulation (adopted in 2004); second, some more long-term aims concerned with structural changes to the actual system of allocation.

The technical amendments EC (793/2004) covered a number of different areas, primarily to make the system more flexible and to strengthen the coordinator's role (EC, 2004) (Table 4.6). They stated that there should be financially independent coordinators at each airport and that there should be better enforcement and monitoring of the slot rules. The legal status of slots was clarified by defining them as permissions rather than property to be owned. There was the retention of grandfather rights and the use-it-or-lose-it rule, but the new entrant threshold was raised to 7 per cent. Another new feature was consideration of environmental constraints, with the possibility of higher priority being given to larger aircraft size or lower priority to services where surface alternatives existed. There were then further EC communications in 2007 and 2008 that clarified certain points relating to slot trading, independency of coordinators, new entrants and local rules.

In the longer term the EC has been looking at more radical changes to the current process (Kilian, 2008; Sorensen, 2008). In 2004 a report considering market-oriented slot-allocation mechanisms and their feasibility was completed for the EC (NERA Economic Consulting, 2004). This led to a period of consultation in 2004 and was followed by a second study in 2006 that focused on secondary trading in more detail, including an assessment of the full economic impacts (Mott MacDonald, 2006). Then in 2011 there was further research by Steer Davies Gleave (2011). This concluded that there was sub-optimal use of capacity at some airports, with some carriers unable to grow their operations to compete with incumbent carriers. It found that at some airports (e.g. Frankfurt, Munich, Heathrow, Paris CDG) the share of grandfather slots was 90 per cent or higher (99 per cent at Heathrow). It concluded that there was inadequate operation of the slot coordination process at some airports, and made a number of key recommendations. This included allowing slot trading; reforming the rules related to new entrants; tightening the rules related to demonstrating use of slots; tightening the rules relating to the independence of the coordinator;

Table 4.6 *Key features of the 2004 amendments to the 1993 EU slot-allocation regulation*

The coordinator is financially independent
The legal status of a slot is a permission, not entitlement or property
There is a broader definition of a 'new entrant'
At a local level the rules can be linked to aircraft size for environmental reasons
At a local level the rules can be linked to other transport modes
There are improved enforcement and monitoring procedures

Source: EC (2004)

increasing the level of transparency on slot transactions; and improving the flow of information between different stakeholders. The research suggested that these proposed changes could be worth €5 billion to the European economy. Also, they could create 62,000 more jobs over the period 2012–25 and would allow the system to handle 24 million more passengers a year by 2025.

Many of these suggestions were incorporated into the EC's so-called 'Airport Package' which contains proposals related to increasing airport capacity, reducing delays and improving the quality of services offered to passengers. Specifically it covers three areas: slots, ground handling and noise. The proposals for slots and noise were agreed by the European Parliament in December 2012 and so now need Council approval. They will allow for the trading of slots between airlines and establish clear conditions for transparent trading to be supervised by national authorities. They will strengthen the independence of slot coordinators and require greater transparency of information. It was proposed that the use-it-or-lose-it rule should be increased to 85 per cent, but this was rejected by the European Parliament in favour of tougher sanctions for the late handing back of slots.

Alternative slot-allocation mechanisms

The discussion so far has provided details of the traditional system related to slot allocation and has outlined the changes that have occurred within Europe. There now follows a broader consideration of the alternative slot-allocation mechanisms that could potentially be used in the future. Undoubtedly the current scheduling committee system is widely accepted and has succeeded in providing a stable environment for allocating slots. However, there is considerable concern that as pressure on runway capacity continues, it may not be the most effective mechanism to manage the scarcity of slots or encourage competition. Critics claim that this procedure gives no guarantee that the scarce airport capacity is used by the airlines that value it most highly, it provides no guide to future investment requirements and is administratively burdensome. Also, many new entrants are prevented from competing at major airports. In addition it can result in wasteful behaviour by airlines who 'warehouse' or 'babysit' slots by operating empty or 'ghost' flights to ensure they retain their slots. The current system, by being based on payment for actual use, provides poor incentives for airlines to actually use slots efficiently. Thus airlines may hold onto slots by using them enough to meet the use-it-or-lose-it criteria, but they may waste the scarce runway resources by not making full use of the slots all the time.

There have been lengthy debates discussing whether a better system could be introduced (e.g. DotEcon, 2006; Czerny *et al.*, 2008). Various regulatory suggestions have been put forward including giving preference to long-haul international flights, which normally have less flexibility in scheduling than short-haul flights because of night closures and other constraints. This could potentially have an environmental benefit by switching short-haul traffic from air to surface transport. Priority could be given to airlines that cause the least noise nuisance. Scheduled airlines could be favoured over charter airlines, and passenger aircraft could have preference over cargo airlines. Alternatively, frequency caps could be placed on certain services once a daily maximum limit has been reached. Another suggestion is to give priority to larger aircraft that make the most efficient use of slots.

While such mechanisms can be useful in pursuing some economic, social or environmental objective, they are still likely to be used in combination with grandfather rights. As a result, any such system will again share the shortcomings of the traditional system by not ensuring that the scarce runway slots are used by the airlines that value them the most and that will most closely serve the underlying passenger demand. Instead, market-based options could be considered for both primary allocation, where the slots are initially allocated, and secondary allocation, where the use of slots may be changed at some later stage. In the latter case this will involve setting up a system of secondary slot trading where airlines are able to buy and sell slots.

The simplest of all market-based options for primary allocation is the use of some charging mechanism, or so-called 'posted prices' to match demand and supply. A fee is attached to each slot, and demand is thus reduced by the raising the cost of using the slot. This could either be a set fee or could be differentiated between peak and off-peaks slots, to reflect the varying patterns of demand. However, as discussed, the market-clearing price would have to be set at a considerably higher rate than is the current practice with airport charges. An alternative suggestion is to use the auction mechanism as a means of allocating slots. These auctions could be held every 6 months, like the scheduling committees, but this would clearly lead to considerable upheaval and disruption for both airlines and passengers. At the other extreme there could be just one auction, selling the slots rights in perpetuity, and then any further changes would have to be implemented through some secondary mechanism. Somewhere in between these two options, slots allocated under long-term lease agreements could be a more attractive compromise. Individual slots or a combination of slots could be auctioned at one particular time.

Alternatively, lotteries for slots could be held. This might potentially overcome the anti-competitive problem caused by slot trading in that all airlines of all sizes would have access to slots, but in practice this could cause havoc with airlines' schedules and be very disruptive. Slots obtained at one end of the route might not match up with those at the other end, and in general there would be a great deal of uncertainty. Also, a major issue with all these primary allocations would be deciding who should retain the money that has been paid for the slots (the airport operator? the government?), and whether it should be stipulated that it is used at the airport for future investment to provide capacity or to reduce the environmental impacts.

The research undertaken by NERA Economic Consulting (2004) considered the potential impacts of these different market-based options. The main focus was on investigating whether such mechanisms would achieve a more efficient use of scarce airport capacity by assessing the effect on passenger numbers. Other factors were considered, including the implementation costs, the potential for instability in airline schedules, the likelihood of increased concentration at hub airports, consistency with existing procedures and risk of international disputes. Five main options were investigated, the first three being secondary pricing and higher posted prices on their own, and then both together. The fourth option was using secondary trading with an auction of the pool slots, and the most radical case assumed that there would be a long lease agreement with an auction of 10 per cent of all existing slots each year in a rolling programme so that each slot would come up for auction every 10 years. This was considered with secondary trading.

It was concluded that all the options would produce higher passenger numbers with a shift in traffic patterns, because the airlines that would value and be prepared to pay most for the slots would tend to be those offering long-haul services with larger aircraft and those with higher load factors. In addition, slot utilisation would be expected to improve as the airlines would be less likely to hold onto slots that they do not need. One of the disadvantages with the higher posted prices is the risk of international disputes. The same is true of the 10 per cent auction and secondary trading option because of its more radical nature. This latter approach would also be the most expensive to implement and be the most disruptive to airline schedules. All scenarios would be likely to lead to an increased concentration of hub carrier slots.

Within the EU, the Airport Package is actually proposing the acceptance of secondary trading. Historically, airlines have not been officially permitted to undertake such practices except with the case of four US airports (see Case Study 4.1). In Europe, slot exchanges are allowed under the EU regulation, but slot trading is not specifically allowed or banned. However, an important decision was made in 1999 by the UK High Court when it ruled that the financial payment from BA to Air UK to 'compensate' for the exchange of some highly demanded slots with some less attractive slots did not invalidate the exchange. This allowed a so-called grey market for slot trading, where valuable slots are bought and very often exchanged for 'junk' or useless slots. Research on secondary trading at Heathrow by Mott MacDonald (2006) for Heathrow found that between 2001 and 2006, 499 slots a week (compared with a total of 8,700) had been traded. Overall it was concluded the UK experience had led to a liquid and flexible market in slots, had fostered new entry and had been supported by the industry, with direct competitors being prepared to trade with each other. It had also improved slot efficiency as a number of short-haul carriers had been replaced with long-haul carriers with larger aircraft.

As capacity at Heathrow has become scarcer, the price for a peak slot has risen sharply (Table 4.7). While the commercial nature of these transactions means it is difficult to get accurate figures, in the early 2000s it was generally thought that airlines were paying up to £10 million (around US$20 million) for a pair of slots in peak times. However, in 2007 the price appeared to have more than doubled, primarily because airlines were very keen to acquire slots at Heathrow to take advantage of the new route opportunities that had arisen because of the EU–US Open Skies agreement which came into effect in April 2008. Although prices may have fallen slightly because of the recent downturn in traffic, the overall estimate in 2010 was a slot pair value of £30–40 million for pre–0900 arrivals, £10 million for 0900–1300 arrivals and much lower values at other times. Meanwhile, the existing experience related to slot trading in other European countries varies. In some places, such as Spain, it is not allowed; at certain other airports, including Frankfurt, Dusseldorf and Vienna, it is thought to have occurred on a few occasions (Steer Davies Gleave, 2011).

While there is now considerable evidence to suggest that some kind of market-based mechanism could make more efficient use of scarce runway resource, there have always been some competition concerns (Office of Fair Trading/CAA, 2005). This is because such an approach will usually increase the dominance of the major airlines at the airports (which has been demonstrated by both the NERA and Mott MacDonald research), even though other second-tier airlines will have better opportunities to compete. In addition, such dominant airlines might place restrictive covenants on how the traded slots can be used to dampen the competition. These factors could be addressed by undertaking market investigations by relevant competition authorities, banning any restrictive covenants and generally increasing the amount of transparency associated with any slot sales. Some argue that such increased concentration may not always be a negative development for passengers. Another potential issue may be reduced competition with short-haul services, and perhaps a loss of regional services which tend to be served with smaller aircraft that are

Table 4.7 Examples of slot trades at Heathrow airport

Buyer	Seller	Date	Number of slot pairs	Approximate total price (million US$)	Approximate average price per daily slot pair (US$)
BA	Air UK	1998	4 per day	25	6
BA	SN Brussels	2002	7 per day	65	9
BA	Swiss	2003	8 per day	55	7
BA	United	2003	2 per day	20	10
Qantas	Flybe	2004	2 per day	35	18
Virgin	Flybe	2004	4 per day	35	9
Virgin	Air Jamaica	2007	4 per week	10	n/a
BA, Qatar Airways, Continental*	GB Airways	2007	4 per day	160	40
Continental, US Airways, BA*	Alitalia	2007	3 per day	140	47
Continentala	GB Airways, Air France, Alitalia	2008	4 per day	210	52

*There is some double counting with these 2007 trades as sale prices for individual airlines were not always available.
Source: Compiled by the author from various sources

less full. In this case use of the European Public Service Obligation (PSO) legislation may help to improve the situation, as might allowing slots to be sold to other bodies, such as regional authorities which could then safeguard slots. In general, making the best use of existing resources while at the same time encouraging or enhancing competition for all is not an easy matter. For example, it may be feasible to focus on competition, but that may cause sudden disruption in schedules. Likewise, it may be possible to protect certain routes through ring-fencing, but this may not produce the most effective use of the scarce runway slots.

GROUND-HANDLING ISSUES

Ground-handling activities at airports are very important to airlines. They have an impact on both an airline's cost and the quality of service they provide for their passengers and freight shippers. Ground-handling services cover passenger handling, baggage handling, freight and mail handling, ramp handling, fuel and oil handling, and aircraft services and maintenance. Such activities are often divided between terminal or traffic handling (passenger check-in), baggage and freight handling, and airside or ramp handling (activities including aircraft loading and unloading, cleaning and servicing). Sometimes these services are offered by the airport operators, although at most airports they are provided by airlines or handling agents. Historically, often the national airline or airport operator may have had a monopoly or near-monopoly in ground handling. Within Europe some airport operators, including Milan, Rome, Vienna and Frankfurt airports, which traditionally were heavily involved in such activities, earned very significant revenues from such activities – sometimes over half the total income of the airport. In other cases the airport operator earned just rental fees and perhaps a small concession fee from the airlines or agents that offered the handling services. Countries in Europe where the national airline used to have a handling monopoly included Spain with Iberia and Greece with Olympic.

For operational reasons, it is far easier to have a number of airlines providing traffic handling rather than ramp handling – given capacity constraints of the equipment and space in the ramp handling areas. Hence providers of monopoly services have claimed that introducing competition, particularly for some ramp handling services, would merely duplicate resources and reduce efficiency, and may also cause considerable apron congestion, particularly at airports that are already at full or near capacity. However, others, particularly airlines, have argued that ground handling monopolies can push up prices and reduce service standards. Within the EU it was argued that air transport could not be fully liberalised unless the ground-handling activities were offered on a fully competitive basis, and this resulted in the EU's adoption of the ground-handling directive EC/96/67 in 1996 (EC, 1996). The long-term purpose of this phased directive was to end all ground handling monopolies and duopolies within the EU by opening up the market to third-party handlers, recognising the right of airlines to self-handle, and guaranteeing at least some choice for airlines in the provision of ground-handling services (Table 4.8) For airports larger than 2 million passengers, this allowed free access to third-party handlers, although for certain restricted categories of services (baggage handling, ramp handling, fuel and oil handling, freight and mail handling) the number of suppliers may be limited to no fewer than two. One of these suppliers has to be independent of the airport or the dominant airline (which handles over

Table 4.8 *Key features of the 1996 EU ground-handling directive*

	General services	Restricted services*
Airline self-handling	All airports	All airports >1 million passengers or 25,000 tonnes. No fewer than two airlines
Third-party handling	All airports > 2 million passenger or 50,000 tonnes	All airports >2 million passengers or 50,000 tonnes. No fewer than two handlers. At least one handler must be independent of the airport operator or dominant airlines with more than 25 per cent of the traffic

*Baggage handling, ramp handling, fuel and oil handling, freight and mail handling.
Source: EC (1996)

25 per cent of the traffic). At all airports airlines are allowed to self-handle for the passenger services, but only at airports larger than 1 million passengers for the restricted services, where again there may be limits with no fewer than two airlines.

A study was undertaken in 2002 to investigate the impact of the directive (SH&E, 2002). The number of third-party handlers had increased although the number of self-handlers had remained the same or even decreased in some cases. It concluded that prices for ground-handling services had dropped, and this was particularly the case where there had previously been handling monopolies or a highly regulated market. This may have been due to the increase in competition between handlers because of the directive, but also because of cost pressures from the airlines. However, as regards quality of service levels there was a more mixed picture. A further study in 2009 found that the number self-handlers and third-party handlers had increased significantly during the period 1996–2007 (Airport Research Center, 2009). Overall between 1996 and 2010, airport operators decreased their market share in ground handling from 25 to 16 per cent, and airlines decreased their share from 68 to 39 per cent. At the same time the independent handlers increased their share from 7 to 45 per cent (ACI Europe, 2011).

While there has clearly been an increase in competition as regards the EU ground-handling markets, recent research (Airport Research Center, 2009; Steer Davies Gleave, 2010) has indicated that there could be improvements made to the efficiency and quality of services offered. In addition some countries, including Spain, Germany, Austria, Belgium and Portugal, have chosen to limit competition in the restricted services to the minimum of two service providers. Therefore the EC included some proposals related to ground handling in the Airport Package. This proposed increasing the minimum number of service providers (in restricted services) from two to three at large airports; allowing member states to go further in protecting workers' rights to maintain a high-quality workforce; strengthening the role of airports as the 'ground coordinator'; and providing them with a new set of tools, for example minimum quality standards, to do this (EC, 2012). This ground-handling part of the package was generally supported by the airlines but not the airports. Unlike the slot proposals, it was rejected by the European Parliament's Transport and Tourism Committee in November 2012. However, in December 2012 the European Parliament referred it back to the Committee for further discussion on how to improve the efficiency and quality of such services.

CASE STUDY 4.1: THE US EXPERIENCE

Airport use agreements

The relationship between airports and airlines in the United States is unique and so is worthy of special consideration (Riconda & Associates *et al.*, 2010). The airports and airlines enter into legally binding contracts known as airport use-and-lease agreements that detail the fees and rental rates that an airline has to pay, the method by which these are to be calculated, and the conditions for the use of both airfield and terminal facilities. A key reason for the existence of these agreements has been that private bond-holders have demanded the security of such formal relationship between the airports and airlines before investing in the airport.

Traditionally there have been two basic approaches to establishing the airport charges: residual and compensatory. With the residual approach the airlines pay the net costs of running the airport after taking account of commercial and other non-airline sources of revenue. The airlines provide a guarantee that the level of charges and rents will be such that the airport will always break even, and so they take considerable risk. Alternatively, with the compensatory approach the airlines pay agreed charges and rates based on recovery of costs allocated to the facilities and services they occupy or use. The risk of running the airport is left to the airport operator. The residual approach is therefore more akin to the single-till practice, while the compensatory approach is more similar to the dual-till approach. Airports have applied these two approaches in various ways to suit their particular needs, and have increasingly adopted hybrid approaches that combine elements of both residual and compensatory methodologies.

The use agreements historically have been long-term contracts, but in more recent years they have become shorter to reflect the more volatile aviation environment. The length-of-use agreement will normally coincide with any lease agreements that the airlines have with the airport operator. In the United States, it is common for airlines to lease terminal space or gates, or even to lease or build total terminals – as in the case of JFK airport in New York. The airlines that carry most of the airport's traffic may also play a significant role in airport investment decisions if they agree to the majority-in-interest (MII) clauses in the use agreement. These clauses, which are far more common among residual agreements, typically mean that these signatory airlines have to approve all significant planned developments or changes at the airport. The anti-competitive nature of such agreements can be a problem if other non-signatory airlines are prevented from gaining access to terminal space and gates. As a result there has been an increasing use of use-it-or-lose-it clauses – the control of assets is returned to the airport if the airline does not use the facilities as intended. Capacity improvements that may bring more opportunities for competition may also not be approved by the signatory airlines. This has meant that some airport operators have tried to reduce the powers of the signatory airlines by requiring MII disapproval rather than approval, or have limited the airlines' influence to only major projects. Some airports have discarded MII clauses altogether.

In a survey undertaken by ACI North America (2012), it was found that 30 per cent of airports used the compensatory approach and 23 per cent used the residual approach, with a hybrid situation existing for the other airports. Comparable figures for 2003 were 21 per cent for compensatory and 26 per cent for residual – showing an increase in the use of the compensatory approach. The decline in length of agreement was also clearly observed with only 16 per cent of agreements lasting longer than 5 years in 2012 compared with 38 per cent in 2003. Two-thirds of airports had MII clauses.

Airport fees and taxes

The landing fees at US airports are normally very simple, being based on a fixed rate per 1000 lb. Signatory airlines may pay less. The charges tend not to vary according to noise levels or peak periods, unlike the practice at some European airports. The level of landing fees tends to be relatively low, partly because the airport operator provides a minimal number of services itself. The generation of aeronautical revenues at US airports is subject to a number of statutory requirements determined by Congress and policy statements issued by the FAA/Department of Transportation. First, there is the federal government requirement for 'fair and reasonable' and not 'unjustly discriminatory' aeronautical fees based strictly on costs. Second, airports are prohibited from using airport revenues for non-airport purposes. This latter requirement is one of the major obstacles in the way of any significant developments towards airport privatisation in the United States (Graham, 2004).

Unlike most other airports in the world, US airports do not have passenger charges – although some of the costs associated with terminal and gate space that are normally incorporated into the passenger fee may be covered by airline lease payments and terminal rental charges. US airports are not legally allowed to levy passenger charges, primarily because of fears that such revenues will be diverted from the airport to be used for non-aviation purposes. However, in 1990 the federal government approved the levying of PFCs. Although the PFCs are legally and constitutionally different from passenger charges levied elsewhere in the world, they have a similar impact on airlines. The initial PFC legislation allowed for airports to levy a US$1, $2 or $3 fee that had to be spent on identified airport-related projects or could be used to back bonds for the projects. In 2001 it was agreed that the maximum PFC could be raised to US$4.50. Airlines have no veto rights when it comes to PFC-funded projects, nor can they have exclusive rights.

Passenger facility charges were first used in June 1992. As of 1 January 2013, 385 airports were approved to collect PFCs, and since their introduction 18 per cent of this total funding has been for airside projects, 34 per cent for landside projects, 4 per cent for noise projects, 6 per cent for access projects and 34 per cent for paying interest. A further 4 per cent has funded the construction costs of Denver airport (Airlines for America, 2013). Some PFCs have been approved for a long time (longer than 30 years) whereas others will be used for as little as 3 years. In addition, there are also a number of government taxes that push up the total amount paid by the airlines and their passengers (Table 4.9). There are the taxes that go into the Federal Airport and Airway Trust Fund, which provides the finance for airport investment grants under the Airport Improvement Program (AIP) (and finance for the air traffic control system). The most significant of the taxes is the domestic passenger ticket tax, which accounts for around half of all the trust fund. Then there are also additional taxes relating to fuel, security, agriculture and health inspection, and customs and immigration services.

Table 4.9 *Taxes at US airports (as of 1 January 2013)*

Type of tax	Tax rate	Unit of taxation
Airport and Airway Trust Fund		
Passenger ticket tax	7.5 per cent	Domestic air fare
Passenger flight segment tax	$3.80	Domestic passengers
International departure & arrival tax	$17.20	International passengers
Frequent flyer tax	7.5 per cent	Sale of frequent flyer miles
Cargo waybill tax	6.25 per cent	Waybill for domestic freight
Commercial aviation jet fuel	4.3 cents	Gallons
Non-commercial jet fuel/gasoline tax	21.8/19.3 cents	Gallons
Local airport projects		
Passenger facility charge	Up to $4.50	Passengers
Department of Homeland Security		
September 11 fee	$2.50	Passengers
Aviation security infrastructure fee	Carrier-specific	
Animal and Plant Health Inspection Service (now CBP) passenger/ aircraft fee	$5.00/$76.75	International passengers/aircraft
Customs user fee	$5.50	International passengers
Immigration user fee	$7.00	International passengers

Source: Airlines for America (2013)

Slot allocation

At most airports in the United States there is no formal slot-allocation mechanism such as the IATA Scheduling Committees, since these would be in conflict with anti-trust laws. This means that, instead, there is open access to the airports barring any environmental constraints, and airlines design their schedules independently taking into account any expected delays. This 'first-come, first-served' system can result in considerable congestion at certain times of day when many flights are scheduled around the same time.

The exception to this practice is at a few airports that have been subject to the 'high-density airport rule'. This rule was introduced in 1969 by the Federal Aviation Administration (FAA) as a temporary measure to reduce problems of delay and congestion at JFK, La Guardia and Newark airports in New York (although it was relaxed for Newark in 1970), O'Hare airport in Chicago and Washington National airport. The traffic was divided into three categories: air carriers, air taxis (now commuters) and other (primarily general aviation), with a different limit on the number of flights during restricted hours for each category. No slot-allocation mechanism was defined, but the relevant airlines were given anti-trust immunity to discuss coordination of schedules.

Initially the rule worked relatively well, but the increase in traffic due to airline deregulation in 1978, and other factors including a major air traffic control strike, resulted in a new allocation system being introduced in 1985. This was the 'buy–sell' rule which effectively meant that after an initial allocation process based on grandfather rights, airlines were then permitted to buy and sell their slots. Airlines were also allowed to 'lease' slots on a short-term basis. This has been the only formal secondary trading market for slots in any part of the world. This trading of slots was limited to domestic operations (international routes being more complex because of international regulation), with air carriers slot being unable to be traded for commuter slots and *vice versa*. Slots used for essential air services were excluded. There was a use-it-or-lose-it rule requirement of 65 per cent, and a slot pool was established for newly available slots. These were reallocated using a lottery – with 25 per cent initially being offered to new entrants. International slots were allowed to be coordinated through the IATA Scheduling Committees.

Over 10 years' experience of this slot trading led to increasing criticism of the system. There had been very few outright sales of air carrier slots, very few new entrants, and regional services had been reduced. The established airlines had increased their dominance at the airports – although this had to be viewed within the context of a US airline industry that itself had become more concentrated (Starkie, 1998). As a result of these concerns, the Aviation Investment and Reform Act (AIR21) of 2000 made substantial changes to the slot rules at these airports. At Chicago O'Hare airport the slot rules were eliminated by 2002 (there is now additional capacity). At the New York airports the rules were withdrawn in 2007.

In anticipation of severe delays following the expiration of the rules, at La Guardia the FAA introduced a temporary control order limiting operations. This was extended in 2009 and 2011. Equivalent restrictions were not imposed initially at JFK and Newark, and as a result there were severe delays and over-scheduling at these airports in 2007. The FAA responded by introducing similar control orders in 2008 at these two airports. These again have been temporarily extended. The orders limit the number of slots, have a minimum use requirement (80 per cent as in Europe) and allow secondary trading through leases, but not on a permanent basis. In 2009 it was planned that there would be an auctioning process for 10 per cent of the slots at the three New York airports, but this was unpopular, particularly with the airlines, was blocked by a federal appeals panel, and in the end was abandoned (GAO, 2012). As yet there is no permanent solution to this capacity problem at these airports.

REFERENCES

ACI (2011) *Airport Economics Survey 2011*, Montreal: Airports Council International.

ACI Europe (2011) *ACI Europe Position on Requirements for a Performing Ground Handling Market*, Brussels: ACI Europe.

ACI North America (2012) *2011–12 Airport/Airline Use and Lease Agreement and MII Survey*, Washington, DC: ACI North America.

Airlines for America (2013) *Economics – Taxes & Fees*. Online. Available HTTP: <http://www.airlines. org/Pages/Econ_Taxes.aspx> (accessed 1 January 2013).

Airport Research Center (2009) *Study on the Impact of Directive 96/67/EC on Ground Handling Services 1996–2007*, Aachen: Airport Research Center.

CAA (2003) *Economic Regulation of BAA London Airports*, London: Civil Aviation Authority.

—— (2008) *Economic Regulation of Heathrow and Gatwick Airports*, London: Civil Aviation Authority.

—— (2012) *Table 06 Major UK Airlines Individual Airline Profit and Loss Account 2010*. Online. Available HTTP <http://www.caa.co.uk/default.aspx?catid=80&pagetype=88&sglid=13&fld=2010_2011> (assessed 10 December 2012).

Czerny, A. (2006) 'Price-cap regulation of airports: single-till versus dual-till', *Journal of Regulatory Economics*, 30(1): 85–97

Czerny, A., Forsyth, P., Gillen, D. and Neimeier, H.-M. (2008) *Airport slots: International Experiences and Options for Reform*, Farnham: Ashgate.

Department for Transport (2008a) *Decision on the Regulatory Status of Manchester Airport*, London: Department for Transport.

—— (2008b) *Decision on the Regulatory Status of Stansted Airport*, London: Department for Transport.

—— (2009) *Reforming the Framework for the Economic Regulation of Airports Decision Document*, London: Department for Transport.

DotEcon (2006) *Alternative Allocation Mechanisms for Slots Created by New Airport Capacity*, London: DotEcon.

EC (1993) *Regulation (EEC) No {95/93} of European Parliament and of the Council of 18 January 1993 on Common Rules for the Allocation of Slots at Community Airports*, Official Journal L14, 22 January, Brussels: EC.

—— (1996) *Directive 96/67/EC of the European Parliament and of the Council of 15 October 1996 on Access to the Groundhandling Market at Community Airports*, Official Journal L272, 25 October, Brussels: EC.

—— (2004) *Regulation (EC) No {793/2004} of European Parliament and of the Council of 21 April 2004 amending Council Regulation (EEC) No {95/93} on Common Rules for the Allocation of Slots at Community Airports*, L138, 30 April.

—— (2009) *Directive 2009/12/EC of the European Parliament and of the Council of 11 March 2009 on Airport Charges*, Official Journal L070, 14 March, Brussels: EC.

—— (2012) 'MEPs to vote on "Better Airports" Package', press release, 6 December. Online. Available HTTP <http://europa.eu/rapid/press-release_MEMO–12–947_en.htm> (accessed 15 December 2012).

Forsyth, P (2008) 'Airport policy in Australia and New Zealand: privatisation, light-handed regulation and performance', in Winston, C. and de Rus, G. (eds), *Aviation Infrastructure Performance*, Washington, DC: Brookings Institution Press.

GAO (2012) *Slot Controlled Airports: FAA's Rules Could be Improved to Enhance Competition and Use of Available Capacity*, GAO–12–902, Washington, DC: General Accounting Office.

Graham, A. (2004) 'The regulation of US airports', in Forsyth, P., Gillen, D., Knorr, A., Mayer, O., Niemeier, H. and Starkie, D. (eds), *The Economic Regulation of Airports*, Farnham: Ashgate.

—— (2008) 'Airport planning and regulation in the UK', in Winston, C. and de Rus, G. (eds), *Aviation Infrastructure Performance*, Washington, DC: Brookings Institution Press.

—— (2013) 'Understanding the low cost carrier and airport relationship: a critical analysis of the salient issues', *Tourism Management*, 36: 66–76.

IATA (2012) *Worldwide Slot Guidelines: Effective August 2012*, Montreal: International Air Transport Association.

ICAO (2012) *ICAO's Policies on Charges for Airports and Air Navigation Services*, Doc 9082, 9th edn, Montreal: International Civil Aviation Organization.

Kilian, M. (2008) 'The development of the regulatory reform of slot allocation in the EU', in Czerny, A., Forsyth, P., Gillen, D. and Neimeier, H.-M. (eds), *Airport Slots: International Experiences and Options for Reform*, Farnham: Ashgate.

LeighFisher (2012) *Review of Airport Charges 2011*, London: LeighFisher.

Littlechild, S. (2012) 'Australian airport regulation: exploring the frontier', *Journal of Air Transport Management*, 21: 50–62.

Lu, C.-C. and Pagliari, R. (2004) 'Evaluating the potential impact if alternative airport pricing approaches on social welfare', *Transportation Research Part E*, 40(2): 1–17.

Mackenzie-Williams, P. (2004) 'A shift towards regulation – the case of New Zealand', in Forsyth P., Gillen D., Knorr A., Mayer, O., Niemeier H. and Starkie D. (eds), *The Economic Regulation of Airports*, Farnham: Ashgate.

Marques, R. and Brochado, A. (2008) 'Airport regulation in Europe: is there need for a European Observatory?', *Transport Policy*, 15(3): 163–72.

Monopolies and Mergers Commission (1996) *A Report on the Economic Regulation of the London Airport Companies*, London: MMC.

Mott MacDonald (2006) *Study of the Impact of the Introduction of Secondary Trading at Community Airports*, Croydon: Mott MacDonald.

NERA Economic Consulting (2004) *Study to Assess the Effects of Different Slot Allocation Schemes*, Brussels: NERA.

Niemeier, H.-M. (2010) 'Regulation of large airports: status quo and options for reform', International Transport Forum, *Airport Regulation Investment and Development of Aviation*, Paris: International Transport Forum.

Office of Fair Trading/CAA (2005) *Competition Issues Associated with the Trading of Airport Slots*, London: The Stationery Office.

Reinhold, A., Niemeier, H.-M., Kamp, V. and Mueller, J. (2009) 'An evaluation of yardstick regulation for European airports', *Journal of Air Transport Management*, 16(2): 74–80.

Riconda & Associates, Anderson & Kreiger LLP and R.W. Block Consulting (2010) *ACRP Report 36 Airport/Airline Agreements – Practices and Characteristics*, Washington, DC: Transportation Research Board.

Schuster, D. (2008) 'Australia's approach to airport charges: the Sydney Airport experience', *Journal of Air Transport Management*, 15(3): 121–26.

SH&E (2002) *Study on the Quality and Efficiency of Ground Handling Services at EU Airports as a Result of the Implementation of Council Directive 96/67/EC*, London: SH&E.

—— (2006) *Capital Needs and Regulatory Oversight Arrangement: A Survey of European Airports*, London: SH&E.

Sorensen, F. (2008) 'The slot allocation philosophy at the EU', in Czerny, A., Forsyth, P., Gillen, D. and Neimeier, H.-M. (eds), *Airport Slots: International Experiences and Options for Reform*, Farnham: Ashgate.

Starkie, D. (1998) 'Allocating airport slots: a role for the market?', *Journal of Air Transport Management*, 4(2): 111–16.

—— (2008) *Aviation Markets*, Farnham: Ashgate.

—— (2012) 'European airports and airlines: evolving relationships and the regulatory implications', *Journal of Air Transport Management*, 21: 40–49.

Steer Davies Gleave (2010) *Possible Revision of Directive 96/67/EC on Access to the Ground Handling Market at Community airports*, London: SDG.

—— (2011) *Impact Assessment of Revisions to Regulation {95/93}*, London: SDG.

Toms, M. (2004) 'UK Regulation from the perspective of the BAA', in Forsyth, P., Gillen, D., Knorr, A., Mayer, O., Niemeier, H. and Starkie, D. (eds), *The Economic Regulation of Airports*, Farnham: Ashgate.

5 Airport operations

This chapter considers the wide range of services and facilities that airports offer in order to meet the demands of their passengers, airlines and other users. Greater competition within the airline industry combined with the more commercially focused airport industry has meant that many airport operators have abandoned their one-size-fits-all approach and instead are differentiating their offer to meet the varying requirements of their diverse users. In addition there have been some major developments in the ways some key processes at airports are provided. This has been partly due to legal and regulatory changes, particularly in the area of security and border control, as the industry has had to adjust to new risks and threats to the business. It has also been a result of technological innovations that have been applied to security and border control and to other areas, most notably check-in. All of this is having major impacts on airport operations and management in areas including space allocation, efficiency and the mix of aeronautical and non-aeronautical revenues. These issues are considered in this chapter; the effects on service quality and the passenger experience are discussed in Chapter 6.

DIFFERENTIATION OF SERVICES AND FACILITIES

Airport operators bring together a wide range of services and facilities to fulfil their role within the air transport industry. Many of these are related to either the airfield or the terminal, with ground-handling facilities providing the link for passengers, their baggage and cargo between the airfield and terminals. There are also a growing number of commercial facilities, including hotels, conference services, entertainment amenities and business parks, that are located outside the terminal. Also, the facilitation of ground transport to and from the airport, including the parking infrastructure, approach roads and surface access links (e.g. direct rail, supply of taxis), takes place beyond the boundaries of the terminal.

There are many different aspects to consider when the physical airfield infrastructure and its technical capabilities are being assessed. This includes the number of runways, their length and configuration; air traffic control services; instrument landing, lighting and weather monitoring systems; ramp and apron space allocation, stand and gate provision; and fire, rescue and policing/security services. The main areas in the airfield (runways, apron, gates) will each have an overall capacity associated with them, and the airfield infrastructure will determine what type of airline is able to use the airport. If airlines then choose to invest in new aircraft types, for example the

500-plus passenger Airbus A380 aircraft, the airport operator may have to make changes to the airfield including reinforcing pavements, extending runway and taxiway widths and enlarging airbridges. Alternatively, it may have to lengthen the runway to accommodate longer-range aircraft. In addition to these physical features of the airfield, slot allocation is clearly important here, but (as explained in Chapter 4) this is not under the direct control of the airport operator.

With the terminal, just as with the airfield area, there is a need for basic decisions relating to the overall design and layout. For example, choices need to be made between linear or curvilinear terminals and piers, as opposed to remote satellites, as well as determining the number of floor levels that will be used. Appropriate levels of service standards related, for instance, to space requirements, queuing and waiting need to be used (see Chapter 6). If airports deal with transfer traffic, they will need the sophisticated and costly passenger and handling systems required for this type of throughput. Likewise, if the airport is handling connecting cargo traffic, it will need to have efficient transhipment facilities. The terminal will contain the services related to the essential processes of security, customs and immigration as well as having commercial or non-aeronautical facilities related to the traditional offer of retail and F&B, and also perhaps newer areas including entertainment, leisure and beauty. Increasingly providing internet facilities, either through wi-fi for laptops or through internet kiosks or workstations, is also becoming the norm.

Historically, most airports offered a fairly common set of services and facilities in trying to serve their airlines, passengers and other users, regardless of the specific needs of the different market segments within these customer groups. Very little segmentation took place at the airports, with product differentiation being limited to separate check-in for economy and business-class passengers, and remote stands rather than airbridges for passengers travelling on charter airlines. This level of segmentation was then increased, with businesses travellers having access to 'fast-track' systems that guide them swiftly through various processes including immigration and customs. At the same time, airline lounges for premium class and frequent flyer passengers became more popular. In spite of these developments, the overall focus was still predominantly on a one-size-fits-all airport for all airport users. However, in recent years stronger competitive forces have led airports to pay far greater attention to differentiating their services and facilities in order to meet the requirements and expectations of different market segments. At the same time, the range of different airline models has become more varied (e.g. alliance member, LCC, cargo specialist).

The needs and requirements of airline alliance customers are different as they want to be able to share and achieve cost economies and brand benefits from operating joint facilities at airports. They want to share check-in and office facilities and have common lounges for all alliance members. Also, where possible they want to have adjacent stand parking with alliance partners to allow for ramp transfers. However, all this may be difficult to achieve because many airports in operation today were built with airlines grouped together according to their type of traffic, most commonly domestic, short-haul and long-haul. While new terminals can be built with these different demands in mind, there is always the potential problem that alliance membership may change. An example here is Manchester airport and the Global Excellence Alliance, which no longer exists. In 1996 the members of the alliance, Swissair, Singapore Airlines and Delta Airlines, were all accommodated in T2. However, now Singapore Alliances, a member of Star, is in T2 – as is Delta, a member of Skyteam. Swiss, also a member of Star, is now in T1. When an airport has to be redesigned to cope with alliance wishes, it can also be particularly challenging to ensure no single alliance group is disadvantaged. A notable case here is Heathrow airport after the opening of terminal 5. Oneworld airlines are based in terminals 3 and 5, and now the airport is redeveloping terminal 2 to provide equivalent facilities for members of the Star alliance. Skyteam members are handled in terminal 4.

To compete effectively as a hub for transfer traffic, as is the situation with airports serving alliance airlines, and others too such as Dubai, the airports need to have an attractive minimum connect time (MCT). This is the minimum interval that must elapse between a scheduled arrival and a scheduled departure for two services to be bookable as a connection. Some airports have one MCT that applies to all services, while in other cases a range of different MCTs may be in operation depending on the airline, terminal, type of passenger and route. For example, at Vienna, Frankfurt and Singapore the MCT for all routes is 30, 45 and 60 minutes, respectively, while at Delhi it is 90 minutes for domestic services and 180 minutes for domestic–international services. At Shanghai airport the MCT value for domestic to domestic traffic is 10 minutes.

Terminal design is important when considering MCTs with multiple terminals that are set some distance apart, not being well suited to connecting traffic. Also, segregating international and domestic traffic, although efficient because of the different processes involved, hinders the speed of domestic–international transfers. In recent years a number of airports have been seeking to improve their transfer product. An analysis of the 18 largest European hubs found that on average transfer times were 10 minutes shorter in 2011 than in 2002 (Copenhagen Economics, 2012). Copenhagen airport was cited as an example of an airport that had sought to improve the quality of its transfer product by entering into a strategic partnership with its main network carrier, SAS, in 2010 with the launch of its World Class Transfer Hub initiative. A major part of this involved reducing its MCT from 40 to 30 minutes, which enabled transfers on 70 extra daily SAS flights. Screens with dedicated transfer information were introduced that showed not only the gate information, but also the walking time needed to get to the gate. In addition a special baggage process was introduced for passengers who had short connections. The result of these various measures was that travelling time on routes via Copenhagen was reduced significantly, for example on Hannover–Helsinki from 5:50 to 3:15, on Hannover–Gothenburg from 5:30 to 2:20 and from Wergen–Bergen from 5:20 to 3:20.

Some airports now pay particular attention to premium traffic when delivering their services and facilities that goes far beyond just check-in differentiation and the provision of the airline lounge. Typically this will involve the provision of dedicated security (and maybe immigration and customs) processes or fast-track lanes for such passengers. They may even guarantee this service, for example again as at Copenhagen airport, where the fast-track system CPH Express guarantees that 99 per cent of passengers will get through the security process in less than 5 minutes. In some regions, for instance the Middle East, it is common to have a completely separate area for check-in, security, immigration and other processes for premium passengers. A relevant case is Bahrain airport, which has designed its premium check-in lounge to be more like a hotel-style foyer, with armchair seating and sofas that eliminate any requirement to stand and queue. There is also the option of providing a whole dedicated terminal for premium traffic, such as the one at Doha International airport opened in 2006. Another example is Frankfurt airport, which in

2004 became one of the first airports to provide such a terminal (in collaboration with Lufthansa) that, as well as providing dedicated processes, also offers a valet service; personal assistants, upper-range catering, and bathroom, sleeping, entertainment and business facilities (Sobie, 2007).

Sometimes the whole airport may be designed with the premium passenger in mind, including airports that are heavily dependent on private jet facilities. London City airport, situated near the business and financial centre of London, is an interesting case of a larger airport being designed to appeal to airlines that serve premium passengers (as well as providing private jet facilities). Overall in 2010, 64 per cent of passengers travelled for business purposes and 65 per cent of business travellers were male. Only 17 per cent were aged under 35 years, and the average income of passengers was high at £105,000. Twenty per cent took trips lasting less than 24 hours, and a further 23 per cent took trips of 1–2 days (CAA, 2011). This market segment is therefore money-rich but time-poor. British Airways uses the airport for its specialist business-only flights to New York. The airport aims to keep process times to a minimum, with a 10-minute check-in policy and a goal of 5 minutes from plane to taxi on arrival. There is fast surface access provided with a chauffeur service or alternatively with a car-parking scheme that allows for unlimited parking and access to the short-stay car park for 12 months. There is also the equivalent of a hotel doorman at the entrance. The commercial facilities are designed with business travellers in mind, and include shoeshine, upmarket fast food, and retail outlets offering merchandise including shirts, ties and business books.

Elsewhere, airport operators have recognised that there may be passengers who are not travelling business or first class, but who would welcome the opportunity to pay extra for some of the service enhancements that premium passengers experience. For example, it is possible to pay for the use of a lounge, as at Kuala Lumpur airport where there is a Plaza Premium Lounge with facilities including high-speed workstations and showers, which can be used for 3-, 6- and 12-hour periods. At other airports there may be specialist lounges for babies and children, such as the Babycare Lounge at Amsterdam airport which has seven semi-transparent cubicles, each with a little bed where the baby can sleep, seating for the rest of the family, and baby baths, baby changing tables, play areas and microwaves. Elsewhere, for instance at the UK regional airports of Manchester, Newcastle, London Luton and Bristol, passengers can pay around €4 to go through a fast-track security queue. At a few airports where passengers choose to self-connect (and thus have no specific airline help), a supporting service may be provided by the airport operator. This occurs at Dublin airport, which offers a €35 Genie Connect service providing an escort to accompany the passenger through all the processes together with access to the fast-track boarding pass channel. This development in paying extra for additional services and facilities is somewhat similar to the trend observed in the airline industry where the product has been unbundled, with passengers having the option to pay for additional services they may want.

Some airports have gone one stage further, offering their regular passengers a chance to pay for privileges or enhanced comfort, including access to lounges and fast-track or priority processes on an annual basis. In particular there are VIP clubs aimed at a limited number of passengers who want special treatment, including help through the airport or access to lounges. Membership fees for these typically vary between US$6,500 and $10,500, and membership numbers are quite low.

Then there are frequent flyer programmes aimed at passengers who require speediness through airport processes, which are cheaper (ranging from US$250 to $1,700) and tend to have more members. A study of 110 global airports found that 10 per cent of airports offered such services, with 70 per cent having several different membership levels (ACI/DMKA, 2012). Examples include Riga International airport which has a RIX Club card that gives access to the business class facilities at the airport for an annual cost of LVL 129 (approximately €185). Likewise, Lyon-Saint Exupéry airport has its Privilys card which provides parking, fast-track and other services, and has three different types: pass (€60 per year), silver (€120 per year) and gold (prices vary). Other airports offering such services include Vienna, Beijing, Nanjing, Milan and Istanbul.

There have also been considerable developments regarding the unbundling of services and product differentiation for LCC operations. This is because LCCs tend to have very different needs from the network carriers to ensure they have quick turnaround times, can raise productivity and can cut down costs. Their focus on point-to-point services means that more complex transfer passenger and baggage handling systems can be avoided (Table 5.1). In general they will tend to require lower-capacity arrivals and departures baggage systems as they discourage checked-in bags, and fewer check-in desks as they tend to focus on online check-in. These different preferences relate solely to the terminal and ramp operations, as in terms of airfield operations the requirements have to be the same for all types of airline to conform with international operational and safety standards and regulations.

For small regional or secondary airports serving urban areas, the arrival of LCCs has often been useful to fill up under-utilised existing infrastructure; at the same time the airlines have benefited from uncongested facilities that help them achieve their fast turnarounds. However, such a strategy may run into problems if demand grows to such a level that new facilities are needed and the airline charges (which will often be reduced initially to encourage LCC use) and the non-aeronautical revenues will not be sufficient to support funding for further investment.

Table 5.1 LCC needs and requirements of airport terminals

Service/facility	LCC needs and requirements
Overall terminal design	Simple, functional with low construction/operating costs
Check-in and baggage facilities	Lower capacity due to online check-in and fewer checked-in bags
Airline lounges	Not needed
Security	Efficient processes so they do not delay aircraft boarding
Transfer facilities	Not needed (no transfer desks or handling systems for baggage transfer)
Airbridges	Preference for steps for quicker boarding and disembarking (with front and back steps)
Airfield buses	Preference for passengers to walk to/from aircraft if possible to save costs
Office accommodation	Simple and functional

Nevertheless, there are many examples of regional airports that have decided to focus purely on serving the LCC market and have subsequently developed the simplified facilities that these airlines require. In some cases, old disused military airports have been developed primarily to serve this LCC sector. This has been the case of London Manston airport (although currently unused by LCCs), Robin Hood Doncaster airport in the UK, Bergamo-Orio al Serio airport in Italy and Uppsala airport in Sweden. Frankfurt-Hahn, a former US airbase, is another example where initially the passenger terminal was a converted officers' club. Ryanair began services from the airport in 1999 and then in 2002 it set up a base there (Schumacher, 2007). However, the volatile nature of the LCC industry has also meant that a considerable number of regional airports have subsequently found themselves fighting for survival when the LCC has left or gone bankrupt, as has been the case of Clermont-Ferrand in France, Malmö in Sweden, Manston and a number of other airports.

When an airport serves both full service and LCCs, it is a difficult task to meet the different and often conflicting needs of these two types of airline. One option is to develop a specialised low-cost terminal (LCT) or pier facility. These have a simple design, with lower service standards than expected in conventional terminals. Limited connectivity to other terminals is required and the focus is on functionality not luxury. Certain costs, for example those associated with the runway, navigational equipment and fire/rescue, will be no different for airlines using the LCTs and so landing charges tend to be the same for all. However, within the terminal the simpler design and lack of sophisticated equipment and facilities, including airbridges, escalators, complex baggage systems and airline lounges, usually results in the airlines that use the terminal being charged a lower passenger charge.

Table 5.2 gives details of some of the LCT and pier facilities now in existence. Some of the LCTs are refurbished existing facilities, including cargo or charter terminals or maintenance buildings, and some are dedicated new terminals. The refurbishment options are particularly popular in Europe and have the advantage of minimising investment costs. Njoya and Niemeier (2011) discussed that a reduction of operating costs in the region of 30–40 per cent can be achieved with these LCTs, with some construction costs being only a quarter of the normal price.

Finavia, the governing body of the Finnish airports, was one of the first organisations to open an LCT at the small airport of Tampere-Pirkkala airport in 2003, and there is now also one at Turku. Marseilles has had a separate LCT (MP2) which has been operational since 2006 and was converted from an old cargo facility at a cost of €16.4 million. Ryanair was the first airline to use MP2 when it established it as its first base in France. Elsewhere in Europe, Budapest developed an LCC terminal at the cost of around €35 million, initially to accommodate Wizz Air and Sky Europe. In Lyon in France, providing an LCT involved refurbishing an existing charter facility at a cost of €1.2 million (Falconer, 2006). A different type of facility is Pier H&M (H for non-Schengen traffic, M for Schengen traffic) at Amsterdam airport. This was built at a cost of around €30 million, has a simple design with no airbridges, and functions with a 20-minute turnaround. The passengers use the normal departure lounge with all the commercial facilities before proceeding to the pier. Similarly, at Copenhagen airport a new low-cost pier facility called CPH Go opened in 2010.

In the USA, Southwest has low-cost facilities at Baltimore-Washington; and at JFK airport in New York, the airport owners (the Port Authority of New York and New Jersey) invested in a

Table 5.2 Examples of LCC facilities and terminals

Airport	Date of opening	Type of terminal	Passenger capacity	Gross area (m²)	Airport charges policy
Tampere-Pirkkala	2003	Refurbished cargo terminal	n/a	n/a	Reduced bundled passenger and ground handling charge
Warsaw	2004	Converted supermarket	n/a	3,414	Closed in 2009
Budapest	2005	Refurbished old terminal	n/a	7,990	Cheaper passenger charges
Amsterdam	2005	New piers off existing terminal	4	6,150	Cheaper landing charge for no airbridges
Marseille	2006	Refurbished cargo terminal	3.5	7,532	Cheaper passenger charges
Kuala Lumpur	2006	New terminal	10	35,290	Cheaper passenger charges
Singapore	2006	New terminal	2.7	25,000	Cheaper passenger charges
Bremen	2007	Refurbished warehouse	n/a	3,200	n/a
JFK	2008	New terminal incorporating old TWA terminal	15	58,000	No difference
Lyon	2008	Refurbished cargo terminal	1.8	n/a	Cheaper passenger charges
Zhengzhou	2008	Refurbished international terminal	n/a	3,800	n/a
Xiamen	2008	Refurbished cargo terminal (short run) refurbished old passenger terminal (long run)	2–3 (short run) 5–8 (long run)	n/a	n/a
Copenhagen	2010	New pier off existing terminal	6	6,700	Cheaper passenger charges
Bordeaux	2010	New terminal	1.5	4,000	Cheaper passenger charges

Sources: Jacobs Consultancy (2007), Njoya and Niemeier (2011), Zhang et al. (2008) and airport websites

new LCT for JetBlue which incorporated Eero Saarinen's iconic 1962 TWA terminal and has an annual capacity of 20 million passengers. JetBlue covers this investment with lease payments for 30 years (Studness, 2007). In Mexico at Monterrey airport, terminal C is an LCC terminal. Outside Europe, and particularly in the Asia-Pacific region, there is more of a scarcity of secondary or regional airports that can be used for the implementation of the LCC business model, with a few notable exceptions including Avalon airport serving the Melbourne area in Australia. Hence airports have also looked to LCTs, including in Zhengzhou and Xiamen in China. There have also been also two major LCTs in South East Asia: Singapore Changi airport (the budget terminal) and Kuala Lumpur airport (the low cost carrier terminal, LCCT), which both opened in 2006. At each airport the passenger charges for the LCT were lower, and the rental charges at Singapore were also claimed to be half those in the main terminal. Both facilities were expanded, notably the budget terminal which increased its capacity from 2.7 million to 7 million passengers in 2009. However, in 2012 Singapore airport announced that it would demolish its budget terminal to make way for a larger passenger building with a capacity of 16 million (terminal 4), due to open in 2017. This will be designed for quick turnarounds with no airbridges, but will have a much wider range of retail and F&B. It will also accommodate wide-bodied aircraft which was not possible with its budget terminal. There is also a new low-cost facility being built at Kuala Lumpur.

While these LCTs have generally been welcomed by the LCCs, the same has not always been true of the full service airlines or network carriers. The latter often argue that these terminals discriminate against carriers who operate in the main terminals, and that airports must ensure all airlines have access to the new terminals. This does assume that all airlines would want to move to the new terminal, a debatable point given the lower service standards they offer. Also, some airlines maintain that airports should be focusing on the reduction of costs for all its airline customers and there should not be differential pricing. Furthermore, it is argued that if there has to be differential pricing, it must be clearly justified by demonstrating the differential costs that exist so that the network carriers do not end up subsidising the LCCs (IATA, 2007). This is particularly relevant as there will be some costs for processes, such as security, that will be difficult to reduce in the LCTs.

Differential pricing and cross-subsidisation concerns have meant that the network carriers have made a number of legal challenges as regards the LCTs. For example, at Geneva airport, where easyJet is a major airline, there were plans to convert an old terminal into an LCT, but Air France–KLM and other airlines objected, claiming that the lower passenger charge would give the LCCs a competitive advantage. The Swiss Federal Court rejected this argument, but nevertheless Geneva abandoned its LCT development. In France, since 2005 the French airport economic framework has allowed airports to have differentiated airport charges between different terminals, which has in turn encouraged the use of LCTs in the country (as is demonstrated by Table 5.2). However, this has not been without problems – for example it led to the 2006/07 passenger charges at the LCT at Marseilles being declared void because of accounting inconsistencies. Nevertheless, the framework was an important development as it paved the way for a similar approach within the EU Charges Directive that was agreed in 2007 (Tatibouet and Doumas, 2008) (see Chapter 4). This permits differential pricing for different facilities as long as these are based on 'transparent', 'objective' and 'clear' criteria (EC, 2009). This can be particularly complex when the airport is run on a single-till basis. Likewise, ICAO (2012, II–2) states that:

States should assess, on a case-by-case basis and according to local or national circumstances, the positive and negative effects of differential charges applied by airports. States should ensure the purpose, creation and criteria for differential charges are transparent. Without prejudice to modulated charging schemes, the costs associated with such differential charges should not be allocated to users not benefiting from them.

LCTs have remained controversial, a notable example being Brussels airport's development of such a facility, which has never actually opened because of fierce of opposition and legal challenges from the other carriers serving the airports. Arguably, LCTs may be an effective and cost-efficient way of coping with increasing demand at airports, if the current terminal capacity is already well utilised. However, if there is still spare capacity in the main terminal, the more favourable option must be to try to persuade the airlines to use this terminal. Providing another terminal means that essential processes, including check-in, security and immigration, need to be duplicated. The worst-case scenario would be when a significant amount of traffic just shifts from the old terminal to the new terminal (perhaps causing congestion and capacity problems), leaving the original terminal under-utilised. This will be at a time when overall costs have increased because of the additional investment and when aeronautical revenues have dropped with reduced charges for the new terminal. Differential pricing principles based on costs may not allow the charges in the main terminal to be reduced to attract traffic back to the original terminal in this situation.

There is also a more general issue related to non-aeronautical revenues at both secondary airports and LCTs. Although the LCTs have commercial facilities, the revenue from these may be lower than would have been achieved in the main terminal because of a more limited retail offer and because the basic terminal may not create the right atmosphere and experience to encourage travellers to shop (Saraswati and Hanaoka, 2012). This is one reason why the budget terminal at Singapore is being demolished and a new terminal is being built. The budget terminal only had limited and basic commercial facilities, including F&B outlets, convenience stores and a few duty-free retailers. Similarly, the new Kuala Lumpur LCT will have a more extensive range of commercial facilities. However, all this will increase the costs associated with such terminals. Hence the key challenge for airport operators in providing such differentiation is in balancing the needs of the different airlines and minimising any tension between these users, while at the same time encouraging the use of commercial facilities to offset the lower charges, and also striving to maintain high passenger satisfaction levels even with the lower service levels. The trade-off between low costs for the LCCs, maximising commercial revenues and satisfying all customers – both passengers and airlines – is a major consideration for all airports serving LCCs (Graham, 2013).

In Europe, the popularity of LCTs seems to be declining as the LCC industry becomes more mature, with the few actual proposals for new LCTs at airports in Tallinn and in Portugal now unlikely to be adopted. However, LCTs continue to be popular in Asia (Zhang *et al.*, 2008). For example, in Japan the recent development of the LCC sector, with airlines including Peach, AirAsia Japan and Jetstar Japan, has encouraged the opening of a new LCT in Kansai airport in 2012. In addition, in 2015 an LCT will open at Narita airport which will be converted from an old cargo building. As regards airports solely for LCC use, there are plans to use Bangkok's old main airport (Don Mueang) as an international LCC airport, as it is currently limited to only domestic LCC flights and international charter flights. There has also been ongoing discussion as to whether Clark airport can be used as a secondary LCC airport for Manila.

CASE STUDY 5.1: A TALE OF TWO LOW-COST FACILITIES

Kuala Lumpur

Kuala Lumpur airport is owned by Malaysia Airports Holdings Berhad. This company operates five international airports, 16 domestic airports and 18 rural airports. It was listed on the Kuala Lumpur stock exchange in 1999. Kuala Lumpur airport opened in 1998, and since then passenger numbers have grown from 13 million to 38 million. The low-cost carrier terminal (so-called LCCT) was designed for Air Asia, whose total traffic for all operations increased rapidly from just 611,000 passengers in 2002–03 to over 5 million in 2006–07. The LCCT originally had a total area of 35,290 m² and a capacity of 10 million passengers. The construction work was fast-tracked and the terminal opened on 23 March 2006, costing in total RM106 million (€23 million). It was on a single floor and had a very simple design, with no airbridges, travellators or escalators, and a basic baggage handling system. A limited number of commercial facilities were also provided. There were no transfer facilities, so if passengers needed to change flights with other carriers they had to travel the 20 km by road to the main terminal. As with other LCTs, the airlines paid the same landing charge but a reduced international passenger charge: RM35 (€7.61) compared with RM51 (€11.09). For a typical operation with an Airbus 319 or Boeing 737–800, this meant total charges paid for operating out of LCCT were about 70 per cent of those for the main terminal.

By 2008, the LCCT was congested and so the terminal was expanded to have a capacity of 15 million. However, because the demand continued to increase and due to the poor location of the terminal, it was decided to replace the LCCT (which had actually only been intended as a temporary solution for accommodating LCC traffic). This new terminal, named KLIA2, will have a capacity of 45 million passengers and is located next to the main terminal building to allow connectivity between the LCCs and other airlines. It will cover an area of 257,000 m² with 60 gates, eight remote stands and 80 airbridges, with a 32,000 m² area to accommodate 225 retail outlets. The terminal will serve Air Asia, many of its subsidiaries, and its sister long-haul carrier Air Asia X as well as up to 10 other LCCs including Cebu Pacific, Lion Air, Tiger Airways and Zest Air. Overall in 2012, in terms of airline capacity offered at the whole airport, LCCs accounted for 48.7 per cent of the total traffic, full service airlines 50.9 per cent and regional/commuters just 0.4 per cent. There have been a number of delays with the KLIA2 and costs have increased, but it is now planned that it will open in April 2013 at a cost of US$1.3 billion (CAPA Centre for Aviation, 2012).

Copenhagen

KLIA2 is on a very much larger scale than the European LCC facilities, with Copenhagen being a prime example where the new facilities cost just $33.6 million.

Copenhagen airport is owned and operated by a public–private company, with the Danish state having a 39 per cent shareholding.

In recent years the airport has started to differentiate its product to meet the needs of its different airline users. This began with a strategic collaboration with its largest network carrier, SAS, which was designed to strengthen its transfer product. Then, due to increased demand from the LCCs, it was decided that a dedicated low-cost pier for these carriers should be built. This facility, called CPH Go, was opened in October 2010. Unlike a separate LCT, it is an integral part of the existing terminal (as at Amsterdam airport) with passengers having access to the same services and facilities. It has six aircraft stands, covers an area of 6,700 m^2 and has an initial capacity of 6 million passengers that can be doubled if needed. Thirteen months after its opening, the number of passengers passing through CPH Go reached 1 million.

The passenger charges are 35 per cent lower than those for the existing facilities, but some airlines, notably Ryanair, still claim that the facility is too expensive and do not use it. In order to maintain the efficiency of the facility, airlines using it were required to meet certain conditions, including a maximum turnaround time of 30 minutes, and 90 per cent passengers checking in online, via mobile phone or at the self-service kiosks. The airlines also had to accept that the check-in area was CPH Go-branded, with no individual airline brands, to achieve better utilisation of the desks (Akerman, 2010). Originally there was also no possibility for transfer traffic, but in December 2011 the Danish Competition Council ruled that this was contrary to competition law and ordered the airport to allow such traffic (and also to handle more types of aircraft) in response to complaints by several airlines.

LCTs are just one example of how airports are becoming increasingly diverse in what they offer their users. Table 5.3 identifies a number of other business models that airports are adopting. A few airports are concentrating on offering connecting facilities for specialist cargo operators and integrators. Examples include Leipzig/Halle airport, East Midlands airport, Paris Vatry and Liege airport. In addition to having reliable and secure connecting processes, they also have other appealing features including good connections to motorways and no night curfews. Another alternative is to develop the airport as an airport city or aerotropolis serving the needs of passengers, and also of local businesses and residents – concepts discussed in Chapter 9. There is also the situation where airports can differentiate themselves by offering pre-clearance with some of the essential services. This is typically the case with flights to the USA, where passengers go through US customs, immigration and agriculture inspections at their originating airport and as a result are treated as domestic passenger when they arrive, allowing a quicker process through the US airport. Such services are offered at Dublin and Shannon in Ireland, a number of Canadian airports, and a few other locations including Bermuda, the Bahamas and Aruba.

Table 5.3 *Examples of different airport business models*

Author	Model
Boston Consulting Group (2004)	Primary hubs, an international origin and destination (O&D) airport, a secondary hubs and O&D airport, and a regional airport
Mercer Management Consulting (2005)	Primary hubs, secondary hubs, major O&Ds, low-cost base and leisure destination airports
Jarach (2005)	Primary hub, secondary hub, regional airports, lowcost airports, cargo airports
Feldman (2009)	Alliance anchor hub, airport city, multi-modal port, airport as final destination, home fortress with satellite, niche player, 'do what others can't', perpetual construction site, offsite/virtual airport
ACI Europe (2010)	Airport network, alliance anchor hub, airport city, multi-modal port, airport as final destination, business traffic, low-cost base, freight platform

In their analysis of airport models, Boston Consulting Group (2004) identified airports as being either a primary hub, an international origin and destination (O&D) airport, a secondary hub and O&D airport, or a regional airport, while Mercer Management Consulting (2005) classified airports as primary hubs, secondary hubs, major O&Ds, or low-cost base and leisure destination airports. Jarach (2005) identified five key market positioning strategies related to primary hubs, secondary hubs, regional airports, low-cost airports and cargo airports. However, he then argued that this is a simplification of the actual situation that exists in the airport industry and explained that there is much higher variance between the market positions. He subsequently listed 19 different types that include airports acting as a county's sole gateway, airports attracting overflow traffic, greenfield airports, airports integrated within a system, and airports operating within the same catchment area.

Feldman (2009) identified nine different types of airport and ACI Europe (2010) had a somewhat similar classification. Within these classifications there are some established models and some more emerging ones. Established alliance anchor hubs are airports where many airline alliance groups connect, including Paris CDG and Frankfurt in Europe, Dallas Fort Worth in the USA, and Singapore in Asia, while a multimodal port is an airport with strong intermodal connections, including Amsterdam. ACI Europe's airport network is the established model of a coordinated airport group as is found, for instance, in Spain, Sweden and Poland. Athens airport is an example of an airport as a final destination, since it has attracted giant warehouse-size retail centres because of its location that provides easy access and parking.

London City airport is defined as an emerging model, classified as a business traffic airport by ACI Europe and a niche player by Feldman. Other niche players (defined as freight platforms by ACI Europe) are the cargo airports of Liège. Feldman's other emerging models include 'do what others can't', which covers the express 24-hour cargo hub at Cologne/Bonn, business aviation at

Farnborough and Biggin Hill in London, and Helsinki with the fastest travel between Europe and Asia due to its strategic location and fast transfer times. Other models that he identified include the home fortress with satellites – giving the example of Manchester airport with its ownership of other smaller airports nearby – and the perpetual construction site, including London Heathrow. He also defined the emerging offsite or 'virtual' airport, where activities including check-in, shopping, and pre-ordering and purchasing of customised services, including parking and lounge access, take place outside the physical site of the airport. Examples include Volaris Airlines' virtual airport in Mexico City, serving Toluca airport, where passengers can complete check-in formalities in a city terminal in a shopping mall; and a similar situation with Etihad at Abu Dhabi airport, where passengers are connected to the actual airport with luxury coaches.

Within this context, Feldman also discussed how airports must embrace three crucial tenets – diversity, differentiation and innovation – needed to survive in today's airport world. In particular he gave examples of mid-sized connecting hubs (including Brussels, Pittsburgh and Milan Malpensa) that have had to rethink their business model. Diversification through the development of commercial facilities may be essential to overcome too great reliance on aeronautical revenues. It may also involve serving various market segments with different needs (e.g. Nice and Cannes airport with network carrier, LCC and business jet traffic) or for some airports, including Singapore Changi, getting involved in the management of other international airports to compensate for a small home market. Differentiation also links to creating a brand and sense of place within the airport, discussed further in Chapters 7 and 8. Another emerging area of differential potential is the airport environmental strategy, an example being Swedavia, the Swedish airport operator, which is the first airport company to become carbon-neutral.

Innovation at airports often involves the use of technology to speed up processes and improve the passenger experience, or the introduction of passenger loyalty schemes. Among a survey of airport companies in 2011 within Europe, Feldman (2011) found that Amsterdam, Copenhagen and Munich airports were considered the top innovators, whereas the airport companies Fraport, AdP and BAA were perceived to lag behind in this area. Indeed, Munich airport has a dedicated innovation team with an innovation budget.

SECURITY AND IMMIGRATION ISSUES

This chapter now focuses on some key processes that take place at airports. Developments within the airfield area are by nature rather technical (and beyond the focus of this book), so the emphasis here is on passenger facilities within the terminal.

Of prime importance are the number of activities at airports involved with the protection and wellbeing of passengers. In this context, airport security needs to be differentiated from airport safety. Airport security is concerned with preventing illegal activities, including terrorism, as opposed to airport safety, which is related to ensuring aircraft are safe, for example by not allowing dangerous goods on board and ensuring there are no hazards on the runway. Only airport security is considered here, as there have been very significant changes in that area in recent years. Table 5.4 summarises the main activities associated with airport security.

Table 5.4 *Main security activities at airports*

Badge regime
Reliability check on applicants for obtaining badge
Checks on access of staff to restricted areas
Checks on passengers and hand baggage
Baggage reconciliation
Checks on hold baggage
Checks on cargo/airmail
Armed protection landside
Armed protection airside
Protection on parked aircraft
Video supervision

Pre-9/11 common minimum standards for airport security were set by ICAO in the Chicago Convention Annex 17. In some parts of the world these were also incorporated into regional standards, as was the case with the European Civil Aviation Conference (ECAC) and its document 30. However, the problem with these standards was that there was no binding mechanism to ensure they were implemented properly, and consequently the level of security offered at airports throughout the world varied enormously. After the Lockerbie disaster of 1988 improved measures had been recommended, including 100 per cent hold baggage screening and baggage reconciliation, but as these were not mandatory requirements they were not adopted everywhere. The turning point for many countries came after 9/11, when much more binding legislation was introduced.

Impacts of 9/11

While security at airports has always been a very important aspect of operations, the events of 9/11 led to its coming under even closer scrutiny, with many additional security measures being introduced. Suddenly, particularly in the United States, airport security became a national concern and high-profile issue that received a considerable amount of media attention. Globally the most immediate affect was the adoption by ICAO in 2002 of an Aviation Security Plan of Action. For this 3-year programme it was agreed that regular and mandatory audits of member states would be conducted to identify and correct deficiencies in the implementation of ICAO security-related standards. In addition, new mandatory security standards were agreed, including locking flight deck doors, sharing information about potential security risks, and ensuring security measures were implemented in a non-discriminatory manner.

The most sweeping changes occurred in the United States, where traditionally security measures were relatively lax compared with many other airports. Congress quickly developed the Aviation and Transportation Security Act (ATSA), signed by President Bush on 19 November 2001. This set a number of important deadlines regarding security that had to be met by the end of 2002 and transferred direct responsibility for security to the federal government with the setting up of the Transportation Security Administration (TSA). Then in 2003, overall control was moved from the Department of Transportation to the Department of Homeland Security, which had been set up to coordinate all security measures in the USA. Previously security at airports had been undertaken by private security company staff who were often underpaid and poorly qualified; the Act provided for these to be replaced by a federal workforce of initially 28,000 properly trained staff (Bacon, 2002).

The new security policies received considerable criticism from the airline and airport industries in terms of the practicalities of introducing enhanced security measures, the feasibility of meeting the tight deadlines, and in relation to how the measures would be financed. One of the major areas of discontent was the deadline for all checked baggage to be screened by explosive detective systems (EDS) by the end of 2002. There were numerous complaints that the new security procedures and rules were inconveniencing passengers and that this significant 'hassle' factor was putting passengers off flying or encouraging them to travel by different modes of transport (Rossiter and Dresner, 2004).

Such fundamental changes to the country's airport security system were costly to implement. The security costs incurred by the airports rose from US$556 million in 2000 to $619 million in 2001, an increase of 11 per cent. They were estimated to have increased to $853 million, a massive 38 per cent rise, in 2002. The TSA authorised $1.5 billion for 2002 and 2003 to allow airports to meet FAA-mandated security expenses. A $2.50 per sector security fee was also introduced to cover some of the costs of the TSA (Ghobrial and Irvin, 2004). The Act gave airports the flexibility to use public money, obtained through passenger taxes, for airport investment (so-called Airport Improvement Program funds – see Chapter 4) to pay for any additional security-related activity required. In 2002 the FAA authorised $561 million of these funds to airports for security projects related to the events of 9/11 (GAO, 2002). Additionally a number of US airports had to redesign many of their commercial facilities in order to conform with the new security measures, which led to a decline in non-aeronautical revenues. For example, new restrictions on the movements of meeters and greeters limited their access to certain retail and F&B outlets, and a number of car parks had to close. In short, the establishment of the TSA has had far-reaching impacts on US airport costs, passenger travel habits and flow patterns through the terminal (Raffel and Ramsay, 2011).

Outside the United States, much attention was also paid to improving security methods at airports and numerous changes were made. ACI research undertaken shortly after 9/11 attempted to quantify the security costs directly attributable to the terrorist attacks and found, for example, that Paris CDG airport estimated this to be US$20 million, Munich airport provided a figure of $5.3 million, Nairobi $3.4 million and Tokyo Narita $2.6 million. In Europe, specifically post 9/11, there was general agreement that security measures should be harmonised throughout the region, and in 2003 Regulation 2320/2002 (based on the recommendations outlined in ECAC document 30) and various complementary implementing regulations came into force (EC, 2002). This covered common security rules and the appropriate compliance monitoring mechanisms. The measures included unannounced airport inspections by independent European Union inspectors, 100 per cent staff searches in restricted areas, improved staff background checks, and more stringent baggage screening methods including limiting personnel 'screen-time'. Each state had to have a national security programme in place (although in most countries these already existed as a result of Lockerbie). In 2008, new legislation (Regulation 300/2008) was approved within

Europe with the aim of clarifying, simplifying and further harmonising the existing rules of the 2320/2002 legislation (EC, 2008). This was thought necessary because it was generally agreed that the original legislation was produced under great political and time pressure in response to the 9/11 events, and could in hindsight have been more flexible and less heavy handed.

The liquids problem

Since 9/11 there have been a number of terrorist threats that have had an impact on airport security – for example the attempted shoe bomb incident in 2001 that led to the removal of shoes at passenger screening – but by far the most significant development has been the changes related to liquids, aerosols and gels (LAGs). This has happened since 10 August 2006, when the security level at all UK airports was raised to critical because of an alleged terrorist plot involving the detonation of liquid explosives carried onto as many as 10 transatlantic services in sports drinks bottles. At that time all hand baggage became prohibited and 100 per cent passenger searches were undertaken. This led to considerable flight delays and cancellations at UK airports. Then, as the security position changed over subsequent weeks, some of the restrictions and rules were relaxed. First, on 14 August, passengers were allowed a small bag (up to 45 cm long, 35 cm wide and 16 cm deep), laptops and electronic devices were permitted, but no LAGs were allowed, except those bought in the airside departure lounge. Then on 22 September internationally agreed hand baggage size (56 by 45 by 25 cm) was allowed again, but still no LAGs could be taken on board (the rules for US flights remained more restrictive).

While these developments were occurring in the UK, a number of other countries, particularly in Europe and North America, also placed restrictions on LAGs and hand baggage, but overall there was no consistent approach. However, by October 2006 the EC agreed Europe-wide rules (Regulation 1546–2006) that came into force at the beginning of November (EC, 2006). This allowed passengers to carry LAGs on board again as long as they were in containers no larger than 100 ml and in a clear plastic bag. Duty-free purchases could continue to be taken on board if they were in standard tamper-evident bags (STEBs), but only from an EU or European Economic Area (EEA) airport. Meanwhile ICAO, in consultation with the EU and US security authorities, started working towards a globally acceptable framework to harmonise all the restrictions on LAGs and agree standards on STEBs.

The most difficult area for any kind of global agreement is in persuading countries to recognise, and have confidence in, the security arrangements that take place elsewhere. If this could happen, then transfer passengers would be allowed to take their purchased goods in STEBs onto their next flight. This does not currently occur in the EU, which means that many unsuspecting transfer passengers have had their duty-free purchases confiscated (see Chapter 7). However, instead in July 2007 the EC introduced Regulation 915–2007 (EC, 2007) which gave unilateral recognition to non-EU countries that had implemented ICAO guidelines on LAGs restrictions, supply chain security and STEBs. Croatia, Malaysia, Singapore and the international airports of Canada and the USA were subsequently approved, which meant that transfer passengers from these countries did not have their liquid purchases over 100 ml confiscated.

These LAGs restrictions were envisaged as temporary, to be lifted when there was suitable technology to screen LAGs for explosives. As a result, a two-stage relaxation of the rules within the

EU was agreed in 2010. The deadline for phase 1 was set for 29 April 2012, when it would have been possible to screen passengers bringing LAG from non-European countries and transferring within a European airport. However, the US government had not agreed to this relaxation and stated that it would require extra screening on US-bound flights. Certain governments and airports within Europe, in countries including the UK, Netherlands and France, expressed their concerns that the LAGs screening technology to be introduced remained underdeveloped and untested operationally. Furthermore, airports in some countries stated that they would not enforce the new restrictions. All of this would have led to a patchy, confused and disruptive situation for passengers when the deadline was reached, so at the last minute the phase 1 policy was postponed. Subsequently, in July 2012 the April 2013 deadline for phase 2, for the screening of all LAGs and the total removal of the LAGs ban, was also postponed. It is now planned that the first phase will be implemented by January 2014, with the total ban lifted as soon as possible after that.

Passenger body scanners and cargo processes

On 25 December 2009 there was a failed attempt to bring down a Northwest Airlines transatlantic flight from Amsterdam to Detroit with a plastic bomb hidden in the underwear of a passenger, which had not been identified by the metal detectors at the airports. This demonstrated that airport security was facing new types of threat that could not be prevented totally with the current technologies employed at the airports. As a consequence there has been consideration as to whether body scanners that use imaging technology to detect both metallic and non-metallic items should be used more extensively at airports. The use of such equipment – which can be based on either X-ray backscatter or millimetre wave technology – has raised a number of concerns. First, the effectiveness of such scanners to image all hidden items on the human body is questioned, along with the high costs involved with this technology (well in excess of €100,000 per machine) and the resulting slowing down of processes. More controversial are the issues related to potential radiation dangers to passengers and airport workers, and privacy requirements of passengers.

A number of countries, including Russia, the USA, Canada, Australia, Japan, Nigeria, India, South Africa, Kenya, China and South Korea, now use scanners or are seriously considering using them. They are also used at some European airports. Largely as a result of the failed bomb attempt, there have been scanning tests at Helsinki, London Heathrow, Manchester and Amsterdam airports, and also in France and Italy. However, within Europe there were many different national operational standards and procedures. As a result, in November 2011 the European Commission adopted a legal framework on security scanners (EC, 2010a). This does not make it mandatory for airports to use body scanners, but if they wish to do so they must adhere to strict operational and technical conditions. To address health concerns, only non-ionising radiation scanners (not X-ray scanners) may be used. To protect passengers' privacy and human rights, the images cannot be stored, copied or printed, with only authorised access to these images being allowed. Passengers must be informed if they are to have a scan and have an option to opt out and be subject to an alternative method of screening. In spite of this framework there continues to be much debate within Europe and elsewhere concerning the benefits, risks and drawbacks related to body scanners. A number of passenger rights groups, for example in the USA and Germany, have been calling for the banning of such machines.

Table 5.5 Key events related to airport security since 9/11

Date	Event	Main impacts
September 2001	9/11 US terrorism attacks	Establishment of the US Transportation Security Administration (TSA) and more stringent security controls worldwide
December 2001	Shoe bomb attempt on a transatlantic service	Introduction of specific security measures to improve screening of shoes
August 2006	Terrorist plot to use liquid explosives on several transatlantic services	Restriction of liquids, aerosols and gels in hand baggage
December 2009	Underwear bomb attempt on a transatlantic service	Increased use of security scanners
October 2010	Two improvised explosives attempts in air cargo consignments bound for EU	Stricter controls on mail and cargo from third countries to the EU

Most of the recent security incidents that have resulted in airports acting in a predominantly reactive manner by introducing new layers of security regulations have been related to passenger activity. However, in October 2010 there was an attempt to hide two improvised explosive devises (home-made bombs) in printer cartridges on air cargo consignments bound for the EU. As a result, in August 2011 the EU adopted new tighter regulations, effective from February 2012, related to securing incoming air cargo and mail from non-EU countries. Table 5.5 summarises the main events related to airport security since 9/11.

Financing security

One of the major consequences of all these tighter security controls has been a sharp increase in the costs of security. This raises a controversial question concerning how the security should be funded. The airports and airlines normally argue that governments should pay, reasoning that as terrorist acts are targeted at states, it is the responsibility of states to finance countermeasures to protect the travelling public. They also argue that the inconsistent approach to funding security, particularly in Europe, distorts competition. For example, the airport operator designs the security measures at airports such as Athens and Helsinki, whereas this is done by the government in Amsterdam and Lisbon, and is shared between these two and the airlines in Munich. As regards the provision of security services, virtually all terminal protection is provided by the government through the police, while in many cases checks on passengers and luggage are under the control of the airport operators. However, for other security activities, including staff access checks/badge control, aircraft protection and cargo checks, a wide range of different organisations, including the airport operator, the airline, the police, or a subcontractor, may play a role (ACI Europe, 2003). The situation may well vary between airports in the same country. For example, in a sample of 21 main airports in the UK, 12 airport operators provided some or all passenger checks, 10 did the hold baggage checks and 16 the access control. Elsewhere these services were outsourced (LeighFisher, 2011).

A study by the Irish Aviation Authority/Aviasolutions (2004) described how European airports (the 15 EC states plus Switzerland, Norway and Iceland), while having a mix of different security providers, could be categorised overall into two basic models: a centralised model, where most of the main security activities are the responsibility of the state via a government body (including Civil Aviation Authority, Ministry of Transport or police force); and a decentralised model, where most of the activities are provided by the airport operator under the supervision of a relevant government body, including the CAA. In this case they may be provided directly or outsourced to a third party. At some airports where the security costs are borne by the government, they may be paid for by a security tax or funded out of general taxation. Elsewhere, where security is paid for by the airport operator this will be covered by normal airport charges or special security fees usually based on passenger numbers. Often there may be a combination of these different types of funding – but with both taxes and charges the passenger is ultimately the main financier of security.

Within Europe, security costs for the airports have increased from around 9 per cent of total operating costs pre-9/11 to 35 per cent now. Forty per cent of airport operator staff are related to security (ACI Europe, 2010). This has primarily been due to new security infrastructure and equipment together with the use of more security staff. As a result it has become more common to have separate security charges. However, there has been some concern about the transparency of such charges, whether they are cost-related and non-discriminatory and whether there is sufficient consultation with airport users. This led in Europe in 2009 to a proposal for a directive on aviation security charges to address these issues, but this has yet to be adopted. The airlines and airports often compare the situation in Europe, where in many cases the air transport industry and its customers bear the majority of the security costs, with the US case where less than half of the TSA funding comes from the passenger security tax. Stakeholders in other countries, for example Australia and New Zealand, have also put pressure on their governments to cover more of the increased security costs. Worldwide, ICAO's charging principles emphasise the need for consultation, cost-relatedness and non-discrimination with security charges (ICAO, 2012).

Risk-based processes

In recent years the security processes at the airports have proved to be one of the most difficult aspects of the passenger experience to improve. The security checks discussed above operate on the principle of using the same processes for all passengers – using the assumption that they all pose a similar security risk. Hence the security resources are evenly distributed across all passengers. As passenger numbers grow, managing such processes without intensifying the inconvenience for passengers will become increasingly challenging.

However, there is an alternative approach: passenger profiling, where passengers of higher risk are identified and then more of the resources and security attention are directed at them. At the same time, the processing of low-risk passengers can become speedier. As a consequence there has been considerable debate as to the merits and effectiveness of passenger profiling techniques and the extent to which they can improve the passenger's experience of security and reduce the perceived hassle factor. Experience with this risk-management approach is limited, the most widespread use being in Israel where it has been implemented for many years. There are many features of such an approach, including using technology in a more targeted manner and having a stronger intelligence focus by increasing the amount of passenger information that is shared between different relevant bodies and countries.

Passenger profiling can be undertaken in a number of ways. This can be done through interview techniques that allow the profiler to screen the passenger's personality, background and various details of their journey. It can also be undertaken through behaviour pattern techniques where the profiler will detect suspicious people by observing any irregular behaviour or unusual body language of the passengers. Then there is passenger profiling based on databases of passenger information, but this raises personal data protection issues. Overall, while passenger profiling has the potential to make screening more effective than using the same process for all passengers, it remains very controversial because of issues related to possible discriminatory treatment or violation of passenger privacy rights.

Passenger name records (PNRs) are data collected by airlines that can be used to identify passengers worthy of special attention. These records contain basic information on the passenger and their itinerary, as well as additional details concerning passenger frequent flyer membership, seat numbers and meal preferences. Since 9/11 a growing number of governments have requested this information from airlines in an effort to combat serious international and organised crime and terrorism. Countries including the United States, Canada, Australia, New Zealand and South Korea are already using PNR data. However, this raises important data protection issues and in the EU, for example, the airlines cannot legally provide PNR data until there is agreement on a clear data protection framework. This has meant that the exchange of PNRs has had to be considered on an individual country basis. Of major significance in this area in Europe was the EC publishing its global approach to the transfer of PNRs to third countries in 2010 (EC, 2010b). Subsequently an agreement was reached between the EU and Australia in 2011, and the EU, the USA (replacing the provisional deal agreed in 2007) and Canada in 2012. Agreements with other countries are being considered. At the same time, various European countries, including the UK, France, Denmark, Belgium, Sweden and the Netherlands, have either enacted legislation related to PNRs for passengers to and from the country, or are testing the processes. However, within the EU there is no harmonisation regarding the obligations of airlines to transmit PNR data. A directive has been proposed, but this has yet to be approved.

There is also advanced passenger information (API) which contains details including date of birth, nationality, gender and address in the destination country. This is more limited in scope and its primary purpose is to improve border control and irregular immigration. Since 2003 the USA (and Canada since 2006) have required this type of data to be sent in advance, which has been very controversial within Europe, again because of privacy and data protection concerns. Many other countries, including Australia, New Zealand, Mexico, Korea and China, also require API data.

Biometric identification and registered passenger schemes

Recent advances in technology have meant that biometric identification can be used in essential processes including security and immigration. Biometric identification involves using unique physical characteristics to ensure a passenger or member of staff is known and is allowed to proceed, for example, through a gate or door. Such techniques can be as simple as a specialised identity card, or as sophisticated as the recognition of retina or iris patterns, fingerprints or speech. This technology concentrates on the individual themselves rather than the more traditional approach of focusing much more on the passenger's baggage. The industry has been developing the technology needed for such biometric processes for some time with the aim of speeding up processing times as well as improving their effectiveness.

There are two types of biometric identification: physiological biometrics (which relies on recognition, for example of fingerprints, retina or iris patterns); and behavioural biometrics (which is associated with aspects of behaviour including signature and voice). Using biometrics for security or border checks can increase the efficiency of the process, save time and enhance customer service. Also, there is no risk of losing, copying, forgetting or having the biometrics stolen. An important use for biometrics is in machine-readable travel documents (MRTD) including passports and visas. A biometric passport or ePassport has the passport's critical information stored on a tiny computer chip. In the past 10 years or so, many countries have issued ePassports with most having passenger information and a digital photo stored on the chip, as this facial recognition was the global standard that ICAO agreed to adopt in 2003 (along with voluntary additional fingerprint or iris recognition).

Biometrics can be used for other processes at the airport as well as border control. It can be used with check-in and boarding to ensure the passenger boarding the aircraft is the same person as the one who checked in. It can be applied at the security checkpoint to confirm the identity of the passenger. It can used for employees to check the identity of those who are entering sensitive and restricted areas. IATA believes that biometrics can be used to help deliver the 'checkpoint of the future' which will bring an end to the checkpoint process designed 40 years ago to stop hijackers, and that will start looking for 'bad people rather than bad objects' (IATA, 2012a). This will be dependent on enhancing the ties between government agencies, airports and airlines to ensure more harmonisation and better sharing of intelligence information (in addition to having a biometric identification in the passport or travel document), so that three different security lanes can be introduced. These will be for known travellers, normal travellers and those requiring enhanced security. IATA claims that this process also has the potential to be combined with outbound customs and immigration.

Some passengers can volunteer (sometimes at a cost) to provide their personal and biometric information to be included in a 'registered passenger', 'registered traveller' or 'trusted traveller' scheme suitable for frequent flyers. These are designed to reduce delays at the airport and to enhance the passenger experience by allowing certain processes to be expedited while maintaining acceptable levels of security and border control. The passenger's background is investigated and if they are approved they will usually receive a smart card that contains their biometric information for use at the airport – as at Singapore airport with the IACS scheme that uses fingerprint recognition. Likewise, at Hong Kong airport there is a frequent visitor card that can be provided free to any visitor who has travelled through the airport three or more times in the past month and allows them to experience quicker immigration clearance. The UK also had its IRIS scheme (based on iris recognition), but this is now being replaced, with more resources being shifted towards machines that automatically read biometric passports. Some schemes offer more, including the Privium scheme at Amsterdam airport. This uses iris recognition and offers three types of membership. Privium Plus (€199 per annum) provides fast-track border control plus other enhancements including priority parking, valet parking and business-class check-in. Premium Basic (€121) offers just the expedited border control, whereas Premium Partner (€73) is available to partners or dependent children.

In the United States there is an initiative called the TSA Pre✓™ which is a risk-based security project. It allows members of certain airline frequent flyer programmes and members of the US Customs and Border Protection (CBP) Trusted Traveler programmes to receive expedited security screening benefits. These so-called Trusted Traveler programmes include Global Entry for international travel, NEXUS for travel between the USA and Canada, and SENTRI for travel between the USA and Mexico. By 2012, 5 million passengers were members and 35 airports were involved with the project (TSA, 2012). It works by having passenger information embedded in the barcode of the passenger's boarding pass which allows access to the fast-track security.

CHECK-IN AND BOARDING PROCESSES

The final part of this chapter discusses developments associated with the check-in and boarding processes. There are now a number of ways that passengers can check in for their flight apart from using the traditional check-in desk. First came self-service check-in kiosks at airports, then remote methods including mobile phones and the internet.

Check-in kiosks at airports began appearing about 15 years ago. They were installed by the airlines primarily for their own use – the so-called dedicated or proprietary kiosks. This was an inevitable development as the airline industry saw how self-service technologies in other industries, such as banking, had lowered costs, increased productivity and reduced customer waiting time. At the same time, better use could be made of the scarce space at airports. This was followed by the development of the common-use self-service check-in (CUSS) kiosks that allowed the airlines to share self-service resources. There had been a similar trend with the traditional check-in desks when common-use terminal equipment (CUTE) was introduced in the early 1980s. The earliest CUSS kiosks were installed at Vancouver and Narita airports in 2002. By 2006 around 29 per cent of all passengers used some type of self-service kiosk (Baker, 2007).

Initially the airlines (and later the airline alliances) developed dedicated desks to differentiate themselves from others and to give themselves a competitive advantage – particularly for their frequent flyers. The kiosks were branded with their name and identity. However, there was no common standard for these dedicated kiosks and so investment and maintenance costs proved to be high – particularly when the airport being served was not a major base for the airline. Hence the CUSS kiosk was developed. This allows the costs to be shared between different airlines and fewer airport counter staff are required. However, the airlines lose individual influence over the check-in process and the costs they incur, and will no longer be able to differentiate this aspect of their product. For the airports, the CUSS system provides more flexibility – just as the CUTE system did when it was introduced – and allows terminal space to be used more efficiently. This may enable a higher volume of passengers to be handled without the necessity of expanding the terminal. The check-in facilities can be placed in the most convenient places in the terminals and spread out if necessary to avoid crowding. In theory, space no longer needed for check-in can be used for retail opportunities, although it may require considerable reconfiguration of the overall space to place these new facilities in an appropriate location. In most cases the airport operator owns the CUSS kiosks and then charges the airlines (or includes CUSS use in other charges, including for CUTE facilities), but in rare cases it may be the airlines themselves or the handling agents.

For the passenger, both types of kiosk provide a opportunity for easier and faster check-in, but the CUSS system gives more flexibility to check in anywhere regardless of the airline and can thus eliminate any confusion arising from multiple dedicated terminals. Kiosks can be placed not only in the traditional check-in areas, but also within other places in the terminal and off-terminal sites, including car parks, train stations, car rental return facilities, hotels and cruise ships, which can reduce check-in queues in the terminal and give passengers extra convenience and control. Las Vegas airport is an interesting example here. It first launched its CUSS programme, Airport SpeedCheck, in 2003, but has subsequently developed it to include remote check-in (Airport SpeedCheck Advance). It has a goal of 10 per cent of passengers with bags checking in remotely. It has kiosks in hotels, the convention centre and a rent-a-car centre that can handle hold baggage. Another example is Hong Kong airport, where there are downtown check-ins at the SkyPier ferry ports. Likewise, Edmonton airport has kiosks in the downtown visitor information centre (Ingalls, 2007). Abu Dhabi airport has off-site kiosks in hotels and in the National Exhibition Centre as it pursues its virtual airport model. Overall, in February 2004 there were only around 10 airports using CUSS kiosks, but by February 2008 this had increased to over 100. The number now has increased very substantially.

Self-service kiosks are also becoming much more sophisticated in the services they offer. Most of the original self-service kiosks could not deal with passengers' bags. Often, once self-service check-in was completed, passengers had to queue up at individual airline desks to check in their luggage, which was a major disadvantage of the machines. However, this problem is being overcome by baggage self-tagging and baggage drops. Self-tagging has increased significantly in the past couple of years in areas including Australia, New Zealand, Canada and Europe. In 2012 approval was given for self-tagging in the United States. Common-use self-service bag drops are also growing in popularity, giving airlines the advantage of cost-sharing and airports better capacity utilisation, just as with the CUSS kiosks. In the future, once more common standards for the bag tagging and bag drop are adopted, the ideal situation would be to have permanent baggage tags or simply home-printed baggage tags that would enable a much faster and simpler bag-drop experience. Many of the new-generation check-in machines can also read travel documents, including passport and visas, allow meal and seat selection, and handle transfer flights, re-booking flights and reporting missing luggage.

For passengers not wanting this self-service method, the development of tablets has enabled mobile agent check-in, where agents can process passengers in any location in the queues or elsewhere, as in the Doha airport premium terminal. Remote online and mobile check-in have also become popular alternatives. This costs even less for the airlines as they do not need to install kiosks and/or use CUSS, and the passengers print their own boarding passes in the case of PC check-in using their own paper. Many airlines actually offer both remote check-in and self-service kiosks, typically giving passengers the chance to print out their boarding pass from the kiosk having already checked in remotely. However, some airlines, for example Ryanair, do not offer this option. Figure 5.1 shows how the use of all self-service methods has increased.

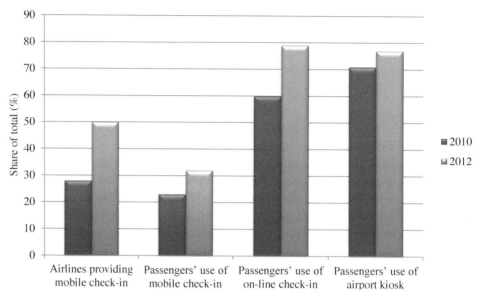

Figure 5.1 *Use of self-service and mobile technology at airports*
Sources: SITA (2012a, 2012b)

For some time there has been a debate as to whether self-service kiosks, which have been around for 15 years or so, have been only an interim solution to improving the check-in process, which eventually will not be needed as checking in remotely using PCs or mobiles is cheaper for airlines and more convenient for passenger (Jarrell, 2007). However, such remote technology may not always available to travellers, particularly if they are away from home. Until there is more wide-spread use of reusable permanent baggage tags such as the radio-frequency identification (RFID) tags of Qantas, or home-printed bag tags, they are also likely to play a vital role for passengers with hold baggage. Also, the self-service kiosks offer opportunities to streamline passenger flows and enhance operational efficiency by being integrated with the other passenger-processing technologies involved with security and border control activities. However, according to the 2012 Airline IT Trends Survey, 71 per cent of airlines believe smartphones and websites will be the dominant channels for passenger processing beyond 2015, with only 39 per cent mentioning kiosks (SITA 2012a).

In addition to check-in, technology is also increasingly being used for other passenger processes at the airport, including transfer kiosks, automated e-gates for check points and self-boarding gates. Boarding passes now use IATA industry standard 2D barcodes that can be accessed from anywhere, including on the internet or a mobile phone. There are also ongoing developments with baggage processing (self-service bag tagging, self-service bag drop, RFID for baggage tracking) and paperless and streamlining processes for cargo, especially as RFID costs continue to decline. Hong Kong airport has pioneered the use of such technology. Tablets can also be used by dispatchers and loaders to capture real-time load data to keep track, for example, of aircraft loaded weight and baggage location. Table 5.6 shows the current and future deployment of some of these developments. By 2015, 79 per cent of airports plan to have self-printing bag tagging. In addition, 74 per cent of airlines and 60 per cent of airports plan to offer automated bag drop, with corresponding adoption rates of 54 per cent for self-boarding.

Table 5.6 Use of self-service technology at airports

Technology	Current deployment (per cent)	Additional deployment by 2015 (per cent)
Airports		
Self-printing bag tag	40	39
Unstaffed bag drop locations	13	47
Transfer kiosks (common use)	8	45
Self-boarding	10	44
Airlines		
Unstaffed bag drop locations	9	65
Transfer kiosks	10	44
Self boarding	4	50

Source: SITA (2012a, 2012c)

Since 2004, the airline organisation IATA has been actively encouraging the use of technology with its Simplifying the Business (StB) initiative to streamline processes and reduce complexity and cost. This has involved a variety of interested parties including airlines, airports, travel agents, technology providers and global distribution systems. Some of the early focus related to areas including e-ticketing, self-service kiosks, barcoded boarding passes and RFID for baggage management. New areas are now being considered covering six main programmes. This includes an e-freight project with a target to create a paperless environment with 100 per cent e-freight use by 2015, and three other initiatives related to mishandled baggage (baggage improvement programme) and airline distribution (new distribution capability) and sales (IATA e-services). Of particular relevance to the discussion here is the passenger facilitation programme, which focuses on the security, border protection, immigration and customs processes with the aim of improving the passenger's end-to-end experience. It covers improving the quality of passenger data transferred from airlines to governments, improving passenger flows at security checkpoints using risk-based approaches, and improving border crossing through the promotion of auto-mated border control using biometric identification. The final key programme, Fast Travel, covers a number of self-service processes that have the potential to speed the passenger flows through airports (Table 5.7). There are currently 106 Fast Travel airline/airport-capable pairs,

Table 5.7 IATA's Fast Travel Initiative

Process	Key features
Check-in	Web, mobile phone and self-service kiosks
Bags ready-to-go	Self-tagging and bag drops
Document check	Self-service kiosks
Flight re-booking	Self-service kiosks
Self-boarding	Automated boarding gates
Bag recovery	Self-service kiosks

Source: IATA (2012b)

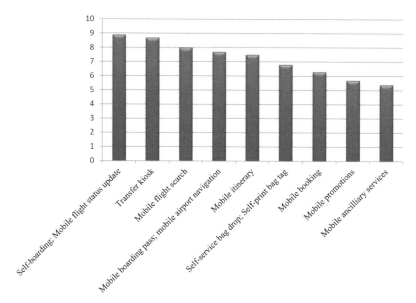

Figure 5.2 *Technology attractiveness index (0–10: low–high)*
Source: SITA (2012b)

including Copenhagen, London Gatwick, Munich, Frankfurt, Madrid, Auckland, Abu Dhabi and Beijing. In total these pairs represent around 10 per cent of global passengers, 6 per cent being in Europe. There is a target to offer 80 per cent of global passengers the complete self-service suite of Fast Travel solutions by 2020 (IATA, 2012b).

Overall, technological developments are seen as a way to improve the passenger experience and reduce stress levels. Figure 5.2 shows that in terms of attractiveness to passengers, technologies that enable passengers to receive flight status updates on their mobile, to self-board and to transfer using self-service are most popular, while mobile ancillary services and mobile promotions are regarded as less important. In the future there will be further developments. A major opportunity is likely to be the use of near-field communication (NFC) with mobile phones. NFC uses a wireless, high-speed, secure data link that allows passengers to perform transactions with the simple touch or swipe of a smartphone onto an appropriate reader. It potentially could be used for a number of processes at the airport, including passenger and baggage check-in, security checkpoint, lounge access and boarding (Amadeus, 2011). NFC promises other applications related to the sale of additional products and services, particularly in the commercial area. The technology could also provide airports with real-time information on passenger flows which could ease congestion problems. The speed of adoption will depend partly on the popularity of NFC-enabled smartphones, but the technology has already been tested, for example at Nice airport with an NFC-based boarding pass project.

In summary, there are a number of current and future developments that will produce a more 'intelligent' airport that are having, or have the potential to have, a major impact on the airport and its passengers (SITA, 2012d). More rigid security procedures can cause disruption to journeys and affect the passenger experience by increasing the hassle factor associated with passing through an airport, reducing opportunities for passengers to use the commercial facilities. Also, increased reliance on technology can have important implications for airport operations and delays if there are malfunctions or breakdowns. On the other hand, more risk-based approaches and biometric identification procedures with border control may speed up certain processes. Likewise, changes in the way passengers check in, drop off their baggage and proceed through the gates, eventually using NFC technology, may also improve the passenger experience. From the airport operator's viewpoint there are also major impacts. Self-service and automated procedures, while expensive to install initially, are likely to have lower operational costs which may be a substantial benefit depending on the airport operator's direct involvement with such processes. They may give the airport an opportunity to reduce congestion, increase capacity utilisation and improve passenger flows. They may also free up space for commercial opportunities, depending on the layout of the terminal, and increase the dwell time for passengers to shop. In short, all aspects of terminal planning will need to consider these changes. Issues related to the passenger experience are developed further in Chapter 6.

REFERENCES

ACI/DMKA (2012) *ASQ Best Practice Report: Airport Loyalty Programmes*, Montreal: Airports Council International.

ACI Europe (2003) *Financing Civil Aviation Security Costs in Europe*, Brussels: ACI Europe.

—— (2010) *An Outlook for Europe's Airports*, Brussels: ACI Europe.

Akerman, A. (2010) 'Copenhagen Airport adapts to low cost market with new pier', *Communique Airport Business*, Winter: 18–20.

Amadeus (2011) *Navigating the Airport of Tomorrow*, Madrid: Amadeus.

Bacon, J. (2002) *The Aviation and Transportation Security Act: The Law and its Implementation*, AAAE/ACI NA Legislative affairs issue brief, Washington, DC: AAAE/ACI North America.

Baker, C. (2007) 'Checking in', *Airline Business*, July: 38–40.

Boston Consulting Group (2004) *Airports – Dawn of a New Era*. Online. Available HTTP <http://www.bcg.com/documents/file14335.pdf> (accessed 30 March 2012).

CAA (2011) *CAA Passenger Survey Report 2010*, London: Civil Aviation Authority.

CAPA Centre for Aviation (2012) 'Low cost airport terminals still popular in Asia-Pacific but declining in significance in Europe', 3 April. Online. Available HTTP <http://centreforaviation.com/analysis/low-cost-airport-terminals-still-popular-in-asia-pacific-but-declining-in-significance-in-europe–81651> (accessed 30 October 2012).

Copenhagen Economics (2012) *Airport Competition in Europe*, Copenhagen: Copenhagen Economics.

EC (2002) *Regulation (EC) No 2320/2002 of the European Parliament and of the Council of 16 December 2002 Establishing Common Rules in the Field of Civil Aviation Security*, Official Journal L355, 30 December, Brussels: EC.

—— (2006) *Regulation (EC) No 1546/2006 of the European Parliament and of the Council of 4 October Amending Regulation (EC) No 622/2003 Laying Down Measures for the Implementation of the Common Basic Standards on Aviation Security*, Official Journal L286, 17 October, Brussels: EC.

—— (2007) *Regulation (EC) No 915/2007 of the European Parliament and of the Council of 31 July Amending Regulation (EC) No 622/2003 Laying Down Measures for the Implementation of the Common Basic Standards on Aviation Security*, Official Journal L200, 1 August, Brussels: EC.

—— (2008) *Regulation (EC) No 300/2008 of the European Parliament and of the Council of 11 March on Common Rules in the Field of Civil Aviation Security and Repealing Regulation (EC) No 2320/2002*, Official Journal L97, 9 March, Brussels: EC.

—— (2009) *Directive 2009/12/EC of the European Parliament and of the Council of 11 March 2009 on Airport Charges*, Official Journal L070, 14 March, Brussels: EC.

—— (2010a) *Communication from the Commission to the European Parliament and the Council on the Use of Security Scanners at EU airports*, COM (2010) 311 final, Brussels: EC.

—— (2010b) *Communication from the Commission to the European Parliament and the Council on the Global Approach to Transfers of Passenger Name Record (PNR) Data to Third Countries*, COM(2010) 492 final, Brussels: EC.

Falconer, R. (2006) 'The low-cost challenge for airports', *Communique Airport Business*, June–July: 21–22.

Feldman, D. (2009) 'Thinking outside the box', *Airport World*, 15 November. Online. Available HTTP from <http://www.airport-world.com/publications/all-online-articles/item/717-thinking-outside-the-box> (accessed 30 March 2012).

—— (2011) 'Leading the way', *Airport World*, 28 September. Online. Available HTTP <http://www.airport-world.com/publications/all-online-articles/item/1029-leading-the-way> (accessed 30 March 2012).

GAO (2002) *Using Airport Grant Funds for Security has Affected some Development Projects*, Washington, DC: General Accounting Office.

Ghobrial, A. and Irvin, W. (2004) 'Combating air terrorism: some implications to the aviation industry', *Journal of Air Transportation*, 9(3): 67–86.

Graham, A. (2013) 'Understanding the low cost carrier and airport relationship: a critical analysis of the salient issues', *Tourism Management*, 36: 66–76.

IATA (2007) *Low Cost Facilities and Services*, Position Statement, Geneva: International Air Transport Association.

—— (2012a), *Checkpoint of the Future*, Online. Available HTTP: <http://www.iata.org/whatwedo/security/Pages/checkpoint-future.aspx> (accessed 15 October 2012).

—— (2012b) *Fast Travel Program*, Online. Available HTTP <http://www.iata.org/whatwedo/stb/fast-travel/pages/index.aspx> (accessed 15 October 2012).

ICAO (2012) *ICAO's Policies on Charges for Airports and Air Navigation Services – Doc 9082*, 9th edn, Montreal: International Civil Aviation Organization.

Ingalls, S. (2007) 'McCarran International Airport: a case study in enhancing processing efficiency', *Journal of Airport Management*, 1(4): 338–47.

Irish Aviation Authority/Aviasolutions (2004) *Study on Civil Aviation Financing* (summary of final report), Dublin: Irish Aviation Authority/Aviasolutions.

Jacobs Consultancy (2007) *Review of Dedicated Low-Cost Airport Passenger Facilities*, London: Jacobs Consultancy.

Jarach, D. (2005) *Airport Marketing: Strategies to Cope with the New Millennium Environment*, Farnham: Ashgate.

Jarrell, J. (2007) 'Self-service kiosks: museum pieces or here to stay?', *Journal of Airport Management*, 2(1): 23–29.

LeighFisher (2011) *UK Airport Performance Indicators 2010/2011*, London: LeighFisher.

Mercer Management Consulting (2005) *Profitable Growth Strategies in the Airport Business*. Online. Available HTTP <http://www.garsonline.de/Downloads/051124/Doering%20-%20Presentation.pdf> (accessed 30 March 2012).

Njoya, E. and Niemeier, H.-M. (2011) 'Do dedicated low cost passenger terminals create competitive advantages for airports?', *Research in Transportation Business and Management*, 1(1): 55–61.

Raffel, R. and Ramsay, J. (2011) 'Aviation security in the United States', in J. O'Connell and G. Williams (eds), *Air Transport in the 21st Century*, Farnham: Ashgate.

Rossiter, A. and Dresner, M. (2004) 'The impact of the September 11th security fee and passenger wait time on traffic diversions and highway fatalities', *Journal of Air Transport Management*, 10(4): 225–30.

Saraswati, B. and Hanaoka, S. (2012) 'Space allocation for commercial activities in low-cost airport terminals', *Journal of Airport Management*, 6(4): 397–411.

Schumacher, J. (2007) 'The latest business model for low-cost airports: the case of Frankfurt-Hahn Airport', *Journal of Airport Management*, 1(2): 121–24.

SITA (2012a) *Airline IT Trends Survey 2012*, Geneva: SITA/Airline Business.

—— (2012b) *Passenger Self-Service Survey Highlights*, Geneva: SITA/Air Transport World.

—— (2012c) *Airport IT Trends Survey 2012*, Geneva: SITA/Airline Business.

—— (2012d) *Make it a Reality*, Geneva: SITA.

Sobie, B. (2007) 'Stress free', *Airline Business*, December: 47.

Studness, L. (2007) 'The role of the airport in the JetBlue business model', *Journal of Airport Management*, 1(2): 118–20

Tatibouet, Y. and Doumas, E. (2008) 'Regulation of low-cost carrier facilities at French airports', *Journal of Airport Management*, 3(1): 4–6.

TSA (2012) *TSA Pre?™ Now Available at 35 Airports Nationwide: Expedited Screening Begins at John Wayne Airport*. Online. Available HTTP <http://www.tsa.gov/press/releases/2012/12/19/tsa-pre%E2%9C%93%E2%84%A2-now-available–35-airports-nationwide-expedited-screening-begins> (accessed 21 December 2012).

Zhang A., Hanaoka, S., Inamura, H. and Ishikura, T. (2008) 'Low-cost carriers in Asia: deregulation, regional liberalisation and secondary airports', *Research in Transportation Economics*, 24(1): 36–50.

6 ■ Airport service quality

CHALLENGES FOR AIRPORT OPERATORS

Chapter 5 discusses how airports are differentiating their offer to meet requirements of their diverse customers and identifies developments related to the main processes. However, in order for airports to change in this manner and meet the demands of current and future users, there needs to be a good understanding of the service quality provided, and in particular the factors that are important for the passenger experience.

Providing satisfactory levels of service for users can be particularly challenging for airport operators because of a number of factors. First, there is usually an uneven spread of demand. For many airports a terminal will look and feel very different on a quiet Tuesday in winter compared with a busy summer Saturday in the school holidays. Likewise, passenger flows in the early morning or evening at an airport dominated by short-haul business traffic will be considerably greater than at other times of day. This is very likely to play a major role in influencing the passenger's perception of the quality of service provided.

The overall service is produced as a result of the combined activities of various different organisations, including airlines, handling agents, customs and immigration officials, concessionaires and so on. These different bodies may have different ultimate objectives and even conflicting views on what determines satisfactory or good service. As a result, the airport operator has only partial control of all the processes that make up the final product or service. Areas of responsibility therefore have to be very clearly identified and the airport operator must define a common goal for all as regards service quality. Even for individual activities, responsibilities may be shared that will increase the complexity. For instance, for check-in an airport operator may provide the equipment while airlines or handling agents actually man the desks.

A further problem is that at many airports, the airport product has to appeal to a very heterogeneous range of passengers unless specialised terminals or products are offered (see Chapter 5). Some passengers may want to get through the airport as quickly as possible with a minimum of distractions, while others enjoy the opportunity of being able to shop and take refreshments. Business and leisure passengers may also have very contrasting requirements. It may even be that the same passenger will have different needs depending on when they are travelling, being a lone business traveller during the week but then travelling for leisure reasons with the rest of the family at the weekend.

In designing airfield facilities, there are many technical specifications to consider that relate primarily to the safe passage of aircraft and their passengers and freight. As a result, the airport operator usually has limited freedom to vary these specifications. However, with the terminal there is more flexibility. The level of service offered to the passenger will be related to two aspects of capacity: static and dynamic. Static capacity relates to the storage potential of the different areas of the terminal. Hence the level of services related to this will be defined as the number of passengers the area will accommodate at any one moment at a defined level of service – for example, a value such as 1.7 m^2 per passenger. By contrast, dynamic capacity is the maximum processing or flow rate of persons through a subsystem in the terminal per unit time. In this case the level of service will be defined as waiting time such as 90 per cent of passengers being processed in 7 minutes or less, or alternatively 180 passengers being processed per hour.

An airport terminal will be a function of the planned level of service: the lower the acceptable level of service, the greater the capacity. IATA has well established level of service (LOS) standards that are related primarily to space, queuing and waiting standards. These are listed in its airport development manual, which has widespread use within the airport industry (IATA, 2004). There are six levels of service: A (excellent), B (high), C (good), D (adequate), E (inadequate) and F (unacceptable); typically most airports design facilities to operate at level C. For example in the holding areas, this assumes that there is 1.7 m^2 for a sitting passenger and 1.2 m^2 for a standing area. At level C the maximum occupancy rate will be 65 per cent, while it decreases to 40 per cent at level A and increases to 95 per cent at level E. Likewise in the baggage claim areas, it assumes that 40 per cent of passengers have trolleys with space allocations of 2.6 m^2 per passenger for level A, 1.7 m^2 per passenger for level C and only 1.0 for level E. While C is generally the industry standard, some of the low-cost terminals and facilities have a lower design LOS – for example, E at Marseille and Hahn; D/E at Kuala Lumpur (the original LCCT) and Amsterdam (Jacobs Consultancy, 2007). While these LOS standards have been used for terminal planning for over 35 years, recent research in the United States has indicated that passengers are still generally satisfied with them (TransSolutions *et al.*, 2011).

The LOS standard will apply only to the planning peak hour in the design year for the airport infrastructure, so at other times the LOS category may actually be higher. Also, rather than using the IATA standards, airports may instead devise their own based on their own specific services and facilities and their unique mix of users. These individual standards will be set and revised in the light of actual user levels of satisfaction. However, in most cases these are not significantly different from those suggested by IATA.

MEASURING SERVICE QUALITY

Different types of measurement

At many airports, measuring the quality of service is just part of the overall quality management system that has become all about the continuous process of identifying customer needs, assessing their level of satisfaction and taking corrective action when necessary. All employees and all processes are considered to contribute to the long-term success of this system. Such an approach is now considered to be a critical element in many service businesses, and is viewed as giving companies a competitive edge and as a way to increase customer confidence. Potential benefits include increased employee motivation and enhanced communication and teamwork within the organisation, with increased productivity and efficiency. Theoretically the 'cost of quality' does not have to be expensive, as good quality management, through quality appraisal and prevention schemes, aims to minimise the costly situation when the service is unacceptable and has to be rectified.

In some cases, airports have chosen to certify their quality management system and gain external recognition by using the ISO 9001 standards. The latest version is ISO 9001: 2008. The ISO standard does not tell the airports how they should set up their system, but simply gives guidance on the elements that should be included. Certification involves inspection by an independent registration body. One of the first airports in the world to obtain such recognition was Aer Rianta (now the Dublin Airport Authority) for its airport operations, maintenance, emergency services, health and safety, retail, administration and human resources. Vienna airport was the first airport to receive ISO 9001 accreditation for the total organisation in 1995. There are now many airports that have ISO 9001 certification for some or all of their activities. There are also awards given by external bodies in recognition of their approach to quality management, including the European Foundation for Quality Management (EFQM) excellence awards and the Malcolm Baldridge Award in North America. The ISO 9001 standard is one of many that airports may seek, including ISO 14001 for environmental management and ISO 20000 for IT service management.

Airports use both objective measures of their service quality (related to service delivery performance) and subjective measures (related to customer perceptions). Objective indicators are connected to the LOS standards, linking to both the static and dynamic measures of capacity and assessing the service delivered. They cover areas including flight delays, availability of lifts, escalators and trolleys, and operational research surveys of factors including queue length, space provision, waiting time and baggage reclaim time. To be accurate, these measures need to be collected regularly and at varying time periods when different volumes and types of passengers are being processed through the airport. The advantages of these are that they are precise, easy to understand and can be related to the levels of service standards.

Most large airports regularly observe their service delivery performance (e.g. waiting time and queue length for essential processes). However, if there is a certain issue related to one aspect of airport operations or one part of the airport terminal, they may want to undertake additional *ad hoc* research. Mystery shoppers may be used for assessing the overall passenger experience in the terminal overall or the quality of the commercial facilities. Other methods may include tracking, when passengers are monitored throughout their journey in the terminal to see where they spend their time and where they are held up with bottlenecks. This may help shed light on how available time influences retail spend, and on any other issues related to passenger flows that have not been identified through other research methods. Bluetooth technology, which enables the identification of an unique electronic ID number with a mobile phone, has made passenger tracking much easier in recent years. Laser technology can also be used to count passengers automatically in and out of a certain area.

However, the objective measures of service quality can cover only a limited range of issues and service dimensions. For instance, while they can measure the reliability of equipment, they cannot tell whether consumers feel safe, assured and satisfied with their use of the equipment. Similarly, a passenger's perception of the time they have spent waiting in a queue may be very different from the actual waiting time. Time and availability measures give no indication of the proportion of passengers receiving poor service and so are not really focused on the passenger experience. Such measures also do not identify priority areas, for example whether or not the availability of a lift that may be covered by a service delivery measure is crucial.

Subjective measures looking at passenger satisfaction ratings are also ideally needed. These measures will enable the quality of service to be assessed through the eyes of users rather than airport management. There are a number of different types of subjective measures, the two key methods being routine comment/complaints feedback (letters, phone calls, e-mails, social networks such as Twitter and Facebook), and customer surveys. Airports may also undertake in-depth interviews, focus groups or panel discussions that give them a chance to discuss certain issues in more depth than could be achieved with a survey. In this case, more qualitative information will be gathered that will typically investigate opinions and attitudes.

As regards the benefits of routine feedback, this information is cheap and immediate. If the comments are favourable they may also provide a positive public relations opportunity. The airport operator, however, has very little control over this type of feedback. The comments will not come from a representative sample of travellers at airports and will usually reflect only extreme views, since users tend not be motivated to comment unless they feel very strongly about their experience at the airport. Hence, while such feedback may be able to identify a weakness that can be rectified swiftly, it is not systematic or scientific enough to be used for quality improvement programmes or target-setting.

In the latter case, consumer surveys are more suitable. Typically such surveys will ask passengers about their usage of facilities and services and their opinion of them in terms of comfort, congestion, cleanliness, value for money and so on. Also, if passenger profile information is collected, the survey findings can be used to investigate relationships between usage and satisfaction of services with demographics, attitudes and experiences of travellers. Consideration has to be given to the sample size, interview time and most appropriate place to survey. Departing passengers may be keen to participate while waiting in their departure lounge having completed all the major essential processes, but tired arriving passengers may be less cooperative – being anxious to find their luggage and return home. The main drawback of surveys is, of course, their high cost. The results are also not so immediate as feedback comments, and may require careful interpretation. Also, passenger perceptions often take some time to adjust once changes have been introduced at an airport, so there may be a lag effect with surveys which does not affect objective measures.

As well as taking into account passengers' views of quality of service, airports need to consider their other customers as well. Airline, concessionaire and tenant surveys may be undertaken to identify the needs of the respective customer groups and to gauge their satisfaction with the airport operator. By way of illustration, Figure 6.1 presents the results of the Spanish airport company AENA's airline surveys for the past 3 years. However, at most airports there is usually a regular dialogue between airlines, concessionaires, tenants and other service providers, so additional information through more formal surveys may not be necessary. Also, the smaller number of organisations involved with all but the largest airports, compared with passenger or

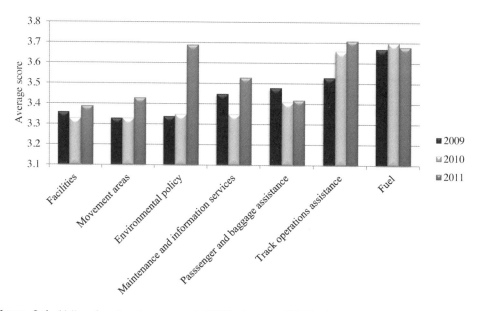

Figure 6.1 *Airline feedback scores at AENA airports, 2009–11*
Note: Score range from 1 (low) to 5 (high).
Source: AENA (2012)

employee groups, means that airports may be able to survey all or most of the target population rather than having to select a representative sample.

As with economic performance, airports now appreciate that it is equally important to make international comparisons and to benchmark themselves against other airports as well as with their past performance. Such an exercise is particularly problematic because of the lack of consistency or common format of each airport's consumer survey. The sample size can also vary significantly, for example ranging from 2,000 passengers a year at Geneva airport to 24,000 at Frankfurt airport, 60,000 at Amsterdam, 46,000 at the Paris airports and 40,000 at Athens airport. There are, however, a few surveys that cover a sample of airports in a consistent manner. The most comprehensive and well established survey is the ACI Airport Service Quality (ASQ), discussed in detail below. In addition, there is the Skytrax airport customer satisfaction survey, based on 12 million passengers and 388 airports, with 39 different airport service and product areas from check-in, arrivals, transfers, shopping, security and immigration through to departure at the gate. While precise details about the methodology are not available, the website states that the research includes passenger-completed questionnaires (online and via e-mail), telephone interviews, business research groups/travel panel interviews and corporate travel questionnaires and interviews. In 2012 Incheon Seoul airport was ranked top, followed by Singapore, Hong Kong, Amsterdam, Beijing, Munich, Zurich, Kuala Lumpur and Vancouver. The best premium airport was Doha, the best low-cost airport London Stansted, and the best improved airport was Delhi. J.D. Power and Associates also produces regional surveys for North America. The 2010 survey ranked Detroit, Denver, Minneapolis/St Paul, Orlando and Phoenix airport as the top five large airports (more than 30 million annual passengers), while Kansas City was the top medium-sized airport (10–30 million passengers) and Indianapolis the top small airport (fewer than 10 million).

Making inter-airport comparisons can enable airport operators to learn from best practice elsewhere. The results, if favourable, can also be used as a marketing tool to promote the airport and give it a competitive edge. However, a number of factors need to be considered when making such comparisons. For example certain airports, including small airports and single-terminal airports, inherently tend to perform better in quality-of-service surveys. This is not just because smaller airports seem more personal, but also because they are usually served by smaller national or regional populations that may view their airport as a local asset and have a much greater pride in it. Some passenger types are likely to complain more than others. For example, in the United Kingdom business travellers, frequent travellers and male passengers tend to be far more critical than foreign leisure travellers, first-time users and female passengers (Maiden, 2008).

CASE STUDY 6.1: ACI AND SERVICE QUALITY

Over the past few years, ACI has been developing measures regarding service quality. First, it has ACI ASQ performance measures that assess the service performance actually delivered by focusing on 16 key measures, including waiting time at check-in, security and immigration, and the number of available trolleys. The data are obtained through a series of observations during peak hours using personal digital assistants (PDAs) with software specifically designed for airport passenger flows. Monthly and quarterly reports are provided that make comparisons with other airports and compare the performance with service delivery targets. The analysis follows the passenger process from check-in to boarding to baggage reclaim in seven steps. Airports included in this research include Abu Dhabi, Cape Town, Dammam, Durban, Faro, Geneva, Johannesburg, Lisbon, Ponta Delgada and Porto.

A much larger project is the ACI ASQ passenger survey, which dates back to 1993. This was initially undertaken by IATA with its Global Airport Monitor, which had just 30 airports and a sample size of 80,000 in its first year. In 2004 and 2005, IATA and ACI joined forces to produce similar research, the ALTEA survey, but from 2006 this survey has been undertaken solely by ACI. The 2011 survey covered over 190 airports in more than 50 countries, ranging from 0.5 million to 85 million passengers in size. Over 250,000 passengers were surveyed on a quarterly basis, with a requirement for each airport to have a minimum of 350 responses per quarter to ensure a representative sample – although in practice most airports survey considerably more passengers. It is a self-completion survey with questionnaires being distributed to passengers at the departure gate. There are 34 service quality aspects included which cover areas including check-in, passport/personal ID control, security, airport facilities, the airport environment and overall satisfaction. There are five scores ranging from 5 (excellent) to 1 (poor). In the 2011 survey Seoul Incheon airport was ranked top, followed by Singapore, Beijing, Hong Kong and Nagoya (ACI, 2012). Table 6.1 presents more detailed results of the survey. ACI provides additional analysis for the airports that contribute to both projects concerning causal links between customer satisfaction and absolute service levels. There is also the newer and more specialist ACI ASQ retail survey, discussed in Chapter 7.

Table 6.1 Overall passenger satisfaction levels: best-performing airports from ACI's 2011 Airport Service Quality survey by airport size and region

	Region						Number of passengers (million)				
	Africa	Asia-Pacific	Europe	Latin America and Caribbean	Middle East	North America	2–5	5–15	15–25	25–49	>40
1	Cape Town	Seoul Incheon	Malta	Cancun	Dubai	Ottawa	Guayaquil	Nagoya	Seoul Gimpo	Seoul Incheon	Singapore
2	Cairo	Singapore	Edinburgh	Guayaquil	Abu Dhabi	Indianapolis	Ottawa	Cancun	Chongqing	New Delhi	Beijing
3	Durban	Beijing	Porto	San Jose	Tel Aviv	Halifax	Halifax	Hyderabad	Hangzhou	Mumbai	Hong Kong
4	Mauritius	Hong Kong	Zurich	Montego Bay	Doha	Austin	Chiang Mai	Hainan Meilan	Salt Lake City	Kuala Lumpur	Shanghai Pudong
5	Johannesburg	Nagoya	Munich	Santo Domingo	Bahrain	Calgary	Grand Rapids	Wuhan	Doha	Shenzhen	Guangzhou

Source: ACI (2012)

An example of how airports use the ASQ passenger survey is provided by Heathrow airport (Ellis, 2012). It has three groups of airports: EU hubs, EU comparators and global comparators. It compares itself with the EU hubs with a clear target of leading within this group, whereas it benchmarks itself with the EU comparators to improve specific attributes. In addition it monitors its performance against the established and emerging hubs in the global comparator group to learn from the 'best in class'. The ASQ results can also be used for target-setting within the economic regulatory system, as is the case in Ireland, and during the consultation for economic regulation, as with the Paris airports.

THE PASSENGER EXPERIENCE

In recent years there has been increased focus on the 'passenger experience' when assessing service quality at airports. This involves consideration of a range of different issues, but of primary importance is a concentration on areas perceived as significant to passengers; more passenger-focused measures (e.g. the proportion of passengers receiving the delivered service rather than just the delivery standards, such as queue length or time); and the measurement of all key services by different providers.

Airport operators need to understand the main drivers that influence a passenger's experience and their satisfaction with the airport. In a passenger survey of the six major airports of Abu Dhabi, Atlanta, Beijing, Frankfurt, Mumbai and Sao Paulo in 2012, unsurprisingly it was found that some parts of the journey were much more stressful than others (Figure 6.2). Security was considered the most stressful by 31 per cent of passengers – nearly twice as many who identified transferring

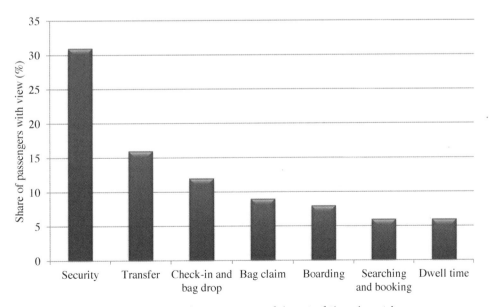

Figure 6.2 *Passengers' views on the most stressful part of the airport journey*
Source: SITA (2012)

flights – with check-in and bag drop ranked third and fourth. Forty-four per cent of passengers said that the main cause of stress was 'loss of time' and consequently the fear of missing the flight. Eleven per cent felt stressed because of unexpected changes, 8 per cent through a lack of control, and 7 per cent through a lack of information (SITA, 2012). Likewise, a study undertaken for Amadeus found that the most common problem, accounted by 25 per cent of passengers, was waiting too long to pass through security. While the second and third most common problems were airline-related (associated with availability of flights and delayed/cancelled flights), waiting too long to check in (16 per cent) and waiting too long to check in bags were also fourth and fifth (Amadeus, 2011).

Linking satisfaction levels to service-quality measures can also provide greater insight into the passenger experience. For example, an analysis of ACI's ASQ in 2008 found that the highest scores for the top 10 airports in the ASQ overall satisfaction table were for cleanliness of terminal, helpfulness of staff, ambience of airport, availability of toilets, efficiency of check-in staff, feeling safe and secure, and wayfinding. By contrast, the lowest scores were for shopping facilities, F&B facilities, banking facilities, IT facilities, value for money with commercial facilities, and opening hours of commercial facilities (CAA, 2009). However, it is difficult to generalise as for each individual airport the most important factors will vary. A case in point is at Lisbon airport, where the critical factors appeared to be ambience, cleanliness of airport, availability of washrooms, helpfulness of staff, thoroughness of security, comfortable waiting/gate areas, business lounges, and arrivals passport inspection. Much lower importance was given to walking distances, parking and internet access (Madeira, 2011).

The implication is that improving areas with low service quality scores may not necessarily improve overall satisfaction and meet passengers' needs. Quite simply, the best way of achieving this is by focusing on areas that are regarded as less than satisfactory, but at the same time important to the customer. For example, ORC International (2009) undertook a 'key drivers of satisfaction' analysis for four UK airports: London Heathrow, London Gatwick, London Stansted and Manchester. For the pre-departure experience, the areas of greatest importance were the ease and time getting from the boarding gate onto the plane, the information provided on flight times and departure gates, cleanliness and maintenance of airport facilities, and ease of getting around the airport. Satisfaction in these areas was also relatively good and so did not suggest that major improvements would have to be made. Likewise, areas that had lower levels of satisfaction, for example the amount of seating and availability and helpfulness of staff, were not considered to be so important and so could be given lower priority.

While using such an approach can prioritise areas for action, it has been argued that too little attention has been given to the overall passenger experience, including transport to/from the airport. All too often, because of the limited control and involvement the airport operator has with certain services or facilities, some areas may be overlooked. However, from a passenger perspective they all contribute to the end-to-end journey experience and should be considered. As Table 6.2 demonstrates, this approach involves taking a more holistic approach to service provision and using performance measures for other providers (e.g. airlines, government agencies) with greater transparency of information (Department for Transport, 2007; CAA, 2009). Some information concerning providers is available, but not in a consistent manner. This ranges from airline delay data (discussed in detail below) and border control data. For example in the United States, the Customs and Border Protection Agency (CBP) monitors and makes available

Table 6.2 The passenger experience

	Getting to/from airport	Getting through airport	Taking off and landing	Getting to destination
Main activities	Driving to airport and parking Using public transport	**Outbound:** Check-in and bag drop Security check Immigration check Getting to gates Shopping, drinking and eating **Inbound:** Immigration check Baggage reclaim Customs check **Transfer:** Dedicated processes	**Outbound:** Push back Taxi to runway Take off **Inbound:** Landing Taxi to stand Disembark	Hiring car Using public transport
Typical delivery accountability	Government departments and organisations, airport operator, commercial operators	Airport operator, airlines, handling agents, commercial retailers, government agencies	Air traffic control, airlines, handling agents, airport operator, slot coordinator	Air traffic control, airlines, government organisations, commercial operators

Source: Adapted from Department for Transport (2007)

on the internet the flight processing time (wait time) for arriving flights at 23 of the busiest international airports. The flight processing time is the length of time from flight arrival to the time the last passenger on the flight is screened by CBP officers in the primary processing area. Minimum, average and maximum processing times are provided per hour as well as the average number of arriving passengers and the average number of booths open. In recent years, some airports have started to provide a wider range of data-related targets for their service providers. For example, as well as information concerning its own performance, London Gatwick shows on its website details by individual airline and handling agent related to the 95 per cent 55-minute baggage delivery target. It also provides data concerning the Border Force agency responsible for passport control checks. There is a target of 95 per cent of EU passengers being processed in 25 minutes or less and 95 per cent of other passengers being processed in 45 minutes.

A number of researchers have tried to develop an overall service quality index for an airport by taking into account the relevant importance of the different aspects of airport operators. For instance, Correia *et al.* (2008) used the example of São Paulo airport in Brazil to assess the statistical relationship between overall passenger satisfaction and individual scores in different areas, while Rhoades *et al.* (2000) surveyed airport directors in North America to gauge their opinion on the most important factors. Yeh and Kuo (2003) surveyed travel agents in Asia to help formulate their index. Elsewhere in the USA, Fodness and Murray (2007) undertook a qualitative and quantitative analysis of airport users, and produced an airport service quality model based on function (effectiveness and efficiency), diversion (productivity, décor, maintenance) and interaction.

Qualitative research, involving in-depth interviews and focus groups, can also be undertaken to understand the main factors affecting the passenger experience in terms of the end-to-end journey. For example, research in the UK divided the issues that seemed important to passengers into six broad themes: end-to-end reliability and efficiency; information and communication; customer care; facilities and entertainment; airport design and maintenance; and cost (Sykes and Desai, 2009). Across all six themes, respondents emphasised the need for a passenger-focused service that incorporates personal control and fairness. Overall, the study concluded that the passenger experience was affected by many interrelated variables, including a range of softer factors that could not be measured with the typical service-quality measures used by airports. For example, queue times and lengths cannot show how queues are managed and how the queuing experience affects the rest of the journey.

This study also recognised the varying needs of different passenger groups – a common characteristic identified in most research. At a very general level, business travellers tend to want to get through airports as efficiently as possible with a degree of comfort. While the same can hold true for certain groups of leisure passengers, others may look at the airport in a different way, as part of their leisure experience. For example, in the above-mentioned survey of passengers at London Heathrow, London Gatwick, London Stansted and Manchester airports (ORC International, 2009), it was found that 84 per cent of business passengers compared with 63 per cent of leisure passengers expected to wait only 10 minutes or less at passport control, with comparable figures of 57 versus 38 per cent and 58 versus 30 per cent for security and check-in/fast bag drop, respectively. A survey of business passengers at Heathrow found that after accessibility and range of flights, the third most important factor was waiting times, which were particularly important for those travelling in the premium classes and frequent flyers (London Economics, 2008). Elsewhere, Copenhagen airport used its annual survey of 130,000 passengers to segment its market into four types related to their travel needs: Experience, Efficiency, Selection and Attention (Copenhagen Airport, 2012) (Table 6.3).

Much of the research consistently identifies wayfinding and information provision as being very influential in affecting the passenger experience. Gresham, Smith and Partners *et al.* (2011) discussed the need to investigate why passengers get lost in order to develop a wayfinding strategy that works to meet the specific needs of users. They then developed wayfinding guidelines that cover all the main areas of the passenger experience. Wayfinding information sources for passengers can include self-help tools (including maps, leaflets and touchscreen interactive kiosks), as at Barcelona and Madrid airports. They can also include staffed facilities including information counters and walking staff, an example being the Changi Experience Agents at Singapore Changi Airport, who speak many languages and each have the support of an iPad. Similarly, Heathrow airport has a journey team consisting of 80 walking uniformed staff who collectively speak more than 40 languages. Interestingly, there are some significant regional differences with the provision of such staff – a recent study found that in Africa, the Middle East

Table 6.3 *Passenger experience segmentation used at Copenhagen airport*

Segment	Share of total passengers (per cent)	Travel frequency at Copenhagen airport	Main characteristics
Experience	44	Medium	Excited traveller seeking experiences, personal contact and wide range of commercial facilities Loves atmosphere of airport Mostly SAS passengers and Scandinavian transfer passengers
Efficiency	22	High	Experienced traveller wanting efficiency and short waiting times Likes automated check-in and uses shops and lounges if delayed Majority are business travellers
Selection	22	Medium	Independent traveller wanting relaxed and calm atmosphere Does not have much need for personal service Majority are women and biggest spenders at the airport
Attention	13	Low	Attention-seeking traveller wanting simplicity, comfort and assistance Arrives early, prefers personal services at check-in and is among first at the gate Includes mostly Danish travellers and long-haul travellers from Asia to USA

Source: Adapted from Copenhagen Airport (2012)

and Asia-Pacific, 84 per cent of airports had walking staff compared with only 56 per cent in Europe (ACI/DKMA, 2011). Some airports, for example London Luton, Manchester, Frankfurt, New York JFK and Boston, have gone one step further by introducing a new kind of airport helper: virtual assistants that are actually life-size holograms.

Many airports recognise the importance of staff training when considering the passenger experience, one such example being Aéroports de Paris (AdP) which opened its service academy in 2011. Initially this is just for AdP staff, but in future this will be extended to other service providers and airlines at the airport. More generally, in their study of airport staff training ACI/DKMA (2012) found that 75 per cent of airports have initial mandatory customer service training for frontline staff that covers communication (93 per cent), courtesy (92 per cent), airport information (90 per cent), behaviour (87 per cent), appearance (80 per cent) and problem solving (70 per cent). Airports try in many other ways to improve the passenger experience. For instance, in 2011 Heathrow airport brought various characters into the terminal to entertain children, and during the Royal wedding period red carpets were laid out to welcome arriving passengers, together with wedding message books that were displayed for well wishers to sign (Adderley, 2012). Another interesting example, out of many, is the Quality Hunters initiative of Helsinki and Finnair. This involved hiring Quality Hunters to travel the world and seek out fresh ideas on quality and on how to improve air travel and the airport experience. Suggestions were also invited from others using a dedicated website and social media tools. Moreover, much can be done physically to improve the passenger experience, including the innovative Video Wall at Vienna airport (as well as other airports including Munich and some in Norway), where 100 screens release a series of letters that cascade down the wall to create the typography of a landscape as passengers approach the security zone.

AIRLINES AND DELAYS

A crucial measure of airport performance for airlines is the level of delays. This is a complicated area, as there are many factors leading to flights being delayed that are outside the airport operator's remit (e.g. *en route* air traffic control, bad weather, technical problems with the aircraft). It is inevitable that aircraft will deviate from the published schedule, which adds an unpredictable element to the time at which any given flight will wish to use the runway. Maximum runway throughput can be achieved only with queuing of aircraft (on the ground for departing flights, or through speed control and stacks in the air for arriving flights) so that there is always an aircraft ready to use the runway. Airports that are operating close to their runway capacity are therefore likely to impose additional delays on flights and exacerbate delays originating from other causes. An airport with spare runway capacity has more scope to accommodate delayed aircraft without disrupting other flights and may be able to avoid queuing aircraft in most cases.

Shortcomings in terminal capacity can also delay aircraft. If there are insufficient stands available, arriving aircraft may be held on the taxiways or apron before they are able to unload. At the day-to-day level, this may be an airline operational decision to await the availability of a preferred gate or avoid bussing passengers from a remote stand. In the longer term, however, airports have the opportunity to expand or upgrade facilities to address these problems. Congestion within the terminals may lead to passengers who have checked in failing to reach the aircraft in time, thus delaying departure; flights may also be held awaiting crew or transfer passengers, creating a knock-on of delays from one flight to another. In the United States, it is common practice for the last flight of the day from a hub to be held much longer than earlier ones as it does not present reactionary problems for subsequent flights and enables as many passengers as possible to get home that night.

The airlines can take account of expected queuing times related to shortages of airport runway capacity in planning their schedule. This enables them to maintain a similar level of punctuality performance at congested airports, but at the expense of longer scheduled flight times and the resultant increase in costs from poorer utilisation of aircraft and crew. Considering the Amsterdam–London Heathrow routes, it can be seen that a morning flight from Amsterdam to Heathrow, scheduled for 1 hour in 1985, had increased to 1 hour 25 minutes by the year 2012 (Table 6.4). At the less congested airports of London City and Luton, the scheduled flight times were less. Airlines thus include a contingency allowance for delays in their schedule. This means that published comparisons of schedule performance tend to understate the total time wasted compared with the theoretical minimum journey time, and airlines can improve their punctuality performance by extending their scheduled journey times. Comparisons between airports and airlines therefore have to be treated with caution. Within Europe in summer 2012, the share of flights delayed on departure (by 5 minutes or more) was 36.3 per cent compared with 39.7 per cent in summer 2011 and 45.7 per cent in summer 2010. Likewise, the comparable figures for arrivals were 33.8 per cent (2012), 37.5 per cent (2011) and 42.4 per cent (2010). Delays due to airline factors represented on average 2.88 minutes per flight, followed by air traffic control (1.29 minutes), airport (0.91 minutes) and the weather (0.32 minutes) (Eurocontrol, 2012). Table 6.5 shows

Table 6.4 *Schedule time: Amsterdam–London, 1985–2012*

From	To	Year	Depart	Arrive	Aircraft type	Sector time (hours: minutes)
Amsterdam	London Heathrow	1985	1200	1200	DC9	1:00
Amsterdam	London Heathrow	2012	1155	1220	A321	1:25
Amsterdam	London City	2012	1130	1135	E90	1:05
Amsterdam	London Luton	2012	1205	1215	A320	1:10

Sources: OAG Flight Guide/ABC World Airways Guide

Table 6.5 *Major European airports with longest delay in summer, 2012*

Airport	Average delay per departure (min)	Average delay per arrival (min)
Lisbon	19.3	19.3
Manchester	15.5	15.8
London Gatwick	13.1	13.7
Antalya	12.2	12.5
Palma de Mallorca	12.0	9.6
Alicante	11.8	9.2
Ibiza	11.8	10.6
London Luton	11.8	10.8
London Heathrow	11.8	11.9
Paris CDG	11.7	8.8
Malaga	11.6	9.6
Istanbul Ataturk	11.3	14.4
Madrid	10.6	13.1
Birmingham	10.6	10.8
Zurich	10.6	(*)
Nice	10.5	(*)
Rome Fiumicino	10.5	(*)
Frankfurt	10.5	8.8
Venice	9.8	(*)
Milan Malpensa	9.4	(*)

*Not in top 20 airports. In addition the following airports experienced average arrival delays: Dublin (10.3), Barcelona (9.4), Cologne/Bonn (9.2), Budapest (8.8), Dusseldorf (8.7)
Source: Eurocontrol (2012)

delay figures for 2012 for the worst affected European airports for both arrival and departures. Lisbon was the worst performing airport for both departures and arrivals; other poorly performing airports for both departures and arrivals were Manchester, London Gatwick, Antalya, Madrid and Istanbul.

Delays are a very difficult area for the airport operator to assess because of the many factors that are beyond its direct control. Nevertheless, it needs to ensure when delays occur, for whatever reason, that they are dealt with in a timely and appropriate manner (e.g. efficient snow clearance of the runway after a snow storm). In addition, a useful development has been the Airport-Collaborative Decision Making (A-CDM) initiative which aims to improve the overall efficiency of operations at an airport, with a particular focus on aircraft turnaround and pre-departure sequencing processes. This is achieved by the real-time sharing of operational data and information between the main stakeholders, including airport operators, airlines, air traffic control and handling agents. It aims to optimise the interactions between these organisations and can lead to better punctuality, for example by reducing taxi-ing time. It can also reduce emissions and produce fuel savings. Munich, Brussels and Paris CDG airports were the first to become A-CDM compliant in 2011. This was followed by more airports including Frankfurt, London Heathrow and Helsinki, and it is eventually planned to be used at all major European airports.

SERVICE QUALITY AND REGULATION

As discussed in Chapter 4, the existence of some form of price cap or other type of economic regulation potentially could lead to a decline in quality as the airport operator tries to reduce its costs to fit in with the requirements of the regulator. As a result, at a number of airports there are formal conditions related to service quality contained within the regulatory framework, although elsewhere the approach may be more informal. For example, in the direct negotiations between Copenhagen airport and its airlines, quality of service is a central discussion point. At Hamburg airport, where there is a price cap, there is a quality monitoring regime, but this does not involve mandatory quality standards. Evidence is collected from passenger surveys and delivery measures.

The UK regulatory system was the first to introduce more formal quality-of-service requirements linked to pricing in 2003, with a system of rebates for airlines if the airports did not meet certain targets or standards. These targets were based on measures of quality of service related to both airlines and to passengers. The airline measures were largely related to existing service-level agreements, with the passenger measures based on BAA's Quality Service Monitor (QSM). It was also decided that regular independent audits of the QSM should be undertaken to ensure the methodology was in accordance with best practices and that representative samples were used. This was because the suitability of BAA using its own survey to give an independent and unbiased measure of its performance had been questioned by many, especially the airlines. At the same time, in 2003 a system of rebates at Manchester airport was agreed based on some central service standards that the airport operator had developed in consultation with its users.

When the service quality conditions were introduced at Heathrow and Gatwick in 2003, it was decided that at some later date, after a period of consultation with the airlines and BAA, a measure should be included to assess aerodrome congestion delay. This was postponed because of the difficulties in finding an acceptable measure of congestion that related only to factors under the control of the airport operator (as opposed to weather, airline operational factors and so on). This measure was finally introduced in 2006, when it was decided that rebates would be payable to airlines when 'material events' occurred that were the responsibility of the BAA or of its contractual agents (including NATS, which provided air traffic control) and that caused a 'material' or significant operational impact in terms of the number of movements lost or deferred. Material events included industrial action; closure of runways or other areas; failure of equipment; and when bad weather had been forecast and materialised but relevant bad weather equipment (e.g. related to fog, ice or snow) had not been used. A material operational impact was defined as causing a deferment (or loss) of more than four cumulative movements. In order to measure this, BAA was required to keep a 'superlog' that recorded all the events that had a material effect, available for review by the airlines on a weekly basis. The maximum impact of these aerodrome rebates was 1 per cent of the regulated airport charge as compared with 1.5 per cent for the airline-related measures and 0.5 per cent for the QSM measures, which meant that in total the rebates were limited to 3 per cent of the charges.

In 2008 the range of service measures subject to financial incentives was broadened and the target performance levels (particularly for passenger security) were raised. Table 6.6 gives an example for some terminals at Heathrow. The maximum level of rebates was increased from 3 to 7 per cent (3 per cent each for passenger-facing and airline-facing services, 1 per cent for aerodrome congestion) and in addition positive financial incentives in the form of bonuses of up to 2.25 per cent were introduced for consistently excellent performance across all passenger-facing measures and all terminals (CAA, 2008). The new UK regulatory system to be introduced in 2014 (see Chapter 4) is also very likely to have new service-quality conditions, and there has been considerable debate as to what these should cover.

Another airport group that has quality conditions built into the regulatory process is AdP. This was introduced when the airport was partially privatised in 2006. In the latest regulatory period (2011–15) there are 11 indicators, chosen because they covered areas where the airport company had considerable control and responsibility. There are four related to availability of equipment, five related to passenger satisfaction, and two other miscellaneous measures. As with the UK system there are financial penalties and incentives related to the indicators. Passenger satisfaction is measured through AdP's passenger survey, its 'Passenger Observatory' (AdP, 2009).

There are also some examples of airports using the ACI ASQ when monitoring passenger satisfaction rates for regulatory purposes. For instance, in Ireland during the latest regulatory period there were a number of targets set for Dublin airport, shown in Table 6.7. This is in addition to SLAs that have been agreed with service providers in the areas of check-in, baggage handling, baggage delivery, stand/gate allocation, trolley availability and security passenger search. In India, the ACI ASQ measures are used as targets for passenger satisfaction (with a target of 3.5 for overall satisfaction) for Delhi, Mumbai, Hyderabad and Bengaluru in the concession and build, operate, transfer (BOT) contracts with the airports. Service delivery standards were also agreed that had to be achieved within a certain time frame (1–5 years) after privatisation. By way of illustration, these are shown for Mumbai airport in Table 6.8.

Table 6.6 *Service quality elements included in the regulation of Heathrow 1, 3, 4 and Terminal East, 2008–13*

	Performance measure	Standard
Stands	Percentage time available	99 per cent
Jetties	Percentage time available	99 per cent
Pier service	Percentage passengers pier served	Linked to expected level of service in each terminal
Fixed electrical ground power	Percentage time available	99 per cent
Pre-conditioned air	Percentage time available	98 per cent
Stand entry guidance	Percentage time available and serviceable	99 per cent
Staff search	Times queue <10 min	95 per cent
Control posts search	Times <20 min	
Departure lounge seat availability	QSM score	3.8
Cleanliness	QSM score	3.9
Way-finding	QSM score	4.0
Flight information	QSM score	4.2
Central security queues	Times queue <5 min	95 per cent
	Times queue <10 min	99 per cent
Transferring passenger queues	Waiting time <10 min	
Arrivals reclaim	Baggage carousel serviceability	99 per cent
Passenger sensitive equipment	Percentage time available	99 per cent
Aerodrome delay: deferment loss of movements	Material events causing deferment/loss of movements	(see text)

Source: Adapted from CAA (2008)

When the Australian airports were privatised in 1997 and 1998 (see Chapter 2), a regulatory framework comprising a package of measures was introduced. This covered aeronautical charges and financial accounting reporting. It also contained specific quality reporting requirements, unlike the UK situation immediately after privatisation. The quality-monitoring programme in Australia was introduced to assist in the review of prices at the airports, to improve transparency of airport performance and to discourage operators from abusing their market power by providing unsatisfactory standards. The Airports Act 1996 provided for the regulator, the Australian Competition and Consumer Commission (ACCC) to monitor the quality of services against criteria defined by the ACCC. It stipulated that records had to be kept in relation to quality of service and that the ACCC should publish the results of the quality-of-service monitoring

Table 6.7 Service quality elements included in the regulation of Dublin airports 2010–14

Service quality measure (per cent weight in price cap)	Target (measurement source: DAA) (per cent)	Service quality measure (per cent weight in price cap)	Target (measurement source: ACI) (per cent)
Security passenger search time <30 min (1.50)	100	Ease of way-finding (0.25)	3.7
Percentage time outbound baggage system unavailable >30 min (0.75)	0	Flight information screens (0.25)	3.8
Percentage time inbound baggage system available (0.25)	99	Cleanliness of airport terminal (0.25)	3.6
		Cleanliness of washrooms (0.25)	3.3
		Comfort of waiting/ gate area (0.25)	3.0
		Courtesy/helpfulness – airport staff (0.10)	3.8
		Courtesy/helpfulness – security staff (0.15)	3.8
		Overall satisfaction (0.25)	3.5
		Communication/ telecom/e-facilities (0.25)	3.1

Source: Adapted from Commission for Aviation Regulation (2009)

Table 6.8 Service quality targets in the Mumbai airport concession agreement

Performance area	Performance target	Target
Transfer process	Minimum connect time	Dom/Int: 60 min Int/Int: 45 min
Terminal services	Handling of complaints	100 per cent response with 2 days
	Response to phone calls	5 per cent answered within 20 seconds

Continued

Table 6.8 *Continued*

Performance area	Performance target	Target
	Availability of flight information	98 per cent available
	Automated services	98 per cent available
	Lifts, escalators	98 per cent available
	Repair completion	95 per cent high priority within 4 hours, 95 per cent others within 24 hours
	Baggage trolleys	100 per cent availability
	Cleanliness	Satisfactory rating for 95 per cent of all inspections
	Availability of wheelchairs	100 per cent within 5 min
	Assistance for disabled	100 per cent within 5 min
Check-in	Maximum queuing time	Business class: 5 min
		Economy class: 20 min
Security check	Waiting time in queue	95 per cent of passengers wait less than 10 min
Customs and immigration	Checking time in queue	95 per cent of passengers less than 20 min
Baggage delivery	Time for bag delivery from aircraft arrival	Domestic: First bag 10 min, last bag 30 min
		International: First bag 15 min, last bag 40 min
International passenger arrival process	Time taken from aircraft arrival to kerbside	95 per cent of passengers less than 45 min
Passenger boarding bridges	Passengers served by bridges	90 per cent of passengers
Runway system	Delays due to arriving/ departing aircraft	Average annual delay per aircraft: 4 min or better
Car parking	Average time to find parking space	95 per cent of drivers take less than 5 min
	Average time to depart from parking space	95 per cent of drives take less than 5 min
Taxis	Maximum waiting time	95 per cent of passengers wait less than 5 min
Gate lounges	Seating availability	Seats for 80 per cent of gate lounge population
Cargo services	Average dwell time	Maximum process time 24 hours

Source: Adapted from Airports Authority of India (2006)

exercise. When price regulation was replaced with price monitoring at the major airports (Sydney, Brisbane, Melbourne, Perth, Adelaide, Canberra and Darwin) in 2002, it was decided that the monitoring process of the ACCC should continue to complement the price monitoring. This measuring of quality of service along the lines of the ACCC monitoring can be incorporated into the airport–airline agreements that have been developed since price monitoring replaced formal regulation.

The ACCC reports on a selection of 'static' or objective measures, including the number, availability and adequacy of particular facilities. In addition, certain airports including Brisbane, Melbourne, Perth and Sydney are required to provide more detailed subjective satisfaction ratings by passengers. Also, the ACCC surveys airlines for their views (and obtains information from the government agencies) (Table 6.9). The rationale here is that passengers' opinions are a direct indication of the quality of service provided not solely by the airports, but also by other bodies including the airlines and ground handlers, while the airlines' views will be much closer to the quality of service provided by the airport operator. This links back to the need for consideration of all service providers and their role at the airport when discussing service quality. As a result of the Productivity Commission's review of airport regulation in 2011, service-quality measures are likely to be reconsidered and maybe revised in some areas in the future.

Table 6.9 *Areas of performance covered in the monitoring of service quality at major Australian airports*

Passenger	Airline*
Check-in services and facilities (waiting time)	Runways
Customs, immigration and quarantine (waiting time)	Taxiways
Security inspection (quality of process)	Aprons
Gate lounges and seating (quality/ availability of seating, crowding)	Aircraft parking facilities and bays
Baggage services and facilities (waiting time, information provision, circulation space)	Ground handling services and facilities
Baggage trolleys (accessibility)	Airbridges
Flight information and signage (display screens, wayfinding)	Check-in services and facilities
Public areas (standard of washrooms)	Baggage processing facilities
Car parking (standard, availability of spaces, time to enter car park)	Management (responsiveness or approach to addressing quality of service problems and concerns)
Airport access (congestion and facilities at taxi kerbside, standard of taxi facilities)	

Source: ACCC (2012)

REFERENCES

ACCC (2012) Airport monitoring report 2010–11, Canberra: Australian Competition and Consumer Commission.

ACI (2012) 'ACI's 2011 ASQ Awards name Incheon International Airport best airport worldwide in overall customer satisfaction', press release, 14 February, Montreal: Airports Council International.

ACI/DKMA (2011) *ASQ Best Practice Report: Airport Wayfinding*, Montreal: Airports Council International.

—— (2012) *ASQ Best Practice Report: Staff Courtesy*, Montreal: Airports Council International.

Adderley, N. (2012) 'Making every journey better: putting passengers at the heart of Heathrow's decision-making', *Journal of Airport Management*, 6(2): 141–50.

AdP (2009) *Economic Regulation Agreement between the State and Aéroports de Paris 2011–2015*, Paris: Aéroports de Paris.

AENA (2012) *Corporate Social Responsibility Report 2011*, Madrid: Aeropuertos Espanoles y Navegacion Aerea.

Airports Authority of India (2006) *Operation, Management and Development Agreement Between Airports Authority of India and Mumbai International Airport Private Limited*, Delhi: Airports Authority of India.

Amadeus (2011) *Navigating the Airport of Tomorrow*, Madrid: Amadeus.

CAA (2008) *Economic Regulation of Heathrow and Gatwick Airports: CAA Decision*, London: Civil Aviation Authority.

—— (2009) *The Through Airport Passenger Experience: An Analysis of End-to-end Journeys with a Focus on Heathrow*, London: Civil Aviation Authority.

Commission for Aviation Regulation (2009) *Determination on Maximum Levels of Airport Charges at Dublin Airport*, Dublin: CAR.

Copenhagen Airport (2012) *CPH and Society 2011*, Copenhagen: Copenhagen Airport.

Correia, A., Wirasinghe, S. and de Barros, A. (2008) 'A global index for level of service evaluation at airport passenger terminals', *Transportation Research Part E*, 44(4): 607–20.

Department for Transport (2007) *Improving the Air Passenger Experience*, London: Department for Transport.

Ellis, D. (2012) 'How Heathrow uses its market research', *University of Westminster Marketing and Market Research Seminar*, London, November.

Eurocontrol (2012) *CODA Digest: Delays to Air Transport in Europe Summer 2012*, Brussels: Eurocontrol.

Fodness, D. and Murray, B. (2007) 'Passengers' expectations of airport service quality', *Journal of Services Marketing*, 21(7): 492–506

Gresham, Smith and Partners *et al.* (2011) *ACRP Report 55: Wayfinding and Signing Guidelines for Airport Terminals and Landside*, Washington, DC: Transportation Research Board.

IATA (2004) *Airport Development Reference Manual*, Geneva: International Air Transport Association.

Jacobs Consultancy (2007) *Review of Dedicated Low-Cost Airport Passenger Facilities*, London: Jacobs Consultancy.

London Economics (2008), *Imagine a World Class Heathrow*, London: London First.

Madeira, C. (2011) 'Building retail practices for the new Lisbon airport', *Journal of Airport Management*, 6(1): 40–50.

Maiden, S. (2008) 'How BAA uses its market research', *University of Westminster Marketing and Market Research Seminar*, London, February.

ORC International (2009) *Research on the Air-Passenger Experience at Heathrow, Gatwick, Stansted and Manchester Airports*, London: ORC International.

Rhoades, D., Waguespack, B. and Young, S. (2000) 'Developing a quality index for US airports', *Managing Service Quality*, 10(4): 257–62.

SITA (2012) *Passenger Self-Service Survey Highlights*, Geneva: SITA/Air Transport World.

Sykes, W. and Desai, P. (2009) *Understanding Airport Passenger Experience*, London: Independent Social Research.

TransSolutions, Strategic Insight Group, Aviation Resource Partners and Kimley-Horn Associates (2011) *ACRP Report 55: Passenger Level of Service and Spatial Planning for Airport Terminals*, Washington, DC: Transportation Research Board.

Yeh, C.-H. and Kuo, Y.-L. (2003) 'Evaluating passenger services at Asia-Pacific international airports', *Transportation Research Part E*, 39(1): 35–48.

7 Provision of commercial facilities

IMPORTANCE OF COMMERCIAL FACILITIES

A major development in the evolution of the airport industry has been the increase in dependence on non-aeronautical or commercial revenues. This chapter discusses the generation of non-aeronautical revenues by looking at the market for commercial services and assessing how the facilities can be planned and managed. It considers the factors that influence commercial performance. Most of the focus is on individual consumers who buy commercial goods/services at airports, although many businesses, including airlines, handling agents and other agencies, also generate rent and property income for airports.

A number of factors have contributed to the growth in dependence on non-aeronautical revenues. First, moves towards commercialisation and privatisation within the industry have given airports greater freedom to develop their commercial policies and diversify into new areas. A more business-oriented approach to running airports has also raised the priority given to commercial facilities. Such facilities were traditionally considered to be somewhat secondary to providing essential air transport infrastructure for airlines. Managers are now eager to adopt more creative and imaginative strategies and to exploit all possible aeronautical and non-aeronautical revenue generating opportunities.

In addition, airlines have been exerting increasing pressure on the airport industry to control the level of aeronautical fees that are being levied. A more competitive environment and falling yields have forced many airlines to focus on major cost-saving initiatives, including outsourcing, reductions in staff numbers and pegging the level of wages. Increasingly, airlines are demanding that airports adopt such cost-cutting and efficiency-saving measures themselves, rather than raising their charges to the airlines. Thus airport charges have become subject to more and more scrutiny from the airlines – particularly from the LCCs. In addition, the ability of some airports to increase aeronautical charges is now, more than before, restricted by formal government regulation which has often been introduced at the same time as privatisation (see Chapter 4). The impact of these pressures on the level of aeronautical charges, either from the airlines themselves or from regulatory bodies, has encouraged the airports to look to alternative ways of increasing their revenues and growing their businesses by giving greater attention to commercial facilities. In effect, the airports have had to broaden their horizons considerably in managing their businesses.

At the same time, increasing numbers of people are travelling through airports and making more frequent trips. Hence passengers are becoming more sophisticated and experienced airport shoppers, and are generally much better informed. As a result of this, airport shoppers are becoming more demanding not only in the quality of service that is provided, but also in the range and value for money of the commercial facilities on offer. This reflects general trends in the high street, where consumers have become more discerning with quality, value and choice at the top of their priorities, and the impact of the additional choice of internet shopping. However, it is difficult to determine entirely whether the raised expectations at airports have been caused by a genuine need or desire of consumers for expanded facilities, or whether airports' drive to maximise their commercial income by becoming shopping centres has merely changed the expectations of passengers. It is also true to say that this increased emphasis on commercial facilities has not been welcomed by all the travelling public, with significant groups of passengers, particularly those from the business community, often desiring a quick route through the airport as uncluttered as possible from the distraction of numerous shops and F&B outlets.

Increasing airport competition, especially between airport hubs, has also played a role in the development of non-aeronautical revenues. The main reason why a passenger will choose a certain airport will normally be the nature of air services offered by that airport and the convenience of the airport's location (see Chapter 8). Consideration of the retail and other commercial facilities is very likely to be secondary. Transfer passengers may, however, be more influenced by the commercial facilities if they cannot perceive any significant difference between the convenience and quality of the choice of connecting flights at different airports. Certain airports, including Amsterdam Schiphol and Singapore Changi, have run high-profile marketing campaigns emphasising the quality and good value of the commercial facilities on offer to transfer passengers. Other airports have gone a stage further. In the Middle East a number of the airports, including Abu Dhabi and Dubai, try to use their duty- and tax-free shops as a way of capturing competing traffic, particularly by using incentives such as raffles with high-value prizes, including luxury cars.

THE MARKET FOR COMMERCIAL FACILITIES

Who buys at airports?

The airport environment is a unique location for shopping and other commercial facilities. The main shoppers, the passengers, make up a large captive market. They often tend to be more affluent than the average and they may have time on their hands to have a quick meal or snack. They may spend spontaneously to acquire a last-minute essential or discount purchase for a holiday, or souvenirs and gifts while returning. They may even spend just to dispose of the last of their foreign currency. Airport retailing is, however, fundamentally different from high street retailing as passengers are going to the airport to catch a flight rather than to shop. Consequently, passengers will be far less familiar with the airport shopping environment than with their neighbourhood shops and this, coupled with a fear of missing the flight and the stress associated with the check-in, immigration and security processes, may impose a considerable sense of anxiety on passengers.

To fully harness the commercial development potential of the airport traffic, the range of facilities on offer and even the product selection should match very closely the preferences and needs of the specific passenger types at the airports. To achieve this aim, airports, together with their retailing and F&B partners, have increasingly been devoting more resources to getting to know their customers. At the most basic level, this involves an analysis of the air services offered and the origin and destination of travellers. Even this detail of information about the market, which is automatically collected at airports, is the envy of most high street retailers. In addition, duty- and tax-free retailers can obtain information about travellers from their boarding passes, shown when purchases are made, known as point-of-sale (POS) data. In many cases this is supplemented by market research, of varying degrees of sophistication, that will investigate the demographic, geographical and behavioural features of passengers. Such research will often aim to determine who shops at airports and what they buy, who does not shop at airports and why, and attitudes towards the range of facilities on offer and the value for money of the products. This type of research needs to be updated regularly as customer demands and perceptions are continuously changing.

Different types of passenger have different spending profiles and preferences. Leisure or charter passengers have traditionally been favourites for impulse buys and the use of F&B facilities. They are encouraged to check in early, which gives them extra dwell time to shop. Long-haul leisure passengers tend to spend more than short-haul leisure travellers, again often because they have more time at the airport. Regular business travellers typically have a shorter dwell time and are less likely to browse in shops. The widespread adoption of airline lounges for business and first-class customers has further discouraged these passengers from having spare time to visit the main terminal shops. As a result, business travellers make purchases relatively infrequently – although their average spend on a purchase tends to be high. Business travellers also tend to make high use of certain facilities, including banks, car hire and airport hotels, and when they use F&B services their spending is less constrained as it is covered by company expenses. They may also use facilities because it is convenient to do this in their busy schedule – for example, buying a new tie for work.

There is considerable debate concerning the spending patterns of LCC passengers, particularly as many airport operators seek to compensate for the reduction in aeronautical revenues by offsetting these with higher non-aeronautical revenues from the increased number of LCC passengers. These passengers are not necessarily budget spenders, tend to be more evenly spread through time, and are particularly good users of the F&B services because of the lack of free in-flight refreshments. They also tend to use car parking because of the relative remoteness of some secondary airports. However, the evidence concerning commercial income from LCC passengers is patchy and inconsistent. For example, Gillen and Lall (2004) observed that non-airline revenue per passenger increased from US$9.70 to $10.55 at Albany airport when Southwest started services. Likewise, the share of non-aeronautical revenues at Luton airport rose from 45 per cent in 1995 to 59 per cent in 2001 as the share of LCCs increased (Francis *et al.*, 2004). Similarly, for Canadian airports it was found that an additional LCC (WestJet) passenger brought C$6.20 of non-aeronautical revenue compared with $1.22 for a non-LCC passenger. However, in a more up-to-date study of UK airports, it was observed that the non-aeronautical spend of LCC passengers was on average £2.87 compared with £5.59 for more traditional passengers (Lei and Papatheodorou, 2010).

Then there are transfer passengers. They are unlikely to make use of facilities including banks and post offices, and obviously will not need car hire or car parking facilities. They may want to make some retail purchases, particularly if the duty- and tax-free prices are competitive, but this will be possible only if there is sufficient time between flights. It is hard for an airport to maximise the commercial opportunities from transfer passengers if it also wishes to maximise its efficiency as a hub by providing swift connections. At most major hubs, there will also be passengers who spend a considerable length of time in the airside area. Various airports have developed some quite imaginative airside facilities to appeal to these passengers. For example, Singapore Changi airport has a swimming pool, sauna, gym and cinema, and if transfer passengers stay for longer than 5 hours they can arrange a bus tour of Singapore. Amsterdam airport has an art gallery and casino. An increasing number of airports are also providing pampering, fitness and health services including reflexology, massage and spa treatments which are particularly appealing to passengers with time to spare when they are transferring.

Nationality will also influence spending and shopping behavioural patterns. For example Scandinavians, who have relatively high duties and taxes, are favourites for buying duty- and tax-free products at airport shops. The Japanese have also tended to have a high spend per passenger which has traditionally been due partly to the buying of gifts to take home to friends and relatives. Americans, although very fond of shopping generally, are not usually expected to do their shopping at airports and so their average spend is much lower. Factors including nationality as well as age, occupation, gender and socio-economic group, in addition to psychographic and behaviour variables, can be used to produce different passenger classifications. For example, research at Taoyaun Taipai airport found that male passengers were more likely to be attracted to brand name products, while passengers under 26 were more likely to shop in souvenir shops and cafés (Perng *et al.*, 2010). A few other examples of classifications are provided in Table 7.1. At Heathrow, four traveller groups associated with UK nationals were identified through specific market research – mass market leisure flyers, young upmarket leisure flyers, older upmarket leisure flyers and time-starved frequent business flyers. A few years ago, Manchester airport segmented its market into six different types. First there was the airport shopaholic, typically a young, happy female on a charter holiday. Next there was the agitated passenger, a young and frustrated middle-income traveller. Then the unfulfilled shopper, a young professional on business or leisure trips; and the value-seeker, a student or pensioner on an annual trip to Europe. The final two categories were the unlikely shoppers, who were frequent business travellers; and the measured shoppers, who were older male travellers. Each of these groups had different characteristics and spending behaviour. Some alternative classifications have been used for Amsterdam and Lisbon, with a somewhat simpler one at Brussels airport.

An assessment of motivation is also important because the primary reason for passengers to come to airports is not to shop, and consequently the motivation to shop at airports will be very different than for other types of shopping. Distinctions can be made between entertainment shopping (gifts/novelty purchases), purposive shopping (confectionery, books, toiletries), time-pressed shopping (last-minute/emergency purchases), convenience shopping (wide choice of known brand names), essential shopping (restaurants/cafeterias, foreign currency exchange, insurance) and lifestyle shopping (high-quality international brand purchases) (Institute for Retail Studies, 1997). Echevarne (2008) described a similar classification devised by Pragma Consulting/ARC Retail Consultants. There was travel necessity (books, toys, music, confectionery), souvenirs (local produce, T-shirts, ornaments), gifts for those at home or destination, personal self-treat (designer label clothing, watches, jewellery, accessories), convenience

Table 7.1 *Passenger segmentation related to shopping behaviour at selected airports*

Amsterdam Schiphol	Lisbon	Brussels	London Heathrow	Manchester	Taipei
Satisfied atmosphere-tasters	Shopaholics	Mood shoppers	Mass market leisure flyers	Shopaholics	Mood shoppers
Certainty-seekers	Supporters	Apathetic shoppers	Young upmarket	Agitated passengers	Apathetic shoppers
Active pleasure-seekers	Pure convenience	Shopping-lovers	leisure flyers	Unfulfilled shoppers	Shopping-lovers
Trendy shoppers	Minimalists		Older upmarket	Value-seekers	Traditional shoppers
Exclusivity-claimers	Controlled		leisure flyers	Unlikely shoppers	
Well-to-do functionals	Value-seekers		Time-starved frequent business	Measured shoppers	
	Unlikely shoppers		flyers		

Sources: Maiden (2000); Geuens *et al.* (2004); Agbebi (2005); Madeira (2011); Martens (2012); Chung *et al.* (2013)

(tie for executive), exclusive opportunity to buy (reduced prices or unique merchandise in the duty-free shop) and trip enhancement (sunglasses for holiday).

Most airport commercial facilities historically have been provided for passengers – or perhaps their pets, as in the case of the 'Park and Bark' dog kennels at Sydney airport. However, many airports have now recognised the commercial opportunities that exist with other consumer groups who use the airport, and have introduced facilities wholly or partially for their needs. The airports have thus exploited their commercial potential of being business or commercial centres that generate, employ and attract a large number of visits – rather than just providing facilities for passengers who choose to use the airport. For example, staff employed by the airport operators and by the airlines, handling agents, concessionaires and government agencies may wish to use airport commercial facilities, particularly as they may not be able to combine a visit to their local shops and their working life at the airport. A survey of a US west coast international airport found that 45 per cent of employees used the F&B facilities daily and 26 per cent used them weekly. Equivalent figures for retail were 4 and 18 per cent, respectively (LeighFisher, 2012). Workers from nearby office complexes or from airport industrial estates may find the airport facilities useful. Popular services include supermarkets, banking services, hairdressers, chemists and dry-cleaners. Some of these services may be used by arriving passengers, another potential market subsegment.

Airports may also be attractive to the local residential community as an alternative shopping centre – especially if the airport is relatively uncongested and easily accessible with good road and rail links. Sometimes local residents will be encouraged to the airport by free parking, or a certain period of free parking, if a purchase is made. The growing popularity of the use of initiatives to encourage public transport use at airports, however, may be in conflict with such commercial strategies. For certain large airports with severe surface access problems, encouraging additional visits to the airport will be the last policy they want to adopt. Opposition may also be voiced by nearby local shopping centres, as has been the case at London Gatwick airport and shopping facilities in the neighbouring town of Crawley. Airports may be particularly popular as alternative shopping centres if there are legal restrictions on shopping hours imposed on the high street. For example, Frankfurt airport was one of the first airports to develop its landside shops into a shopping mall concept, benefiting from downtown shopping hour limits that were only relaxed in the mid-1990s.

Accompanying visitors, known as 'meeters and greeters', 'well wishers' or 'farewellers and weepers' will also need F&B services and, perhaps, additional facilities including florists, gifts and souvenir shops. Car-parking revenue can be generated from them. International and long-haul flights for passengers who are travelling for leisure purposes generally tend to attract the most meeters and greeters. For example, at Los Angeles airport only 20 per cent of business passengers were accompanied compared with 24 per cent of vacation passengers and 35 per cent of 'other' passengers (AMPG, 2007). Likewise, at Heathrow airport only around 1–3 per cent of business passengers had people waving them off, whereas for leisure this was around 6 per cent (CAA, 2012). Air travel still holds a unique fascination for certain people, and for these enthusiasts specialist shops and merchandise can be sold. Viewing platforms, tours and exhibitions can also be provided on a commercial basis, and can have a dual purpose in acting as a public relations function or service to the community. For instance, Munich airport visitors' park is one of

Bavaria's most popular day-trip destinations, consisting of an interactive multimedia centre, an observation hill, a 'behind the scenes at the airport' display, guided bus tours, and F&B and retail facilities. Other airports, for example Dusseldorf, also provide airport tours. Visitors may also be attracted to airports if leisure facilities are provided. A notable example is Kuala Lumpur airport, where among the leisure facilities within the boundary of this airport is a Formula 1 motor-racing track. Stockholm Arlanda airport has even become a popular destination for weddings, where almost 500 marriage ceremonies took place in 2009.

For the business community, conferences and meeting facilities can be provided. The good transport links that airports generally possess can make them ideal for international business events. These facilities can be shared by business passengers, local businesses and other customers. A survey in 2011 showed that just over two-thirds of the airports provided business, conferencing and/or event facilities (Halpern *et al.*, 2011). Many airports have also expanded beyond the boundaries of the traditional airport business by using neighbouring land for hotels, office complexes, trade centres, light industries, freight warehousing, distribution and logistics centres and business parks. If such development occurs, the airport is often called an airport city. Way back in 1994, Amsterdam airport defined itself as an airport city, and later adopted this concept at Brisbane airport which it partially owned. Many other airport cities also now exist. If the airport city continues to develop outwards, the boundaries between the airport and its surrounding urban area may become increasingly blurred, and a new urban form known as an aerotropolis can emerge. This is discussed further in Chapter 9. In summary, Table 7.2 lists the main markets for commercial facilities.

Geographical characteristics

On average, European airports generate the highest volumes of non-aeronautical revenue. This is due to a number of general factors, including the large international traffic volumes within Europe and the relatively high income per capita. European airports have also led the way in

Table 7.2 The different markets for commercial facilities at airports

Market segment	Facilities provided
Passengers (departing/arriving, terminal/transfer, low-cost/full-cost, business/leisure, different nationalities, ages, etc.)	Wide range of retail, F&B and other essential and leisure services dependent on passenger type
Workers at the airport and in surrounding areas	Convenience shops, banks, chemists and other essential services
Local residents	Shops, F&B, leisure services
Visitors – meeters, greeters, farewellers	F&B, gift and souvenir shops
Visitors – air transport enthusiasts	Specialist aviation shops, tours, visitor terraces, exhibitions, F&B
Local businesses	Office/meeting facilities, land for business development/light industry

terms of commercialisation and privatisation trends, with the development of non-aeronautical revenues being one of the most notable outcomes of these more advanced evolutionary stages of the airport industry. European airports as a whole generated US$12 per passenger from non-aeronautical sources in 2010 compared with a global mean of $8 (ACI, 2011) (Figure 7.1). Retail was the most important single item, followed by car parking (Figure 7.2).

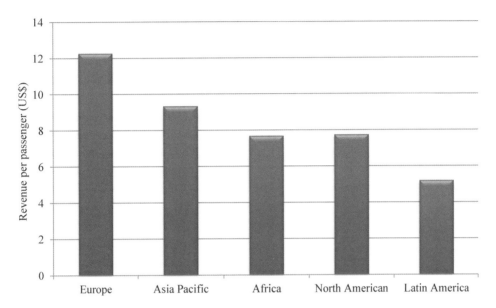

Figure 7.1 Non-aeronautical revenue per passenger at ACI airports by world region, 2010
Source: ACI (2011)

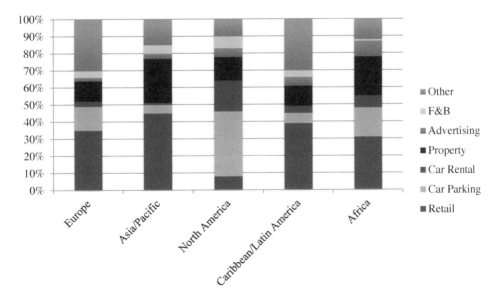

Figure 7.2 Non-aeronautical revenue at ACI airports by revenue source, 2010
Source: ACI (2011)

Non-aeronautical revenue per passenger for North American airports is much less than in Europe – averaging less than US$6. These airports are dominated by domestic passengers who spend less. Also at hub airports, emphasis is placed on swift, efficient connections rather than providing passengers with the time to browse and shop. Dependency on the car and the lack of adequate public transport access to many airports means that the two single most important non-aeronautical sources are car parking and car hire (Figure 7.3). Retail is much less important and proportionally F&B is much more significant. Appold and Kasarda (2006) estimated that at US airports typically 54–68 per cent of passengers use F&B facilities, while only 11–37 per cent make a non-food/drink purchase. Also, duty- and tax-free sales are not very significant at most North American airports, with the exception of certain airports including San Francisco, Los Angeles and Honolulu which handle a large proportion of Asian traffic.

By contrast, in Asia duty- and tax-free income is much more important and there are arrival duty- and tax-free shops at many of the major Asian airports. Airports including Singapore Changi, Kuala Lumpur's Sepang and Hong Kong's Chek Lap Kok are known worldwide for their extensive commercial facilities. In addition, the passenger profile at a number of Asian countries which have been developing rapidly in recent years (e.g. Indonesia and the Philippines) has changed as the traditional upper-class high-spending Asian nationals have been joined by a large volume of Asian travellers who are of a younger average age and are from fast growing middle classes. Inbound passengers in this area are also now a much more diverse, more cost-conscious group of travellers. Elsewhere in Africa and in Latin America there generally tends to be less reliance on non-aeronautical income. This is partly because many of the airports in these regions have relatively small numbers of passengers and also because the spending power of the local population is more limited. Furthermore, the airport management, often closely tied to its government owners, may have neither the expertise nor the commercial pressures to fully exploit the non-aeronautical opportunities at these airports.

APPROACHES TO THE PROVISION OF COMMERCIAL FACILITIES

Most airports have come a long way since they provided just the generic newspaper, book and gift shop, the traditional duty-free shop with its internationally branded products and the bland F&B services with no recognisable identity. It was way back in the 1980s when many European airports began to recognise the attraction of speciality retail outlets and the advantages of using familiar brand names. The specialist retail chains that had grown so quickly in the high streets started to appear at airports. Branding provided reassurance for the traveller, who was aware of the quality and price level of the goods within the branded outlet. More variety was also introduced into the F&B outlets by again bringing in famous brand names such as McDonald's and Burger King. The F&B area began to be split into a number of different, sometimes competing individual outlets. In most cases the large sit-down restaurant, which took up considerable valuable floor space, became a relic of the past.

However, the widespread adoption of branding at airports has meant there is now greater similarity between the shopping facilities at many airports, and less diversity. Brand fatigue can become a problem – particularly for the frequent traveller who can find that airport shopping can become rather dull and boring. Hence most airports are trying to blend famous brand outlets together with local outlets that can give the airport some kind of identity and distinguish it from other airports. The character and culture of the city or country the airport serves can be represented by selling local merchandise or gourmet products such as cheese from Switzerland, chocolates from Belgium or Parma ham from Italy. A flavour of the local environment can also be provided by theming the commercial facilities. For instance, at Las Vegas airport a number of the outlets are themed after hotels and entertainments in the city. There are slot machines everywhere (even before arriving passengers reach the baggage reclaim) and gaming accounts for over 10 per cent of total concession revenue. At Orlando airport there are shops representing the major theme parks in the area, and Memphis airport is themed around the blues, rock and roll and Elvis Presley. (There is even an Elvis-themed bar in Prestwick airport in Scotland, which is the only place in Great Britain that Elvis visited.) Vancouver airport is themed to represent the physical characteristics and cultural heritage of British Columbia, while Santiago airport in Chile tries to depict Chile's diverse geography from desert to Antarctic conditions. At Austin airport there are 15 weekly live music performances in five airport venues to reflect the city's strong association with the music culture.

Fundamentally, the skill is in finding the correct balance between international recognised global brand retailers and local shops and F&B outlets that give the airport an individual identity. Brands also need to be appropriate for passenger spending capabilities – too expensive a brand may deter spending, but on the other hand too cheap a brand may mean suboptimal revenue is generated. In addition, even when global F&B brands are used, local tastes should be taken into account. An example of a few years ago is Subway, which increased its vegetarian offerings in Indian airports and made greater use of chilli sauce at Changi Singapore airport. Similarly, to accommodate local preferences for coffee, Caffè Ritazza focused on strong filter coffee in Sweden, latte macchiato in Germany and strong espresso in Italy (McCormick, 2006). Some airports have chosen to enforce and promote an airport brand rather than the individual brands of the high street retailers. For example, at Amsterdam airport all the shops in the airside area are branded under the 'See Buy Fly' identity.

A survey of North American airports found some interesting results concerning branding (ACI North America, 2012). Overall, F&B was more likely to be branded (either internationally, regionally or locally) compared with news shops and speciality retailing. For F&B, it found 43 per cent of airports using national/international brands, 36 per cent using regional/local brands and the remaining 21 per cent having airport brands or no brands. From the passenger viewpoint another survey, albeit from just one individual airport in the United States, found that 49 per cent of passengers favoured a mixture of national and local brands for F&B compared with just 12 per cent for mainly national, 5 per cent for mainly regional/local, and the remaining 35 per cent did not consider the brand to be important (LeighFisher, 2012).

The development of airport terminals into shopping centres has not been universally popular. Certain passenger types, particularly business travellers who are seeking a quick transit through the terminal, favour a more streamlined airport service. Also the airlines, while welcoming the fact that non-aeronautical income can reduce an airport's reliance on aeronautical charges (particularly if a single till is adopted), have periodically expressed concerns that the shopping function of the airport has interfered with the normal flows of passengers through the airports. Clear signage to gates, for example, is difficult to achieve if the airport is cluttered with retail and F&B signage and branding. There have been claims that passengers have delayed flights because they have been lost in the duty-free shops – so many airports have now placed flight information display systems (FIDS) in the commercial outlets as well. Some airlines have also complained that airports have been giving too much attention to developing commercial facilities while ignoring basic operational requirements. A correct balance between commercial and operational space is needed so that the non-aeronautical revenue is optimised without compromising operational effectiveness – but this is no easy matter.

As well as adopting high street preferences for speciality shopping and branded products, airports have also applied other tried-and-tested retail practices. This has been helped by an increasing number of airports employing professional retail managers from the high street rather than from within the airport business itself, as historically used to be the case. Many airport operators have encouraged loyalty purchases at airports by introducing loyalty schemes. As with high street shopping, the schemes not only provide the airport operators and their retailers with a mechanism to encourage repeat buying and to encourage spend, but also enable airport operators to find out about their customers and their purchasing habits. This allows airport operators to communicate with scheme members when new products and services are being introduced, perhaps even providing customised offers. With these schemes, points are earned from travelling and spending at the airport, giving benefits including discounts on parking and the commercial facilities, and access to fast-track systems and airline frequent flyer mileage.

A study of 110 global airports found that 16 per cent of the airports offered loyalty schemes, with these being concentrated in the three regions of Europe, Asia-Pacific and North America (ACI/ DKMA, 2012). Milan Malpensa airport has two linked schemes: ViaMilano Program and the Club SEA ViaMilano Program, the latter being more focused on premium travellers. Elsewhere Singapore Changi airport has Changi Rewards, Bristol airport has Bristol Airport Rewards, Dubuque airport has FlyDBQ Rewards Program, Venice airport has Club il Milione, Nice Côte d'Azur airport has Club Airport Premier and Wellington airport has Wellington Airport VIP. Also in the USA there is the loyalty card 'Thanks Again' that can be used at over 100 airports and gives discounts on parking, shopping and eating as well as at local businesses and attractions. In addition, many airports have value and money-back guarantees that have been commonplace on the high street for many years. These are seen as particularly important because of the perceived expensive 'rip-off' reputation of many airports. For example, Singapore Changi airport has two such guarantees, one offering a 100 per cent money-back guarantee and the other offering a double refund on the price difference of any product that is found to be more expensive than at popular downtown shopping areas.

The airport's website can be viewed as an important revenue-generating opportunity as it can offer hyperlinks to the booking pages of airlines and the travel trade, and earn commission. It can also generate income from advertising. The internet can bring many opportunities for airports if strategies are developed in conjunction with the terminal facilities. For instance, most airport websites now give details of the commercial facilities available so passengers can be more prepared when they visit the airport. They may be better able to plan their shopping in the limited time they have available. Special offer vouchers can be made available on the internet to encourage passengers to buy at the airport. At an increasing number of airports, products and services can be pre-ordered for collection at the airport – particularly foreign currency and car parking. However, it is important to note that many purchases at airports form part of the travel experience and are made on impulse (Crawford and Melewar, 2003; Lin and Chen, 2013). Therefore the use of mobile devices to promote commercial facilities while passenger are actually at the airport is seen to offer even more opportunities for increasing passenger spend. For example, a survey of US airports found that a third had mobile apps for their website, with 73 per cent using these to promote concession sales (ACI North America, 2012). Future developments in this area are discussed below.

The airport website is just one of a wide range of advertising opportunities that airports can use to generate additional non-aeronautical revenue. In general, airport advertising is often seen as attractive because of the high volume of passengers and the cosmopolitan and higher socio-economic group of many travellers. However, it is always important with airport advertising, as with the provision of all commercial facilities, to ensure it does not inhibit ease of movement through the airport or irritate the passengers. In practice, the amount of advertising varies quite significantly between airports, with the income depending on factors including the volume and characteristics of passengers and the design and layout of the airport.

Car parking facilities, particularly for North American and Australian airports, are an important source of commercial revenue. Generally these can be split into different categories depending on their location, the duration of stay, and whether or not additional services are provided. There will be short-stay (or term) and long-stay terminal car parks that are normally within walking distance of the terminal, and for that there will be a premium price, particularly for the short-stay. Then there may be off-site long-stay, usually accessible only by shuttle bus. This will normally be the cheapest option for the passenger and the least profitable area for the airport operator, particularly if there is competition from other non-airport operator suppliers. The final category of car parking is the high-end product. This includes additional services such as providing dedicated spaces close to the terminal or a reservations system where business travellers, by paying a premium, can reserve a convenient space. In a study of 132 global airports it was found that they all provided short-stay terminal car parks, 89 per cent provided long-stay terminal car parks, 50 per cent off-site parks and 34 per cent high-end car parks. On average the off-site parks were 37 per cent cheaper than the long-stay terminal ones, while the high-end ones were 42 per cent more expensive. Airports offering these high-end facilities include Helsinki, Copenhagen, Baltimore, Atlanta, Dallas, Boston and Indianapolis (ACI/DKMA, 2009).

The demand for car parking services will depend on factors including the passenger profile, the airport site and location, the public transport available, the amount of transfer traffic and the number of meeters and greeters – this is explored further in Chapter 10. While the traditional approach to car parking – paying a fixed price on the day of travel – is still popular, there is increasing use of pre-booking on the internet with the use of dynamic pricing or revenue management to manage demand and supply and maximise sales, just as with air tickets (Jacobs Consultancy, 2009). Processes associated with car parking are also being streamlined, for example with automatic number plate- and mobile phone-recognition technologies.

In addition to the concession and car parking income, the property income at airports can be significant. This can include very diverse revenue streams, for example those generated from the renting or leasing of terminal areas such offices, business lounges, ticket desks and check-in desks, as well as off-airport space including aircraft maintenance, hangars, training centres, cargo facilities and light industrial buildings. The income will vary according to the type of facility or property, its location and competing off-airport rents, and in recent years many airports have paid much more attention to maximising their income from these sources. However, this can be a complex aspect of airport management that may involve a number of different stakeholders from both the private and public sectors (Armstrong *et al.*, 2011). Property policies may link with broader strategies, for example with an airport's desire to develop as an airport city.

THE COMMERCIAL CONTRACT AND TENDER PROCESS

There are various ways in which commercial facilities can be provided at airports. Most airports have chosen to contract out these services to specialist retail and F&B companies. This lower-risk option is usually chosen because the airport operator does not have specialist skills required or a detailed understanding of the market environment, and may not have the bulk buying power and well established supply infrastructure that the specialist companies will have. Some airports, particularly smaller ones and those in the United States, may opt to offer their airports as a total retail or F&B package to a master concessionaire, who in turn will seek specialist operators to run the individual outlets.

There are a few airport operators, for instance Dubai airport, Dublin airport, Malaysia airport and Hyderabad airport, who have chosen to provide some facilities themselves, including duty- and tax-free products, either directly or through a wholly owned subsidiary. A few regional airports also do this, including Florence airport with duty-free and Venice airport with F&B. A larger number of very small airports run their own facilities, which makes sense with small operations where it would be difficult to attract external specialists. Car parking tends to be the only commercial activity that is provided by a substantial number of airport operators themselves, since it generally requires fewer specialist skills and also greater capital investment by the airport operator. For example, out of the 21 major airports in the UK, 13 operate all their own car parks (LeighFisher, 2011).

When airport operators contract out their commercial facilities, they usually enter into a concession contract with the companies providing the services. This typically involves the concessionaire paying a percentage of sales to the airport operator, often in addition to agreeing a minimum annual guaranteed amount. The turnover fee may vary from as little as 5 per cent for some landside commercial activities to up to 50 per cent for facilities with higher profit margins – notably duty- and tax-free sales. The fee may also increase at a faster rate than the level of turnover in the belief that concessionaires will be in a better position to pay higher fees once all basic fixed costs have been covered. LeighFisher (2012) found that for large hub airports, concession fees for F&B average 13–14 per cent, for news/gift and speciality around 15–16 per cent. Many airports with advertising receive 60–70 per cent. Globally the revenue yield (revenue to the airport as a percentage of gross sales) averages around 20 per cent (Moodie Report, 2009).

The airport operator will usually provide only the shell for the outlet and it will be up to the concessionaire to provide the capital investment for fitting out the facility. A typical length for the concession will be around 5 to 7 years, although this can vary considerably and there may be options for renewal. If the contract is too short there will be no time to develop the business, whereas if the contract is too long the airport may miss out on the increased revenues and opportunity to react to retail trends that the signing of a new contract may be bring. There may be longer contracts (up to 10 years) for F&B to take account of the investment required, and occasionally shorter contracts may be issued for experimental facilities. For example in North America, for large hub airports contracts for F&B were around 10 years, duty-free and news/gifts around 7 years and speciality retail and advertising closer to 6 years (LeighFisher, 2012). Generally concession contracts will be relatively low risk for the airport operator, who will tend to have little responsibility over the commercial facilities and be assured of a certain amount of revenue. However, since this revenue stream will be linked to the concessionaire's sales rather than profit volumes, there is no guarantee that the concessionaire will aim to maximise its sales as it may be more concerned with profit margins. An increasing number of such contracts also include service-level agreements. These cover areas including staffing levels; staff training and other policies; marketing and after-sales service; store quality, maintenance and refurbishment schedules; and product innovation and pricing policies.

Alternatively, the airport operator may choose to enter into a management contract that involves greater financial risk for that operator. These contracts have been used for car parking facilities at airports for many years, but are not a popular approach for other commercial activities. In this case the specialist operator will be paid a monthly fee in return for maintaining certain agreed standards, including accurate financial accounts, high quality of cleanliness and professional staff appearance. The ability to build in guaranteed service levels is important, especially with car parking where competition from off-airport parking may be present.

A third option is to have a joint venture arrangement where the airport operator enters into a partnership with the specialist retailer or some other organisation to provide the commercial facilities. The advantages of such an approach are that the airport and retailer develop a long-term relationship, and all the transaction costs and time associated with a concession contract can be avoided. In this case the risk, profits and capital expenditure can be shared between the airport operator and specialist, and longer-term security for the specialist can be gained. Examples include the joint retail venture of Aéroports de Paris and Aelia, Hamburg airport which has a joint venture with F&B, TAV airports with Gebr Heinemann at Istanbul airport, and Delhi airport's duty-free provision which is a combined venture between the airport operator, India Duty-Free and Aer Rianta International. This type of practice is comparatively rare, but it does offer opportunities for airport operators wishing to expand their involvement to other airports. Dublin Airport Authority (through its subsidiary Aer Rianta International) is the best example of this, where the operator has entered into a number of joint venture agreements in order to provide commercial facilities in areas including the CIS and the Middle East.

At many airports, concession contracts are automatically put out to tender when they come up for renewal. This is usually the most effective way of ensuring the best contractual arrangements. Having a tendering process will give existing retailers incentives to improve their performance if they want to win the contract again. It also gives the airport a chance to introduce new concepts in retail and F&B as fashions change, and perhaps the opportunity to generate more revenue if new concessionaires are prepared to pay a higher fee. In bidding for a concession contract, the specialist needs to be fully aware of the different operating environment that they face compared with high street shopping, particularly relating to staffing and operating hours, security and supply chain issues.

While selection criteria will vary from airport to airport, generally the evaluation of offers will consider both the financial terms (the concession fee paid) and more qualitative terms (experience, quality, vision, innovation). Some airports may just choose the bid that will generate the highest revenue, but this may lead to overbidding. While in the short run this will benefit the airport operator with high levels of concession revenue, such a situation will not be sustainable in the longer term. The concessionaire will lose money and have to renegotiate conditions with the airport operator or be forced to abandon its airport operations completely. Sometimes this issue may be overcome by setting a maximum percentage fee. The problem of overbidding was one of the key reasons behind ACI Europe's development of a best practice charter for concession tenders. This covers areas including the information that airports should collect and that retailers should provide, what should be done before and after a contract is awarded, the types of contract that can be used, and service-level agreements (Airport Business Communique, 2005).

FACTORS DRIVING SUCCESS

Choosing the right concessionaire and negotiating the most appropriate contractual agreement is crucial if an airport is going to fully exploit its commercial opportunities. However, there are many other factors that will also play a role (Martel, 2009). The airport operator may be able to influence some of these factors, but by no means all of them. Also, the nature of the airport traffic and its spending capability need to be taken into account. For instance, an airport handling predominantly domestic business travellers is likely to be in a less favourable position for generating commercial income than an airport with many long-haul leisure passengers. Therefore understanding the mix of passengers and planning the facilities to match their needs and preferences as closely as possible is paramount to maximising the revenue-generating opportunities and return on investment. If an airline starts new services, or changes terminals, this may change the mix. Market research ideally needs to be undertaken, not only of passengers but also of staff, meeters, greeters and visitors, to enable their preferences and experiences to be examined. Focus group research may be particularly useful in identifying trends and future issues.

Figures 7.3 and 7.4 show the comparative importance of different retail items at Heathrow and Stansted airports. Heathrow has a large share of scheduled long-haul traffic and consequently duty and tax-free is a significant revenue source. By contrast, it is less important at Stansted as the majority of traffic is to the EU, where no such sales are allowed; here F&B is more substantial, presumably at least in part because of the predominance of LCCs at the airport. As regards other types of consumers, LeighFisher (2012) estimated that just 0–5 per cent of arriving passengers spent on F&B and retail, compared with 40–60 per cent of transfer traffic and 30–40 of meeters and greeters. They also estimated that employees spend 10–20 per cent on F&B compared with departing passengers, and 5–10 per cent on retail.

Small airports with limited passenger traffic are at a distinct disadvantage since they will not have the critical mass, typically around 5 million passengers, necessary to diversify and support specialist retail and F&B outlets. Airports go through different evolutionary stages as regards their commercial income, depending on their size. Small airports can only really offer the basic facilities including a duty-free shop, newsagent and F&B outlets, especially as the volume of traffic tends to be unevenly spread with just a few flights a day. Focusing just on airside shopping will not be viable as often there will not be enough passengers to

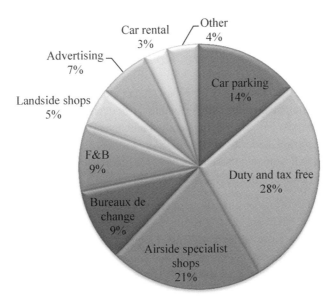

Figure 7.3 *Airport concession revenue at Heathrow airport, 2011*
Source: Heathrow Airport Ltd (2012)

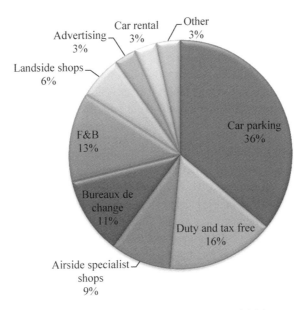

Figure 7.4 *Airport concession revenue at Stansted airport, 2011*
Source: Stansted Airport Ltd (2012)

sustain such businesses. The airports are unlikely to be able to attract global specialists, and the fees and rentals are likely to be lower than at large international airports. As the airport grows, more specialist shops can be added until finally the airport can be considered as a shopping centre.

Spending by all passengers will be influenced by the general economic climate. Factors to consider include growth in gross domestic product (GDP) and consumer expenditure, level of taxation, inflation rates and foreign currency fluctuations. The level of sales taxation will also play a role. In addition, purchasing patterns will be affected by delays at an airport. A delay of an hour or so for a departure slot may give passengers extra time to visit the shops or F&B outlets. Such a delay may be popular with the commercial department, but not with anyone else. On the other hand, congestion and lengthy operational delays within the terminal, including long queues for passport control, security or immigration, will have the reverse effect and reduce or even eliminate the dwell time that passengers have for browsing in the shops and having something to eat or drink (Torres *et al.*, 2005).

Then there is the competition for airport commercial facilities that can come from a variety of different sources. First, there are other airports. Notable examples of airports in a particularly competitive situation are those in the Gulf, including Dubai, Abu Dhabi and Doha, and some Asian airports serving destinations including Incheon, Singapore, Kuala Lumpur and Hong Kong. There is also competition from the in-flight sales of airlines. Some of the airlines allow pre-booking of goods in order to catch some business before the passengers can see what the airport competitor has on offer. In addition, competition can come from downtown tax-free outlets for international travellers, which are allowed in a number of countries, particularly in Asia. In Europe and North America, competition exists with discounted electrical and other high street businesses and from the growth of factory outlets. Internet shopping is a major competitor: customers are now far more likely now to search on the internet to see what bargains they can purchase rather than waiting until their next airport visit to shop. All this means the airports need to ensure they keep up to date with retail trends and fashions and that they constantly monitor competitor prices. A study of North American airports found that 46 per cent of airports stated they had pricing comparable to the high street, 38 per cent had a high street plus a percentage methodology, and 9 per cent had prices comparable with other airports (ACI North America, 2012). Research undertaken by LeighFisher (2012) confirmed similar percentages.

Just as in the high street, the outlet number, size and mix are very important. For example, too many outlets may reduce sales per outlet and create excess competition. The mix should be determined by the type of customer, the commercial viability of the outlets and the different space requirements needed. Again using the example of Stansted and Heathrow, Stansted which serves predominantly LCC demand has much 'grab-and-go' F&B, whereas London Heathrow which has a substantial amount of long-haul and transfer traffic has many more designer retail stores and sit-down restaurants. Another key factor is the location, space and design of facilities. A large proportion of the airports in use today were designed without taking sufficient account of the commercial opportunities that airport terminals can offer. All too often, concession planners become involved at much too late a stage of the terminal design and development process. This has meant that commercial facilities very often are not ideally situated or have been added on later as an afterthought.

Successful concession planning, at least when passenger purchases are being considered, is all about providing facilities close to passenger flows and not in areas that are dead ends or are too far from passengers' view. A change in the flow line of passengers can have a dramatic impact on concessionaires' sales. The outlets should ideally be on the same floor levels as the departure gates, as having to go through the inconvenience of changing levels may deter some passengers from visiting the commercial facilities. Using the same logic, shops aimed at business travellers should be allocated near the business lounges. There is also a popular trend to have facilities that require passengers to walk through them to get to the departure lounge or gates. These walk-through shops can increase footfall at airports to 100 per cent, but such shops are difficult to introduce into a terminal unless new infrastructure is being provided. Other strategies can include using popular facilities, including duty-free shops, to attract passengers and act as an anchor for a concession hub. At all times, however, the commercial facilities must not hamper the passengers' ability to wayfind around the airport as this may well increase their anxiety. Likewise, when product promotions spill out of the retail units into other parts of the terminal they must not obscure passengers' lines of sight to the next essential airport process.

Particular problems can arise from terminals that are of a linear design, such as terminal 1 at Munich airport, because very often facilities have to be duplicated which can be costly until there is sufficient throughput of passengers to support all the facilities. This was the situation with the fourth terminal at London Heathrow Airport when it first opened. Problems have also occurred for airports in European countries that have signed up to the Schengen agreement and have abolished immigration controls with other Schengen countries. At some airports this has caused unnecessary duplication of facilities, resulting in reduced custom for each outlet. A similar situation exists at certain Canadian airports, including Toronto, where there are three different passenger channels: domestic, US and other international, which have to be separated from each other. In some cases where there is more than one terminal, passenger flows can be combined to go through a central security area that is situated near a commercial area. This means the airport can minimise the amount of duplication in its retail offer while at the same time giving a greater choice for passengers. For example, this happened at Toulouse airport a few years ago, where the passengers of the newer terminal 3 were combined with the passengers of the existing terminal 2 and one larger commercial area for around 4 million passengers has been constructed (Entwistle, 2007). Likewise, this was experienced at Hamburg airport, where a walk-through shopping centre (the Plaza) was built between terminals 1 and 2 to accommodate all the passengers. Usually any way that involves consolidating space and passenger flows, for example with centralised security or by integrating different passenger flows, will be beneficial for commercial operations.

The amount of time a passenger has at an airport will obviously influence their shopping behaviour. This dwell time is affected by the check-in procedures and control and departure processes. Thus developments including self-service check-in, more stringent security rules and the tendency of some low-cost carriers to make early calls for their passengers to the gates (or for LCC passengers to go near to the gates in order to select a good seat on the aircraft) will all have an impact on dwell time. Different types of passenger spend varying times in the lounge, with BAA calculating that the incremental airport spend for each additional 10 minutes available time is £0.80 for domestic passengers and £1.60 for international passengers (Maiden, 2008). Figure 7.5 shows the average dwell time from the 2012 Airport Commercial Study (Moodie Report, 2012). On average, domestic passengers spend 91 minutes with 68 per cent of this time airside. The remaining 32 per cent of time in the landside area is split relatively evenly between pre-check-in (e.g. seeing off friends and family), post check-in and security. By contrast, on average intra-EU passengers spend 115 minutes in the terminal and non-EU passengers 126

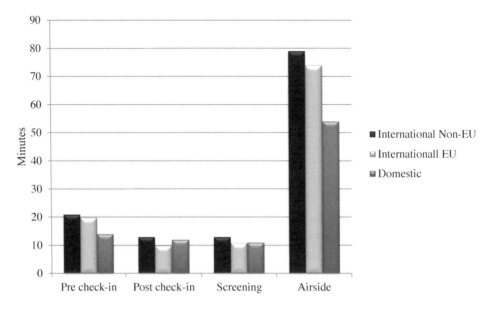

Figure 7.5 *Dwell time by journey stage, 2011*
Source: Moodie Report (2012)

minutes. Slightly less of the total time (63–64 per cent) is spent airside compared with domestic passengers, which may well be partly due to additional processes related to immigration and customs control which these passengers may have to experience.

Passengers also need to feel relaxed when they shop, and tend to prefer to buy from outlets situated within the vicinity of the departure gates – once all essential processes including check-in and security screening have been completed. They will not want to walk long distances to be able to shop. Throughout their time at the airport, passengers' stress levels will fluctuate depending on where they are within all the airport processes, and this will have a direct impact on their spending patterns. As discussed, security is usually the most stressful experience. Passenger stress levels will vary according to other factors, for instance whether they are travelling alone or with their family. If they are travelling for leisure purposes, their excitement levels will often increase as they go through the airport, which should encourage spending in the airside area (Bork, 2006). However, boredom levels may also be important. As a result, factors that need to be considered to create the right atmosphere for shopping include the architectural aesthetics, the temperature, and other possible enhancements including music and entertainment. An interesting case here is the research that Manchester airport undertook in preparation for its revamping of terminal 1 in 2009, which included new commercial facilities. It undertook an in-depth study into passengers' state of mind as they travelled through the airport, with psychologists analysing their body language and feedback in order to gain a total picture of the passenger experience and key stress points before designing the new facilities.

Planning landside shopping is different from airside shopping, as convenient locations must be found not only for passengers, but also for staff, meeters, greeters, farewellers and local residents. If there is too much landside shopping, passengers may spend too much time in this area, which can reduce their purchases in the airside area where average spend tends to be higher. On average, 60 per cent of retail space is in the departures airside area and a further 26 per cent in the departures landside area. Only 12 per cent is in the arrivals area (3 per cent airside and 9 per cent landside) and 2 per cent outside the terminal (Moodie Report, 2009). The split between airside and landside varies significantly, however, with Dubai airport, for instance, having very few landside facilities, while the split at Zurich is almost equal because this later airport been very active in developing facilities for non-travelling customers. At most airports it is the sales in the airside area of the airport that still brings in the most revenue for the airport operator. Some landside facilities, including post offices, travel agents or booking agencies, may not bring in huge amounts of revenue to the airport, but may be perceived as adding value to the airport product from the point of view of the passenger and other consumers.

A few airports have developed very successful arrival duty- and tax-free shops. This has tended to happen in developing countries where there are large numbers of returning expatriate workers. For example, in Colombo in Sri Lanka and Manila in the Philippines over half the duty- and tax-free sales have tended to be on arrival, primarily due to spending by returning nationals from the Middle East. Oslo airport in Norway also has substantial sales from its arrivals shops because it is the only Scandinavian country still to sell duty- and tax-free goods within Europe as it is not a member of the European Union. Arrivals shops overcome the security problems related to LAGs and can be considered to be more environmentally acceptable as, unlike goods from departure shops, they do not increase the overall weight on the aircraft and consequently cause less emissions. However, it is usually very difficult to get passengers to shop on arrival because they are anxious to get through the airport as quickly as possible and to focus on the essential processes, including baggage reclaim. For this reason, Buenos Aires Ezeiza airport has TV screens in the arrivals shop that show when the baggage is ready to be collected.

F&B outlets can compete with passengers' dwell time in shops and so they need to be positioned near to the retail facilities, but must not interrupt the flow. This is particularly important as most shop purchases are made on impulse. Shops and F&B outlets have to be large enough not to give a congested and overcrowded image, but not so large that consumers may be deterred by an appearance of inactivity and empty space. In the airside area it is useful to have as many of the F&B facilities as possible situated by the outside wall to preserve views of the runway and keep the natural light. Average spend on F&B tends to be low and the spend per square metre is also less; more space is required for the kitchen, food storage and eating areas. Typically the duty-free sales per square metre can be in the region of US$23,000–47,000 compared with values of $4,000–8,000 for F&B (Moodie Report, 2012). However, while F&B tends to account for a fairly small share of total airport commercial revenues and profit levels, more passengers tend to use F&B facilities than shops and so they can have a major impact on a passengers image and perception of the airport. Thus if F&B is considered to offer poor value for money, the customer may assume the same is true for the shops. Figure 7.6 shows that the average penetration rate for F&B is between 30 and 40 per cent compared with around 25 per cent for duty-free and only 5 per cent for bureau de change. In general, maximising income will involve assessing the passenger preferences, space requirements, spend levels, concession fees and penetration rates of the different facilities. For instance, regarding duty-free, the average spend and concession fee tends to be high and the penetration rates are significant, although such shops do tend to take up considerable space. By contrast, the space requirements and demand for both currency

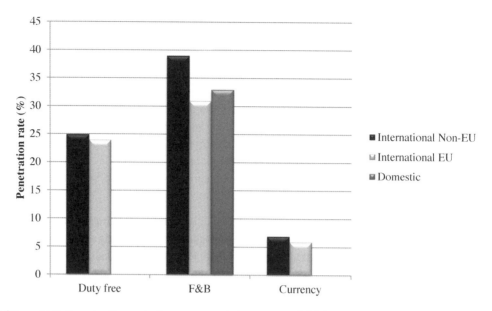

Figure 7.6 *Penetration rate by commercial category, 2011*
Source: Moodie Report (2012)

exchanges and car hire are less, but with average revenue tending to be high for exchanges and low for car hire.

Finally, the commercial performance of an airport will be influenced by a wide range of laws and regulations. These will include the duty- and tax-free limits set by governments and also any regulations related to legal contracts and the bidding process. There may also be local planning regulations, particularly if the airport is competing with nearby shopping centres. Then there are security rules, which have had a major influence on airport retail and F&B in recent years (see Chapter 5).

MEASURING NON-AERONAUTICAL PERFORMANCE

Airports, with their concessionaire partners, have become increasingly active in monitoring their non-aeronautical performance. This is partly due to a drive for better performance monitoring of all aspects of the industry and also because retail experts, with experience of assessing retail performance at other locations, are now commonly employed at airports. Consumer satisfaction levels and perceptions of value for money are assessed by many airports through customer surveys (as described in Chapter 6). For example the ACI ASQ retail measures passenger satisfaction survey focuses on three main areas: F&B, duty- and tax-free, and general retail. There are 30 measures that cover performance aspects (e.g. the number of passengers spending at outlets and the amount spent) and passenger characteristics, satisfaction and behaviour (e.g. who are the typical shoppers, how many shops did they visit, how much time did they spend there, whether purchases were planned or on impulse). This is a bi-annual survey that was launched in 2012.

In addition, airports use indicators including sales per passenger, passenger penetration levels and sales per square metre to analyse the economic performance of their commercial facilities. The latter measure has the advantage that it can be used to compare airport performance with other retail facilities at other sites, including shopping malls. However, making inter-airport comparisons is difficult because of the commercially sensitive nature of the information required and a lack of reliable industry-wide data. One of the most comprehensive benchmarking studies is the Airport Commercial Revenues Study which has been undertaken since 1998. For the 2011/12 research there were 116 airports covering Europe (48), Asia-Pacific (26), North America (28) and the Middle East (14), with 35 airports having more than 30 million annual passengers, 37 recording 10–30 million annual passengers and the remaining 44 airports having fewer than 10 million passengers. The study looked at performance indicators including sales per passenger and per square metre by different commercial activity, and other indicators including yield and penetration rates. In addition it also had a number of management indicators examining how the airports manage and control the retail function, which considered factors including concession structures, dwell time and the marketing undertaken (Table 7.3).

Table 7.3 Key indicators used in the Airport Commercial Revenues Study, 2012

Activity	Indicator and measures
Duty-free and duty-paid	Sales per international departing passenger (IDP)/ departing passengers
	Sales per square metre
	Yields (airport income/sales)
F&B	International airside sales per departing passenger
	Domestic airside sales per departing passenger
	Sales per departing passenger
	Sales per square metre
	Airport income per departing passenger
	Airport income per square metre
	Yield
Currency exchange	Sales and airport income per IDP
Advertising	Income per departing passenger
Terminal space/property rental	Airport income per departing passenger
Car parking	Income per departing passenger
Car rental	Income per departing passenger
Dwell time	Time in minutes by airport processing stage
Penetration rate	Penetration rate by activity category
Retail marketing	Budget, airport and concessionaire contribution
Management	Reporting structure
	Number of staff
	Fastest-growing retail segment
	Level of private ownership
Shop fit-out cost	Costs paid by airport and concessionaire
Concession structure	In-house operations, single/multiple concessions, guarantees, revenue structure, approach, sales target, term, high street comparisons

Source: Moodie Report (2012)

Table 7.4 Average sales per departing passenger by category and airport size, 2008

Sales per departing passenger ($US)	Small hub	Medium hub	Large hub
F&B	3.49	4.50	5.34
Convenience retail	2.17	1.95	1.88
Speciality retail	0.27	1.21	1.71
Duty free	0.00	1.36	7.05
Total	5.93	9.02	15.97

Source: LeighFisher (2012)

A one-off detailed study of commercial revenues was recently undertaken for the US Transportation Research Board (LeighFisher 2012). Table 7.4 shows the average duty-free sales and F&B per square metre from the research. It clearly shows the lower sales for F&B and also the impact of size (e.g. large airports having more sales). In North America there is also an annual concessions benchmarking survey undertaken by ACI North America. This looks at measures including income per passenger and per square feet as well the types of concession agreement, length of contract, the staff involved and the branding used.

CURRENT DEVELOPMENTS AND FUTURE TRENDS

Generating commercial revenues at airports over the past decade or so has become much more challenging. As discussed in Chapter 3, globally non-aeronautical revenues as a share of total revenues increased from 46 per cent in 1995 and 1996 to 52 per cent in 1997 and 1998, and peaked in 2001 at 54 per cent. Since then it has dropped back to around 47–48 per cent in the past 5 years. Likewise, specifically within Europe non-aeronautical revenue has dropped from its peak of 50 per cent 10 years ago to 47 per cent.

There are some general factors, notably the abolition of EU duty- and tax-free, and security developments, that may have had a key influence. In addition, for each individual airport there may be specific events that may have played a negative role, as can be demonstrated with Zurich airport (Table 7.5). In 2001, not only did 9/11 have an impact, but also the largest airline serving the airport (Swissair) was grounded in October. These combined effects reduced traffic levels, overall sales and airport revenues, although individual passenger spending remained relatively constant. In 2004 the new airside centre was opened, which appears to have increased passenger spend although passenger numbers remained fairly constant. However, in more recent years the impact of the poor global economic situation on sales per passengers can be clearly seen, although the strength of the Swiss franc may have been another contributing factor.

EU developments

Duty- and tax-free shops in Europe had been in existence for many decades. The first duty- and tax-free airport outlet was opened in 1947 at Shannon airport in Ireland. In 1951, another shop was opened in Prestwick airport in Scotland. These shops were designed to be attractive to

Table 7.5 Retail and F&B sales performance at Zurich airport, 2001–11

Year	Total passengers (millions)	Sales (CHF millions)	Airport revenue (CHF millions)	Sales per departing passenger (CHF)
2001	21.0	346	54	33.0
2002	17.9	296	46	33.0
2003	17.0	287	52	33.7
2004	17.3	305	56	35.4
2005	17.9	350	65	39.1
2006	19.2	391	73	40.6
2007	20.7	435	82	42.0
2008	22.1	481	91	43.5
2009	21.9	459	83	41.8
2010	22.9	482	86	42.1
2011	24.3	479	88	39.4

Source: Zurich Airport (2012)

transatlantic passengers on refuelling stops (Freathy and O'Connell, 1998). The shops sold a small range of alcohol, tobacco and perfumes and a few other items. By the 1960s, other airports had opened similar shops and had started to expand the range of merchandise on offer. For example, in 1957 shops were opened in Amsterdam and Tel Aviv, in 1958 in Brussels and Miami, in 1959 in London Heathrow, Frankfurt and Dusseldorf, and in 1960 in Osaka and Oslo. This was primarily in response to the rapid increase in passenger traffic at that time and particularly the growth in package holidays and other forms of leisure travel. Amsterdam Schiphol airport was one of the first airports to offer tax-free electronics and photographic material. Then came a retail boom in duty- and tax-free shopping, with many airports substantially increasing the area dedicated to such shops and offering a much more diverse and varied product selection, ranging from the traditional alcohol, tobacco and perfume products to camcorders, watches and jewellery, sports clothing and other fashion accessories.

The 1990s were a period of uncertainty for most EU airports. It was originally intended that all EU duty- and tax-free sales would be abolished on 1 January 1993 as the single market was 'born'. The rationale was that it was illogical and incompatible to have such a system when the EU should be behaving as a single market with open borders. In addition, these shopping privileges were considered to distort competition between modes of transport with no access to these sales, including rail, and to be unfair trading in relation to downtown shopping. It was argued that EU consumers were subsidising not only duty- and tax-free outlets, but also air and ferry travellers. In response, the airports, charter airlines, ferry companies and associated manufacturing industries collectively argued that duty-free privileges did not distort or hamper the development of the single market and that abolition would result in millions of jobs being lost. It was claimed that the cost of travel would have to rise substantially to compensate for the loss of income, which would have a knock-on effect throughout entire national economies. Through active lobbying of government ministers, the proponents of the abolition managed to achieve a 6.5-year extension of these sales until 30 June 1999, when eventually these sales were abolished.

Many of the EU airports, in partnerships with their retail concessionaires, absorbed the value added or sales tax themselves – effectively offering the merchandise still at 'tax-free' prices. A few airports sold a selection of liquor products at duty-free prices, but at most airports cheaper tobacco was no longer available to EU passengers. Different strategies were adopted by airports, including having dual pricing or different facilities for the different types of passenger. In 2004, 10 new European countries joined the EU which reduced the potential for duty and taxes free sales to and from these countries, and this was followed by Bulgaria and Romania joining in 2006. It is very likely that this is one of the main reasons for the drop in the share of non-aeronautical revenue. For example, at 17 UK airports non-aeronautical revenue per passenger (in 2007 prices) decreased from £6.43 in 1998/99 to below £6 in 1999/2000 and then to £5.14 in 2006/07 (Graham, 2009). In the future, if other countries including Turkey become members of the Union, clearly the opportunities for duty and tax-free sales to and from these countries will also be reduced. A further EU development has been the adoption of the euro in 2002 by the majority of the EU countries. This has decreased the need for currency exchange outlets at the airport and, combined with the widespread use of automatic teller machines (ATMs) to access cash, has reduced the prospects of generating revenue from exchanging money.

Security issues

Shortly after the abolition of EU duty-free, airport commercial managers had to face a new challenge: the impact of 9/11. This had a number of different effects on the airport industry, particularly in the United States. There were fewer passengers to generate commercial revenues, and revenues also declined because of the additional time spent on the essential processes due to more stringent security requirements. Some airports were quite innovative in providing F&B kiosks and carts for passengers waiting in long security queues. However, these security queues at some airports blocked important retail areas that previously had been in prime locations. It was estimated that in the USA overall non-aeronautical revenues declined by 4.5 per cent in 2002 compared with 2001 for the whole airport industry (ACI North America, 2002). Many of the US airports had to redesign commercial facilities in order to conform with new security measures. For example, previously meeters, greeters and farewellers had been permitted to accompany passengers right up to the gates, but this practice was then stopped. Most of the commercial facilities were near the gates, and so this caused a reduction in the commercial revenue generated by non-passengers. Also certain car parks near the terminal, which generated large amounts of income, had to be closed or reallocated for security reasons after the FAA brought in a 300-foot rule that prevented any vehicle being parked within that distance of the terminals.

The other security event that has had a major impact on the commercial performance of airports has been the LAGs restrictions (see Chapter 5). The 100 ml rule for LAG in hand luggage is thought to have encouraged passengers to buy lower-value and essential travel items airside that they previously would have bought landside or packed in their hand luggage. This may very well have reduced the money and dwell time that they have airside to make more high-value and impulsive purchases. Passengers are also confused as to what they can take on the aircraft. At the same time, more stringent and more time-consuming security measures at many airports have caused congestion, taken up more space and reduced dwell time for shopping. The problems of different LAGs security rules in different regions or countries have also led to a loss in sales and more confusion among passengers. When the rules were first introduced many unsuspecting passengers from outside the EU had their LAGs purchases confiscated at EU airports if they were transferring onto a different flight. For example, in 2007 Frankfurt airport confiscated 2,500 liquids a day, and Amsterdam and Madrid airport removed around 1,000. Zurich estimated that it took away US$29,540 worth of alcohol and perfume from passengers daily, while at Heathrow this figure was around $211,000 (Jane's Airport Review, 2007). It is hoped that when screening of LAGs is finally introduced in the EU, the current problem, which is reducing passenger spend and damaging overall consumer confidence in airport shopping, will be overcome.

Future prospects

The poor economic climate of the past few years has had a significant impact on commercial revenues, particularly in areas such as Europe where there has been a dampening of demand and less spending by passengers who are still actually travelling because of less disposable income. This was shown in Table 7.5 for Zurich airport, where sales per departing passenger peaked in 2008 and have yet to return to that level, even though the past passenger throughput has returned. Another example is Amsterdam airport, where airside spend per departing passenger reduced from €15.59 in 2007 to €15.13 in 2009 and only partially recovered in 2011 with a figure of €15.55. Likewise, concession income per departing passenger declined from €5.41 in 2007 to €5.11 in 2009, rising back a little to €5.26 in 2011 (Schiphol Group, 2012). In the future, economic factors will continue to play an important role, as with the general retail sector. Lifestyle trends are also likely to be influential, for example with greater emphasis on healthy living having an impact on the type of F&B facilities provided, and encouraging more health/fitness treatments and personnel/pampering services including manicures, pedicures and massages. There is also likely to be continued pressure on tobacco and alcohol sales because of health concerns (Ghee, 2011). For instance, in 2012 both the European Travel Retail Council (ETRC) and the Asia-Pacific Travel Retail Association (APTRA) agreed codes of conduct to ensure retailers and producers do not encourage excessive consumption or misuse of alcohol.

Airline developments will also continue to play a central role. The ongoing pressure on airport charges is likely to mean that airport operators will remain committed to seeking new ways to increase their non-aeronautical revenues. However, this may become more challenging if airlines themselves continue to increase their focus on ancillary revenues. At the same time, F&B is likely to continue to be a growth area for airports because of the airline trend to serve less free F&B on board. Also, a 'one-bag rule' policy has been introduced by a number of LCCs in Europe, which prohibits passengers from carrying retail and F&B purchases on board the aircraft unless they fit into the traveller's single cabin bag. As a result passengers have to throw away their purchases or pay a significant premium to bring them into the cabin or put them in the hold. This is considered to be having a detrimental impact on commercial incomes, particularly at airports where this policy is strictly enforced, where drops in sales of 40 per cent have been recorded (Spinks, 2011). This development has also introduced a considerable degree of confusion among passengers as the rules tend to be enforced sporadically at different airports. Meanwhile, in the United States Spirit Airlines now allows only a very small item on board free of charge – a policy that, if adopted by other airlines, would again be likely to affect passenger commercial spend.

An important factor to consider for the future is the dwell time passengers will have. This will clearly be influenced by the passenger experience through the essential processes of check-in, security and border control. Chapters 5 and 6 discuss how technology and automation are being used to speed up these processes, although at the same time additional features have been added in the security area. The overall impact on dwell time in the future will depend, to a certain degree, on how passengers respond to these developments and how prepared they are to shift their behaviour, for example related to the time they typically plan to spend at airports. Another impact of these technology developments is that they can potentially free up space for more commercial facilities, although the new space may not be located in the optimal position unless some major reconfiguration of all airport facilities is undertaken.

Finally, the internet has undoubtedly had a major impact on commercial revenues in a number of different ways, and will continue to do so. As regards shopping in general, the internet has enabled passengers to become much more informed consumers, and internet shopping has become a major competitor to airports in terms of both prices offered and ease of purchase. As a result, airports have had to develop the retail features of their own websites and a number now offer pre-ordering of goods, collection of goods on arrival, or money-off vouchers.

There are also many commercial opportunities offered by airport mobile apps, particularly integrated with social media sites. Passengers can receive details of special offers while using their smart phone devices in the terminal. Figure 7.7 shows how the use of mobile apps and social media to sell airport services and promote commercial facilities is likely to increase significantly by 2015. One of the most significant technology developments in the future is likely to be the widespread use of NFC, as discussed in Chapter 5. This will provide the passenger with the all-in-one technology needed to use their phone to check-in, navigate and board the aircraft, as well

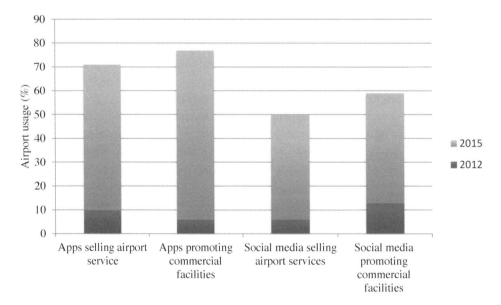

Figure 7.7 *Airport use of mobile apps and social media for commercial facilities, 2012–15*
Source: SITA (2012)

as being informed of specific mobile promotions based on their precise location and being able to use their phones to make purchases (Amadeus, 2011).

CASE STUDY 7.1: DUBLIN AIRPORT AUTHORITY AND AER RIANTA INTERNATIONAL: AN INTERNATIONAL AIRPORT RETAILER

Dublin Airport Authority (DAA) (formerly known as Aer Rianta) is an interesting example as it was one of the first airport companies to expand beyond national boundaries and become involved with the management and operations of commercial facilities at other international airports. DAA is the Irish state-owned airport company that has been responsible for managing the country's three major airports, Dublin, Shannon and Cork, since 1937 (Shannon became a separate company in 2013). It has a long history with the provision of commercial facilities, as the world's first duty-free shop was opened at Shannon airport in 1947. It continues to operate its own duty-free shops at its own airports.

In 1988, Aer Rianta International (ARI) was set up as a wholly owned subsidiary of Aer Rianta. With a population of less than 4 million, Aer Rianta recognised the limits of its own market and aimed to use ARI to promote commercial activities in locations outside Ireland. The first undertaking was a joint venture company, Aerofist, with Aeroflot Russia, the Moscow airport authority and ARI each having a one-third interest in the company. Aer Rianta had originally developed links with the Soviet Union in the early 1970s with an agreement whereby Aeroflot would trade airport charges for fuel at Shannon airport. In 1988, Aerofist opened the first duty-free shop at Moscow airport. It also began offering in-flight duty-free sales on international flights operated by Aeroflot out of Moscow. In the next few years, joint venture companies with ARI involvement were also set up to manage duty-free shops at St Petersburg and Kiev airports as well as downtown shops in Moscow and two shops, now closed, on the Russian–Finnish border.

In 1991, ARI expanded its involvement into the Middle East area with the setting up of a joint venture company with local investors in Bahrain to be responsible for designing the duty-free shops, overseeing their fitting out and their day-to-day management. ARI further expanded operations in this region by getting involved in the management of the duty-free shops at Karachi airport in 1992 and at Kuwait airport in 1994. In 1997, other new duty-free shop contracts were awarded in Beirut, Qatar (in-flight F&B for Qatar airways), Damascus and Egypt. In Europe, ARI's first retail operation outside Ireland in Europe was at the terminals of the Channel tunnel. The organisation provided duty-free facilities from the tunnel opening in 1994 until the abolition of duty-free sales in 1999. In addition, ARI opened two shop in Cyprus in the late 1990s – one at Larnaca airport in 1997 and one in Paphos in 1998.

In 1998, ARI expanded into North America for the first time by acquiring the duty-free division of Canada's United Cigar Stores and the concession for duty-free shops at Montreal, Winnipeg, Edmonton and Ottawa airports. In 2002 ARI took over the duty-free concession at Halifax airport as well. ARI has continued to expand and now has a role in 24 airports in 14 countries, employing in the region of 3,500 staff (Table 7.6) Most recent developments include its involvement, starting in 2010, with Delhi Duty Free Services (DDFS), a joint-venture company with DIAL (Delhi International Airport Limited) and IDFS (Indian Duty Free Services). This is now the single largest duty-free retailer in India. Then in 2012 ARI opened 11 duty-paid outlets at the new Kunming Changshui International Airport in the Yunnan province of China. It secured this contract following the signing in 2010 of a strategic collaboration agreement between Yunnan Airports Group in 2010. Previously in the 1990s, ARI had been involved with retail consultancy services at Hong Kong and Beijing airport.

Table 7.6 Aer Rianta International's involvement in international retailing activities, 2012

Region	Location
Europe	Larnaca airport
	Paphos airport
CIS	Sheremetyevo and Domodedovo airports, Moscow
	Borispol airport, Kiev
Middle East	Bahrain International airport
	Beirut International airport
	Muscat International airport
	Qatar Airways (in-flight)
Asia	Delhi airport
	Kunming airport
America	Montreal airports
	Winnipeg airport
	Halifax airport
	Ottawa airport
	Barbados airport

Source: Dublin Airport Authority (2012)

CASE STUDY 7.2: DUBAI AIRPORT: NON-AERONAUTICAL STRATEGIES FOR A COMPETING AIRPORT

Many of the Gulf airports are in fierce competition for transfer traffic. They are very interesting airports as regards non-aeronautical strategies, as they probably have done more than any other airport in the world to attract passengers by promoting the duty-free facilities on offer. Dubai airport is the largest airport in the region. In 2011 it handled 51 million passengers compared with just 4.5 million in 1989. It works closely with the national airline, Emirates Airline, which is based at the airport. The airport serves Dubai, which has become the major trading and tourism base of the Gulf region as well as being used as a transfer stop for intercontinental services.

The airport is government-owned, as is the duty-free shop operator Dubai Duty Free (DDF), and DDF works very closely with the airport management. The first DDF shop was established in December 1983 and then, in 1987, arrival duty-free shopping was added. In 2012 the sales turnover was around US$1.6 million. representing a 10 per cent increase over 2011. Perfumes are the most popular goods, accounting for 15 per cent of sales, but gold has third position (after liquor) with an unusually high share of sales at around 10 per cent. The average spend per departing passenger in 2009 was US$49 and there are 350 cash registers to handle an average of 57,000 sales transactions per day with over 3,000 employees working on the shop floor (Staunton, 2010). As with Emirates Airline, sponsorship and the support of international events has always been an integral part of DDF's marketing strategy, and in recent years the company has diversified to operate a hotel and a border shop.

An interesting development occurred in November 1989 when DDF launched its 'Dubai Duty Free Finest Surprise' to mark the expansion of its shopping complex. This promotion offered a Rolls-Royce Bentley Mulsanne car to the winner of a raffle, and has remained ever since with a continuous high-profile display of luxury cars in the airport concourse. The tickets, sold exclusively at the airport or online, were US$139 in 2012 and are limited to 1,000 per draw. In excess of 1,000 travellers have won luxury cars. Other competing airports in the Middle East, including Abu Dhabi and Bahrain, have undertaken similar promotions. There is now a motorbike promotion with a cheaper ticket. Also in 2000, a new duty-free area was opened at the airport, and to commemorate this and the millennium the airport launched another promotion, the 'Dubai Duty Free Finest Cyber Surprise'. This promotion offered US$1 million to winners of the 'Millennium Millionaire Draw'. Originally this was planned as a one-off event, but it has now become an ongoing promotion with over 130 passengers having been made millionaires.

REFERENCES

ACI (2011) *Airport Economics Survey 2011*, Montreal: Airports Council International.

ACI/DKMA (2009) *ASQ Best Practice Report: Parking Facilities*, Montreal: Airports Council International.

—— (2012) *ASQ Best Practice Report: Airport Loyalty Programmes*, Montreal: Airports Council International.

ACI North America (2002) *State of the Industry Report*, Washington: ACI NA.

—— (2012) *2012 ACI NA Concessions Benchmarking Survey Summary Results*, Washington, DC: ACI NA.

Agbebi, Y. (2005) 'How do traffic structure and leisure preferences drive airport retail and investment strategies?', *Hamburg Aviation Conference*, Hamburg, February

Airport Business Communique (2005) *ACI Europe Best Practice Charter*, ACI Europe, May.

Amadeus (2011) *Navigating the Airport of Tomorrow*, Madrid: Amadeus

AMPG (2007) *2006 Air Passenger Survey Final Report: Los Angeles International Airport*, Los Angeles: AMPG.

Appold, S. and Kasarda, J. (2006) 'The appropriate scale of US airport retail activities', *Journal of Air Transport Management*, 12(6): 277–87.

Armstrong, Scout Marketing Group and Lynxs Group (2011) *ACRP Report 47: Guidebook for Developing and Leasing Airport Property* Washington, DC: Transportation Research Board.

Bork, A. (2006) 'Developing a retail marketing strategy to promote both airport and retailers', *Journal of Airport Management*, 1(4): 348–56.

CAA (2012) *CAA Passenger Survey Report 2011: A Survey of Passengers at Birmingham, East Midlands, Gatwick, Heathrow, Luton, Manchester and Stansted*, London: Civil Aviation Authority.

Chung, Y.-S., Wu, C.-L. and Chiang, W.-E. (2013) 'Air passengers' shopping motivation and information seeking behaviour', *Journal of Air Transport Management*, 27: 25–28.

Crawford, G. and Melewar, T. (2003) 'The importance of impulse purchasing behaviour in the international airport environment', *Journal of Consumer Behaviour*, 3(1): 85–98.

Dublin Airport Authority (2012) *Aer Rianta International*, Online. Available HTTP: <http://www.daa.ie/gns/doing-business-with-us/aer-rianta-international.aspx> (accessed 20 December 2012)

Echevarne, R. (2008) 'The impact of attracting low cost carriers to airports', in Graham, A., Papatheodorou, A. and Forsyth, P. (eds), *Aviation and Tourism: Implications for Leisure Travel*, Farnham: Ashgate.

Entwistle, M. (2007) 'Customer service and airport retail: stimulate passenger spending', *Journal of Airport Management*, 1(2): 151–57.

Francis, G., Humphreys, I. and Ison, S. (2004) 'Airports' perspectives on the growth of low cost airlines and the remodelling of the airport–airline relationship', *Tourism Management*, 25(4), 507–14.

Freathy, P. and O'Connell, F. (1998) *European Airport Retailing*. London: Macmillan.

Ghee, R. (2011) 'ETRC dedicated to overcoming travel retail challenges', *Communique Airport Business*, Spring: 62–64.

Gillen, D. and Lall, A. (2004) 'Competitive advantage of low-cost carriers: some implications for airports', *Journal of Air Transport Management*, 10(1): 41–50.

Graham, A. (2009) 'How important are commercial revenues to today's airports?', *Journal of Air Transport Management*, 15(3): 106–11.

Geuens, M., Vantomme, D. and Brengman, M. (2004) 'Developing a typology of airport shoppers', *Tourism Management*, 25(5): 615–22.

Halpern, N., Graham, A. and Davidson, R. (2011) 'Meeting facilities at airports', *Journal of Air Transport Management*, 18(1): 54–58.

Heathrow Airport Ltd (2012) *Annual Report and Financial Statements for the Year ended 31 December 2011*, London: Heathrow Airport Ltd.

Institute for Retail Studies (1997) *Airport Retail Economics*, Stirling: University of Stirling, IRS.

Jacobs Consultancy (2009) *ACRP 24: Guidebook for Evaluating Airport Parking Strategies and Supporting Technologies*, Washington, DC: Transportation Research Board.

Jane's Airport Review (2007) 'Duty-free industry fears security restrictions pose risk to revenues', *Jane's Airport Review*, May: 4.

Lei, Z. and Papatheodorou, A. (2010) 'Measuring the effect of low-cost carriers on regional airports' commercial revenue', *Research in Transportation Economics*, 26(1): 37–43.

LeighFisher (2011) *UK Airport Performance Indicators 2010/2011*, London: LeighFisher.

—— (2012) *ACRP Report 54: Resource Manual for Airport In-Terminal Concessions*, Washington, DC: Transportation Research Board.

Lin, Y.-H. and Chen, C.-F. (2013) 'Passengers' shopping motivations and commercial activities at airports: the moderating effects of time pressure and impulse buying tendency', *Tourism Management*, 36: 426–34.

McCormick, C. (2006) 'Bringing home the global brand', *Airports International*, March: 34–35.

Madeira, C. (2011) 'Building retail practices for the New Lisbon airport', *Journal of Airport Management*, 6(1): 40–50.

Maiden, S. (2000) 'Getting to know the market at airports', *University of Westminster Marketing and Market Research Seminar*, London, December.

—— (2008) 'How BAA uses its market research', *University of Westminster Marketing and Market Research Seminar*, London, February.

Martel, F. (2009) 'External factors and their impact on non-aeronautical revenues', *Journal of Airport Management*, 3(4): 337–44.

Martens, H. (2012) 'How to win back markets', *ACI Economics and Finance Conference*, London, March.

Moodie Report (2009) *The Airport Retail Study 2008/09*, Brentford: Moodie Report.

—— (2012) *The Airport Commercial Revenues Study 2012*, Brentford: Moodie Report.

Perng, S.-W., Chow, C.C. and Liao, W.-C. (2010) 'Analysis of shopping preference and satisfaction with airport retailing products', *Journal of Air Transport Management*, 16(5): 279–83.

Schiphol Group (2012) *Annual Report 2011*, Amsterdam: Schiphol Group.

SITA (2012) *Passenger Self-Service Survey Highlights*, Geneva: SITA/Air Transport World

Spinks, K. (2011) 'The cost of one bag', *International Airport Review*, 15(2): 44–47.

Stansted Airport Ltd (2012) *Annual Report and Financial Statements for the Year ended 31 December 2011*, London: Stansted Airport Ltd.

Staunton, S. (2010) 'Increasing revenue generation by improved customer flow and sale points: Dubai Duty Free', *Journal of Airport Management*, 5(1): 7–8.

Torres, E., Dominguez, J., Valdes, L. and Aza, R. (2005) 'Passenger waiting time in an airport and expenditure carried out in the commercial area', *Journal of Air Transport Management*, 11(6): 363–67.

Zurich Airport (2012) *2011 Full Year Financial Results*, Zurich: Zurich Airport.

Airport competition and the role of marketing

8

It used to be commonly believed that most major airports were monopolies with significant market power, with their precise role being determined by the passenger demand in the catchment area. Airline choice was considered to be limited to particular airports because of government bilateral agreements. While this may still be true in a few markets, there are now many opportunities for airports to compete for passengers, freight and airlines. The modern-day airline industry, which has been transformed in many places from a regulated and public sector-controlled activity into a liberalised and commercially orientated business, has played a major role in this changing airport situation. Certain airline developments, including the formation of global alliances and the emergence of the low-cost sector, have been particularly important in creating new views on airport competition.

Airport competition is a complex area because there are many different aspects that need to be considered (Graham, 2006; Forsyth *et al.*, 2010). There is the competition between airports and competition within airport groups. Then there is the competition inside airports, including the competition for the provision of a certain service or competition between airport terminals. This chapter begins by discussing all of these. They have major consequences for many key areas of the airport business, including pricing and quality management, which are considered elsewhere in this book. However, one other very important issue related to competition that has yet to be covered is the role of marketing, investigated in the second part of this chapter.

AIRPORT COMPETITION

Competition between airports

There are a number of main ways in which airports can compete (Cranfield University, 2002). If airports are physically close, their catchment areas may overlap for certain types of traffic. For short-haul routes, passengers tend to choose the most convenient, nearest airport that has suitable services. For long-haul flights, passengers may be more willing to travel further distances to an airport that they regard as offering a more desirable or superior long-haul service. However, if airports are located on small islands or in remote regions, there will be very little competition.

In some major urban areas or cities there are a number of situations when more than one airport serves the population. Notable examples are the European cities of London and Paris and the

American cities of New York and Washington. Sometimes the airports may be under the same ownership, as with Aéroports de Paris (AdP), which owns Charles de Gaulle, Orly and Le Bourget airports; and the Port Authority of New York and New Jersey, which owns JFK, La Guardia and Newark airports. Such common ownership arguably may reduce the amount of potential competition. Elsewhere, in London for instance, the BAA airports Heathrow, Gatwick and Stansted used to compete with the independently run London City and London Luton airports, although this situation has now changed. In Washington, the Metropolitan Washington Airports Authority airports of Dulles and National compete to a certain degree with Baltimore airport, which is owned by the State of Maryland. The San Francisco bay area also has three airports that compete for domestic traffic. Another example of an area where neighbouring airports compete for large volumes of traffic is the Pearl River delta region of China and the airports of Hong Kong, Guangzhou and Macau.

In many cases where there are overlapping catchment areas, one airport tends to become the dominant player in a preferred location with the other airports playing a more secondary role. In the London area, for example, Heathrow airport is considered by many passengers, particularly those travelling on business, to be *the* 'London airport' in spite of a range of services being offered at the other London airports. The secondary airports tend to fulfil more specialised roles. They may act as overspill airports when the major airport has inadequate capacity, as has happened to a certain extent in London when airlines that cannot get into Heathrow go to Gatwick or Stansted instead. Alternatively, centrally located secondary airports may be able to attract a certain amount of domestic or short-haul traffic, particularly business-related traffic. These types of passenger favour the convenience and generally less congested environment that a city centre airport such as London City may offer.

Then there are the airports that market themselves as low-cost alternatives to the major airports – having been encouraged by the rapid development of European low-cost carriers (Table 8.1). In recent years some of these alternative airports have had a significant impact on the market share of the nearby major airports. For example, between 2002 and 2010 the total market share of Milan Linate and Malpensa airports with the alternative airport Bergamo reduced by 17 per cent. Likewise, at Stockholm's Arlanda and Bromma airports with the nearby alternatives Skavsta and Vasteras, the market share dropped by 22 per cent, and at Oslo Gardermoen with Sanderfjord and Moss as alternatives it fell by 8 per cent (Copenhagen Economics 2012). Outside Europe there are similar airports, including Avalon as an alternative for Melbourne and Hamilton for Toronto, although this use of secondary airports is not so widespread in other areas. In general, as discussed in Chapter 5, these alternative airports offer faster turnarounds, short walking distances from the terminal to the aircraft, and fewer delays, all vital elements of the low-cost model. They are also usually in a position to be more flexible on pricing and maybe to enter into long-term pricing agreements if desired by the low-cost carriers. In many cases they are situated substantially further from the town or city they are serving compared with the competing airports. Sometimes these airports may be owned by the same operator who has control of the competing airports; for example, AENA owns Barcelona, Girona and Reus; and Aeroporti di Roma owns both Fiumicino and Ciampino. Elsewhere separate ownership patterns exist. Some low-cost airlines, including Ryanair, have even argued for competing terminals at airports run by different operators, especially at Dublin.

Table 8.1 Examples of alternative low-cost airports within Europe

Low-cost airports	Competing major airports	Under same ownership?
Beauvais	Paris – CDG and Orly	No
Bergamo	Milan – Linate and Malpensa	No
Charleroi	Brussels National	No
Girona and Reus	Barcelona	Yes
Hahn	Frankfurt	No
Lübeck	Hamburg	No
Prestwick	Glasgow International	No
Rome – Ciampino	Rome – Fiumicino	Yes
Sandefjord and Moss	Oslo – Gardermoen	No
Skavsta and Vasteras	Stockholm – Arlanda and Bromma	No
Weeze	Dusseldorf	No

Problems can arise when a new airport is built and is perceived as providing an inferior service to the old one – perhaps being in a less conveniently situated location. A notable much quoted example is Montreal Mirabel's airport, which was built in the 1970s to provide extra capacity in addition to Dorval airport, but never managed to attract the volume of traffic that was forecast. Milan is a more recent case where there has been considerable reluctance for carriers to transfer from the Milan Linate airport, which is closer to the city centre, to the newer expanded Milan Malpensa airport. Unless effective regulation is introduced, the only feasible way of ensuring that traffic will transfer to the new airport is by actually closing the old one, which has happened in locations including Munich, Hong Kong, Oslo and Denver (Caves and Gosling, 1999). Competition for the new Athens airport is even more limited as not only has the old airport closed down, but also no new airport development within the same catchment area is allowed.

Competition tends to be weakest at airports that have a high concentration of both short-haul and long-haul services. These airports appeal most to the traditional scheduled carriers who have networked services. In these cases it is difficult for other airports to provide effective competition. This is unless the airport is competing as a hub by providing good flight connectivity and efficient passenger transfers. Key prerequisites for a hub are a central geographical position and adequate runway/terminal capacity to enable a 'wave' system of arriving and departing flights to take place. Certain airports can compete as hubs for cargo operations especially for express parcel services, particularly if they are open all night and have a good weather record. Ultimately all hub airports are, however, very dependent on the operating strategies of airlines. While many medium- and large-sized airports have aspirations to become a hub, in reality there is now less opportunity for this to happen as a result of the growing concentration within the airline industry through developments including global alliances, joint ventures and code-sharing. An alternative may be just to try to encourage airlines to base themselves at an airport, because this will be normally mean that the airline will offer more flights and make better use of all the other airport facilities.

In most cases, passengers will have a specific destination in mind when they travel. The exception may be with some intercontinental traffic when passengers might be more indifferent. For example, Americans visiting Europe may not have a strong preference as to whether they start their European tour from Paris, London or Frankfurt. Airports serving these cities can therefore compete for this traffic. The same can be true with cargo traffic. This is particularly the case within Europe, where most long-haul freight is trucked to its final destination. A somewhat similar passenger example in North America is airports that compete as embarkation points for cruise holidays.

When an airport's relative competitiveness is being assessed, the substitution possibilities need to be considered. First, the prospect of new competing airports emerging has to be investigated. This is generally low because of the large investment that is needed for the new infrastructure and because of the long and complex planning and regulatory processes that frequently have to be followed in order for approval of any new development to be given. In many areas of the world it is increasingly difficult to find suitable locations for new competing sites, although in some regions, including Europe, the existence of a number of obsolete military airfields (e.g. Finningley and Manston in the UK) have provided some opportunities for new airport development in recent years. In addition, barriers to entry for new airports may also be high because of the existence of cost economies of scale although, as discussed in Chapter 3, these may disappear once the airport reaches around 3 million passengers and at then some stage diseconomies of scale may actually develop.

At a broader level, the amount of substitution from other transport modes needs to be considered. High-speed rail is probably the greatest threat. For regional airports, the introduction of high-speed rail services can have a significant impact on air services to major airports. However, at major capacity-constrained airports, increased usage of high-speed rail for short-haul trips may free up capacity for other long-haul services – although this may have a detrimental impact on the airport's ability to act as a hub and attract transfer passengers. Improvements to the road and rail infrastructure to major airports may also reduce the necessity for feeder services from regional airports.

The amount of substitution that exists depends on the type of traffic that is being served. For example, as discussed in Chapter 4, different types of airline have varying degrees of sensitivity to price. Airport charges can be substantially more important for short-haul operations as they are levied more frequently. For low-cost and charter operations they can be even more significant because these airlines will have minimised many of the other airline costs. In these cases, airport price competition can be very real, particularly if additional pricing incentives (discussed below) are offered. There are numerous examples of LCCs cutting services or abandoning airports entirely, giving high airport costs as the only reason, or one of the key reasons, for this action. Recent examples include Ryanair closing its Marseille base in 2011 and cutting services at Edinburgh and Budapest airports in 2011. Elsewhere, easyJet moved its base from Madrid in 2012 citing reasons of high charges and overcapacity. As regards passengers, those on leisure trips are the most likely to be willing to shift between origin airports because of airline price or product differences. Those on holiday may even have a choice of destination and hence a choice of airport, whereas those travelling for business or visiting friends and relatives (VFR) will probably be more limited in their ability or desire to shift destination airports.

When the Productivity Commission in Australia recently reviewed the price-monitoring process it considered these three substitution issues (airport, modal and destination). By way of illustration, these findings are summarised in Table 8.2. The substitution possibilities generally seemed low, with the exception of Canberra airport because of surface transport competition, and Darwin which competes with other airports for holiday passengers. An additional element for the airport operator that is not covered here is the competition for commercial facilities. Some airports with a large share of transfer traffic, including Dubai and Singapore, may compete directly with their retail offering. While airports have the advantage of a captive and often fairly affluent passenger market, the substitution possibilities with high street and internet shopping are quite considerable.

As discussed in Chapter 5, price regulation has traditionally been introduced when competition is not considered strong enough to deter airports from abusing their position of market power. This is most relevant for large city airports, as smaller regional airports, especially in high population-density countries, will tend to have overlapping catchment areas and be in a sufficiently competitive environment so as to not need regulatory intervention. One of the key issues, however, is determining that airports have substantial market power. It cannot simply be related to airport size, but also has to take account of competitive factors including market share, pricing, quality of service, capacity provision and substitutions possibilities.

An interesting example here is the United Kingdom, where two price-regulated airports, Stansted and Manchester, were investigated by the government with a view to possibly having the price control removed. The criteria that was used in the UK for price-regulated airports was that they must possess substantial market power, that EU and domestic law would provide an insufficient tool to remedy any abuse, and that the incremental net benefits of regulation could be shown to outweigh its costs. In the Manchester case it was decided that the airport did not hold a position of substantial market power since local airports, including Liverpool airport, provided a meaningful substitute; there was spare capacity at Manchester and competing airports; the market share of Manchester was declining; high service quality was provided at Manchester; the airport and the airlines effectively and constructively engaged with one another; and finally

Table 8.2 Substitution possibilities at Australian airports

Airport	Main market segments (per cent)			Substitution possibilities		
	Holiday	VFR*	Business	Airport	Modal	Destination
Adelaide	23	27	44	Low with no nearby airports	Low for business travellers but some for VFR and holiday travel	Relatively low as mostly business and VFR traffic
Brisbane	22	28	44	Moderate with both the Gold Coast and Maroochydore airports nearby	Low for business travellers but some for VFR and holiday travel	Relatively low as mostly business and VFR traffic

Continued

Table 8.2 Continued

Airport	Main market segments (per cent)			Substitution possibilities		
	Holiday	VFR*	Business	Airport	Modal	Destination
Canberra	17	18	59	Low with no nearby airports	High as three-quarters of visitors to Canberra arrive by car and go by surface to Sydney then fly to a holiday destinations	Relatively low as mostly business and VFR traffic
Darwin	40	23	33	Various by market segment: low for visits to the 'top end' but higher for those visiting several areas within the Territory	Low for business travellers but significant for holiday travel	High as mostly holiday traffic can choose to go to other tourist destinations
Melbourne	33	24	40	Generally low but Avalon airport used by LCCs for some of its flights	Low for business travellers but some for VFR and holiday travel	Relatively low as mostly business and VFR traffic
Perth	24	26	45	Low with no nearby airports	Low as Perth is relatively isolated	Relatively low as mostly business and VFR traffic
Sydney	26	25	45	Low with no nearby airports	Low for business travellers but some for VFR and holiday travel	Relatively low as mostly business and VFR traffic

*VFR, visiting friends and relatives.
Source: Productivity Commission (2011)

pricing and quality of service decisions appeared to have been determined more by competitive forces than by the price cap (Department for Transport, 2008a). For Stansted it was concluded that the airport already had substantial market power by virtue of BAA's common ownership and that it was likely to acquire more market power in the future (Department for Transport, 2008b). As a result, the government decided to remove the price control for Manchester, but not for Stansted. For the new regulatory system that is being introduced in 2014, the CAA has developed new criteria for assessing market power (CAA, 2011a). In general, because of the changing competitive environment, there has been increased interest in developing methodologies for assessing airport market power (e.g. Maertens, 2012).

A major report published in 2012 considered competition at European airports (Copenhagen Economics, 2012). It found that airlines had become more footloose, both able and willing to switch away from airports if conditions are not right. This high degree of switching was demonstrated, with many routes opening and closing. There was also evidence of passengers having more choice, for example with nearly two-thirds of Europeans being within 2 hours' drive of at least two airports, and more choice for local departing and transfer passengers. Even at the larger airports there was evidence that the share of European destinations that were also offered at another nearby airport had increased significantly between 2002 and 2011 (Table 8.3).

This led to the conclusion that for all airports competition is increasing in Europe as market power weakens, which raises the important question as to whether specific economic regulation at European airports is still needed.

Competition within airport groups

When airports are operated as a system or a group rather than individually, there is an important issue as to whether this inhibits competition (Forsyth, 2006). As discussed in Chapter 2, particularly when privatisation of groups takes place, decisions have to be made as to whether the group

Table 8.3 Share of European destinations with overlap at another nearby airport, 2002 and 2011

Airport	Share of European destinations (per cent)	
	2002	2011
Amsterdam	17	32
Brussels	77	82
Paris CDG	30	48
Dusseldorf	53	73
Rome Fiumicino	3	20
Frankfurt	35	54
London Heathrow	78	85
Milan Malpensa	53	64

Source: Copenhagen Economics (2012)

should be privatised in its entirety or split up. Arguments for keeping the group include the ability to share resources and expertise, reduce costs due to scale effects and adopt a strategic and coordinated approach to airport development. In Australia the government decided on individual privatisations for the major international airports (even though most of them were at least 800 km apart): in Argentina the airports were privatised as a group; and in Mexico the airports were divided into four different groups with a mixture of small and large airports in each group. While issues related to competition and airport groups especially tend to be raised when airport privatisation is taking place, clearly it is an ongoing issue that is relevant to both public and private airports alike. An interesting example of this as regards a public sector group is the Dublin Airport Authority (Case Study 8.3).

CASE STUDY 8.1: THE UK SITUATION

The UK is an interesting case to consider as regards airport competition (Bush, 2009). BAA was privatised as a single entity in 1987, but this remained a controversial issue. At the time of the privatisation of BAA, the arguments in favour of the retention of this single airport group, as opposed to separation, included the existence of very limited competitive pressures because of product diversity at the airports and the dominance of Heathrow; the small effect of airport charges on airline costs; economies of scale in airport operations; less uncertainty and a higher share price; and less risk of under-investment with an overall investment strategy. It was claimed that group ownership was needed to enforce the government's traffic distribution rules (TDR) which redirected traffic from congested Heathrow to elsewhere, and to fund investment at Stansted airport. Opponents, however, argued that Gatwick and Stansted could compete for charter traffic, that the former was developing into a credible alternative airport to Heathrow, and that the group sale would give BAA much less incentive to provide any extra capacity than would have been the case with individual airport sales.

Since the privatisation of BAA, the UK airline regulatory environment has become progressively more liberal, providing more opportunities for airport competition. Consequently there were various governmental reviews investigating whether BAA should be split up, but these generally concluded that the additional benefits of competition would be more than offset by the disbenefits of loss of economies of scale and fragmentation of financial strength together with the dispersion of expertise (Toms, 2004). Interestingly, however, this UK policy did not seem entirely consistent, as a few years after BAA privatisation, Belfast International airport wanted to buy the neighbouring Belfast City airport but was prohibited from doing so by the government as it was seen as anti-competitive. Then, in 2005, the owners of Bristol airport (Ferrovial/Macquarie) were selected as preferred bidders for nearby Exeter airport, but pulled out when it was announced that there would be a detailed investigation to ensure this situation did not have a negative impact on competition in the region.

In 2006, the UK airports market was investigated again, this time by the Office of Fair Trading (OFT). By then BAA was just under new ownership and was coming under increasing criticism from both airlines and passengers regarding its responsiveness to customer needs. As a result the OFT inquiry concluded that the BAA group should be referred to the Competition Commission for more detailed investigation, as the OFT identified joint ownership as a factor that could be preventing, restricting or distorting competition. The Competition Commission reached its decision in 2009 (Competition Commission, 2009). Its main conclusion was that common ownership of airports in south-east England and lowland Scotland did give rise to adverse effects on competition in connection with the supply of airport services by BAA. However, it did also identify a number of other features that affect the competition, including Heathrow airport's position as the only significant hub airport in the south-east UK; aspects of the planning system and other areas of government policy; and the economic regulatory system for airports. It therefore concluded that Gatwick and Stansted airports should be sold to different airport operators as well as either Edinburgh or Glasgow. In 2009, BAA completed the sale of Gatwick airport that it had begun before the final outcome of the Competition Commission's inquiry was known. BAA subsequently undertook a number of appeals, but none overturned the Competition Commission's decision. As a result Edinburgh airport was sold in 2012 and the sale of Stansted airport was completed in 2013.

As regards competing terminals, in the two most recent regulatory reviews in the UK, the introduction of competing terminals has been discussed. In 2003 the CAA concluded that the benefits of regulatory intervention to stimulate intra-airport competition were most likely to be outweighed by the operational and regulatory disbenefits. For the 2008–13 review, the issue was again considered and while some stakeholders, including the airlines at Stansted, very much favoured competition between terminals, there was no overall consensus of views and consequently this idea was again not developed any further (CAA, 2008). Subsequently this issue was explored again in the government review of airport economic regulation (Department for Transport, 2009). Some airlines, including easyJet, were in favour of moves towards terminal competition, and British Airways agreed that the option should be kept open. Others, including the airports, opposed the idea. In the end the government concluded that inter-terminal competition should not be precluded under the new regulatory regime if the CAA considers that it will bring benefits to passengers.

Competing facilities and terminals

As discussed in Chapter 3, many airport services, including air traffic control, security, ground handling and the provision of commercial facilities, can be provided either by the airport operator or by a third party. The way in which they are offered, and whether there are competing services, can have a major impact on an airport's competitive situation in both price and service quality terms. Competing services tend to be the most established in the commercial areas, including airport retail outlets, F&B, hotels and car parks. A major airport service for airlines is ground handling, and the issue of competition with the provision of handling services has always been controversial as traditionally it has been quite common for the national airline or airport operator to have a monopoly or near-monopoly in providing these services. This resulted in the introduction in 1996 of the ground handling directive in Europe (see Chapter 4), but elsewhere the extent to which ground handling services are offered on a competitive basis varies from country to country.

Potentially the greatest competition within airports could be achieved by having competing terminals under different ownership offering competition in terms of price and service quality. Varying quality standards and facilities could be offered to different services, including low-cost, short-haul, long-haul or business – although the more specialised the terminal, the less scope for competition with other terminals. However, strategic planning could be much more difficult with the lack of a single ownership, and economies of scale could be lost. In addition, coordinating the essential passenger processes could be more challenging – in particular ensuring that there are clearly defined and allocated accountabilities for the delivery of security in the different terminals. Fundamentally, competing terminals might not always bring about the best use of capacity, which for many of today's airports is a crucial consideration as they have limited space to expand. There could also potentially be an anti-competitive issue if the airlines control the competing terminal and limit access to rival airlines.

There is only limited and insufficient industry evidence to conclude whether it is possible to have successfully competing airport terminals. In 1986, terminal 3 at Toronto airport was handed over to a private consortium to provide new investment. However, in 1996 it was bought back under the responsibility of the Greater Toronto Airport Authority to allow for the development of the airport master plan. Elsewhere, at Birmingham airport, the Eurohub terminal was at one stage operated separately, but has now been brought back under single management at the airport. In Brussels there were not competing terminals but the management of the airside and the terminal was split. However, in 1998 this dividing of management was reversed with the establishment of the Brussels International Airport Company. These cases suggest that the experience of competing terminals or split management was not too favourable. On the other hand, in the United States, and particularly at JFK airport in New York, there are permanent examples of different terminals being operated by airlines. Likewise in Australia, some of the domestic terminals have been run directly by the airlines. However, in these cases the situation is really more to do with allowing the airlines to operate their own facilities rather aiming to provide greater competition. The country where competing terminals have probably been given the most consideration is Ireland, and this is discussed in greater detail below. Experience here has shown that attempts to introduce competition can also significantly lengthen the process of planning and constructing additional capacity.

THE BIRTH OF AIRPORT MARKETING

Having debated the extent of competition that exists at airports, this chapter now focuses on airport marketing. It needs to be acknowledged that airport marketing as a concept did not really exist at most airports until the 1980s. Prior to this, the role of the airport as a public service meant that very often airport management would merely respond to airline requests for new slots by providing published charging and use-of-facility information rather than initiating talks to attract new services. In most cases, the airports considered it was solely the role of the airline to identify opportunities for new or expanded services. It was up to the airport to provide an efficient and safe airport with good facilities for aircraft and travellers. Promoting the air services at the airport was also not considered to be a responsibility of the airport, the view being that this should be undertaken by the airlines and travel agents selling the products. It was rare to find airport marketing managers, and generally the resources allocated to marketing activities were very small. Airport promotion tended to be very basic, typically consisting of the production of a timetable and publicity leaflets, and reactive responses to press enquiries about the airport. In essence, even if there was some potential for competition between airports even at this early stage of the evolution of the airport industry, there were very few airports that recognised and exploited this.

This passive approach has long since gone at most airports. Airports have become much more proactive in their outlook and have developed a wide range of increasingly sophisticated techniques for meeting the demands of their complex mix of customers, including passengers, airlines, freight forwarders, tour operators and so on. Within any commercially run business, marketing is considered to be a core activity and one that is a vital ingredient for success. The airport sector is no longer an exception, and in most cases marketing is now seen as an integral part of the airport business.

Deregulation of air transport markets has made the airport business much more competitive. Airlines in Europe, for example, are much freer to operate out of any airport they choose without being constrained by bilateral restrictions. They are thus much more susceptible to aggressive marketing by airports. Many airports have actively sought to attract the new low-cost carriers through a range of marketing techniques. The increase in demand for air transport due to deregulation and other more general factors, including economic growth, has meant there have been enhanced opportunities for more airports to share in this expansion of the market. This has provided airports with greater incentive to develop innovative and aggressive market strategies so that they can reap some of the benefits from this growth. A number of airports are close to capacity and unable to offer attractive slots for new services, which means there may be attractive prospects for other airports to promote themselves as alternative uncongested airports.

The travelling public have also become more demanding and more sophisticated in their travel-making decisions and their expectations of the airport product. Airports have had to develop more sophisticated marketing strategies and tactics to meet the needs of travellers and adopt contemporary approaches, including relationship marketing, e-marketing and social media marketing. In addition, deregulation, privatisation and globalisation trends within the airline industry have increased the commercial pressures being faced by airlines which, in turn, has encouraged airports to recognise the need for a professional marketing-oriented approach when dealing with their airline customers.

By the late 1990s, the majority of airports were devoting considerable resources to marketing activities. It is difficult accurately to quantify this increased emphasis on the role of marketing, but some indication of this trend can be gleaned from an analysis of staff employed in the marketing area. For UK regional airports the number of passengers per marketing staff decreased significantly between 1991 and 1997. For instance, the number of marketing staff at Manchester airport increased from 16 to 27, and at Birmingham airport from 10 to 24. This meant that the number of passengers per marketing staff decreased from 631,000 to 562,000 at Manchester and from 325,000 to 227,000 at Birmingham (Humphreys, 1999). Copenhagen Economics (2012) gave further examples. Marketing staff at Copenhagen Airport increased from two full-time employees in 2000 to four in 2005 and eight in 2012, while expenditure on sales, marketing and administration at Zurich Airport increased from CHF17.6 million in 1999 to CHF39.1 million in 2011. Along with increased industry activity in this area, there has also been a growing interest in airport marketing as an area of academic study. Kramer *et al.* (2010) provided a marketing guidebook for small airports; Jarach (2005) examined the new management vision of airport marketing; and Halpern and Graham (2013) applied principles of marketing within the airport industry by integrating key elements of marketing theory with airport marketing in practice.

If marketing is defined in its broadest sense of satisfying customer needs, there are various other activities (discussed in other chapters) that can also be considered as airport marketing. These activities include quality assessment and improvement, and environmental neighbourhood communication initiatives. In addition, the development of non-aeronautical activities can be treated as a marketing role. However, this chapter offers a more narrow consideration of satisfying customer needs by assessing how general marketing concepts and techniques can be applied to the airport industry.

MARKETING CONCEPTS

The market for airport services

The focal point of any marketing system is always the consumer of the services. For the airport product, demand comes from a variety of markets each with their own specific requirements. From a marketing perspective, it is useful to divide this demand into two: the trade, including airlines, who buy the airport facilities direct; and the general public or travellers who merely consume or utilise the airport product. The marketing techniques used for these two types are very different. Most airports would probably now agree that both airlines and passengers are key customers, whereas some airlines may tend to think of passengers as their customers and themselves as customers of the airports. Airlines are key drivers of the overall air travel business – unless they provide a suitable product, passengers and freight shippers will not be able to use a certain airport. Freathy and O'Connell (2000) discussed how airlines could be considered as primary customers with passengers as secondary customers, but argued that in practice this distinction is difficult to maintain because the boundaries of responsibility between airport operators and airlines are often obfuscated in the mind of the passenger.

As discussed in Chapter 7, passengers enable airports to generate significant amounts of non-aeronautical revenues which, in turn, can be used for airport operations and development. Therefore one view is to consider modern airports as so-called two-sided businesses or markets, which offer services to both passengers and airlines (Gillen 2011). Such businesses provide platforms for two distinct customers who both gain from being networked through the platform. The positive interdependence means that airport operators will be incentivised to compete for airline traffic and passengers, as these will influence both their aeronautical and non-aeronautical revenues. If passengers stay away, this will affect the airlines, which might have to leave the airport; if airlines reduce or withdraw these services, this will reduce passenger numbers and consequently non-aeronautical sales.

In addition to passengers and airlines, a broader assessment of the airport market can include other segments, including local residents and businesses, whose needs must be met. Concession-aires, tenants and other organisations, including handling agents, can also be considered customers of the airport. Hermann and Hazel (2012) divided airport customers into five groups: airlines, passengers, non-travellers (employees, visitors and retail customers, meeters and greeters and neighbours), tenants/service providers (retail, car park, ground handling, adver-tisers), and potential development partners (real estate developers, hospitality, transportation service providers, government). Table 8.4 shows a simpler classification that defines customers as trade, end users and 'other'. Each of these needs to be further subdivided into much smaller discrete segments so they can be targeted appropriately and so that the airport's marketing efforts can be the most effective.

A common way to segment trade customers is by product type. For example, with passenger travel this would include a full-cost traditional service, a low-cost service, regional airlines and a charter service. Airline alliances could well be given special consideration. In the cargo area, the market may be segmented into integrators, cargo airlines, passenger airlines and other freight companies. In addition, at some airports general aviation may be an important market. This can cover many activities including flight training, police aviation, air ambulance, aerial fire-fighting, surveying and crop spraying, as well as private flying and leisure pursuits including skydiving, aerobatics and gliding. Another significant area may be private business or corporate aviation. Other trade customers include tour operators who traditionally have sold charter airline seats as part of a package tour. Hence the tour operator may make the decision as to which airports should be served, while the charter airline will pay for, and consume, the airport product. In this respect tour operators can be considered as separate customers from charter airlines, although this is a grey area with many charter airlines and tour operators belonging to large integrated travel companies. Travel agents indirectly sell certain parts of the airport's product by selling airline seats and so can be considered both as customers and distribution intermediaries. For cargo traffic there are other intermediaries, including freight forwarders or global logistics suppliers, who provide the interface between the freight shipper and airline. They will often make decisions regarding which airport to use to transport the cargo.

Table 8.4 The airport's customers

Trade	End users	Others
Airlines	Passengers	Tenants and concessionaires
General aviation	Freight shippers	Handling agents
Tour operators		Visitors
Travel agents		Employees
Freight forwarders		Local residents
		Local businesses

The end-users – the passengers and owners of cargo that is being transported – are another group of customers. Passengers are clearly of central importance to airports not only because they consume the product that the airline provides, but also because they are direct customers for airport commercial facilities. By contrast to passengers, the end-user in the cargo market rarely comes into contact with the airport itself. Instead, freight shippers tend only to deal with the forwarder or integrator away from the airport. There are many ways in which passengers can be segmented at airports. The easiest and most basic way is to use the airline types or models (e.g. alliance, LCC). Passengers can also be segmented according to the type of airline service. For instance, domestic and international passengers have needs for different facilities (including customs and immigration) and may have access to additional commercial facilities (including duty-free and tax-free retailing). A distinction can be made as to whether they are terminal or transfer passengers. There are other variables related to travel characteristics that can be used, including group size, length of stay and seasonality. One of the most popular variables is trip purpose. At the most basic level, passengers can be grouped by business and leisure and then each of these categories can be further subdivided. Business passengers can be grouped according to whether they are travelling for internal business, meetings with external customers, conferences, trade fairs or exhibitions. Leisure passengers may be going on short breaks, long holidays, package tours, VFR, or travelling to study. Linked to this, there can be segmentation by travel class (including premium or economy). Each segment can be broken down further, such as at Amsterdam Schiphol Airport where leisure passengers are divided into three groups: price-seekers (42 per cent), comfort-seekers (35 per cent) and short distance-seekers (23 per cent) (Martens, 2012).

Airports may also use general demographic and geographical variables, including nationality, income, age, gender, life stage, education and occupation, to segment demand. Sometimes they may use psychographic and behaviouristic market segmentation in order to match more closely the needs of each market segment. For example, Young (1996) suggested that there are 'agora-phobics' who have the lowest level of need, have a fear of flying and of missing the plane, and do not want to be distracted from the departure monitor. Then there are the 'euphorics' who are the once-a-year holidaymakers who arrive early at the airport and spend money as part of the holiday experience. Next in the order of needs are the 'confident indulgers' who are frequent leisure fliers who are familiar with the airport product and want to be pampered. Most complaints come from 'airport controllers' who are typically frequent business passengers flying economy with their families on holiday and feel aggrieved that they do not have the privileges they normally experience when flying business class. Then, finally, there are the 'self-controllers', frequent business fliers who just want to be processed through the airport as quickly and as efficiently as possible. The amount of time that these types of passenger spend at the airport varies from considerable in the case of the agoraphobics down to the minimum possible for the self-controllers. Another useful way to segment the market is by loyalty to the airport. Freathy and O'Connell (2000) discussed such a classification, devised by Ballini, which identified the passengers as loyalists, defectors, mercenaries and hostages.

One classification that Amsterdam airport used defined passenger segments according to their likely propensity to switch between Amsterdam and other airports (Martens, 2012). It divided the market between users and non-users. Within the user groups there were committed customers (entrenched or average) and uncommitted customers (shallow or convertible). Among non-users there were open non-customers (available or ambivalent) and unavailable non-customers (weakly unavailable or strongly unavailable).

The 'other' customer category includes all individuals who will use some features of the airport product, but will not be direct customers of the airlines. This includes employees at the airport who work for the airport operator, airlines, ground handlers, commercial concessionaires and other organisations. These individuals may use airport commercial facilities primarily because of their convenience and other facilities, including car parking. In addition there will be the accompanying visitors known as 'farewellers and weepers', 'well wishers' and 'meeters and greeters'. These visitors may use the retail and F&B facilities in the terminal and the car parks. The size of this market will depend on the purpose of trip and length of haul of the associated passengers, and will be influenced by other factors including culture and nationality. International and long-haul flights for passengers who are travelling for leisure purposes generally attract the most accompanying visitors. There will also be visitors who are not directly related to air transport activity. For instance, there may be aviation enthusiasts who visit the airport to view aircraft, buy specialist merchandise and perhaps have a tour of the airport. Local residents may also visit the airport to use the retail and F&B facilities, or businessmen and women may use conference and meeting facilities. This customer category includes concessionaires who typically provide the terminal commercial facilities including shops and F&B. Other organisations, including handling agents, can also be considered as customers of the airport.

Some of these different customer groups will inevitably be interdependent – hence the view of the airport as a two-sided business. If the number of airlines serving the airport decreases, this is likely to reduce the volume of passengers, employees and accompanying visitors and could ultimately, if the decline is sufficiently large, make the airport less attractive to other customers, including the providers of commercial facilities. It is also certainly true that the different customer groups, especially the airlines and passengers, will view airports from different perspectives. In most cases, given the competitive nature of the airline industry, the interests of airlines will align quite closely with the interests of passengers. However, this may not always be the case, for instance with airlines giving too much attention to higher-yielding premium passengers, or not supporting expansion plans that might benefit passengers but increase airline competition. Cambridge Economic Policy Associates (2010) argued that the circumstances in which there may be a misalignment of interests between airport passengers include when airlines have market power; when developments that may increase the degree of competition are being contemplated; and airports are subject to economic regulation.

For each type of customer, choosing an airport is the result of an amalgam of many decision processes (Table 8.5). For passenger airlines (and tour operators if relevant), one of the most important factors is the size and nature of the catchment area, especially if point-to-point services are the main focus. Depending on the type of route being considered, key factors are the business and tourist appeal of the catchment area for incoming passengers and the characteristics and purchasing power of those residing in the catchment area. The opportunities for carrying cargo (preferably in both directions) on passenger flights may need to be assessed. If an airline wants to develop or maintain a hub and draw on traffic beyond the immediate catchment area, it will also look for a central geographical location in relation to the markets it wants to serve.

Table 8.5 *Factors affecting the choice of airports*

Passengers	Airlines
Destinations of flights	Catchment area and potential demand
Flight fare	Slot availability
Flight availability and timings	Capacity for growth
Frequency of service	Competition
Image and reliability of airline	Network compatibility
Airline alliance policy and frequent-flyer programme	Airport fees and availability of discounts
Surface access to airport cost	Other airport costs (e.g. fuel, handling)
Ease of access to airport	Marketing support
Car parking cost	Range and quality of facilities
Range and quality of shops, F&B and other commercial facilities	Ease of transfer connections
Image of airport and ease of use	Maintenance facilities
	Environmental restrictions

The airport product has to be able to meet the needs of the airline. There must be sufficient capacity and slots to enable the airline to operate the services that it wants now and in the future, and other airfield physical capabilities, including runway length, need to be appropriate. The infrastructure also needs to fit the requirements of the specific airline, including fast turnarounds for LCCs or reliable transfer facilities for network carriers. Warnock-Smith and Potter (2005) undertook a survey of LCCs, who were asked to rank the most important factors that influenced their choice of airport. After the existence of high demand, the next factors were quick and efficient turnaround facilities and convenient slot times. Corporate aviation operators will look for a swift, efficient and personalised service for their company executives. There are also commercial factors to consider, including the presence of other airlines and the amount of competition that exists at the airport, the fit with the rest of the airline's network and the potential for its passengers to feed onto other services, or for other services to provide feed for them. Just as important will be the total visiting costs of operating from the airport. Undoubtedly the level of aeronautical charges and other marketing support that the airport offers is very important. In addition, airline choice will be influenced by other costs, including for handling and refuelling, over which the airport operator will generally have less control. If the airline is planning a significant presence at the airport, or wants to develop the airport as a base, this will involve recruiting local staff and so the cost of labour may be important.

With regard to cargo operations, airports need to have strong demand for such services or be centrally located to operate as a cargo hub. Visiting costs can again be very important as cargo traffic can be highly price sensitive and easily shifted from one airport to another by freight forwarders, as long as they can meet the delivery requirements of the shippers. More specific factors will be the ability of the airport to operate at night, to have quick customs clearance times, to have a good weather record and convenient road access so that cargo can be efficiently trucked to its final destination. All-cargo flights often use large aircraft that need specialist loading and transfer equipment. In addition, certain types of cargo, including livestock, dangerous or perishable goods, may require specialist handling and storage facilities that may not be available at all airports. For integrated carriers, factors including the weather record to ensure high reliability and space to build dedicated facilities that are needed for such operations may be vital. Gardiner *et al.* (2005) undertook a survey of non-integrated carriers who were asked to rank the most significant factors that influenced their choice of airport. Night operations were the most important, followed by costs, the airport's reputation and local demand.

For passengers, clearly the nature of air services on offer (in terms of fares, destinations, schedules and so on) – in effect the airline product – will be the key influencing factor as no one will choose to fly from an airport unless it offers the required travel opportunities. Hence what seems like airport competition is in effect competition between airlines. For example, two airports may be described as being in strong competition with each other, but this may be because they are served by airlines that themselves are in fierce competition. From a passenger viewpoint, airport competition will be closely linked to the amount of airline competition that exists (Morrell, 2010).

Factors including the distance, cost and ease of surface access to a certain airport, as well as cost and convenience of car parking at the airport, can also be very important to passengers. The quality of the airport product can have an impact, but usually only after these other factors have been taken into account. For business passengers, facilities including fast-track processes and airline lounges may affect choice, while for customers with special needs, for example disabled passengers, the quality of the provision of wheelchairs, lifts and general assistance may be important. Then there are other factors that are more difficult to explain and quantify. For example, in many European countries there will be a preference for the established capital city airport even if there are alternative airports that offer a comparable service. This is especially the case among the business community. In some instances, this may be because of better flight availability and frequency at the main airport, but not always. It may be because of ignorance about the other airports or because of some other factor, including the traveller's choice of a certain airline in order to add to their frequent flyer points. Passenger choice may also be influenced by personal preferences for a certain airport because of factors related to the airport product and the overall experience. For example, in a qualitative study of UK passengers, Sykes and Desai (2009) found that passengers preferred smaller airports because they were less formal, offered better customer care, were less congested and allowed passengers to feel more in control. Familiarity and reliability were also considered to be important factors, especially for business travellers. Passenger choice may also be influenced by the involvement of third parties or intermediaries, including travel agents or corporate travel offices, during their decision process.

Figure 8.1 shows passenger choice factors for four London airports, Heathrow, Gatwick, Stansted and Luton, in 2011. Routes and frequency factors were much more important at Heathrow airport than the other airports, reflecting its role as the UK's main hub airport with a higher share of business passengers. By contrast, cost was much more important at Stansted and Luton airports, which are predominantly served by LCCs. The route network was the second and first choice factors for UK and foreign business and VFR passengers, respectively, but not so important for leisure passengers; by contrast, cost was not among the top five choice factors for UK business passengers and only positioned fourth for foreign business travellers (Table 8.6). These

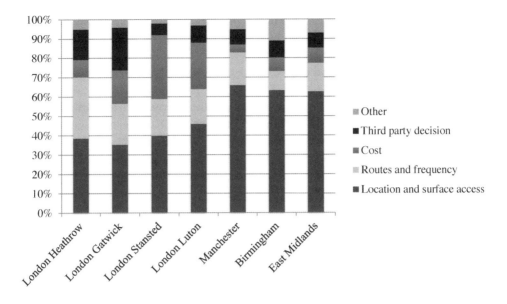

Figure 8.1 *Reasons for passenger airport choice at UK airports, 2011*
Source: Adapted from CAA (2012)

Table 8.6 *Main reasons for airport choices at London Heathrow, Gatwick, Stansted and Luton airports by purpose of travel, 2011*

UK residents	Reason for choice (per cent)	Foreign	Reason for choice (per cent)
Business			
Nearest to home	33	Nearest to business	38
Route network	20	Third party decision	20
Third party decision	14	Route network	16
Nearest to business	11	Cost	8
Timing of flights	10	Timing of flights	7
Leisure			
Nearest to home	31	Cost	36
Third party decision	27	Third party decision	17
Route network	18	Nearest to leisure	17
Cost	15	Route network	15
Timing of flights	4	Nearest to home	7
Visiting friends and relatives			
Nearest to home	36	Cost	28
Route network	25	Nearest to leisure	26
Cost	20	Route network	20
Nearest to leisure	5	Nearest to home	10
Timing of flights	4	Third party decision	5

Source: Adapted from CAA (2011a)

results are confirmed by Accent (2011), which found that in the UK, availability of flight was identified as a reason for choice of airport by 63 per cent of business passengers compared with 55 per cent of leisure passengers, while only 23 per cent of business passengers mentioned the cost of the flight in contrast to 35 per cent of leisure travellers. Only 8–10 per cent of both groups identified airport facilities as being a significant factor. Similarly, a survey of the three Washington airports (Baltimore Washington International, Dulles International and Reagan National) also demonstrated the importance of accessibility, especially for the centrally located Reagan National airport, with 72 per cent of passengers citing 'closest airport' as a reason for their choice. The cost of air travel at Baltimore airport, which offers an alternative to Washington and has the LCC Southwest as one of its main airlines, was given as a reason by 27 per cent of passengers compared with 16 per cent at Dulles and only 7 per cent at Reagan National (Canan and Mohammed, 2010).

The airport product

The airport product consists of a supply of services, both tangible and intangible, to meet the needs of different market segments. Urfer and Weinert (2011) classify the tangible features as being the airside infrastructure (runways, taxiways, navigational aids), landside infrastructure (terminals, parking facilities, ground transport interchanges), airport support infrastructure (aircraft maintenance, in-flight catering services, police and security facilities) and support areas including industrial areas and duty free zones. The intangible components are defined as the organisational, structural and operational aspects including state support, administration (airport management, airport planning, air traffic control), operations (air traffic control, airport safety and security), airport maintenance and external factors including regulations and the environment.

Marketing theory often divides the product into core, actual or physical, and augmented elements to relate the product to customer needs and expectations. The core product is the essential benefit that the consumer is seeking, while the actual product delivers the benefit. Product features, quality level, brand name, design and packaging will all make up the physical product. The augmented product is then additional consumer services and benefits that will be built around the core and actual products, and will distinguish the product from others. Much of the competition will typically take place at the augmented level (Kotler *et al.* 2008). Sometimes the physical product is referred to as the 'generic' product, with the 'wide' product representing the augmented elements (Jarach, 2005).

Each market segment will perceive these product levels very differently. For the airline, the core is the ability to land and take off an aircraft, while for the passenger it will be the ability to board or disembark an aircraft. For freight forwarders it will be the ability to load and unload the freight on the aircraft. In order to provide the core product for the airline, the actual product will need to consist of the runway, the terminal building, the freight warehouses, the equipment and so on – and the expertise to provide all these facilities efficiently and safely. For the passenger, the actual product will include check-in desks, baggage handling and other features including immigration control which will enable the passenger to fulfil his/her need to board or disembark the aircraft. The actual product will also include adequate transport services to and from airport and the provision of outlets selling essential travel goods, as well as other facilities including information desks and toilets. At the augmented level the airport may, for example, offer marketing support or pricing incentives to the airlines or may formalise some agreement about the exact service levels to be expected. For the passenger, the range and diversity of shops, F&B and other commercial facilities as well as other features, including ease of transfer between different aircraft, could all be considered part of the augmented product.

It is difficult to apply this marketing concept to the airport sector because of the composite nature of the airport product. From a passenger viewpoint, the airport product includes the airline product as well as the product of the concessionaire, handling agent and so on. Another way of looking at the airport product is by considering its 'raw' and 'refined' features. The raw product consists of both physical tangible elements (including the runway, buildings, apron, lighting, navigation aids, fuel, fire and rescue) and intangible service elements provided by the airport operator's own staff and those of the customs, immigration and security agencies. To produce the refined product involves adding the services provided by concessionaires and other tenants and the air travel elements, both tangible and intangible, provided by the airlines.

Chapter 5 has already provided a number of examples of how airport operators are increasingly differentiating their product to appeal to different market segments. Related to such product differentiation is the idea of an airport brand. In marketing theory a brand is represented by a name, logos, design, signing, merchandising and advertising, which all give the product an identity. These tangible and intangible features of the identity differentiate the product from its competitors. Within the airport sector it is certainly true that there are widespread attempts to create a corporate identity with the use of catchy publicity slogans and eye-catching logos and designs on promotional information and within the terminal itself. For airport operators that own more than one airport, use of similar signposting, colour schemes and interior design may also be used for all their airports. However, whether such branding actually gives an airport any competitive edge is open to debate, especially as there will usually be other brands of retailers, airlines and alliance groups displayed within the terminal. The brand effects may also be diluted by advertising on blank wall space, which airport operators encourage to boost their commercial revenues. So the airport operator needs to ensure there are not too many brands that may confuse passengers and have a negative impact on the passenger experience.

Airport operators often give considerable attention to the name of the airport. Many regional airports like to be called 'international' airports to demonstrate that they serve international as well as domestic destinations – even if in some cases there may be only one international route. On the other hand, as airports become more developed and well known for their range of services, they might choose to drop the international part of their name, as Birmingham Airport did in 2010. Other airports will include the name of the nearest large city or town, even if it may not be particularly close and there may be more conveniently located airports. This may result in many airports seemingly serving one city. A prime example is London, which appears to be served by eight airports: London Heathrow, London Gatwick, London Stansted, London City, London Luton, London Southend, London Biggin Hill and London Ashford. This is also typically the case with secondary airports that serve LCCs. Examples include Stockholm Skavsta airport which is 100 km from Stockholm; Frankfurt Hahn airport which is 120 km from Frankfurt; Chicago Rockford which is 145 km from Chicago; and Brussels South Charleroi airport (BSCA) which is 46 km south of Brussels. Including the nearby city name may well make the airport easier to market and will give routes served by it better placing in the airline computer reservation systems and internet searches. However, it can also be misleading to passengers and disliked by rival airports. A relevant case here was in 2003 when the German court blocked Weeze airport from using the name Dusseldorf which is more than 70 km away – although this name is still used by some of the airlines when they are selling their services.

Giving an airport a name that is based on geographical characteristics, natural or man-made attractions or aspects of historical importance may raise the visibility and profile of the airport. These may be natural (e.g. Lakselv Banak North Cape Airport and Annecy Haute-Savoie Airport Mont Blanc) or man-made (e.g. Bardufoss Snowman International Airport). The name Euro-Airport for Basel-Mulhouse airport was devised to reflect its central European location and bi-national ownership characteristics. Knock airport in Ireland was rebranded as Ireland West Airport Knock in 2005 to emphasise its importance as an access point to the West of Ireland. Other airports use famous people associated with the location, which may include members of the royal family (King Abdulaziz International airport), politicians (John F. Kennedy International airport), composers, entertainers and musicians (Warsaw Chopin airport) or artists (Leonardo da Vinci-Fiumicino airport). In the UK there are also now 'John Lennon' Liverpool airport, 'Robin Hood' Doncaster airport and 'George Best' Belfast City airport. However, there has been some debate as to whether the name 'Robin Hood' is appropriate for Doncaster Sheffield Airport, given that this legendary figure is more strongly linked with Nottingham; and likewise whether the naming of the George Best airport is the most appropriate, given that he was closely associated with Manchester United football team. There can be a problem if the name is too distinctive and encourages certain traffic types. For example, Rovaniemi airport in Finland became known as Santa Claus airport in order to contribute to the Santa-based tourism in Finnish Lapland, initially after BA took a Concorde flight of 100 passengers there in 1994. However, this type of traffic is very seasonal and is dominated by charters, so this name may discourage other airlines that might provide a more regular service. Another example of an airport that has had a particular problem with its name and geographical position is the airport in the UK that up until 2003 was called East Midlands airport. In 2003 it decided to change its name to Nottingham East Midlands to make its location seem more specific. However, there are two other towns, Leicester and Derby, that are nearer to the airport than Nottingham and the new name was therefore not popular there. Eventually in 2006 the airport was given another new name, East Midlands airport – Nottingham, Leicester and Derby.

A comprehensive study of 1,562 world airports gives some insight into the typical use of names (Halpern and Regmi, 2011) (Figure 8.2). Unsurprisingly, nearly 80 per cent include a place name, and just over 40 per cent include an indication of the services (e.g. international, regional). Using famous people or attractions is less popular.

This study also found that one-tenth of airports used slogans, and this was most common in North America. Typically these may relate to the connectivity that the airport provides, including Dallas/Fort Worth International Airport 'The world connected', Munich Airport 'Service non-stop', Budapest airport 'Where everything takes off', Brussels airport 'Welcome to Europe', Macau International Airport 'Gateway to China', Aéroports de Montréal 'Where Montreal meets the world', Cheddi Jagan International Airport 'The gateway to South America', and Miami Airport 'Gateway to Miami, to Florida and to the Americas'. They may also relate to the travel and

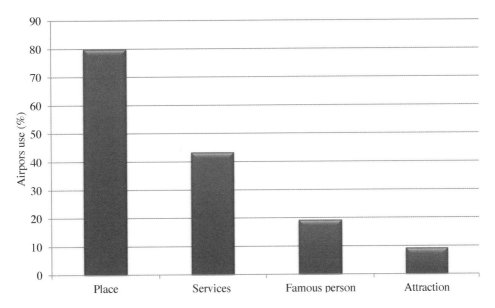

Figure 8.2 *Use of different types of airport name*
Source: Halpern and Regmi (2011)

passenger experience, including Helsinki-Vantaa Airport 'For smooth travelling', Singapore Changi Airport 'The feeling is first class', and Moscow Domodedovo airport 'Happy Landings'. Airports may adopt a new slogan when there is a significant change to their product, for example London Gatwick airport used 'Your London Airport Gatwick' to differentiate itself from London Heathrow Airport when it came under new ownership, and Kuala Lumpur airport used to slogan 'KLIA Next Gen Hub' to prepare for new facilities, particular the new LCC terminal.

AIRPORT MARKETING TECHNIQUES

Successful airport marketing involves focusing on understanding and responding to the needs of the various customer segments. Every airport is unique and needs to be marketed in its own specific way. At small airports, all marketing tasks may be undertaken by a couple of staff, whereas at larger airports there may be separate departments for coping with different customers, including the passengers and airlines, and different teams looking at different marketing activities, including market research, sales and public relations. Once an airport gets to a certain size, the marketing focus is likely to change. Small airports may concentrate on growing specific services that appear to offer opportunities for the airport. Larger airports, that already have a reasonably developed route network, may be more concerned with putting forward a good positive image for the airport and building on a corporate identity. The marketing of airports aiming to be hub or feeder points is totally different from marketing an airport that relies on point-to-point services including charter or low-cost services. Airports with considerable spare capacity will adopt different strategies from congested airports. Smaller airports competing with major capital city airports will probably find that they are always faced with an uphill struggle, nevertheless a considerable amount of proactive and aggressive marketing may achieve results.

Airlines

At the most basic level, airports promote themselves to airlines by producing general publicity information, by placing advertisements in trade journals, and by being represented at exhibitions, travel trade seminars and workshops, roadshows and other similar events. The aim here is to increase awareness among the airlines. It must be borne in mind, however, that this activity will usually only reach a general audience and may be very costly. Developing regular contact with key airlines through visits by airport sales staff, or with regular mailshots and other promotional activities, may also be effective.

However, very often airports deal with potential airline customers in a much more direct and personal way as well. This hard or personal-selling approach, called route or air service development, was developed in the 1980s owing to the realisation that airports were actually in a good position to identify new route opportunities for airlines. This was a task previously left solely to the airlines. The airport operators analysed passenger and catchment area data which gave them adequate information to suggest new route opportunities to potential operators. Many of the airports had the advantage that they already kept at least some of these data for their own passenger marketing and forecasting. They also benefited from certain cost economies by being able to consider all different markets and routes simultaneously. For a small airline interested in operating just one or two new routes, the cost of undertaking such research could well have been too prohibitive.

So the airports started to take a leading role in initiating interest from airlines with this more direct route development approach. From their databases, they would provide airlines with information about potential routes and the size of the market, and perhaps other factors including the likely requirements for frequency and aircraft size and route cost and yield considerations. By the 1990s, airline presentations from the marketing departments of airports to route planners in airlines had become commonplace. Typically, the presentation would give a detailed analysis of the new route or routes and usually an approximate financial evaluation. This would be supplemented by information about the catchment area in terms of the characteristics of residents and its tourist and business appeal for incoming passengers. Information would also be given about the airport's facilities and accessibility by transport links.

Times have now moved on in the air transport industry, and both airports and airlines have developed more sophisticated marketing techniques. The airline presentation can still be an important element of an airport's marketing, but it has to be highly focused. The emphasis must be very much on the potential demand at the airport (including an assessment of any newly stimulated traffic and the impact on existing routes) and the level of services that is needed in terms of frequency and capacity, with the quality of facilities taking second place. Emphasis on architectural excellence and best quality facilities could even have a negative impact, with airlines being concerned that the cost of such infrastructure may be passed on to them. The airlines themselves have become awash with route studies from numerous airports and so have become much more skilled in using this information to back up and verify their own research.

An interesting development regarding airline marketing has been the route development forums that provide networking opportunities for airline route planners and airport operators through one-to-one meetings. The airport operator will typically use their market research to demonstrate opportunities for new routes or expansion of services, and will sell the virtues of their catchment areas and facilities and services. In turn the airlines will explain their expansion strategies to the airports. The first forum was 'Routes' in 1995, which is now an annual global event that has been joined by region-specific meetings including Routes Regional Americas, Routes Regional Asia, Routes Regional Europe and Routes Regional Africa. In North America there are similar events called Network USA and the JumpStart Air Service Development Program. There are also other events in Europe, including French Connect. The 2012 Global Routes event attracted 3,200 delegates (including 650 airline delegates) who had more than 16,000 meetings over the 4 days. Airports pay different fees for eight to nine meetings depending on whether they have fewer than 1 million passengers annually, between 1 and 4 million, or over 4 million. Airports are also able to pay additional fees for additional meetings and separate fees are available for cargo airports, commercial suppliers, consultants, economic development agencies and tourism authorities. Airlines are not required to pay a registration fee.

More recently there has been the opportunity to explore route development opportunities online. For example, in 2008 the anna.aero website, previously dedicated to airline network news and analysis, launched the Route Shop. With this, airports can provide details about unserved routes and other information, including the catchment area, marketing support, airport infrastructure and services, and freight opportunities. In December 2012 there were 3,387 unserved routes and over 150 airports. Around the same time, the organisation involved with the Routes events launched the online Route Exchange. With this website airlines are invited to submit a request for proposal (RFP) that will include their requirements for a new route related to target markets, data needs and desirable support. Airports can access this and respond directly with a confidential proposal to the specific airline. The airports can also provide full details of their profiles which are available on the website. As of the end of December 2012, Route Exchange had 195 listed airlines and 211 listed airports.

Copenhagen Economics (2012) discussed a survey that considered how airports marketed themselves to airlines. It found that 96 per cent of European airports attended route development conferences, and 80 per cent met airlines in their office, or invited them to the airport (77 per cent), or sent them a bespoke report (68 per cent). A smaller share sent out general marketing material or presented themselves on route development websites.

One of the most important aspects of the route development process will be pricing incentives which the airport operator will offer to encourage the airline to serve the airport (Fichert and Klophaus, 2011). In Europe about a third of all airports offer these (Malina *et al.*, 2012). Usually they involve reduced fees over a certain period (Table 8.7). These can be particularly important, and may be crucial particularly for LCCs. Such discounts will usually diminish as traffic grows and the service becomes sustainable. One of the most popular methods is to waive or reduce the landing fee in the first few years of operation so that the airline only pays for the passengers it carries. If demand at the start of a service is initially low, the airline will pay very little. This means the airport will share more of the risk when the airline is developing the route. There may also be discounts on passenger and parking charges. Alternatively, the three charges may be replaced with a set charge per passenger, which again is a more risky option for the airport as it has the effect of relating the charge solely to passenger numbers, which drive airline revenues. As well as these new route incentives to encourage greater connectivity for the airport, there may

Table 8.7 *Types of airport charge discounts*

Discount	Objective
Landing charge discount on flights to new destinations	Encourages new routes
Landing charge discount on all additional flights or larger aircraft	Encourages new frequencies or additional capacity
Landing charge discount for replacing one-stop service by non-stop	Encourages new direct routes
Landing charge discount for positioning flights	Encourages airlines to base aircraft at the airport
Transfer passenger discount	Encourages growth of transfer passengers
Passenger charge discount	Encourages new routes and more frequencies/capacity
Passenger and landing charge discounts for off-peak/daytime flights	Encourages new routes and frequencies/ capacity while avoiding congestion and night noise
Aircraft parking charges discount	Encourages new routes and more frequencies/capacities and basing of aircraft

Source: Adapted from STRAIR (2005)

be incentives to persuade airlines to offer more capacity, or to increase frequencies, or to operate non-stop services. Incentives may be offered to support airlines to use the airport as a base. Not all these incentive schemes are published, but Table 8.8 contains a sample of those that are, to give an indication of the range of incentives on offer. Here some airports consider new routes or greater volume in general, while others give priority to certain services (including charter or intercontinental).

Airports may be able to make themselves appear particularly attractive if they guarantee that the overall package of costs that an airline is faced with at the airport will be reasonable. In many cases, airports will be able to offer discounted airport charges, but will have no control over handling or fuel charges. However, a few airports, including Abu Dhabi in the Middle East, offer a one-stop approach when there is a single contract for all ground services at the airport. Since all the facilities, including aircraft fuelling, are owned by the government, the airport is in a position to do this and to have complete control over what it offers to the airlines. Bahrain airport also operates a comprehensive package of incentives which includes reduction in fees, discounts on hotel accommodation for crews and low fuel prices. STRAIR (2005) described how all the promotional efforts at Bahrain were channelled through the 'Single Co-ordinated Group' that included Bahrain Airport Services, Bahrain Petroleum Company, Air BP and Bahrain Duty Free. A number of smaller regional airports are also able to offer low-cost airlines deals that include the handling charges as well as providing these services themselves.

As well as offering reductions on charges, airports very often provide financial help for marketing or will pool resources so that joint advertising and promotional campaigns may be run to promote

Table 8.8 *Examples of airport discount schemes, 2012*

Bangkok	New international charter routes: 3-year discount 95 per cent, 95 per cent, 95 per cent on landing and parking fees, and a rebate of THB 120 p/passenger Growth on existing charter routes: Bonus of THB 120 p/passenger over the previous year
Copenhagen	New routes: Up to 5-year discount (80–100 per cent, 70–90 per cent, 60–80 per cent, 20–40 per cent, 10–20 per cent) on take-off fee depending on MTOW. Up to 5-year discount (80–90 per cent, 60–70 per cent, 40–50 per cent, 20–30 per cent, 10–20 per cent) on passenger fee depending on number of passengers
Dusseldorf	Passenger volume rebates: 500,000–1 million (4 per cent), 1–2 million (5 per cent), 2–3 million (5.5 per cent), 3–4 million (6.0 per cent), 4–5 million (6.5 per cent), 5–6 million (7 per cent), >6 million (7.5 per cent)
Geneva	New route discount on landing charges: Period 1 (80 per cent), 2 (60 per cent), 3 (40 per cent) 4 (20 per cent). Period is a year for long-haul and 6 months for short-haul
Hamburg	New route discount on landing charge: year 1 intercontinental (100 per cent), Europe (75 per cent) year 2 intercontinental (75 per cent) Europe (50 per cent) year 3 intercontinental (50 per cent)
Hong Kong	New routes: 1-year rebate on landing charges (75 per cent months 1–6, 25 per cent months 7–9, 25 per cent months 10–12)
Incheon	New route: 3-year discount (100 per cent, 75 per cent, 50 per cent) on landing fees Increased frequency: 3-year discount 50 per cent on landing fees Night flight (23:00–05:00): 3-year discount 25 per cent on landing fees

Source: Compiled by the author from various sources

the new services. For example, all Swedavia airports offer support for airlines and tour operators that start a new route with at least 20 departures or expand their service on an existing route by at least 20 departures during a 12-month period. Costs may also be shared for exhibitions and trade fairs. Very often stakeholders, including local governments, regional agencies and tourism boards, can become involved at this stage, which is quite common in the United States (Weatherill, 2006) (see Chapter 9). In addition, non-financial incentives can be offered, including information provision, for example regarding the regulatory situation and market characteristics or useful contacts lists for local travel agent, tour operation, ground handling, recruitment agencies and media sectors. Airports may give advice on scheduling decisions, particularly if an airline is to benefit from connecting traffic from other airlines. The airport may also promise to help lobby government to remove environmental or traffic rights regulatory obstacles. Finally, another way an airport can put together an attractive deal for an airline, and be cost-effective in its marketing, is by pairing up and cooperating with the airport at the other end of a route that has been identified as having potential. Extending this idea further may lead to airport sister agreements, discussed in Chapter 2.

A very visible indication of what low-cost carriers are looking for from an airport was illustrated in 2005, when easyJet took the unusual step of advertising on its website the criteria that it uses for airport selection. These were:

- Does the airport serve a large population of people within 1 hour or serve an attractive destination?
- Does the airport support rapid aircraft turnarounds?
- Can the airport support services to other easyJet destinations?
- Is low-cost part of the airport strategy?
- Is the airport seeking to improve the efficiency of its business?

If the airport could answer yes to all these questions, it was invited to send detailed information about the demand characteristics and facilities at the airport. This helped easyJet in choosing some additional bases.

The most common airlines to benefit from a total package of measures are the low-cost carriers. Airports are willing to enter into such agreements due to the additional commercial revenues that hopefully the extra passengers will bring and the impact such services will have on raising the profile of the airport and encouraging other new carriers. For a number of regional airports, this may also be a way of filling airport capacity that was under-utilised. If the airport is under regional public ownership, the new services may be supported because of the potential broader economic benefit they could bring to the whole region – for example in terms of encouraging tourism and inward investment. However, this raises the issue of whether state aid should be used in this way to support certain airlines. For instance, as a result of a complaint by Air France in 2003, the Strasbourg court ruled that the marketing support given by the publicly owned Strasbourg airport to Ryanair was illegal. Ryanair pulled off the route and opened a route from Baden-Karlsruhe in Germany instead, which had a very negative impact on the traffic levels at Strasbourg. A similar, but in the end much more significant, example that has had wide-ranging impacts in Europe is the Brussels South Charleroi airport (BSCA) case (Case Study 8.2).

CASE STUDY 8.2: THE BRUSSELS SOUTH CHARLEROI (BSCA) AIRPORT CASE

Charleroi airport is a regional airport formerly owned by the Walloon government which is 46 km south of Brussels. Between 1990 and 1996, its passenger levels fluctuated around 50,000. Then, in 1997, Ryanair began to operate two flights a day to Dublin and the airport passenger numbers increased dramatically to 200,000. Ryanair's passenger numbers increased from 86,000 in 1997 to

178,000 in 2000, but the airport still remained very much a small regional airport. The most significant change came in 2001 when Ryanair decided to make Charleroi its first continental base and began operating 10 routes with 19 daily frequencies. This changed its status from that of a regional airport serving passengers on charter airlines originating from the Walloon region to a larger secondary airport with a much greater traffic base in the whole of Belgium and also cross-border regions in France and Germany. It was at this time that the name was changed from Charleroi Airport to Brussels South Charleroi Airport (Jossart, 2006).

The airport offered Ryanair a very favourable deal because it felt the presence of Ryanair could substantially grow its non-aeronautical revenues and attract other airlines to the airport. For example, it transformed the coach shuttle from the Airport to Brussels City from a loss-making into a profitable activity and generated a substantial amount of revenue from car parking since it introduced parking charges in 1999. It also expanded the duty-free and catering outlets to cope with the additional passengers and increase the overall non-aeronautical revenues.

Table 8.9 shows the reported details of the arrangement made between BSCA and Ryanair. Ryanair paid very low landing and handling charges starting at €1 per passenger, which was planned to go up to €1.13 in 2006 and €1.30 in 2010. In addition, BSCA contributed towards other expenses incurred by Ryanair which,

Table 8.9 Elements of agreement between Ryanair and BSCA

Annual payments	Amount (euros)	Cost assumptions (euros)	Other assumptions (euros)
Ryanair to BSCA			
Landing fees	1,000,000	Landing fees/pax: 1.00	Annual pax: 1 million
Handling fees	1,000,000	Handling fees/pax: 1.00	
Total	2,000,000		
BSCA to Ryanair			
Marketing fees	2,000,000	Marketing contribution/pax: 2.00	
Hotel costs	250,000	Hotels costs/year: 250,000	
New route payment	1,920,000	Payment/new route: 160,000	New routes: 12
Recruitment payment	768,000	Recruitment/training (one-off): 768,000	

Continued

Table 8.9 *Continued*

Annual payments	Amount (euros)	Cost assumptions (euros)	Other assumptions (euros)
Office costs	250,000	Estimated office costs/year: 250,000	
Hangar costs	250,000	Estimated hangar costs/year: 250,000	
Total	**5,438,000**		
Net benefit	**3,438,000**		

Source: Aviation Strategy (2001)

together with the low charges, resulted in a net benefit to Ryanair. The expenses covered by BSCA included marketing support, incentive payments for each route started, and Ryanair's costs for local crew hiring and training. Office and hangar space was also provided for a minimal cost. For this support from BSCA, Ryanair agreed to base two to four aircraft at the airport and to operate at least three departing flights for each aircraft over a period of 15 years – if not it would have to repay the incentives.

However, in 2001 a complaint was lodged with the European Commission concerning these incentives and whether they were anti-competitive, and an investigation was undertaken concerning the state aid that had been given by the Walloon region to Ryanair. Two issues were considered. First, according to Article 87 of the Treaty of Rome and European transport policy, aid is allowed if it encourages the development and use of under-utilised secondary airport infrastructure. On the other hand, state aid is not allowed when it can be proved that a private airport operator would not behave in the same manner – the so-called private market investor principle. A decision was reached in 2004 when it was decided that Ryanair could keep some of the aid, but the remaining amount had to be paid back (EC, 2004). The EC determined that no private operator in the same circumstances as Charleroi airport would have granted the same advantages to the airline, hence the private market investor principle had not been followed. However, the EC took the view that some aspects of the aid could be compatible with European transport policy. Thus the EC allowed Ryanair to keep some of the aid intended for the launch of new air routes (including marketing and publicity) and other one-off incentives, including recruitment payments. However, other aid that took no account of the actual costs of launching such routes was not allowed, nor were the fee discounts because they had not been allocated in a non-discriminatory and fully transparent manner and were planned for a very long period of operation. Ryanair launched an appeal against this judgment.

Following on from this case, and to clarify the application of state aid principles to airports, the EC issued guidelines on financing of airports and start-up aid to airlines departing from regional airports in 2005 (EC, 2005). This stipulates that the aid can be offered only by airports with fewer than 5 million passengers, and it must in most cases be limited to 3 years and be regressive (Table 8.10). However, these are not law, but only guidelines of the EC's interpretation of how the law should be applied. It is important to emphasise that it only applies to publicly owned airports in Europe, whereas the growing number of private airports are free to offer whatever incentives they feel are suitable. Since the issuance of the guideline the EC has investigated a number of airports and their incentive schemes for airlines. Most recently, in 2012 it concluded that the financial arrangements between Tampere Pirkkala in Finland and Ryanair did not constitute state aid. There are also ongoing investigations at Alghero airport in Italy, Beauvais, Carcassonne and Angouleme airports in France and Dortmund airport in Germany. The EC guidelines are currently being reviewed, in part because Ryanair successfully won its appeal in 2008 against the original decision in 2004.

Table 8.10 Key features of the 2005 EU guidelines on financing of airports and start-up aid to airlines departing from regional airports

---

Supported routes must usually be between EU airports of fewer than 5 million
 passengers

The aid must only apply to new routes or to increased frequencies which lead to
 an increase in passengers

The aid must be linked to the net development of the number of passengers
 carried

The route must be shown to be viable after the aid has expired

The aid must be linked directly to the start-up costs or increased costs of the
 airline in operating the new route or increased frequencies

The aid must be digressive and granted for maximum period of three years
 (five years for remote airports)

The aid must not exceed 50 per cent of the total eligible costs in 1 year and the
 total aid must not exceed an average of 30 per cent of all eligible costs

---

Source: EC (2005)

Travel trade

Airports also need to promote themselves to the travel trade including travel agents, tour operators and freight forwarders. Again this can be done by producing general publicity electronic and paper information, by placing advertisements in trade journals and by going to trade exhibitions such as ITB Berlin and the World Travel Market in London. In spite of the increased use of the internet and other direct-booking methods, travel agents can still be highly influential in some cases when passengers go through the process of selecting and assessing possible travel options. Some of the general sales promotions directed at the airlines may be targeted at the travel agency sector as well and may help to give exposure to the airport and the services that it offers. Regular mailshots by post and electronically to agents may enhance that awareness.

In many cases, however, this is not enough. Numerous airports, particularly the regional and smaller ones, have found that it is particularly important to spend some time and effort in developing close, personalised links with travel agents serving the direct catchment area. This usually involves regularly sending out a sales representative who can talk to the agents about new developments at the airport and explore the agents' knowledge and views of the services on offer. This one-to-one contact can be supplemented with frequent, personalised e-mails giving details of promotions, new facilities, up-to-date timetables and other information. Very often, airports will also organise competitions, airport tours and other social events to encourage greater interest in the airport and to forge closer links with the agency sector. Familiarisation trips and launch parties for new routes for key business and travel trade representatives are particularly important. There are stories of regional airports discovering that their neighbouring travel agents are unaware of some of the services they offer, with agents advising passengers to travel instead via a larger airport further away. Cardiff airport in the United Kingdom overcame this problem by buying a chain of 22 local travel agents in an attempt to promote flights from its airport. Norwich airport, also in the UK, went one stage further by not only opening its own travel agencies, but also operating its own charter flights to some of the main leisure destinations in Europe in the late 1990s. However, this policy was abandoned a few years later, having been successful in persuading the tour operators and airlines that there was a demand for direct services and to subsequently take over the destinations themselves (Eady, 2007).

Passengers and the local community

Generally a much more soft-sell approach is adopted for passengers. Advertising is used to create awareness and communicate messages to a mass audience. It is undertaken by producing general publicity information (internet and mobile sites, information leaflets, stickers and T-shirts) and advertising in a range of media (print, radio, television, outdoor and electronic media). Travel brochures and adverts, produced jointly with tour operators or airlines, can be circulated or offered online. Sponsorship and fundraising events may also be used as a means of advertising, although this perhaps could be considered more as public relations than actual advertising. Likewise, airports may organise open days, air shows and exhibitions.

The choice of media will depend on the relative costs, the target audience and the message the airport operator wants to put across. A basic message or idea can be successfully communicated through a simple advert, whereas more detailed information, for example, timetable or flight materials, needs to be presented in more detailed written form. Airports adopt various approaches to woo passenger to their airports. Most commonly, airports try to increase the consumer's awareness of flights and closeness of the airport by listing the destinations on offer or by focusing on the convenience of the public transport links. More specific messages may relate to a certain service or facility at the airport, particularly airport shopping, or a certain market segment, including business travellers. Advertising can be particularly important when a new route is launched. In general, the ultimate aim of advertising activities is to sell a product, but the airport has a rather unique relationship with its passengers as it is not selling a product directly to them. The passenger will not go to the airport unless the required airline service is there, and so this more limited role of advertising needs to be recognised. For this reason, mass market advertising aimed at passengers focusing just on the airport product is not very common. However, examples include Heathrow airport, which recently ran an advertising campaign using various media including outdoor billboards and those on the London underground, with messages including 'Can't stop thinking about your holiday? Neither can we'; 'Everyone gets a smoother take-off at Heathrow'; and 'How the Great British getaway will getaway this Easter'. However, there are generally more examples of promotional activities aimed at passengers undertaken primarily to increase non-aeronautical revenues at airports rather than directly influencing their choice of airport.

Some airports have gone further by developing loyalty schemes for their passengers. These can be viewed as part of the airport's customer relationship management which also covers other areas including enhancing passenger travel and communications (Halpern and Graham, 2013), considered in Chapters 5 and 6. Loyalty schemes typically give rewards or points that can then be used in the future to gain discounts or other benefits. For airports they can provide greater insight into the needs of their customers, reduce marketing costs by being more focused on familiar customers, and incentivise customers to buy more products. Regular e-newspaper or mobile messages can be sent to those passengers who are involved with the schemes. However, compared with other industries including supermarkets, hotels or even airlines with their frequent points, the impact of these is likely to be less significant at airports, again because of the more limited impact that the actual airport product (as opposed to the airline product) can have on passenger choice. There are generally two types of schemes: paid membership schemes based on frequent flyer programmes that focus on helping passengers travel through the airport more comfortably and swiftly (Chapter 5), and free schemes that tend to concentrate on incentivising passengers to spend more in the commercial areas (Chapter 7). A recent study of airports showed that a quarter of all airports provided such schemes, with 10 per cent having a paid frequent flyer programmes and 16 per cent having a free loyalty scheme (ACI/DMKA, 2012).

All airports have a need for public relations activities – airports have major impacts on the local community not only by providing local flights for residents, but also by generating jobs and other economic benefits. On the other hand, the environmental impacts including noise and pollution are of major concern. Generally, the aviation industry still holds a fascination and wonder for some and a fear for others. For all these reasons, airports tend to receive extensive coverage, both favourable and otherwise, in the press. It is worthwhile for airports to put considerable effort into trying to capitalise on the general interest people have in airports and to create a degree of goodwill between airports and the community, particularly should anything so wrong, when crisis management techniques will be needed. Developing good links with local, regional, national and in some cases foreign media is crucial, and hosting events for journalists and travel writers can increase interest in the airport and stimulate press coverage. Arranging school visits and other trips will also be an essential public relations activity.

MARKET RESEARCH AND ROUTE DEVELOPMENT

A fundamental element of marketing is market research so that organisations can have a thorough understanding of the characteristics and needs of their market. Most research will cover two areas: market characteristics in terms of market size, share, segmentation and trends; and the more subjective area of passenger satisfaction. Chapter 6 considers passenger satisfaction, so the emphasis of the discussion here is very much on the first area. In practice, many small airports will not have the resources to undertake all the market research that is needed, so strategic partnerships with tourism and regional development agencies may be vital so that resources can be pooled.

There are a number of different data sources that airport operators can consult to gain knowledge about their market (Table 8.11). Passenger volume data are easily available from the airport itself, and in addition many airports undertake periodic surveys of their passengers to find out details including origin and destination, age, sex, socio-economic group, flying frequency and so on (these surveys may be tied in with the quality surveys described in Chapter 6 so that correlations between passenger profiles and levels of satisfaction can be made). In some countries, surveys may be undertaken by the national civil aviation authorities or government transport departments instead of, or in addition, to those carried out by the airport operators. For example, in the United Kingdom the CAA regularly surveys passengers at all main airports. This has the advantage of producing survey data that are directly comparable for different airports. Information about the characteristics of existing travellers may also be obtained from tourism statistics that may be available from local or national government agencies or from the World Tourism

Table 8.11 *Types of data used for route development research*

Data	Typical sources	Information obtained
Airport traffic data	Airport or government departments	Passenger, freight and aircraft volumes
Airport passenger survey data	Airport or government departments	Passenger characteristics such as origin/destination, purpose and frequency of travel, socio-economic group
Tourism data	World Tourism Organization (UNWTO), tourist boards or government departments	Tourist numbers and tourist/trip characteristics
Airline booking and sales data	Computer reservation system market information data tapes (CRS-MIDT) and billing and settlement planning data (BSP)	Travel details such as passenger origin/destination, connecting airports, routing patterns
Airline schedule data	Official airline guide, airlines	Current routes, frequencies/ schedules and seat capacity data

Organization (UNWTO). While these can give an indication of the volume of tourists and current trends, they may have limited use if they are not available by mode of transport and if they are not available for outbound as well as inbound flows. More in-depth information about current services and particularly any underserved destinations can be also gleaned from other organisations including travel agents, local businesses and freight forwarders.

Most of the market analysis undertaken is based on revealed preference techniques, that is by assessing the passenger's current behaviour to determine future travel patterns. The alternative is to use stated preference techniques, where passengers are asked to state their preference between a number of different scenarios. These techniques have been used to look at airport choice and also transport modal choice for surface access. For instance, passengers might be asked how they would trade off higher journey cost to an airport against journey time. Such information can give airports invaluable insight into how passengers rate the factors that influence passenger choice. While stated preference techniques are widely used for other transport modes, their application within the airport industry is more limited. A few years ago the UK CAA undertook a stated preference survey at Stansted airport which helped to estimate the price elasticities of the passengers (CAA, 2005). More recently, the CAA used stated preference to investigate passenger preferences to switch London airports when prices were increased (CAA, 2011b).

An important area of airport market research is associated with the marketing of new services (STRAIR, 2005; Martin, 2008). For this, the airport operator will typically go through an air service or route development process that will have different data and research requirements at each stage. The overall task is to identify potentially viable routes that are not currently being served and ultimately to produce route-by-route forecasts and a feasibility assessment. Halpern and Graham (2013) define the seven stages of the route development process:

- define catchment area
- undertake market assessment and leakage analysis
- identify unserved or underserved routes
- produce growth forecast for potential routes
- choose possible airlines to operate the routes
- undertake a financial viability assessment of the route
- present the business case to the airline.

The first stage of this route development process involves defining the catchment area of the airport. This relates to the geographical reach of the airport services to the surrounding population and economy that they serve, and so is the area to which most inbound passengers are travelling, or from which most outbound passengers have originated. The most basic approach to defining a catchment area is by using a certain drive-time period criteria – typically 1 or 2 hours. This area can be called the primary catchment area, where most travellers are likely to consider the airport their first choice based on proximity. Isochrones of longer times may represent weaker secondary or even tertiary catchment areas, where the airport will not necessarily be the first choice. For example, Toronto, Copenhagen, Prague and Cancun airport all use 30-, 60- and 120-minute drive-time definitions. More complex definitions may make distinctions between drive time and public transport time. With such definitions, improvements in the road infrastructure or the quality of public transport may change the catchment area. Alternatively a distance criterion may be used, for instance 100 km for Dubrovnik airport, 250 km for Rome Fiumicino airport, and 10, 40 and 50 miles for Dublin airport. In defining the catchment area, airport operators need to take into account the willingness of passengers to travel certain times or distances to or from the airport and the nature and purpose of their journey. For instance, more time-sensitive business passengers will tend to demand shorter travel times than leisure passengers, while long-haul (or perhaps international) travellers are likely to be less concerned with this element of travel time compared with short-haul (or perhaps domestic) travellers, as it accounts for a smaller share of their overall journey time.

Once the catchment area has been defined, the level of air travel demand needs to be estimated. This will depend on factors such as the economic, business and tourist activity within the area, the demographic characteristics of the residents, and past immigration patterns. However, this level of demand will be only a hypothetical maximum measure of the traffic-generating power of the area, as it will fail to take account of nearby competitor airports and the impact such airports will have on potential traffic volumes. In reality, many airports have overlapping catchment areas and so potential passengers within these areas will make their choice of airport dependent on a number of factors, including fare levels, service levels (frequency, or whether the service is nonstop or connecting), preferred airlines, parking and so on. For short-haul travel to popular destinations, there may be significant competition from other airports and so catchment areas will probably overlap considerably, whereas this may not be the case for less popular or longer-distance destinations. Overlap typically occurs with regional airports or when there is more than one airport serving a major city. The larger the overlap of the two catchment areas, the higher the likelihood that the two airports will compete directly for the same passengers. In fact the notion of catchment areas for large capital city airports is not generally so applicable, as in many cases these airports may offer the only link to the destination under question in the whole country.

When traffic is lost or diverted away from its 'natural' catchment area to another airport, due to factors including insufficient airline capacity or frequencies, higher air fares, or a lack of non-stop services at the airport in question, this is defined as traffic leakage. Reverse leakage is the opposite situation, when passengers will use a given airport even though they have not been directly associated with its catchment area. A number of LCCs have been particularly successful in attracting passengers from outside catchment areas and causing leakages because of the lower prices that they offer. This has been especially the case with leisure passengers because of the lower value of their own time. For example, Dennis (2007) described how Stansted originally operated as a regional airport for East Anglia, but has now been transformed into a major airport serving the London area. Another example cited is Charleroi, where only 16 per cent of Ryanair passengers resident at the Charleroi end of services come from the natural catchment area of the airport. However, Dennis also observes how demand levels can contract as the provision of low-cost services increases – giving the example of the low-cost services to Barcelona from East Midlands that began in 2002, but 2 years later had competing services from the nearby airports of Leeds/Bradford, Birmingham and Manchester. Pantazis and Liefner (2006) also observed how LCCs have caused reverse leakage at Hanover airport.

The airport operator needs to estimate these leakages when going through the route-development process. However, the problem with most sources of traffic data is that they do not normally show the true origin and/or destination (O-D) of a passenger, as they will not take into account leakage when passengers have travelled out of their way to another airport to reach the same destination. While the data will include passengers who are connecting at both ends, they will not count passengers who have flown indirectly between the two points. This leakage problem may be partly overcome by using airport survey data for neighbouring airports. However, these data exist only for some countries, such as the UK, and additionally will not help identify indirect passengers. For these reasons, booking data are often used. There are two major sources: market information data tapes (MIDT) that come from the global distribution systems (including Sabre and Amadeus) used by high street and online travel agents; and billing and settlement plan (BSP) data from IATA and its accredited travel agents. For example, Nice airport used BSP data to calculate that in 2011, 84 per cent of passenger traffic from Nice to other European countries was direct while the share to other regions was much less, for example the Middle East (34 per cent) and North America and Africa (27 per cent). There were no direct services to South/Central America or Asia/Oceania (Route Shop, 2012).

However, there are a number of shortcomings with these data. They do not cover tickets sold through direct distribution channels including airline call centres and internet sites, and so do not provide complete coverage – particularly with the trend towards more direct internet selling. Also they do not cover charter activity. Therefore the total market size may have to be estimated, typically by using schedule data. Also, with the booking data it is assumed the place of issuing the ticket represents the passenger's residency, but now in many cases travel agencies process bookings through a centralised office that will invalidate this assumption. Also, the cost of obtaining such information may be beyond the reach of the marketing department budgets of many small airports.

Once the airport operator has assessed the market within its catchment area and the associated leakages, it can determine the adequacy of air services at the airport and identify routes that are not served satisfactorily. By weighing up the factors that passengers take into account when considering different flight and airport options, including air fares, frequencies and schedules and accessibility of the airport (in terms of cost and time), the airport operator can estimate the likely market share of new services to and from the airport. There is a statistical tool called the quality service index (QSI) that airports may use, which estimates passenger behaviour by quantifying the relative attractiveness of different flight options. It has traditionally been used by airlines when assessing their networks, but a number of airports have chosen to develop their own QSI models, even some small ones including Grenoble airport and Chambéry airport. The future demand for the route can then be estimated, typically by taking into account key drivers of demand including income, population, propensity to travel and journey purpose. The airport operator subsequently can identify which airline would be most suitable to operate the route, and undertake a financial and operational feasibility assessment of the route that can be discussed with the airline, either at a formal presentation or through physical or electronic route development networks.

THE ROLE OF THE INTERNET AND SOCIAL MEDIA

Ninety-four per cent of world airports now have their own website or feature on a corporate website of some kind (Halpern, 2012). The internet potentially can offer numerous marketing and revenue opportunities, and an increasing number of airports are taking full advantage of this.

In addition, many airports have developed their own mobile applications (apps) designed to run on smartphones and tablet computers. In Europe about one-third of airports either have an app or are planning to have one, with this figure rising to 56 per cent for airports with more than 10 million passengers (ACI Europe, 2012). As discussed previously, the future use of NFC will provide many more opportunities for airports to exploit mobile technology.

Initially as airports started to develop their websites, most of the information was aimed at passengers, and while airport websites now have additional roles, this continues to be an important feature. This includes airport location details, car parking and local transport information, with perhaps opportunities for pre-booking car parking space or buying public transport tickets online. A study of 102 global airport websites found that only 15 per cent did not provide a map, and this was usually for smaller airports where wayfinding was not considered to be an issue (ACI/DMKA, 2011). Real-time flight information, flight delay details and check-in requirements are usually provided. There will also often be a list of the commercial facilities, including shops and F&B, perhaps with pre-ordering possibilities (see Chapter 7). Tourist and other information and travel tips about the airport's catchment area might be included. There may also be links to airlines and other products including car hire, hotels and tourist boards. There may even be the possibility to book flights directly, with the website acting as a distribution channel itself.

However, information provision for passengers is just one role of the airport website. It also provides aviation information for trade customers such as airlines, general aviation, freight forwarders and tour operators. This will include technical and facilities information, traffic data, airport charges, details of incentive schemes and marketing support, and perhaps market research information related to the catchment area and potential demand which can be used to investigate route development opportunities. Details about customs requirements and handling and warehousing facilities available to cargo customers can also be provided. Moreover, airports are increasingly turning their attention to the non-aviation business opportunities that the airport website may offer. This includes selling advertising space, hiring out meetings facilities, providing details of property and real estate services, and listing other commercial and consultancy services the airport may offer.

The final main role of the airport internet is in using it as a platform for corporate communications to inform and develop good relations with a number of different stakeholders including local residents, local businesses, shareholders, employees and the media. Local residents may be able to find out about achievements in environmental protection or social responsibility areas. Shareholders can track the performance of their shares and have instant access to the airports' financial reports. Employees may be able to explore career and training opportunities.

Figure 8.3 presents the top 15 items of content according to the proportion of airports that provide such content on their website, based on a study of European airports in 2011 (Halpern and Regmi, 2013). Most of these focus on the passenger. In general, while passenger information and corporate communications were provided by all airports, non-aviation business areas were only covered by 46 per cent of airports. In addition, 60 per cent of airports provided technical information for airlines and only 41 per cent gave details about airport charges.

Nearly 30 per cent of airport websites provide links to airport social media accounts, allowing the airport to interact with users rather than just providing information or selling services. In recent years airports, like most other organisations, are increasingly using social media to market

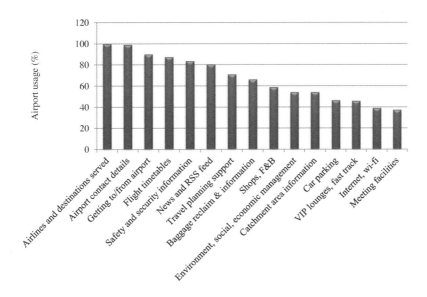

Figure 8.3 *Top 15 items of content on airport websites*
Source: Halpern and Regmi (2013)

to their customers (Nigam *et al.*, 2011). As with the internet, passengers are typically the main focus for social media initiatives at airports, although airports do also use them to communicate with other stakeholders. Halpern (2012) investigated the use of social media at 1,559 airports worldwide, considering four main categories. These were social networking sites including Facebook and Google+, blogs (e.g. airport's own blog or Twitter), professional business networking sites (e.g. LinkedIn, XING) and content communities where multi-media information is shared (e.g. YouTube, Flickr). Nineteen per cent of all airports used at least one type of social media representing 52 per cent of the total airport traffic, the most popular being Facebook (13 per cent), Twitter (12 per cent), LinkedIn (7 per cent) and YouTube (4 per cent). The top five airports in terms of Facebook 'likes' were Singapore, Cleveland Hopkins, Akron-Canton, Los Angeles and Frankfurt, while the top five for Twitter followers were London Heathrow, London Gatwick, Manchester, Dublin and Edinburgh Airport. This research was undertaken at the end of 2010, so it is likely that social media use is much greater now. Research by AirGate Solutions (2012) indicated that there are now around 500 airports using Facebook and Twitter.

Specifically within Europe, a study by ACI Europe (2012) showed that 57 per cent of airports (77 per cent of total passengers) used social media in 2012. Over half of these airports used both Facebook and Twitter (Table 8.12). Five main uses of social media were identified: corporate communications as a tool to raise awareness; crisis promotion to communicate quickly and directly during times of crisis; commercial promotion to sell products and services; informal engagement to build relationships with customers; and customer service to act as a virtual customer service desk. Corporate and crisis communications were the most popular uses. Commercial promotions are discussed in Chapter 7. Numerous examples of different and imaginative social media initiatives exist, including those identified by AirGate Solutions/SimpliFlying (2012), whose 10 top airports for 2012 were Aberdeen, Amsterdam, Dublin, Helsinki, Kansas City, London Gatwick, Melbourne, Singapore, San Diego and Warsaw.

Table 8.12 European airport use of social media, 2012

	Share of airports (per cent)
European airports social media use	57
Europe airports Facebook or Twitter use:	
Facebook only	35
Twitter only	9
Both	56
European airports purpose of social media:	
Corporate communications	89
Crisis communication	87
Commercial promotions	82
Informal engagement	74
Customer service	51
Other uses	22

Source: ACI Europe (2012)

CASE STUDY 8.3: COMPETITION AND MARKETING ISSUES AT THE IRISH AIRPORTS

There have been a number of interesting competition and marketing issues at the Irish airports that make it a valid case study. In 1937, the Irish state-owned company Aer Rianta was established as a holding company for the national carrier Aer Lingus. It also took control of Dublin airport, with this becoming a statutory responsibility in 1950. Then in 1969 it also took over the management of Cork and Shannon airports, and in 1988 Aer Rianta International was established to pursue international projects (see Chapter 6). The three airports handle over 95 per cent of all air traffic to, from and within the Irish Republic, and Dublin airport accounts for around 80 per cent of all the traffic of the three airports. Traffic rose rapidly in the late 1990s, very much helped by the economic boom that was occurring at the time (McLay and Reynolds-Feighan, 2006).

During these early years, Aer Rianta had one of the most complex published discount schemes in existence at the time. The airport operator gave discounts on new routes and growth on existing routes, which reduced over time. In the initial years, airlines could be paying as little as 10 per cent of the standard landing and passenger charge. Various airlines, especially Ryanair, benefited significantly from this scheme – particularly because of the short-haul nature of their services and the price sensitivity of its leisure passengers. However, Aer Rianta terminated their discount scheme at the end of 1999, largely in preparation for the demise of EU duty- and tax-free sales.

This was greeted with considerable opposition from the airlines, particularly Ryanair, which announced it would abandon any new route development from Dublin. As a consequence the Commission for Aviation Regulation was established in 2001 and the level of fees is now controlled with an RPI-*X* single-till approach. However, the level of fees has continued to be a very controversial area, with both the airport operator and the airlines at various times being critical of the Regulator's decisions.

After 9/11, new discount schemes were introduced to stimulate new routes, and are still in existence today. For example at Cork airport there is a long-haul route support scheme that gives annual discounts of 100, 90, 75, 50 and 25 per cent on passenger charges, aircraft parking, airbridge and landing charges over a 5-year period. For short-haul routes there is a 3-year initiative (100, 75 and 50 per cent reductions). There is also a growth incentive scheme that offers a full rebate on passenger charges for traffic growth over a 3-year period. Additional marketing support is also offered depending on certain criteria shown in Table 8.13.

Another issue is group state ownership. While privatisation has been discussed at various times, this option has not become a reality. However, a less radical move was introduced by the State Airports Act of 2004 which created the Dublin Airport Authority (DAA) to replace Aer Rianta and also established new authorities for Shannon and Cork. The split was welcomed by a number of the airlines, but was heavily criticised by management and the trade unions who feared it would weaken the company and lead to job losses in Cork and Shannon. These two airports formed separate boards of directors, but it was not until the end of 2012, after a considerable amount of debate, that Shannon airport was separated from DAA and made a separate state entity (Shannon Airport Authority). Traffic at Shannon airport has fallen from 3.6 million in 2007 to 1.6 million in 2011. Cork airport remains under the direct control of DAA.

Table 8.13 *Cork airport marketing support development criteria, 2012*

Weighting	Criterion
1	Network development potential (new, key developing market or existing market)
2	Capacity origin (new or redeployment)
3	Country (served or not)
3	Commercial revenue potential (high or medium)
3	Aircraft capacity (< or > 250 seats)
3	Tourism potential (high, medium, low)
3	Availability of new route (annual, seasonal)
4	Route (new or existing)
5	Operator commitment to Cork (high, medium, low, predatory route, entry)

Source: Cork Airport (2012)

For a number of years there has also been the issue of the second terminal at Dublin. Before this was built, Ryanair argued that it should have the right to run its own separate terminal rather than to put up with what it claimed to be the costly and inefficient operation of Aer Rianta, which had led to the unjustified high charges. Partly as a result of this pressure and because of the need for extra capacity due to the high growth rates, in 2002 the Irish government asked for expressions of interest from organisations that might wish to develop an independent/competing terminal at Dublin airport. Thirteen companies responded, including international airport groups and airlines. The government appointed an independent panel to scrutinise these proposals and advise on the feasibility of the concept, and in 2003 this panel decided in favour of an independent terminal. It concluded that this could bring effective competition at Dublin through increased capacity and quality of service (Department of Transport, 2003).

This was followed by the Irish government approving the building of a new terminal in 2005 which would be commissioned by the DAA and would have a tender process to select an operator for the new terminal. So although the principle of the second terminal being operated on a competitive process was accepted, the recommendation of the panel of 2003 to also have this terminal designed, built and owned separately was not adopted. While DAA welcomed this decision, Ryanair opposed it, claiming this would mean the terminal would be too costly and badly designed. There were a number of appeals, but eventually the terminal was opened in 2010. However, the suitability of this terminal to suit the needs of airlines, especially given the significant downturn in traffic due to the poor economic conditions, continues to be debated, particularly by Ryanair, in relation to its cost and overall size.

REFERENCES

Accent (2011) *2131 Consumer Research*, London: Accent.

ACI/DMKA (2011) *ASQ Best Practice Report: Airport Wayfinding*, Montreal: Airports Council International.

—— (2012) *ASQ Best Practice Report: Airport Loyalty Programmes*, Montreal: Airports Council International.

ACI Europe (2012) *Digital Report 2012*, Brussels: ACI Europe.

AirGate Solutions (2012) *Airports Using Twitter*, Ontario: AirGate Solutions. Online. Available HTTP: http://www.airgatesolutions.com/index.php?option=com_content&view=article&id=109&Itemid=98 (accessed 15 December 2012).

AirGate Solutions/SimpliFlying (2012) 'Top 10 Social Media Initiatives by Airports', Ontario: AirGate Solutions. Online. Available HTTP: http://simpliflying.com/2012/top-10-airports-on-social-media-2012-edition (accessed 15 December 2012).

Aviation Strategy (2001) 'Ryanair, just too good a negotiator', *Aviation Strategy*, July–August: 3.

Bush, H. (2009) 'The development of competition in the UK airport market', *Journal of Airport Management*, 4(2): 114–24.

CAA (2005) *Demand for Outbound Leisure Air Travel and its Key Drivers*, London: Civil Aviation Authority.

—— (2008) *Economic regulation of Heathrow and Gatwick Airports*, London: Civil Aviation Authority.

—— (2011a) *Guidance on the Assessment of Airport Market Power*, London: Civil Aviation Authority.

—— (2011b) *Passengers' Airport Preferences: Results from the CAA Passenger Survey*, London: Civil Aviation Authority.

—— (2012) *Heathrow: Market Power Assessment: Non-Confidential Version*, London: Civil Aviation Authority.

Cambridge Economic Policy Associates (2010) *The Extent to which Airlines' Interests are Aligned with those of Passengers*, Cambridge: CERA.

Canan, T. and Mohammed, A. (2010) *2009 Washington–Baltimore Regional Air Passenger Survey*, Washington, DC: Metropolitan Washington Council of Governments.

Caves, R. and Gosling, G. (1999) *Strategic Airport Planning*, Oxford: Elsevier.

Competition Commission (2009) *BAA Airports Market Investigation*, London: Competition Commission

Copenhagen Economics (2012) *Airport Competition in Europe*, Copenhagen: Copenhagen Economics.

Cork Airport (2012) *Cork Long-Haul Route Support Scheme (RSS) 2012*. Online. Available HTTP <http://www.corkairport.com/gns/about-us/doing-business-with-us/aviation-marketing/route-support-incentives.aspx> (assessed December 15).

Cranfield University (2002) *Study of Competition between Airports and the Application of State Aid Rules*, Cranfield: Cranfield University.

Dennis, N. (2007) 'Stimulation or saturation? Perspectives on the European low cost airline market and prospects for growth', *Transportation Research Record: Journal of the Transportation Research Board*, 2007: 52–59.

Department for Transport (2008a) *Decision on the Regulatory Status of Manchester Airport*, London: Department for Transport.

—— (2008b) *Decision on the Regulatory Status of Stansted Airport*, London: Department for Transport.

—— (2009) *Reforming the Framework for the Economic Regulation of Airports Decision Document*, London: Department for Transport.

Department of Transport (2003) *Dublin airport – Review of expressions of interest for an independent terminal – Panel report to Minister for Transport*, Dublin: Department of Transport.

Eady, T. (2007) 'Developing a travel product for regional airports', *University of Westminster Regional and Low Cost Air Transport*, London, July

EC (2004) *Commission's Decision of 12 February 2004 concerning Advantages Granted by the Walloon Region and Brussels South Charleroi Airport to the Airline Ryanair in Connection with its Establishment at Charleroi*, OJ L 137, 30 April.

—— (2005) *Community Guidelines on Financing of Airports and Start-Up Aid to Airlines Departing from Regional Airports*, OJ C 312, 9 December.

Fichert, F. and Klophaus, R. (2011) 'Incentive schemes on airport charges – theoretical analysis and empirical evidence from German airports', *Research in Transportation Business and Management*, 1(1): 71–77.

Forsyth, P. (2006) 'Airport competition: regulatory issues and policy implications', in Lee, D. (ed.), *Competition Policy and Anti-Trust*, Oxford: Elsevier.

Forsyth, P., Gillen, D., Mueller, J. and Niemeier, H.-M. (eds) (2010) *Airport Competition*, Farnham: Ashgate.

Freathy, P. and O'Connell, F. (2000) 'Market segmentation in the European airport sector', *Marketing Intelligence and Planning*, 18(3): 102–11

Gardiner, J., Ison, S. and Humphreys, I. (2005) 'Factors influencing cargo airlines' choice of airport: an international survey', *Journal of Air Transport Management*, 11(6): 393–99.

Gillen, D. (2011) 'The evolution of airport ownership and governance', *Journal of Air Transport Management*, 17(1): 3–13.

Graham, A. (2006) 'Competition in airports', in Papatheodorou, A. (ed.), *Corporate Rivalry and Market Power: Competition Issues in the Tourism Industry*, London: I.B. Tauris

Halpern, N. (2012) 'Use of social media by airports', *Journal of Airline and Airport Management*, 2(2): 66–84.

Halpern, N. and Graham, A. (2013) *Airport Marketing*, Oxford: Routledge.

Halpern, N., and Regmi (2011) 'What's in a name? Analysis of airport brand names and slogans', *Journal of Airport Management*, 6(1): 63–79.

—— (2013) 'Content analysis of European airport websites', *Journal of Air Transport Management*, 26: 8–13.

Hermann, N. and Hazel, B. (2012) *The Future of Airports: Part 1 – Five Trends That Should Be on Every Airport's Radars*, New York: Oliver Wyman.

Humphreys, I. (1999) 'Privatisation and commercialisation: changes in UK airport ownership patterns', *Journal of Transport Geography*, 7(2): 121–34.

Jarach, D. (2005) *Airport Marketing: Strategies to Cope with the New Millennium Environment*, Farnham: Ashgate.

Jossart, L. (2006) 'The airport's relationship with low cost carriers', *University of Westminster/Cranfield University Airport Economics and Finance Symposium*, London, April.

Kotler, P., Armstrong, G., Wong, V. and Saunders, J. (2008) *Principles of Marketing*, 5th European edn, Harlow: Prentice Hall–Pearson Education.

Kramer, L., Fowler, P., Hazel, R., Ureksoy, M. and Harig, G. (2010) *ACRP Report 28: Marketing Guidebook for Small Airports*, Washington, DC: Transportation Research Board.

McLay, P. and Reynolds-Feighan, A. (2006) 'Competition between airport terminals: the issues facing Dublin airport', *Transportation Research Part A*, 40(2): 181–203.

Maertens, S. (2012) 'Estimating the market power of airports in their catchment areas – a European-wide approach', *Journal of Transport Geography*, 22: 10–18.

Malina, R., Albers, S. and Kroll, N. (2012) 'Airport incentive programmes: a European perspective', *Transport Reviews*, 32(4): 435–53.

Martens, H. (2012) 'How to win back markets', *ACI Economics and Finance Conference*, London, March.

Martin, S.C. (2008) *ACRP Report 18: Passenger Air Service Development Techniques*, Washington, DC: Transportation Research Board.

Morrell, P. (2010) 'Airport competition and network access: a European Analysis', in Forsyth, P., Gillen, D., Mueller, J. and Niemeier, H.-M. (eds), *Airport Competition*, Farnham: Ashgate.

Nigam, S., Cook, R. and Stark, C. (2011) 'Putting the joy back into the airport experience: can social networking platforms make a genuine contribution to increasing commercial revenues and engaging customers?', *Journal of Airport Management*, 6(1): 7–11.

Pantazis, N. and Liefner, I. (2006) 'The impact of low-cost carriers on catchment areas of established international airports: the case of Hanover airport, Germany', *Journal of Transport Geography*, 14(4): 265–72.

Productivity Commission (2011) *Economic Regulation of Airport Services*, Canberra: PC.

Route Shop (2012) *Nice Côte d'Azur Airport*. Online. Available HTTP: http://www.therouteshop.com/nice-airport (accessed 20 September 2012).

STRAIR (2005) *Air Service Development for Regional Development Agencies*, Brussels: STRAIR.

Sykes, W. and Desai, P. (2009) *Understanding Airport Passenger Experience*, London: Independent Social Research.

Toms, M. (2004) 'UK regulation from the perspective of BAA plc', in Forsyth, P., Gillen, D., Knorr, A., Mayer, O., Niemeier, H. and Starkie D. (eds), *The Economic Regulation of Airports*, Farnham: Ashgate.

Urfer, B. and Weinert, R. (2011) 'Managing airport infrastructure', in Wittmer, A., Bieger, T. and Muller, R. (eds), *Aviation Systems: Management of the Integrated Aviation Value Chain*, Heidelberg: Springer.

Warnock-Smith, D. and Potter, A. (2005) 'An exploratory study into airport choice factors for European low cost airlines', *Journal of Air Transport Management*, 11(6): 388–392.

Weatherill, J. (2006) 'North American airline incentives: best practices and emerging trends', *Journal of Airport Management*, 1(1): 25–37

Young, D. (1996) 'Knowing your customer', *ACI Europe Good Communication and Better Airport Marketing*, April.

The economic and social impact of airports

THE WIDER PICTURE

The focus of this book shifts in the next two chapters from the internal environment within which the airport operates to considering the wider consequences of the airport business. This chapter looks at the economic and social impact of airports, while Chapter 10 discusses the environmental effects. A key issue for any airport operator is how to optimise the economic potential of an airport while providing acceptable environmental protection. This may be a particular problem when the economic benefits of airport development may be perceived as being the most relevant within a regional or national context, whereas the negative environmental impacts may be hardest felt by the local community.

Many airports undertake economic impact studies and they do this for a number of reasons. They may want to inform debates about strategic economic investment and to make the economic case for investment in new airport facilities or off-site infrastructure, including roads or rail links. Alternative expansion options may be evaluated with consideration of the relative economic benefits that they will bring. Impact studies may be used to obtain financial support or for planning purposes to assess whether there is enough land for new commercial projects in the vicinity of the airport, or whether there is a sufficient supply of labour and associated housing to support such developments. Impact information may also be used for lobbying purposes, to gain regulatory approval, for example for more direct services. Such studies can play an important public relations role in educating policy-makers, airport users and the general public as to the economic value of airports. Figure 9.1 presents the results of a survey in the United States that shows the most common reasons for undertaking airport economic impact studies.

There are basically two types of economic impact at airports. First, the income, employment, capital investment and tax revenues that airport operations can bring by virtue of the fact that they are significant generators of economic activity. Second, the wider catalytic or spin-off benefits, including inward investment or the development of tourism, that can occur as a result of the presence of the airport. These can contribute to the economic development of the area surrounding the airport. Thus within an economic context airports have a role to play both by being a significant economic activity in their own right and by supporting business and tourism activity.

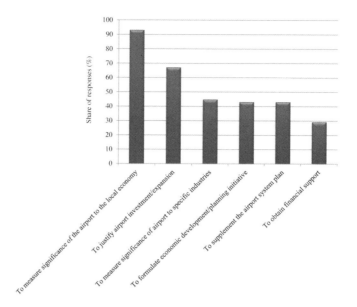

Figure 9.1 *Popular reasons for airport economic impact studies*
Sources: Hoyle, Tanner & Associates and RKG Associates (2008)

At the most basic level, a key indicator of an airport's economic impact is the number of jobs generated. This is the most readily understandable measure and can be used, albeit in a very simplistic manner, to determine an airport's relative importance within an economy. In addition, there are 'income', 'earnings', or 'gross value added' measures. These relate to the value that airport-dependent activities add to the economy in terms of wages, salaries, interest and profits. These indicators can be related to an area's total income or GDP to assess the relative contribution the airport makes to wealth generation. Past economic income studies have shown that the share of GDP varies quite significantly, from less than 1 per cent in Delhi, to 2 per cent in Sydney and around 5 per cent in Hong Kong (NCAER, 2012). Then there is the economic/business activity or output measure which is the sum of the gross revenues of all the businesses that depend on the airport. Indicators related to capital investment and tax revenues can also be considered.

AIRPORTS AS GENERATORS OF ECONOMIC ACTIVITY

Economic effects can be classified as direct, indirect and induced impacts. The direct or primary impact is the employment and income generated by the direct operation of the airport. This is the most obvious economic impact and the most easily measured. This impact is associated with the activities of the airport operator itself, the airlines, the concessionaires providing commercial facilities, the handling agents and other agencies that provide services such air traffic control, customs and immigration and security. Some of these activities, including car parking, car hire, in-flight catering, freight forwarders and hotels, may be located off-site in the surrounding area of the airport.

However, the economic impact of an airport is not limited just to these direct, airport-related effects, although this is the impact that is most frequently quantified and studied. The role of the suppliers to the airport industry also needs to be considered. This requires an examination of the indirect impact, which is defined as the employment and income generated in the chain of suppliers of goods and services to the direct activities located both at and in the vicinity of the airport. These types of activity include the utilities and fuel suppliers, construction and cleaning companies, and food and retail good suppliers. In addition, the impact that these direct and indirect activities have on personal spending also needs to be taken into account. This so-called induced impact can be defined as the employment and income generated by the spending of incomes by the direct and indirect employees on local goods and services including retail, food, transport and housing. The indirect and induced effects are together often known as the secondary effects (Figure 9.2).

These indirect and induced impacts are clearly much more difficult to measure, involving an understanding of how the airport interacts with other sectors within the economy. Their combined impact can be assessed by the economic multiplier. This concept takes account of the successive rounds of spending that arise from the stimulus of the direct impacts and assumes that one individual's or organisation's spending becomes another individual's or organisation's income in the next round. Some of the money spent on airport-related activities will be re-spent on purchases from suppliers of goods and services – the indirect effect – with a proportion of this leaking out of the economy as imports. Much of the remainder will be spent on labour or will go to the government in the form of taxes. The suppliers will then make purchases locally, import goods and services, distribute wages and salaries, and pay government taxes. During each round of spending a certain proportion of the money will accrue to local residents in the form of wages, salaries and profits. Some of this money will then be re-spent again, producing the induced effects. The rest will be saved and not recirculated within the economy. Eventually, the successive rounds of spending will become so small that they will be considered negligible.

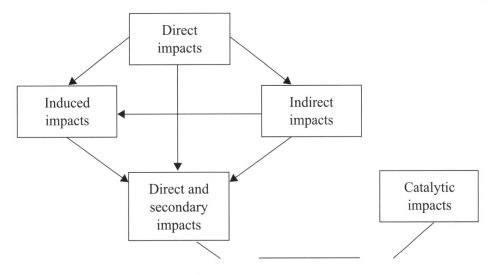

Figure 9.2 *The economic impact of airports*

The multiplier analysis thus quantifies the economic value and jobs from the financial transactions that take place within any economy.

There will be new investment associated with these direct, indirect and induced activities in the form of airport facilities, IT systems, maintenance facilities, offices and so on. Airport activities can also have a significant impact on local, regional and national government revenues. Employees will pay income tax and sales transactions will be subject to sales or value-added taxes. Airports, particularly in the private sector, will probably also be subject to other taxes including property or land taxes and business or corporation taxes. On one hand, some airports in the public sector may be exempt from these but may, on the other hand, pass over a considerable share of their profits to their government owners. In return, many government owners have traditionally allocated considerable public sector funds to aid airport development. Then there are the taxes collected through airport charges. These may be required to cover some specific airport services, including immigration and public health inspection as in the United States, to provide funds for investment including the US transportation tax, or just to boost public sector funds as in the United Kingdom with the air passenger duty. Conversely, in the duty- and tax-free sales area of operation it can be argued that the airports and their passengers receive a direct tax subsidy.

MEASURING THE DIRECT, INDIRECT AND INDUCED IMPACTS

Direct impacts

There are a number of different techniques, of varying levels of sophistication and accuracy, available to airports that want to measure their economic impacts. It needs to be noted that while many areas of airport management, including financial and operational performance, are monitored at least annually, the difficulties involved with assessing economic impacts, as well as the additional resources required, tend to mean that the data are collected less frequently. As a result, some of the examples provided below may not relate to the most up-to-date year.

Direct impacts are the easiest of all the impacts to measure. Employers at the airport can be asked to provide details of their employees, how much they earn and where they live. Information concerning purchases of goods and services, location of suppliers, revenues, expenditures and capital expenditure also needs to be gathered. While such a process for on-site airport activities should not pose too many difficulties, the off-site data collection may be more difficult. First, a definition of 'off-site' needs to be established – a rule-of-thumb figure is an area within a 20-minute drive time. Then the relevant companies within this area need to be identified by taking into account the knowledge of the airport operator and other industry bodies and, perhaps, by direct visual inspection. Many airports regularly measure the direct economic impacts, particularly the employment effects. For example, at London Heathrow airport there is a full employment survey carried out every 5 years, supplemented by an annual or biennial survey that provides an overview of the size of the Heathrow workforce. The full survey is divided into two parts: an employer and an employee survey.

The direct employment at an airport will vary according to a combination of factors including the volume and mix of passenger traffic, the amount of freight, and the actual capacity utilisation of the airport. The role of the airport also has to be considered, for example whether it is a major hub, whether it acts as a base for airline activity, and/or whether it provides other opportunities including office or other commercial development. Globally the Air Transport Action Group (ATAG, 2012) estimated that in 2010, of the 8.4 million jobs directly generated by the air transport industry, 0.5 million were employed by airport operators, in airport management, maintenance and security, and also there were 4.9 million other jobs on-site at airports – for example in retail outlets, restaurants, hotels and government border agencies. In addition, 2.2 million worked for airlines or handling agents, including flight crew, check-in staff and maintenance crew.

A study of employment at European airports showed that the airline and handling agents were, on average, the largest employers at the airport, followed by the airport operators and concessionaires (York Aviation, 2004). Figure 9.3 shows a similar situation at Heathrow in 2008/09. Overall there tends to be a regional difference in the share of airport staff to total on-site airport employment. On average the share is around 9 per cent, but for Europe it is around 14 per cent, for Asia-Pacific 11 per cent, but for North America 3 per cent (ACI, 2008). The percentage is much smaller for North American airports because many more activities are outsourced, and higher in Europe primarily because of direct involvement of airport operators in activities including handling and security.

For meaningful airport comparisons to be made, airport direct employment is often related to the traffic throughput of an airport to produce an employment density figure. This is usually equivalent to the number of employees per million passengers per annum (jobs per mppa) or per WLU if freight is an important activity at the airport. A figure of 900–1,000 jobs for every million passengers or WLU equal to a density figure of 900–1,000 tends to be the rule-of-thumb figure generally accepted by the industry, although it obviously masks

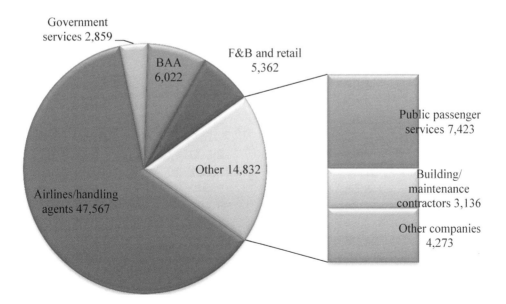

Figure 9.3 *Employment at Heathrow airport, 2008/09*
Source: Adapted from Heathrow Airport Ltd (2010)

wide variations in employment at different airports. Globally, in 2007 it was estimated that there were 4,300,000 employed at global airports. This gave an overall employment density figure of around 1,100 – the equivalent number in 2001 was 1,600 (ACI, 2002, 2008). This shows a drop in density that has decreased in recent years and is likely to continue in the future.

For smaller airports, the average employment density may be higher due to the fact that they are unable to achieve economies of scale. Other factors, including capacity utilisation, the existence of airline bases and development opportunities, may have an impact. For example it was observed that airports including Malaga, Edinburgh, Gothenburg, Nice and Cork had much lower density values because of limited development at the airports, high utilisation and no base airlines. By contrast, airports including Paris CDG, Amsterdam, Frankfurt and Copenhagen had high values because they are major airline bases and have substantial development (York Aviation, 2004). Airports serving low-cost carriers tend to have lower values because the number of airline staff employed by LCCs at the airport is kept to a minimum and often other services provided at the airport will be more basic. Tables 9.1 and 9.2 show direct employment density for UK and German airports and, although there is quite a considerable variation in the values, the average is fairly close to the rule-of-thumb figure of 900–1,000.

In general, density figures are declining for a number of reasons. The airport and airline industry has become more productive, which has been helped, for example, by having larger and fuller aircraft that may not require any increase in cabin crew. More and more airlines are also

Table 9.1 Direct employment at UK airports, 2004

	Passengers (million)	Direct employment	Jobs per 1 million passengers
Aberdeen	2.64	2,716	1,029
Belfast City	2.13	807	379
Birmingham	8.86	9,071	1,024
Bristol	4.65	4,747	1,021
Cardiff	1.89	1,932	1,022
East Midlands	4.38	4, 512	1,030
Edinburgh	8.02	2,300	287
Gatwick	31.47	23,761	755
Glasgow	8.58	5,442	634
Heathrow	67.34	68,427	1,016
Luton	7.54	7,756	1,029
Manchester	21.25	18,000	847
Newcastle	4.72	4,855	1,029
Stansted	20.91	10,592	507
Other	20.63	21,116	1,024
Total	214.98	185,900	865

Source: Oxford Economic Forecasting (2006)

Table 9.2 Direct employment at German airports, 2004

	Passengers (million)	Direct employment	Jobs per 1 million passengers
Berlin	14.9	12,890	865
Bremen	1.7	2,508	1,475
Dresden	1.6	1,498	936
Dusseldorf	15.3	12,986	849
Frankfurt/Main	51.1	61,579	1,205
Frankfurt/Hahn	2.8	2,487	888
Hamburg	9.9	5,679	574
Hannover	5.2	6,245	1,201
Cologne/Bonn	8.3	11,487	1,384
Munich	26.8	23,220	866
Munster	1.5	1,529	1,019
Nurnberg	3.6	4,016	1,116
Stuttgart	8.8	7,804	887
Total	151.5	153,928	1,016

Source: Klophaus (2008)

cutting back on the frills – as with the LCC sector – which reduces the manpower requirement, for instance with in-flight catering. In addition, technology developments and, in particular, shifts to a greater self-service role for passengers have also caused a drop in the density measures.

Indirect and induced impacts

There are different approaches to estimating the multiplier effect and measuring the indirect and induced impacts. The first, rather basic method involves using multiplier values that have been calculated by using information gathered from surveys of on-site and off-site employers, and by making assumptions about the tax rate and the share of purchases that are imported.

A more sophisticated approach involves using an input–output model. This model looks at the linkages that exist within any economy by considering the relationships between the different economic sectors (agriculture, manufacturing, construction and services) within a certain area. This methodology involves constructing a transaction table that shows, in money terms, the input–output relationships for the sectors in the economy. Each sector is shown as a column representing purchases from other sectors and as a row representing sales to the other sectors. From this table, coefficients or multiplier values can be obtained for each economic activity. This technique will allow the impact of additional spending in any one specific economic activity to be identified sector by sector as well as for the area as a whole. Sometimes the indirect impacts are called the production-induced effects and the induced impacts are called the consumption-induced effects. Also, some studies identify two types of multiplier: type 1 and type 2. The former covers just the indirect effects, while the latter includes both the indirect and induced impacts. One country that has extensive experience of using the input–output method to measure impacts is the United States. There are three models that are most commonly used: the US Department of Commerce RIMS II model; the Minnesota IMPLAN Group, Inc. model; and the Regional Economic Modeling, Inc. (REMI) model (Hoyle, Tanner & Associates and RKG Associates, 2008). These have been used widely in the United States to estimate regional impacts in both the public and private sectors, and form the basis of many airport economic impact studies.

In 2012 the IMPLAN model was used to estimate the overall impact of the US airport industry (CDM Smith, 2012). This study estimated an employment multiplier in the region of 2.4 (for every 1,000 direct jobs there were another 2,400 induced and indirect). In general the multiplier effects need to be related to the size of the economy under consideration, depending on whether the national, regional or local situation is being assessed. The indirect impacts tend to increase with the size of the study area, as this increases the likelihood of goods and services required by airport-related companies being supplied within the area rather than being imported from outside. The choice of study area will depend primarily on the role and size of the airport and the reason for measuring the impact. Large capital city and main international airports tend to have such an important impact on the overall economy that it makes sense to assess their impact within a national context. Specific issues, however, particularly related to the employment market, may be more appropriately considered at a regional or local level. The impacts of smaller airports usually need to be considered within a narrower context. Within Europe it has been found that 1,000 direct jobs support 2,100 jobs nationally, 1,100 jobs regionally or 500 jobs subregionally (York Aviation, 2004). The differences in the indirect and induced employment impacts when different surrounding areas are chosen can be seen clearly at Heathrow airport (Figure 9.4).

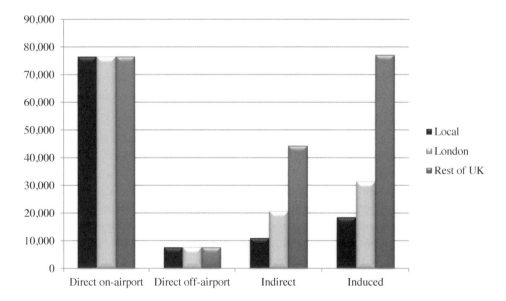

Figure 9.4 *Employment impacts of Heathrow airport, 2010*
Source: Optimal Economics (2011)

Multiplier values at individual areas will depend on many factors, including the nature of the traffic at the airport, propensity to travel characteristics, employment sector mixes and the role of the airport. They will also depend on the methodologies used and the precise definitions adopted. For example, sometimes all off-site impacts are considered as indirect impacts, irrespective of whether the activities are directly airport-related. This makes it very difficult to compare multiplier values. Then there is the problem of how to treat any activities that are based at the airport but not actually related to airport operations. Very often the split of activities on- and off-site will depend on whether or not the actual site is constrained. One of the major areas of discrepancy is in the treatment of jobs associated with leisure and business tourists who arrive via the airport. These jobs are in tourism industry activities, including hotels, restaurants, attractions, conferences and exhibitions. Some airports, particularly in the United States, treat these as indirect jobs, which can have a dramatic effect on the overall magnitude of indirect impacts. Other studies separately identify the visitor impacts, or adopt a more qualitative approach to assessing this effect. Another area of inconsistency between airports occurs with the treatment of construction activities. Sometimes the temporary staff employed in the construction industry will be included in the impact figures and sometimes they will not. When there is a major capital investment programme, including a new runway or terminal, airports tend to identify the impacts separately to add additional support to the case for new capacity.

By way of illustration, Table 9.3 presents some individual multiplier values that have been calculated for Delhi, Vancouver and Sydney airports. There are some very varied findings, which undoubtedly reflect the unique characteristics of the three airports, albeit that they are also likely to be influenced by the adoption of different detailed methodologies.

One of the problems with the multiplier and input–output analysis is that it is a static measure which takes a snapshot of the economic situation and does not take account of the interaction between all elements in the economy if there is a change in the inputs or outputs. An alternative approach is to use computable general equilibrium (CGE) models which are dynamic and more flexible, and can be applied to analyse the effect of any change through the whole of the economy. Although overall these models are becoming more popular, their use in the airport sector is still comparatively rare, although some examples exist, for example with a recent economic impact study of Canberra airport (ACIL Tasman, 2011).

In general all these measures can help to assess an airport's significance within the economy. However, it is important to emphasise that the impacts that have been discussed are not necessarily net benefits, as so often is wrongly implied by economic impact studies. The employment impacts are a good example, as while the promise of greater employment may be seen as a positive outcome of airport expansion in relatively underdeveloped areas, the views on airport employment may be different at a major established airport. In this case the presence of the airport may already mean there is full employment in the region and hence extra job vacancies would be hard to fill, especially as many of the jobs are not seen as very attractive as they tend to be low-skilled and are likely to involve anti-social hours because of the 24-hour nature of operations. The impact assessments do not identify the costs involved, both internally related to airport operations and externally especially related to environmental problems, including noise and air pollution. Moreover, all these have to be considered to reach a conclusion about the net benefits (benefits minus costs).

Table 9.3 *Economic impacts at Delhi, Vancouver and Sydney airports*

	Direct	Indirect	Induced	Direct:indirect ratio	Direct:induced ratio	Passengers (million)	Passengers per direct employee
Delhi airport (2010)						29.9	467
Employment	64,074	452,026	1,061,600	1:7	1:17		
Value added (Rs billion)	42.90	77.20	194.70	1:2	1:5		
Output (Rs billion)	71.50	128.7	291.00	1:2	1:4		
Vancouver airport (2010)						16.8	777
FTE employment	21,633	22,072	13,696	1:1	1:0.6		
GDP (C$ billion)	1.9	2.1	1.3	1:1	1:0.7		
Output (Rs billion)	9.5	(included in direct)	2.2				
Sydney airport (2007)						31.0	698
FTE Employment (000)	44,389	28,193	47,581	1:06	1:1		
Value added (C$ billion)	7,969	3,636	4,675	1:05	1:06		
Output (A$ billion)	14,759	6,499	8,604	1:04	1:06		

Sources: URS (2008); Vancouver Airport Authority (2011); NCAER (2012)

AIRPORTS AND ECONOMIC DEVELOPMENT

The airport's catalytic role

As well as being a generator of economic activities in its own right, an airport can also play a role in attracting and sustaining wider economic activity in the surrounding area – in terms of both business and tourism development. This is the catalytic, magnetic or spin-off impact. This impact can be defined as the employment, income, investment and tax revenues generated by the wider role that an airport can play by acting as an economic magnet for the region it serves. Airports can give a company easy access to other parts of the company as well as to suppliers and customers, and can offer speed and security for goods being transported. Hence airports can play an important role in influencing company location decisions. They can encourage inward invest-ment and the relocations of businesses by attracting industries that rely on quick and convenient access to air services for both people and goods. These businesses will not rely directly on the airport for their operation, but they will have a preference for a location near an airport because of the accessibility benefits that can be gained.

Airports can also help retain current businesses or encourage them to expand. By providing access to a wide range of both passenger and freight services, an airport can enhance the competitiveness of the economy and can contribute to the export success of businesses located in the vicinity of the airport. In some cases the airport can be the lifeline to local economies, as has been the situation in some developing countries in Africa and Latin America, where air travel has enabled the export of fresh and perishable fruit and flowers to Western economies.

The trend towards globalisation, in terms of both multinational companies and greater reliance on imported components and products, has increased the importance of locating in the vicinity of an international airport. Some of the fastest growing knowledge-based industrial sectors, including computing, electronics, communications and pharmaceuticals, are the most inter-national and are heavily reliant on air travel for the transportation of their high-value/low-weight products. The increasing reliance on just-in-time inventory systems for these expanding industries and more traditional sectors, including car manufacturing, has meant that air travel has become a critical element for a quick and efficient distribution system and rapid delivery times. In short, airports have become increasingly important for businesses operating in the global marketplace.

In economically disadvantaged areas, where unemployment is high and there is a narrow, declining economic base, airport development is often seen as a way of generating new employ-ment, creating wealth and regenerating the area. These arguments are frequently used to gain approval for airport expansion or development. Airports undoubtedly play an integral part in economic development, and for areas that are relatively inaccessible by air this will be a distinct economic drawback. Certain regions will find it difficult to attract inward investment if their airports have not reached the critical mass needed to provide an adequate range of services. Thus airports are often considered a vital component of a regional development policy and can be viewed as giving a real advantage to competing regions. However, it is very difficult formally to establish the causality between the expansion of an airport and wider economic development (Caves and Gosling, 1999). In many cases it is impossible to establish whether it is the nature of the surrounding economy of an airport, in terms of wealth and population size and distribution, that has encouraged airlines to operate from the airport, rather than the development of air services influencing the economy. It is particularly difficult to assess the overall impact of LCCs and their impacts on the regions surrounding the airports they serve (Graham and Shaw, 2008; Williams and Baláž, 2009).

In general, it is certainly true that investment in airport infrastructure is not usually sufficient in itself to generate sustained increases in economic growth. The wider economic benefits will depend very much on the scale of the airport and, very critically, its ability to attract air services. In the end, it will be the airlines that will determine the success of an airport and broader economic impacts, in choosing whether to operate from the airport or not. As discussed in Chapter 8, their primary concerns will usually be whether sufficient passenger demand exists and the nature of the airport's strategic and geographical location (Graham and Guyer, 2000).

It is extremely difficult to isolate and quantify the economic effects that are due to the presence of the airport from the wide range of other factors that will affect a company's location decision. The exact location of any business activity will be only partially related to the existence of any nearby airport services, with other factors being the availability, quality and cost of any potential development sites, the nature of the local labour market, tax incentives, trade policy, and the supporting communications and transport infrastructure. The situation is made more complex by the fact that many economic regions are served by a number of airports, with either complementary or competing roles.

Airports can play a role in encouraging both business and leisure visitors to the surrounding area. There are many examples of countries, particularly in developing areas including the Caribbean, Asia and Pacific, where the tourism potential of a destination has been realised only after direct services and suitable airport infrastructure have been provided. The increase in visitor numbers may then have a spin-off effect on the income and employment generation in tourism industry activities such hotels, restaurants, attractions, conferences and exhibitions. Tourism markets that are particularly dependent on air travel include package holiday travel, city break tourism, long-haul travel and the conference business. Also the low-cost airlines, particularly in Europe, by flying to airports in relatively unknown regions have had the effect of transforming some of these into new international tourism destinations. Table 9.4 shows some of these airports that have been served by LCCs.

Causality between airport growth and tourism development, as with business development, is very difficult to prove. For example, is it new air services at a resort that encourage new hotel development; or do more bedspaces encourage more frequent flights? Some impact studies, particularly in the United States, have a separate visitor impact category. An estimate of spending is often calculated by multiplying the visitor numbers by average daily spend and length of stay. Other airports choose to categorise the visitors' impact as indirect. Admittedly, many of these tourism businesses will be reliant on air services for their tourism demand, but it is unlikely, except in an isolated island situation, that this tourism industry would not exist if a certain airport was not present. It thus seems inappropriate to include these tourism impacts as indirect impacts. Instead, it is preferable to consider them alongside the catalytic impacts causing business development.

Table 9.4 *European airports served by LCC that have encouraged new international tourism flows*

Austria	France	Ireland	Norway	Sweden
Graz	Limoges	Knock	Haugesund	Malmö
Linz	Carcassonne	Derry		Nykoping
Klagenfurt	Tours	Kerry		
Belgium	**Germany**	**Italy**	**Slovakia**	**United Kingdom**
Charleroi	Karlsruhe-Baden	Bari	Kosice	Blackpool
	Münster	Palermo		Bournemouth
	Erfurt	Trieste		Newquay
Denmark	**Finland**	**Poland**	**Spain**	
Esbjerg	Tampere	Gdansk	Bilbao	
		Poznan	Girona	
			Santander	

Source: Adapted from ELFAA (2004)

The airport city or aerotropolis

The existence of an 'airport city' in the surrounding area of a number of airports may be an additional factor that companies take into account when choosing their location. Airport cities are developed when airports expand beyond the boundaries of the traditional business in the terminal and diversify by developing facilities including office complexes, business parks and free-trade zones; distribution and logistics centres; sport, cultural and entertainment amenities; shopping centres; and medical services (Morrison, 2009). Such initiatives are driven not only by the airport operators' desire to grow non-aeronautical revenues, but also by the commercial sector's pursuit of affordable, accessible land, by increased passenger and traffic throughput, and by the recognition of the ability of an airport to act as a catalyst and magnet for landside business development. So, as a result of this commercial expansion and diversification, there are these multimodal and multifunctional businesses called airport cities. Way back in 1994, Amsterdam airport defined itself as an airport city, and later adopted this concept at Brisbane airport which it partially owned. However, there are now numerous other examples (Kasarda, 2009).

Some airport cities have continued to develop outwards, with the boundaries between the airport and its surrounding urban area becoming increasingly blurred. As a consequence, a new urban form, known as an aerotropolis, has emerged. This development, similar to a traditional metropolis, consists of a central city core (the airport city) surrounded by rings or clusters of business and residential suburbs extending as far as 30 km outwards from the airport, connected with corridors of transport links and efficient communication systems. Initially, many of these airport cities and aerotropolises had limited planning behind them and grew in a rather haphazard, uncontrolled and organic manner. However, as these developments have matured and as competition has become fiercer, it has been recognised that in order to fully exploit the potential benefits, much greater attention must now be given to planning and strategic management decisions (Reiss, 2007; Poungias, 2009).

Airport cities and aerotropolises now exist in Asia, the Middle East, Australia and Europe, but this trend has been less evident in the USA until quite recently. They are particularly popular in Asia and the Middle East, where there tend to be newer airports surrounded by a large amount of open land. Notable examples are Hong Kong's SkyCity, Incheon's Air City and Kuala Lumpur's Gateway Park; and there are many others currently under development, including Beijing's World City and Dubai World Central. The actual type and nature of development can vary significantly, as van Wijk (2009) illustrated in his detailed study of the monocentric airport city of Amsterdam, compared with the polycentric airport city of Frankfurt and the sprawling aerotropolis of Narita in Tokyo. Nor are these concepts confined to just the large global hubs of the world; there are an increasing number of airports on a smaller scale, including Dublin, Washington Dulles, Vancouver, Helsinki and Zurich, that have also given priority to this type of commercial development. An example of an airport city that is being planned for a smaller airport is at Manchester airport, the first in the UK (MAG, 2012). It became fully operational in April 2012 and will be created through phased delivery during the next 15 years, at a cost of £650 million. It will have space for businesses involved in manufacturing, logistics, accommodation, retail and leisure, across a 150-acre regeneration site. It has also been designated as an enterprise zone which gives relief from business taxes, support for inward investments, a simplified planning process and fast broadband connections.

Measuring the catalytic impacts

While an airport city undoubtedly can be an attraction to businesses, it remains very difficult to prove direct causality between airports and broader business and tourism development. Therefore it is not usually feasible or suitable to identify with any certainty the exact number of jobs, or the amount of income generated from these catalytic or spin-off impacts. A more qualitative approach is often adopted which will involve investigating factors including the significance of the airport to location decision, competitiveness and business performance by surveying and holding discussions with relevant businesses in order to gain a closer understanding of the nature of the interaction between the airport and the wider elements in the local economy.

In a survey of 500 European companies' views of leading business cities in 2011, 42 per cent stated that transport links with other cities were an absolutely essential factor for locating a business. Only three other factors – availability of qualified staff (53 per cent), proximity to markets (60 per cent) and quality of telecommunications (52 per cent) – were selected by a higher percentage of companies. Also, the top five cities for external transport links with other cities, London, Paris, Frankfurt, Brussels and Berlin, were also rated as 1, 2, 3, 8 and 5 in terms of best city in which to locate a business (Cushman and Wakefield, 2011). Likewise, a survey of 165 UK companies examined the most important factors in determining the country in which the organisation chooses to invest, and around 40 per cent stated that the air transport network was vital or very important. Again, only three other factors were selected by more organisations – size of local market, availability of skilled labour and the extent of government regulations on business (Oxford Economic Forecasting, 2006). Other more specific surveys have found that 31 per cent of companies relocating to the area around Munich airport cited the airport as the primary factor in their location decision, and 80 per cent of businesses in the Hamburg area reported air service connections as important to getting customers to look at their products. At London

City airport, 70 per cent of businesses stated that air services were critical for business travel (York Aviation, 2004).

A potentially useful tool for assessing these business development impacts is the value connectivity index. This seeks to examine the relative 'connectedness' of an airport in terms of its route network's ability to service business-focused destinations. In other words, it looks at whether the airport is connected to important business destinations, rather than to just any destinations. It thus provides a proxy indicator of an airport's ability to support catalytic or wider economic benefits in its catchment area economy. The index compares the destinations served by an airport against established rankings of world cities which indicate their usefulness and importance as business destinations. An airport's connection to any of these cities is then weighted according to the frequency of service to that destination. Figure 9.5 shows some values for Manchester airport that place it a good position within the UK context, but with lower connectivity values than a number of fairly similar European airports.

As regards measuring the business and leisure tourism effects, again the importance of the role of the airport can be discussed among industry experts. A difficulty with this interview approach is to ensure that respondents give genuine comments. They will often have a very positive, but perhaps not totally realistic, view of the value of new air services, for example, since the respondents will bear no direct costs associated with the new services but may benefit from the gains. Alternatively, the impact of opening up specific new routes can be considered in order to see how air services have a direct impact on business or tourism development (Button and Taylor, 2000). For example, in the San Diego region it was estimated that a new domestic flight would produce additional annual visitor spending of US$1.7 million that would not have occurred if there was no new flight (i.e. these visitors would not have used other means, including connecting flights

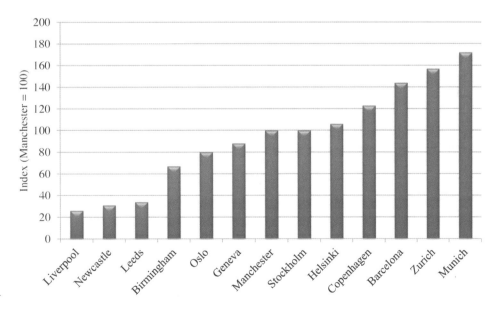

Figure 9.5 *Airport value connectivity index*
Source: York Aviation (2008)

or other modes, to travel to the region). For an international flight this figure was $5.4 million (San Diego International Airport, 2008).

Again it is important to emphasise that *net* benefits should be considered. For example, airports do not only encourage visitors to the local region, but also enable local residents to holiday abroad rather than staying in the local region. Similarly, the availability of nearby direct air services may increase the use of imported goods and services at the expense of local products. The impacts should ideally be compared with possible alternative, non-airport-related economic activities, with an assessment being made of the comparative economic benefits and opportunity costs. Alternative developments could have a better overall impact on the economy. The cross-over effects on other industries, for example the impact on other modes of transport, all need to be considered. Increased industrial and economic activity around an airport may merely be draining resources from other areas, including city centres. The negative or adverse potential impacts of airport development, including extensive urbanisation and industrialisation, over-heating of the economy and consequences of local labour shortages, also need to be taken into account. The overall impact on the local community of tourism development related to aviation activity also needs to be assessed. The positive effects may not be very substantial if the tourism industry has to be supported by a substantial level of imports and foreign investment.

Aviation can have a multitude of impacts on society as well. In the broadest context, it is often claimed that air travel brings wider benefits to society in the form of strengthening ethnic and cultural links between countries, enhancing opportunities for travel and increasing consumer choices for foodstuffs and other products. These are all very general impacts, which are extremely difficult to quantify or contribute to any one airport. In acting as a catalyst for economic development, airports will also have a major social impact on the surrounding area. Employment and living patterns will change, with implications for housing, health, education and other social needs. An overheated economy associated with a successful airport development may bring problems of labour shortages, insufficient housing and rising prices.

In addition to all these impacts, it must be remembered that since airports can provide accessibility and mobility, they can have a major role in promoting social inclusion – especially for remote and island communities. These social impacts are very difficult to quantify, but undoubtedly without such airports, certain communities would suffer and would have a reduced quality of life. Airports can enable regions to have access to essential services including hospitals and higher education. They can also make the communities more attractive places to work and can contribute to attracting and retaining skilled labour in the area. For example, a survey of residents in the Highlands of Scotland found that 50 per cent felt the existence of air services made the area a better place to live, with 75 per cent agreeing that they made it less remote, and 40 per cent saying that they made it more likely that they would remain there (York Aviation, 2004).

Overall, there is little doubt that airports have a substantial economic and social effect on the region in which they are located. While concepts including the multiplier or catalytic effects are reasonably straightforward to understand, they are very difficult to quantify with any degree of confidence, and there are still considerable inconsistencies in the terminologies and methodologies used. However, there is a growing need to develop more effective and accurate measures, not only so that airports can justify their existence when facing increasing pressure from the environmental lobby, but also so that incentives that are used to encourage economic development through air transport growth can be used in the most effective way. The next part of this chapter considers the nature of these incentives.

INCENTIVES TO ENCOURAGE ECONOMIC DEVELOPMENT

Chapter 8 describes how various airport operators may offer financial and other incentives to encourage new carriers or more services. This may be undertaken purely to grow the airport business – particularly if the airport is privately owned. However, if the airport is publicly owned such incentives may be adopted because of the broader catalytic impacts that additional services to the surrounding region may bring. Alternatively, regional development agencies, chambers of commerce or tourist boards may contribute directly to supporting airline services. For example, a few years ago Ryanair developed a number of such arrangements with the regional and local authorities in Spain. In Girona, the Generalitat (local government), through its Departments of Commerce, Tourism and Consumer Affairs and Public Land and Development; the Girona Government Council; the Girona Chamber of Commerce, Industry and Navigation; and the Hotel Federation of the province signed an agreement for 2 years where €6.2 million was provided to the airline to help promote the Girona region. Nearby in Reus, €2 million was provided by a group of municipalities and the chamber of commerce. In Granada, it was agreed that €300,000 would be paid to the airline for a publicity and promotion campaign in 2005, rising to €700,000 in 2006 and €1 million in 2007. In return, Ryanair guaranteed the arrival of a minimum of 90,000, 240,000 and 370,000 passengers in these 3 years, respectively. This type of marketing aid, where the airline commits itself to promoting the destination, for example with links on its website, has the advantage of not being covered by the EC guides for state aid for airlines from regional airports (Travel Trade Gazette, 2005).

It is common practice for public bodies in North America to provide marketing support to airlines that offer new services. These so-called co-op marketing funds are used to promote the new air service at the same time as the region. Risk-sharing mechanisms, including revenue guarantees, are also used. In this case, public and private institutions as well as local businesses in a region raise a minimum amount of money as a guarantee to an airline to cover the costs associated with provision of the service during a limited period. There are also community ticket trusts or travel banks which require the airport operator and/or public institutions to persuade the major airline customers in their region to commit to booking a minimum number of tickets during the early stages of operation of a new service (Martin, 2008). Companies may be prepared to do this if it means the local air services will improve. Again, this will reduce the risk for the carrier and will not necessarily involve any extra cost to the public authorities. However, many airlines are not in favour of trust funds as they find them cumbersome to administer and it is difficult to ensure the pledged funds are actually used on air services (STRAIR 2005; Weatherill, 2006). However, in spite of this a study of small airports in the USA found that travel banks had been used by a number of airports, including Stockton (California), Pensacola (Florida), Augusta (Georgia) and Wichita (Kansas). Revenue guarantees had also been used by Durango, Gunnison, Montrose and Telluride in Colorado, New Haven in Connecticut, Tallahassee in Florida, and again Wichita (Kansas) (GAO, 2003).

Since airlines have different economic impacts, the incentives must be designed to appeal to the airlines that will bring the public agencies the specific economic benefits that they desire. For example, network or legacy carriers can bring much business traffic to an area, and often link the region to their global air service networks through hubs. By contrast, LCCs may be able to encourage inward tourism, but may also promote outbound tourism – which in the end might have a net negative economic impact. Charter carriers can also bring in extra tourists, but they may have the disadvantage of being highly seasonal.

The UK route development funds (RDF) are an interesting example of funds provided by regional development bodies to support new services that were deemed beneficial to the region's overall economic development by encouraging better business links or inbound tourism. Such funds were designed to have a catalytic impact in that airlines potentially could share the same based aircraft on these supported routes that brought inbound benefits, using them on additional non-subsidised outbound leisure services. The funds need to comply with UK and EU law, especially with respect to state aid and competition policy. Of particular relevance here are the EC guide-lines on start-up aid to airlines departing from regional airports (see Chapter 7). These guidelines resulted in a protocol for the RDFs being agreed with the EC in 2006, which allowed the funding allocated before the guidelines were established to continue until June 2007.

The first RDF, which ran from November 2002 to May 2007, amounted to £6.4 million and was created by the Scottish Executive and managed on a partnership basis by Scottish Enterprise, High-lands and Islands Enterprise and VisitScotland (Pagliari, 2005). This was followed in 2003 by a £3.6 million fund that was set up by the Northern Ireland Department of Enterprise, Trade and Investment and managed by Invest Northern Ireland. Then, in the UK Airports White Paper of December 2003, other regional development agencies and the Welsh Assembly government were invited to consider such funds. Subsequently the Welsh Assembly government and One Northeast (the regional development agency of the north-east) set up RDFs in June 2006 (CAA, 2007).

In order to examine the likely benefit of the route proposals to the economy as a whole, an economic appraisal framework was established. The first stage of this was to undertake the net user benefits of the new route. This involved looking at the net present value to users by consid-ering generalised cost savings from journey time savings and air fare savings. It also involved calculating the benefit/cost ratio by considering the benefits to users compared with the cost of funding support. If either the net present value was negative or the benefits: cost ratio was less than one, the proposal was rejected. Otherwise it was assessed according to a route appraisal score. This was calculated by quantifying the business efficiency benefits (in terms of service frequency, hub connectivity, business centre links): the tourism impacts (in terms of net additional tourism employment): the direct employment impact; the social impacts (in terms of connectivity): and the environmental impacts (in terms of aircraft noise and carbon dioxide emissions). The final appraisal score was calculated by weighting these impacts according to the strategic priorities and primary drivers for the route development funding. A risk assessment was also undertaken to investigate the risk that the route would not be sustained by the airline in the long term by consid-ering the airline's financial position and route network. If this score was greater than some threshold or calibrated score, the route proposal was recommended for support (STRAIR, 2005).

Figure 9.6 shows the routes that were set up as a result of the RDFs – although a number of these are no longer operated. In general the RDFs do seem to have helped improve the connectivity of the more peripheral UK regions, but experience has been varied according to which specific region decided to adopt such a fund. Related to Scotland, Smyth *et al.* (2012) found through

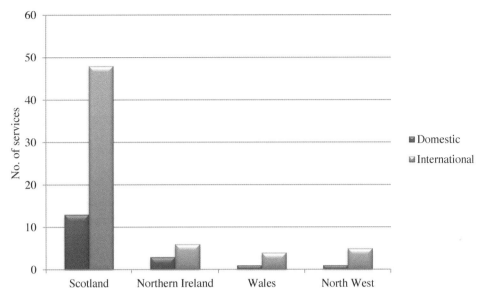

Figure 9.6 *Services funded by the UK Route Development Fund*
Source: CAA (2007)

surveys that two-thirds of non-Scottish businesses saw the RDF services as instrumental in maintaining connectivity and competitiveness in Scotland. Nearly three-quarters of non-Scottish businesses stated that the RDF-supported flights had reduced the feeling that Scotland was remote from the centres of business activity. However, the more restrictive conditions that have applied since June 2007 have meant that all these funds are now closed.

THE IMPACT OF PASSENGER TAXES

While the above discussion illustrates how public money may be used to encourage air services and economic development, the imposition of additional government taxes potentially could have the opposite effect. This is a topical issue because of the increasing number of airports that have introduced passenger or ticket taxes which are often defined as environmental or eco-taxes. These tend to be highly controversial and have been fiercely debated (ACI Europe, 2011). This is particularly because such taxes are generally considered to be a rather blunt instrument in terms of tackling environmental problems, and the money tends not to be used on any environmental projects (see Chapter 11).

As discussed in Chapter 4, in 1994 the Air Passenger Duty (APD) was introduced in the UK and now ranges from £13 to £184 (Table 9.5). In France in 2006, a 'solidarity tax' of €1 (economy) and €10 (premium) for European passengers and €4/€40 for intercontinental passengers was introduced to fund development aid in poorer countries. In 2008, the Dutch government started levying a passenger tax of €11 for European travel and €45 for long-haul travel. Then in 2009, a tax in Ireland was introduced. Originally it was €10 for destinations further than 300 km and €2 for shorter flights. However, in 2010 the EC found this discriminatory as almost all cross-border flights were charged at the higher rate whereas all domestic flights were covered by the lower

Table 9.5 UK Air Passenger Duty (as of April 2012)

Distance between London and capital city of destination country	Reduced (economy class) (£)	Standard (business and first) (£)
Band A (0–2000 miles)	13	26
Band B (2001–4000 miles)	65	130
Band C (4001–6000 miles)	81	162
Band D (over 6000 miles)	92	184

rate. As a result, from 2011 there was a single rate of €3 per passenger, regardless of the destination of the flight. Also in 2011, Germany imposed a tax of €8 on short-haul trips, €25 for medium-haul and €45 on long-haul, and a similar tax (€8 short-haul, €35 long-haul) was introduced in Austria in the same year.

While the exact impact of these taxes on passenger demand is not entirely clear, there is evidence in the Netherlands to suggest that they can have a significant impact on an airport's competitive position if there are alternative airports nearby. Research found that the tax reduced the number of Dutch passengers departing from airports in the Netherlands, especially Amsterdam. A survey of 3,000 passengers was undertaken, with questions related to whether the tax had affected their choices. Fourteen per cent said that the tax had influenced their travel behaviour, with about half of these saying they had chosen not to travel, or to travel by car or train. The other half said they had switched to another airport, with Dusseldorf being the most popular (36 per cent) followed by Weeze and Brussels (Figure 9.7). An analysis was also undertaken of the traffic figures before and after the tax, where it was estimated that there had been a decrease of 2 million passengers when the tax had been in force. This resulted in estimates of traffic going to Dusseldorf of 450,000, to Weeze 275,000, to Brussels 175,000 and to Charleroi 75,000 (KiM Netherlands Institute for Transport Policy Analysis, 2011). Veldhuis (2012) also found that the tax had little environmental benefit and provided little net revenue for government. The tax was abolished in 2009.

In Ireland, SEO Economic Research (2009) estimated that revenue from the tax would have been approximately €130 million per annum if no demand reduction had occurred as a result of the tax. In addition, if airline capacity had been maintained at the previous levels and the tax passed on in full to the passengers in the form of higher fares, it was estimated that the total resulting demand reduction would be between 0.5 and 1.2 million departing passengers. The study concluded that there would be a direct loss of jobs of at least 2,000 to 3,000 affecting airports, airlines and the tourism industry, dependent on the extent to which companies were willing to accept the inherent diseconomies of scale from a reduction in demand. In addition, it was concluded that the reduction in passengers would give rise to significant reductions in income tax, corporate tax and sales tax. Therefore the analysis concluded that the tax would result in a decline in revenue to specific sectors of the Irish economy of a far greater magnitude than the amount of tax likely to be collected. This was similar to findings in the Netherlands, although in the Irish case there would be few shifts to surface modes or foreign airports.

Figure 9.7 *Passenger use of alternative airports to Amsterdam after the introduction of the passenger tax*
Source: Adapted from KiM Netherlands Institute for Transport Policy Analysis (2011)

Relevant experience also exists in other countries. Denmark had a tax, but because of negative impacts on traffic it halved it in 2006 and then abolished it entirely in 2007. Belgium has proposed such a tax, but has yet to introduce one. An interesting example of the potential impact of taxes on airport competition can be found in the UK with the air passenger duty (APD). Largely as a result of Continental Airlines threatening to shift its North Atlantic services from Belfast to Dublin in Ireland (where the tax is much lower), it was agreed in 2012 that passengers would be allowed to pay the lower short-haul rate on long-haul services from Belfast International Airport to help maintain its competitive position. From January 2013 all direct long-haul flights from Northern Ireland will have no tax. There has also been fierce opposition to this tax elsewhere, particularly in Scotland and some areas of northern England, where again it has been argued that the beneficial economic impact for governments is outweighed by the impact on traffic, tourism and business.

REFERENCES

ACI (2002) *ACI Airport Economics Survey 2001*, Montreal: Airports Council International.
—— (2008) *ACI Airport Economics Survey 2007*, Montreal: Airports Council International.
ACI Europe (2011) *ACI Europe Position on Aviation Taxes in the EU*, Brussels: ACI Europe.
ACIL Tasman (2011) *Economic Impact of Canberra Airport 2010 to 2030*, Canberra: ACIL Tasman.
ATAG (2012) *Aviation: Benefits beyond Borders*, Geneva: Air Transport Action Group.
Button, K. and Taylor, S. (2000) 'International air transportation and economic development', *Journal of Air Transport Management*, 6(4): 209–22.
CAA (2007) *Air Services at UK Regional Airports: An Update on Developments*, CAP 775, London: Civil Aviation Authority.

Caves, R. and Gosling, G. (1999) *Strategic Airport Planning*, Oxford: Elsevier.

CDM Smith (2012) *The Economic Impact of Commercial Airports in 2010*, Cincinnati: CDM Smith.

Cushman and Wakefield (2011) European Cities Monitor 2011, London: Cushman and Wakefield.

ELFAA (2004) *Liberalisation of European air transport: The Benefits of Low Fares Airlines to Consumers, Airports, Regions and the Environment*, Brussels: European Low Fares Airline Association.

GAO (2003) *Factors Affecting Efforts to Improve Air Services at Small Community Airports*, GAO-03-330, Washington, DC: General Accounting Office.

Graham, B. and Guyer, C. (2000) 'The role of regional airports and air services in the United Kingdom', *Journal of Transport Geography*, 8(4): 249–62.

Graham, B. and Shaw, J. (2008) 'Low-cost airlines in Europe: reconciling liberalization and sustainability', *Geoforum*, 39(3): 1439–51.

Kasarda, J. (2009) 'Airport cities', *Urban Land*, 68(4): 56–60.

KiM Netherlands Institute for Transport Policy Analysis (2011) *Effects of the Air Passenger Tax: Behavioural Responses of Passengers, Airlines and Airports*, The Hague: KiM Netherlands Institute for Transport Policy Analysis.

Klophaus, R. (2008) 'The impact of additional passengers on airport employment: the case of German airports', *Journal of Airport Management*, 2(3): 265–74.

Heathrow Airport Ltd (2010) *Heathrow: On-airport Employment Survey 2008/09*, London: Heathrow Airport Limited.

Hoyle, Tanner & Associates and RKG Associates (2008) *ACRP Synthesis Report 7: Airport Economic Impact Methods and Models*, Washington, DC: Transportation Research Board.

MAG (2012) *Airport City Manchester*. Online. Available HTTP: <http://www.airportcity.co.uk/opportunities> (accessed 15 December 2012)

Martin, S.C. (2008) *ACRP Report 18: Passenger Air Service Development Techniques*, Washington, DC: Transportation Research Board.

Morrison, G. (2009) 'Real estate, factory outlets and bricks: a note on non-aeronautical activities at commercial airports', *Journal of Air Transport Management*, 15(3): 112–15.

NCAER (2012) *Economic Impact Study of Delhi Airport*, Delhi: NCAER.

Optimal Economics (2011) *Heathrow Related Employment*, London: Optimal Economics.

Oxford Economic Forecasting (2006) *The Contribution of the Aviation Industry to the UK Economy*, Oxford: OEF.

Pagliari, R. (2005) 'Developments in the supply of direct international air services from airports in Scotland' *Journal of Air Transport Management*, 11(4): 249–57.

Poungias, P. (2009) 'Airport city developments: an airport investor's perspective', *Journal of Airport Management*, 4(1): 14–22.

Reiss, B. (2007) 'Maximising non-aviation revenue for airports: developing airport cities to optimise real estate and capitalise on land development opportunities', *Journal of Airport Management*, 1(3): 284–93.

San Diego International Airport (2008) *Airport Economic Impact*, San Diego: San Diego International Airport.

SEO Economic Research (2009) *The Implications of the Irish Air Travel Tax*, Amsterdam: SEO Economic Research

Smyth, A., Christodoulou, G., Dennis, N., Al-Azzawi, M. and Campbell, J. (2012) 'Is air transport a necessity for social inclusion and economic development?', *Journal of Air Transport Management*, 22: 53–59.

STRAIR (2005) *Air Service Development for Regional Development Agencies*, Brussels: STRAIR.

Travel Trade Gazette (2005) 'Ryanair's cushy number: over 20 million euros in grants', *World Travel Market TTG Edition*, November.

URS (2008) *The Economic Impact of Growth at Sydney Airport*, Sydney: URS.

Vancouver Airport Authority (2011) *Vancouver International Airport 2010 Economic Impact Report*, Vancouver: Vancouver Airport Authority.

Weatherill, J. (2006) 'North American airline incentives: best practices and emerging trends', *Journal of Airport Management*, 1(1): 25–37.

Williams, A. and Baláž, V. (2009) 'Low-cost carriers, economies of flows and regional externalities', *Regional Studies*, 43(5): 677–91.

van Wijk, M. (2009) *Airports as Cityports in the City-Region: Spatial–Economic and Institutional Positions and Institutional Learning in Randstad-Schiphol (AMS), Frankfurt Rhein-Main (FRA), Tokyo Haneda (HND) and Narita (NRT)*, Utrecht: Netherlands Geographical Studies 353.

Veldhuis, J. (2012) 'The implications of airport taxes in Europe', *University of Westminster Airport Economics and Finance Symposium*, London, February.

York Aviation (2004) *The Economic and Social Impact of Airports in Europe*, Maccelesfield: York Aviation.

—— (2008) *Economic Impact of the MAG Airports Update Report*, Macclesfield: York Aviation.

10 The environmental impact of airports

GROWING CONCERNS FOR THE ENVIRONMENT

The airport industry, like all other industries, is facing the effects of increasing environmental pressure. The level of environmental concern varies from country to country, or from one airport to another, depending on views about aviation and other social and political attitudes. In many countries increased prosperity has led to greater expectation for the quality of life and more sensitivity to the environmental impacts of airports. For this reason it has become progressively difficult substantially to expand airport operations or to build new airports. All indications are that this will become even more difficult in the future as concern for the environment grows. At the same time, continual long-term growth in demand is putting greater commercial pressures on airports to develop further. The problems are particularly acute for airports that are popular because of their proximity to local population centres, but in turn this means that a significant proportion of the community is affected by airport operations. In short, environmental issues must be seen as one of the greatest challenges to, and possible constraints on, the future activities of the air transport industry.

The environmental impacts have to be considered at two levels: global and local. Within a global context, the role aviation plays in contributing to world problems, including global warming and ozone depletion, is increasingly under scrutiny. These are long-term issues that society as a whole has to address. The meeting of governments in Kyoto in 1997 was one of the first attempts to introduce constraints on environmental impacts at the global level – although international aviation was excluded from this. At a local level, impacts associated with noise and air quality have to be considered. In some areas of operation, airport operators may be legally required to minimise the adverse effects, whereas elsewhere many airport operators are increasingly voluntarily introducing measures to mitigate the impacts. It is the local problems that airport operators mostly have to address on a day-to-day basis. The focus of this chapter, therefore, is very much at this level, although some investigation of the global developments has also been made to put the local issues into a broader context.

Consideration of the environmental impacts at airports is made more difficult because of the many different bodies involved in, or affected by, airport operations. These include the airport operator, the airlines, governments and statutory organisations, amenity and conservation groups and local residents. These will have a complexity of different and often conflicting interests.

Issues including resident safety or loss of wildlife habitat can cause anxiety among certain sectors of society and generate considerable emotive concern. Other impacts may require complex technical data to be assessed, which may be difficult for all interested parties to understand fully. Some impacts cannot be measured adequately. Then, when mitigation measures are considered, most standard procedures have to be adapted to suit each airport's individual circumstances because of variations in aircraft use, night flights, land-use rules, closeness to residential areas and overall environmental sensitivity of the community.

THE MAIN IMPACTS

The main environmental impacts can be divided into five categories:

- noise
- emissions
- water pollution and use
- waste and energy management
- wildlife, heritage and landscape.

Noise

Aircraft noise has traditionally been considered the most important environmental problem at airports, and in many cases public tolerance of aircraft noise has been diminishing. This is despite the fact that over the years the noise levels associated with aircraft movements have been declining. This reduction has been due primarily to the development of less noisy aircraft and the pressure of more stringent requirements for noise certification of new aircraft types. Noise certification was first introduced in 1969 by the United States in the Federal Aviation Regulations Part 36 (FAR Part 36). ICAO adopted similar international standards in 1971. These standards were included in the Environmental Protection Annex 16 of the Chicago Convention. The initial standards for jet aircraft, based on the maximum noise level given a certain flight procedure, became known as chapter 2 or stage 2 in the United States. In 1977 more stringent standards, known as chapter or stage 3, to be applied to all new aircraft designs, were adopted by ICAO. Chapter 2 aircraft include the Boeing 727, DC-9 and older types of Boeing 737 and 747. Newer aircraft certificated under chapter 3 included the Boeing 757, 767, 777 and all the airbus family of aircraft.

Since 1990, the first generation of noisy aircraft (chapter/stage 1), including the Boeing 707, have been prohibited. After that the second-generation chapter 2 aircraft were the noisiest types. They were phased out completely in the United States at the end of 1999 and worldwide in 2002. An issue that complicates this noise certification process is the treatment of hush-kitted or re-engined jets. These are chapter 2 jets that have been modified to comply with the chapter 3 rules. They are the noisiest of the chapter 3 aircraft and so there have been pressures, particularly in Europe, to phase them out. However, this has been opposed elsewhere, especially by the United States, which has been a major supplier of the hush-kitted equipment and up until recently has had a high proportion of hush-kitted aircraft used by its airlines. In 2001 it was decided by ICAO that a new chapter 4 standard would apply to all new aircraft designs, beginning in 2006, which cumulatively have to be 10 decibels quieter than chapter 3. In 2013 it is expected that a new chapter 5 standard will be defined.

At the same time as establishing the 2006 standard, ICAO agreed the concept of a 'balanced approach' to noise management, comprising four principal elements:

- reduction of aircraft noise at source
- land-use planning and management measures
- noise abatement operational procedures
- local noise-related operating restrictions.

Within Europe in 2002, the EC adopted a new directive (2002/30/EC) which incorporated ICAO's balanced programme (EC, 2002a). In the same year the EU Environmental Noise Directive (2002/49/EC) was agreed, which is not specifically related to airports but requires all major ones to prepare strategic noise action plans and submit them for government approval (EC, 2002b). The former directive identified the need to follow ICAO's four principles in any deci- sions concerning noise-mitigating measures as these can have significant impacts on areas including capacity and airline operations. However, in practice it has been found that there had been too many inconsistencies in the assessments of whether such measures were the safest they could be; produced excess impacts on capacity; created holding patterns; or even encouraged inappropriate residential development (EC, 2008). Therefore changes have been proposed in the Airports Package (discussed in Chapter 4). These include bringing the legislation up to date in line with technological developments to make it easier to phase out the nosiest planes; and increasing the transparency in the process of setting noise-related restrictions at airports, including an oversight role for the EC.

Undoubtedly the first principle of ICAO, the reduction of aircraft noise at source, which has been brought about by international certification, has had an impact on reducing overall aircraft noise levels. The newest generation of aircraft, including the A380 and Boeing 787, are the quietest yet and research continues into researching new technology solutions to reduce noise from jet engines. However, such reductions of noise at source can take a considerable length of time to achieve – given the heavy investment needed by both aircraft manufacturers and airlines and the long lifetime of an aircraft. This is why other measures, detailed in the balanced approach, are also needed.

The appropriate control of land use near the airport is vital when the mitigation of noise impacts is being considered. This is in order to prevent the gains achieved by using quieter aircraft being offset by people living closer to the airport. To overcome this problem, noise zoning is often applied to airports. This involves defining a certain area, or noise buffer, around an airport where the construction of new houses and other noise-sensitive buildings is not allowed. In a study of European practice, it was found that 33 out of 52 airports had some land-use planning or manage- ment controls, including London Gatwick, London Heathrow, Vienna and Athens airports (MPD Group Ltd, 2007).

Individual airports can also introduce unilateral noise-abatement operating measures that can reduce the annoyance caused by aircraft noise (Girvin, 2009). For example, many airports have introduced preferred noise routes (PNRs) (or noise preferential routes, NPRs) to minimise the noise impact on the surrounding population. This is usually done by directing aircraft away from the most densely populated areas. Airports may also choose to place restrictions on flight procedures by requiring, for example, reduced power and flap settings for take-off or approach. Other noise-abatement procedures may involve having favoured runways with flight paths over uninhabited areas, and continuous descent approach (CDA), which entails having a continuous steady descent to a runway rather than a number of short descents to set cleared altitudes, as was traditionally required by air traffic control. Similarly, there are continuous climb departures (CCDs), and take-off gradients can be increased, as at Brussels airport where there is a requirement for a gradient of at least 7 per cent. Runways can also be operated in segregated rather than mixed mode, as is the case at Heathrow airport.

Flight-track monitoring equipment combined with airport surveillance radar is used to improve airline departure and arrival procedures and to monitor adherence to the PNRs. In some cases airport operators may impose financial penalties on airlines that deviate from their required flight track. Money from penalties may be used for soundproofing or other community projects. For example, there is a £500 fine during the day and £750 at night at Manchester that goes to the Manchester Airport Community Trust Fund. There may be difficulties with this, however, because airlines quite legitimately may be required to depart from their preferred route for ATC reasons. Most airports also use noise-monitoring equipment. This can be used to measure local noise levels and calculate noise contours, or to enforce noise limits. The information gathered from the noise- and track-monitoring procedures can be provided for the airlines, local community, governments and other interested parties, and a growing number of airports publish the results. There can even be further incentives, for example San Francisco airport has a 'Fly Quiet' programme where it awards airlines that perform particularly well in relation to noise pollution.

There is also the noise from airline engines running, especially during maintenance. To reduce the noise emission levels, a number of airports have introduced mufflers or noise-attenuating walls and special noise-attenuating hangars. Restrictions have been placed on when and how engine tests can be undertaken. Limits have also been imposed on the use of reverse thrust by airlines. However, the noise problem is not confined to aircraft landing, taking off, taxi-ing or engine testing. There is also noise from ground vehicles and auxiliary power units (APUs). Noise has been reduced at a number of US airports that have mostly fixed rather than auxiliary power units, as is increasingly the case at many European airports. There are also various restrictions on APU use, for example at Athens, Madrid, Beijing, Brussels, Incheon and Kansai airports.

The fourth aspect of the balanced approach is local noise-related operating restrictions. A common measure is a night curfew or limitations on night flights. This may involve a blanket ban on all aircraft (including at London City, Wellington and Bermuda airports) or a limit on the noisier aircraft (including at Manchester, Bahrain, Lisbon, Madrid, Brussels, Toronto and Geneva). At a number of Australian airports, including Sydney and Adelaide, the airport is closed at night to all except very small aircraft. Other airports, for instance Beijing and a number of US airports including Lambert-St Louis and Las Vegas, do not allow movements on certain runways at night. However, night constraints may have a significant impact on the development of freight or charter traffic, which often relies on night movements, and make scheduling long-haul services more difficult. A recent example of a night ban is at Frankfurt airport, which has been strongly opposed by the German aviation industry especially because of Frankfurt's strongly competitive position in the cargo market.

The application of a 'noise budget' is also a noise-related operating restriction. In this case the budget will restrict the overall noise during a certain period at night, such as a season or year. For instance the UK airports including Heathrow, Gatwick and Stansted use a noise budget called a Quota Count (QC) system. The quota count is based on the aircraft's noise performance, with noisy aircraft receiving a higher quota count than a quieter one. For example a 747-400 has a QC count of 4 on departure and 2 on arrival, compared with a 777-200 aircraft which has a QC count of 1 and 0.5. The sum of all the QCs is then the noise budget or noise limit for the specified time. At Amsterdam, Copenhagen and Brussels airports, noise budgets are also set based on different aircraft usage within the day and night. Long Beach airport in California is one of the few US airports that has a similar system. Marginally compliant chapter 3 aircraft have also been banned at a number of airports, including the major Australian airports in 2010 and Madrid airport in 2012. At other airports (e.g. Manchester and Paris CDG) such aircraft are banned at night or heavily restricted.

Many airports also impose noise surcharges for noisier aircraft and an incentive to use quieter aircraft. These charging policies are, however, unlikely to influence an airline's choice of aircraft unless the fee differential is very large. Frankfurt, Heathrow, Gatwick and Manchester were among the first airports to introduce such charges in the 1970s. Noise charges are now used in many countries, particularly in Europe but also at Gimpo airport in South Korea, Toronto in Canada and a number of Australian and Japanese airports. There is, however, no consistency in the way these noise charges are structured. In addition, at many airports, such as Brussels, Oslo, Amsterdam and those in Germany, the landing charges are higher at night. Overall, a survey in Europe found that around half of airports used landing charges that differentiated by noise category and around half also had day/night time differentiated charges (MPD Group Ltd, 2007). By way of illustration, Table 10.1 shows the charges for Paris where the basic charge varies by noise levels during the day by 0.7–1.3 and at night by 1.05–1.95 The landing fees are multiplied by a noise level coefficient based on the aircraft's noise classification according to certain specifically defined acoustic groups.

Table 10.1 *Landing and noise charges at Paris CDG airport, 2012*

Aircraft category	Price per landing (€), day (06:00–22:00)	Price per landing (€), night (22:00–26:00)
MTOW <40 tonnes	168.01	
MTOW >40 tonnes	$168.01 + 5.734 \times (t - 40)$	
Acoustic group	Noise level coefficient	
1	1.300	1.950
2	1.200	1.800
3	1.150	1.725
4	1.000	1.500
5a	0.850	1.275
5b	0.700	1.050

In spite of all these measures to reduce noise levels, there will always be some residents who will be subject to noise annoyance, and for this reason many airport operators will fund or assist in the funding of noise insulation for properties in the vicinity of the airport – either voluntarily or because it is a legal requirement. Housing and buildings including schools and hospitals may be insulated. In most cases the cost of insulation will be covered by the airport operator alone, but sometimes national or regional governments will also contribute, as is the case at Copenhagen and Milan. Sometimes the funds may come from specific noise taxes, as at Amsterdam airport. There is also a noise tax in France, where the costs of house insulation is financed primarily by the state, but unlike at Amsterdam these tax revenues are not directly earmarked for insulation costs.

Emissions

Global impacts

Through the combination of the development of quieter aircraft and noise abatement operating procedures, most airports are attempting to contain many of the problems arising from aircraft noise. However, a newer environmental threat that has been growing in recent years is that of aircraft emissions and their impact on climate change (Gossling and Upham, 2009). By consuming fuel, aircraft are producing emissions of carbon dioxide (CO_2), nitrogen oxides (NO_x) particles (mainly soot) of sulphur oxides, carbon monoxide and other effects including water vapour trails and induced cloudiness.

At a global level, CO_2 is the most important of all the greenhouse gases and is the emission for which there has been the most developed and conclusive research. One of the most comprehensive studies of aviation emissions, albeit rather old now, found that globally aviation's contribution to the world total of human-made CO_2 was fairly small in the 1990s, at around 2 per cent. If other less scientifically certain effects are also taken into account, including the NO_x emissions and the creation of vapour trails, it was estimated that the radiative forcing or global warming effect of all aircraft emissions would be around 3.5 per cent (this excluded possible damaging unknown changes in cirrus clouds). However, because of the growth of air transport and the relative ability of other industrial sectors to reduce their emissions, by 2050 this global share was predicted to rise to around 4–15 per cent, depending on different growth scenarios and other assumptions (Intergovernmental Panel on Climate Change, 1999).

More recently, the International Transport Forum (2010) found that in 2007 CO_2 aviation emissions were considered to contribute to 2.5 per cent of global emissions and 12 per cent of all transport emissions. Total aviation impacts were in excess of 3 per cent. However, aviation emissions had grown at a much higher rates, for example in the EU by 85 per cent between 1990 and 2007 compared with total growth of emission of 7 per cent. Higher relative growth is also expected in the future compared with other sectors. Various statistics also exist for individual countries, for example in the UK where aviation accounted for 6 per cent of total greenhouse gas emissions in 2009 compared with 6 per cent in 1990. This 2009 figure compares with 19 per cent for road transport (Department for Transport, 2011).

Emissions from international flights (but not domestic flights) were excluded from the Kyoto Protocol which was adopted in 1997 and came into force in 2005 – and instead ICAO, through its Committee on Aviation Environmental Protection (CAEP), was given the responsibility for developing proposals on international aviation emissions. In 2010, ICAO agreed overall targets related to future emissions that included an average improvement in fuel efficiency of 2 per cent per year up to 2050 and a cap on CO_2 emissions from 2020 to ensure carbon-neutral growth (ICAO, 2010). These targets are similar to those agreed by IATA (2009) which included an average improvement in fuel efficiency of 1.5 per cent per year from 2009 to 2020, a reduction in CO_2 emissions of 50 per cent by 2050 relative to 2005 levels, and again a cap on emissions from 2020.

Lighter airframe materials and more efficient engines will help reduce emissions. However, it is generally agreed that future global air traffic will increase at growth rates that will outperform the impact of any technology improvements that will reduce engine emissions. In addition, while more fuel-efficient aircraft may produce less emissions including CO_2, the higher combustion temperatures needed for greater efficiency may actually produce more NO_x emissions. All this also has to be viewed within the global context where major CO_2 reduction efforts are taking place in other industrial sectors.

At present there does not appear to be a viable commercial alternative to jet fuel. There has been some experimentation with non-carbon-based biofuels that have been tested by a number of airlines including Virgin, Qatar, Air New Zealand, Finnair, Lufthansa, Thomson and Japan Airlines. However, important questions remain regarding the cost of biofuels and problems associated with their wide-scale production and distribution, together with issues related to sustainability and land/water availability needed to produce the fuel. In Europe a consortium of industry members called 'Biofuel Flightpath' is seeking to produce 2 million tonnes of sustainably produced biofuel by 2020 (EC, 2012). Improved operational procedures, including more efficient air traffic management and flight operations, perhaps with larger and fuller aircraft and coupled with reduced airport and airspace congestion, could also bring about a further reduction in fuel burn. European and US ATC projects, including Single European Sky Air Traffic Management (SESAR) and NextGen, should help in the area of ATC, as should the adoption of airport collaborative decision-making when airport delays are being considered.

However, all these developments will not by themselves reduce emissions to an acceptable level. As a consequence, IATA now has a four-pillar strategy for reducing emissions, covering the three areas that have already been discussed – technology investment, more efficient infrastructure and more efficient operations – and a fourth area, 'positive' economic or market-based options or measures (MBMs), which many industry experts now feel are an essential feature of any emissions reduction policy.

There are a number of MBMs, including a kerosene tax. Currently aviation kerosene fuel is exempt from tax on international flights under the 1944 Chicago Convention, and many bilateral air service agreements between countries prohibit such a tax. (Domestic fuel taxes are allowed and are in fact levied in a few countries, including the USA, India, Japan and the Netherlands.) Some time ago, the EC undertook some detailed research of the effects of taxing EU airlines and concluded that it would give them a distinct competitive disadvantage and produce fairly marginal emission savings. The environmental effectiveness of taxing all routes would be far greater, but it was concluded that this option would be very difficult to implement because of the legal and political implications (EC, 1999). The case of emissions trading (discussed below) demonstrates clearly the international political obstacles that the EC can face.

Within this context, it is worth revisiting environmental passenger taxes (see Chapter 9) which are growing in popularity. Taxing on a per passenger basis is a very blunt instrument for tackling the emissions problem, as each passenger pays the same regardless of the level of emissions from the aircraft and how full it is. In the UK there have been two attempts to replace it with a tax payable per plane rather than per passenger, which would take account of the carbon impact of each aircraft type and its occupancy. However, in both cases it eventually did not prove feasible to introduce. In addition, the passenger taxes are criticised as the taxes are not normally used on any environmental projects. An alternative is an emissions charge that could be levied as part of the airport or ATC charge (CE Delft, 2002).

A more attractive option to many industry stakeholders appears to be emissions trading or a 'cap-and-trade' system. In this case an overall target for emissions is set and then individual participants can choose to meet the target; reduce their emissions below the target and sell excessive emissions allowance; or keep their emissions above the target and buy more emissions allowance. There is either a closed system where individual companies just buy or sell emission certificates from others in the same sector; or a more radical open system where companies can buy/sell from other industries. Overall it is felt that this gives a much greater incentive to monitor and regulate emissions than the other options.

Since 2005 a multi-sector emissions trading scheme (ETS) has been applied in the EU to fixed-source energy-intensive installations. Since 2012 aviation has been included in this scheme. This covers all flights to and from EU airports, with the total allowances being capped at 97 per cent of the average 2004–06 value. It is an open scheme with 18 per cent of the allowances auctioned and the rest issued free based on the historic share of tonne-km traffic in 2010. This has been greeted with some opposition from European carriers, who are opposed to the auction as they regard this as a tax and are fearful of how the money, which has to be spent to mitigate climate change, might be spent. A few airlines, notably Ryanair, have introduced a new ETS charge of €0.25 per passenger. However, the greatest opposition has always been from the non-EU airlines (especially the Americans, Indians and Chinese) who have argued that the EU ETS is illegal under international law and that the industry ought to adopt a global approach through ICAO. Retaliatory trade measures from some of these countries were threatened, and in November 2012 the scheme was temporarily suspended for non-EU flights in anticipation of a meeting of ICAO in 2013 that is planning to discuss all global MBMs.

Local impacts

While the global impacts of aircraft emissions have attracted a great deal of attention in recent years, clearly they are not the only impacts that need to be considered. At a regional level the emissions from aviation are thought to contribute to acid rain. At a local level the air quality of the area in the immediate vicinity of the airport can be affected – primarily due to emissions of hydrocarbons, carbon monoxide and nitrogen oxides. Many airports monitor their local air quality, although the monitoring systems vary considerably in their level of sophistication and accuracy. Some airports use these systems to help them model predicted air quality in the future.

Since 1981, ICAO has laid down standards for four categories of engine emissions: smoke, hydrocarbons, carbon monoxide and nitrogen oxides. These standards are aimed at local air pollution problems as they are based on the aircraft landing and take-off (LTO) cycle and do not cover emissions during the cruise phase. Over the years these standards have been strengthened, the latest 2008 standards being 12 per cent lower than the previous standards. However, they are not legally binding and it is up to member states to include these standards in their laws. Local air quality may also be regulated by general national or international laws related to air quality. For example, within Europe the 1996 Framework Directive on Ambient Air Quality has limits for NO_x that became binding after 2010. These standards may be breached by some airports as traffic grows. For example, a few years ago there was considerable debate as to whether this would occur if there were was a third runway at London Heathrow which was being considered at that time.

A few airports have introduced emissions charges (Scheelhaase, 2009). This happened initially in the late 1990s at the Stockholm airports of Arlanda and Bromma, some other Swedish airports, and the Swiss airports of Zürich, Basel-Mulhouse, Bern and Geneva. Aircraft were initially classified according to their specific emissions, with five classes in Switzerland and seven classes in Sweden. Emissions charges have subsequently been introduced at Heathrow, Gatwick, Luton, Copenhagen, Munich, Hamburg, Dusseldorf and Frankfurt, based on the ERLIG formula which provides a methodology for calculating NO_x and hydrocarbons emissions from different aircraft engines. CE Delft (2008) found that the level of charges varied widely from 6 per cent saving on landing fees for cleanest aircraft at Basel (and rebates for low emissions at Heathrow/Gatwick) to 40 per cent surcharge for the dirtiest aircraft at Zurich.

Just as with noise abatement measures, airport operators and airlines can work together to reduce emissions, and very often certain practices such as CDA will reduce noise and emissions. Likewise, the length of time that engines are run on the ground can be reduced, fixed ground power can be used and taxi-ing times can be minimised. As with the noise issue, the problem at airports is not limited to aircraft operations – the local air quality may also be affected by ground service vehicles which traditionally have tended to be fuel-powered. At some airports, electric vehicles that are more economically and environmentally favourable have been used. Then there are emissions from maintenance and cleaning processes, auxiliary power units, and cars and other surface transport modes.

London Heathrow is one of many airports where a considerable amount of ground-level NO_x is from landside vehicles. For this reason, in 2002 BAA established its so called Clean Vehicles Programme. This had 45 members and encouraged them to use lower-emission vehicles and to increase fuel efficiency. In 2006 it launched an incentive scheme with a total fund value of £100,000 in response to calls from members for financial assistance with implementing technologies, including replacing old diesel vehicles with electric alternatives or fitting cleaner technologies to existing vehicles. Elsewhere, Hong Kong airport has a 'Green Apron' policy that involves replacing the existing fleet with alternative fuel or low-emission vehicles; similar policies exist, for example at Amsterdam, Dallas/Fort Worth and Bristol airports which have mixtures of electrical and biodiesel vehicles. Phoenix airport uses compressed natural gas for its car and bus fleet, while Fraport has been undertaking tests on hydrogen-powered vehicles.

Water pollution and use

Water pollution at airports can occur for a number of different reasons. Surface water discharge or run-off that goes into local watercourses from runways, aprons, car parks and other land development may be contaminated by anti-icing and de-icing fluids, including glycol, used during the winter months. The chemicals used in maintaining and washing aircraft and vehicles, as well as fire training activities and fuel spillages, can contribute to this pollution. Leakages from underground tanks and pipes, and grass fertilisers used in landscaping activities, can contaminate the soil. Then there is the normal wastewater from buildings and facilities including domestic sewerage. An increasing number of airports now monitor water quality as well as air quality and have adopted various measures to minimise water pollution. These include revised operational practices to reduce the use of harmful chemicals, to improve cleaning processes and to minimise spillage and leakage. For example, at Hamburg airport de-icing takes place only on sealed apron surfaces to ensure the fluid run-off does not leak elsewhere; at Munich airport this is done in a specially designated remote area so that the de-icing fluids can be recovered for recycling. A by-product of this recycling process is heat which can be used to help warm the terminal. Many other airports, including Detroit, Seattle and Dallas/Fort Worth, also recycle de-icing fluid. Balancing reservoir treatment may be undertaken before the surface water joins local watercourses, including at Auckland airport.

Waste and energy management

Waste pollution is also an issue. In many cases there may be general legislation related to waste management. However, airports are also faced with specific operating restrictions because of the nature of the aviation business. For example, airports need to incinerate or send to a controlled landfill site all 'international' food waste from aircraft. In addition, the transfer of waste from airside to landsite at airports is problematic because of security, customs and insurance restrictions.

The waste at airports is generated by airlines, airport operators and other airport-related companies. While most of the waste comes from the airlines, it is usually the airport operators who have overall responsibility for waste management for the entire airport activities. Most of the individual companies, especially the airlines, do not have enough space for waste management facilities, and there are cost economies of scale to be gained by having communal recycling and other waste management procedures. Improvements can usually be brought about by an assessment of on-airport treatment methods and the scope for reducing, re-using or recycling waste. In-flight catering waste, with the disposable nature of most of the packaging, is considered a particular problem. Off-airport disposal methods that typically involve incineration and landfill also need to be considered.

Most airports now have recycling initiatives. One of the earliest airports to undertake this was Zurich airport, which introduced an airport-wide waste management concept in 1992. Other examples range from concrete recycling at Jersey airport to recycling food waste at Hong Kong airport to produce compost for airport landscaping, re-using cut grass instead of fertiliser at Stansted airport, airline pillow recycling at Oakland airport, and re-use of excavated soil at Dallas/Fort Worth airport. At Los Angeles airport the food waste is used to produce methane gas which is turned into electricity; at Seattle it is given to a food bank in the city. Other airports, including Canberra, recycle their water.

Energy management associated with the provision of heating, ventilation, air conditioning and lighting is also very important. Many airports undertake energy audits. With energy conservation, as with waste and water management, there are good financial reasons why airports should address these issues, since environmental improvements may bring about considerable cost savings. Some airports, including Vancouver, Chicago and San Francisco, have installed solar panels, whereas La Palma airport in Spain has wind power generators.

Wildlife, heritage and landscape

There is also a need to protect the wildlife, heritage and landscape of the local environment, and there are many examples of how specific airport operators in the past have tackled the disturbance of certain wildlife habitats – particularly during the construction of a new airport or during airport expansion. While the Chek Lap Kok airport in Hong Kong was being built, a 1-km exclusion zone for dolphins was set up to ensure their sensitive hearing was not harmed during blasting work. At Indianapolis airport, 3,000 new homes for Indiana bats had to be installed due to a new maintenance building that displaced the bats. At Perth airport, development was halted when a rare western swamp tortoise colony was discovered. At Miami airport, the death of four manatees beneath the runway forced the airport operator to take action to protect this endangered species. At Manchester airport, badger sets had to be relocated and a rare breed of newts had to be protected when the second runway was being built. At Oslo Gardermoen airport, a bridge had to be built to prevent the 1,000 moose who annually migrate across the region from wandering onto the airport approach roads. At Stansted airport, some great crested newts had to be moved to a habitat especially created by the airport operator, while Tallahassee airport in Florida also developed an onsite conservation area for the gopher tortoise. Many more examples exist.

Heritage may also be affected by airport development. For example, historic buildings may be situated within the area that has been allocated for airport expansion. In the case of Manchester and Copenhagen airports, this meant moving such buildings brick by brick to other locations. In addition, landscapes can be radically changed by airport developments which can disturb the ecosystem and may be visually intrusive. To compensate for this, some airports have established 'green areas', including Athens airport where there are five such projects that cover a total area of 6 hectares and include features including walking paths, playgrounds and planted areas. Detroit airport has developed a wetlands area, whereas at Southwest Florida airport a nature reserve has been established.

Community impacts

Airport environmental impacts may have a detrimental impact on the quality of life for residents in the vicinity of the airport. The major areas of concern are aircraft noise, air pollution, fuel odour, ecological damage and the safety of aircraft. While the exact relationship between human health and wellbeing and these factors is still not entirely clear, an area that has received particular attention is the problem of sleep disturbance due to night flying. It is for this reason that many airports restrict aircraft movements at nights or ban noisier aircraft types. The rising number of aircraft movements has also increased concerns about aircraft safety and has resulted in some airports establishing risk contours around airports associated with third-party death and injury.

Forging strong links with the community and ensuring continual public dialogue with all interested parties is often considered an important role. Airports become involved in community relations, including the provision of information about environmental and other developments, offering a complaints-handling service, supporting and sponsoring local arts, culture and sports events, and developing educational links. Some airports set up residents' forums. Many airports also have consultative committees with representatives from local government, amenity groups, local commerce and industry and airport users. These may be a legal requirement. Another important stakeholder to consider here will be the airport employees, and issues including equal opportunities, ethics policies, skills training and workplace safety and security.

Increasingly, most airports are addressing such social and community issues within the framework of a broader sustainability or corporate responsibility strategy that considers all stakeholders and all impacts, both positive and negative (Berry *et al.*, 2008). A growing number of airports are publicly reporting their sustainability or corporate responsibility performance against the Global Reporting Initiative (GRI) guidelines. These give stakeholders a universally applicable and comparable framework in which to understand the disclosed information about economic environmental and social performance. The ultimate aim is that such reporting will become as routine as financial reporting.

THE ROLE OF OTHER TRANSPORT MODES

Returning more specifically to the environmental aspects of airport operators, an important considerations is that of other transport modes. There are two ways in which the use of other modes can affect the direct and indirect environmental impacts of airports. First, there may be some opportunity for passengers on short- and medium-distance flights to be diverted onto high-speed rail services. In the 1980s and 1990s there was continuing growth in the number of high-speed rail services, notably in France and Germany in Europe and Japan in Asia. Various studies showed that a quick city centre to city centre rail service had been quite successful in attracting a certain share of the population away from competing air services. For example in Europe, it was estimated that the rail share of traffic on the Frankfurt–Munich route increased from 30 to 37 per cent in the first year of operation, with a drop in airline share from 27 to 23 per cent. On the Stockholm–Gothenburg route, the rail share was estimated to have increased from 40 to 55 per cent in the first 4 years of operation, and the first TGV route in France between Paris and Lyons was claimed to have gained a 90 per cent market share (CAA, 1998). More recent research on routes from the UK airports to Paris and Brussels shows that traffic declined annually by 6 per cent between 2004 and 2007, while passengers travelling on the Eurostar rail service across the Channel increased by 5 per cent per year over the same period. In terms of market share, in 2005 rail share of point-to-point traffic between London and Paris/Brussels was below 70 per cent, but by 2010 it had increased to 80 per cent. Another example is in France, where the TGV Mediterranean was introduced in 2001 between Paris and Marseille. In 2001 rail held a market share of only 22 per cent of the combined Paris–Marseille air/rail market, but by 2005 this had increased to 65 per cent (Copenhagen Economics, 2012).

However, switching from air to rail is feasible only when dense routes are being considered. Such rail links also require huge capital investment. In the end passengers will choose the rail option when the time, fare, frequency and access characteristics of the service offers them an advantage. Rail services are not usually an attractive option for transfer traffic unless the high-speed network is linked to airports. An interesting development occurred in Germany when, in 1998, Lufthansa and the railway company Deutsche Bahn (DB) signed a memorandum of understanding that enabled them to produce their AIRail product on completion of the high-speed train link. This involved a partnership on the high-speed routes of Frankfurt–Stuttgart from 2001 and Frankfurt–Cologne from 2003. There was a code-sharing agreement between Lufthansa and DB, and similar agreements now exist with other airlines. At Paris CDG, a number of airlines have similar agreements with the French railways, SNCF. The services are also operated with through baggage check-in and the same transfer times as at the air terminal. This initiative has switched passengers to high-speed trains and reduced the use of feeder flights as well as shifting some demand from cars and local urban rail services (Fakiner, 2005).

The individual airport operator has far greater control in influencing the mode of surface travel used by passengers, employees and others to reach the airport – the other aspect of surface transport that needs to be considered. Ground transport makes a major contribution to the overall noise levels and air pollution at an airport, with the impacts rising as the transport system becomes congested. Many airports are trying to develop more effective public transport alternatives to the car for accessing the airport. They have also introduced many initiatives to encourage passengers and airport employees to use public transport – or at the least to use electric cars, as demonstrated by Brussels airport which has installed free charging points.

Historically, most passengers arrived at airports by private car or taxi, with only a small proportion using bus or coach transport. With airport growth in the 1970s and 1980s, some existing suburban or local rail services were extended to reach the airport. They are still the most common form of rail link today, with many examples being found in North America (e.g. Cleveland, Boston, Atlanta and Chicago) and other airports including Munich, Stuttgart, Barcelona, Malaga, Rome Fiumicino, London Luton, Changi Singapore and Shanghai. There are also underground or light rail links at some airports such as London Heathrow, Madrid, Newcastle, Nuremberg, Bremen, London City, Portland Oregon and Baltimore.

Many of these services are relatively slow, with a rather basic quality of service, and are not dedicated links to the airport. They may be popular with employees, but are less attractive to passengers. This has meant that a number of airports, particularly those with large traffic volumes or a long journey away from the city centre, have instead developed high-speed dedicated links. Such links bring environmental benefits and alleviate road congestion as well as bringing extra convenience for passengers. Arlanda, Stockholm airport's third runway, was approved only subject to a rail link being built. Other dedicated airport rail link examples include Gardermoen in Oslo, Heathrow in London, Chek Lap Kok in Hong Kong, Milan in Italy, Brussels in Belgium, Nagoya and Narita in Japan, Incheon in Korea and Kuala Lumpur in Malaysia. A recent completed link is for Johannesburg airport in South Africa and others are planned – including for Bengaluru airport in India.

A number of airports have also developed high-speed links connecting airport terminals to international routes, including Charles de Gaulle in Paris, Lyon, Frankfurt, Zürich, Cologne and

Dusseldorf. Some airports also have integrated regional and high-speed rail links – Paris CDG being a good example. Frankfurt airport has three railway interfaces. There is a regional train station below terminal 1, the AIRail terminal for the long distance services and a rail connection to Cargo City South. A few airports also have rail links for the carriage of cargo, a more recent idea as historically the only cargo transported was aviation fuel. Remote baggage services are also available in Europe, one of the most developed examples being the Fly Rail baggage system in Switzerland that provides check-in and delivery of baggage at all rail stations.

A growing number of airport operators have recognised that encouraging passengers onto public transport is very much more than just consideration of journey time. It also includes looking at the accessibility of the surface modes, ease of transfer to the airport and arrangements for baggage. Some airports are designing better interchange processes between public transport and the airport and offering more remote check-in, as in Switzerland. Others have tried making improvements in marketing, signage and the availability of information. A few, such as Pittsburgh airport in the USA, have dedicated buses and high-occupancy bus lanes to discourage individuals from using their cars. Reducing car use is a key way in which airports can yield important environmental benefits, but matching such reduction policies with the commercial pressures to maximise the revenue potential of airport parking can be very challenging (Ison, 2008).

Figures 10.1 and 10.2 show the public transport use at a number of airports worldwide. The highest shares are achieved at airports in Europe and Asia, particularly Oslo, Hong Kong, Narita and Shanghai, where at least half the passengers use public transport. In the United States and

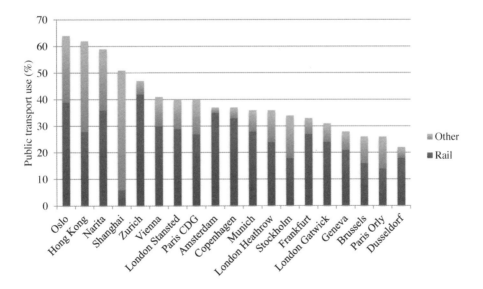

Figure 10.1 *Public transport use at European and Asian airports*
Note: the year under consideration varies, it is for the latest available when the research was undertaken.
Source: Coogan (2008)

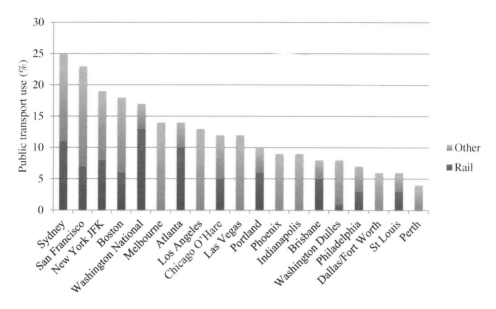

Figure 10.2 *Public transport use at US and Australian airports*
Note: the year under consideration varies, it is for the latest available when the research was undertaken.
Source: Coogan (2008) and Department for Infrastructure and Transport (2011)

Australia, higher dependence on the car generally and the smaller number of specific rail links mean that public transport use is generally less – even below 10 per cent for a number of airports. More details of the specific transport mode used in the UK are provided in Table 10.2. Even within the London area there is considerable variation; more passengers use the private car for Manchester airport, reflecting its role serving the surrounding region where car travel tends to be more convenient.

Table 10.2 *Mode of transport to selected UK airports, 2011*

Transport use (per cent)	London Gatwick	London Heathrow	London Luton	London Stansted	Manchester
Private car	42	29	48	38	57
Hire car	2	3	3	3	2
Taxi	13	27	18	9	26
Rail	35	12	15	25	12
Bus/coach	7	12	16	24	2
Tram/tube	0	17	0	0	0
Other	0	1	1	0	0
Total	100	100	100	100	100

Source: Department for Transport (2012)

Employees also tend to make heavy use of private transport to travel to and from the airport. For example, research in the UK found that there were only three major airports (London Gatwick, London City and Birmingham) where the public transport share for employees was above 10 per cent (Humphreys and Ison, 2005). Likewise, in the USA typically very few employees travel by public transport, with a few exceptions including Boston, Chicago and Denver (Coogan, 2008). However, some European airports, including Amsterdam, Frankfurt and Zurich, achieve a higher share of public transport use. For instance in 2011 the share at Amsterdam airport was 28 per cent, with 20 per cent using the train and 8 per cent using buses (Schiphol Group, 2012).

Many airport operators have been trying to encourage more airport employees to use public transport. Inherently there are a number of characteristics of airport employment that encourage the use of private car. Many of the jobs tend to be on a shift basis, often at unsociable times when public transport services are inadequate. Employees' residences tend to be dispersed around the vicinity of the airport, which makes it much more difficult to provide an effective public transport system. Airport employees traditionally have been provided with free parking spaces at airports, thus increasing the attractiveness of car transport (Ison *et al.*, 2007). Staff initiatives to encourage public transport use include discounted bus and rail travel, dedicated airport workers' buses, the development of cycling networks, and park-and-ride schemes. Manchester airport is an example of an airport that provides cycling facilities and services including bike parks, showering facilities and loans for purchasing bikes. When car use is still necessary, car sharing has been encouraged at some airports. Restrictions on car use within the airport area have also been introduced. One of the many examples of a staff travel plan is the 'lift' plan at Auckland airport, which had an initial goal of encouraging staff to car-pool once a week or use public transport once a fortnight, and subsequently has developed into a significant initiative for car-pooling. The internet has greatly improved the opportunities for car-pooling systems.

A third group of car users at the airport are visitors and meetings and greeters. These generate so-called 'kiss-and-fly' journeys. With these users, for every flight there are four vehicle trips (dropping off and collecting) rather than two if passengers drive themselves. These journeys also put extra pressure on airport roads and kerb space, which can lead to increased congestion and raised levels of emissions and so are particularly problematic for airports (Budd *et al.*, 2011). Traditionally these users paid nothing at the airport, but some airports are now charging or limiting such practice because of security concerns.

Many airports have developed strategies to encourage better public transport use by all users of the airport. For example, from 1998 in the United Kingdom all airports with scheduled services have been required to form airport transport forums (ATF) and prepare airport surface access strategies (ASAS) as part of a national policy framework for integrated transport. The ATF has three specific objectives:

- to agree to short- and long-term targets for decreasing private car usage to and from airports
- to devise a strategy for achieving these targets
- to oversee implementation of the strategy.

The ATF consists of the airport operator and representatives from local businesses, local government, transport operators, the local community and other interested parties. In preparing an

Table 10.3 *Key features of the Edinburgh Airport Surface Access Strategy, 2012*

Strategy area	Overall aim
Public transport use	Work with others to achieve a 35 per cent public transport mode share target
Transport infrastructure	Work with others to deliver enhanced external roads infrastructure and future transport interventions
Bus travel	Seek to enhance and add to the bus network to and from the airport, review bus charging and bus stance allocation, and further promote staff travel by bus
Taxi travel	Look into consolidating existing taxi ranks to improve passenger choice and experience
Tram travel	Assist in promoting the tram and review how it contributes to access options 1 year after it becomes operational
Bike travel	Continue to support and promote cycling as an option for accessing the airport
Cargo areas	Seek to enhance access to the cargo areas
Car parking	Continue to review car-parking strategy to reflect changing trends and passenger profile
Coach parking	Continue to offer coaches parking close to the terminal, and overflow facilities
Employee schemes	Continue to offer the Ride 2 Work scheme to Edinburgh Airport staff and to promote the car-share scheme

Source: Edinburgh Airport (2012)

ASAS, the forum has to ensure the proposals are consistent with the broader integrated transport plans for the area (Humphreys *et al.*, 2005). By way of illustration, the targets for Edinburgh are shown in Table 10.3.

ENVIRONMENTAL MANAGEMENT

For most airport operators, environmental policies are a very important component of their overall business strategy. Environmental pressures from governments, users and other bodies have made it essential for airports to address environmental issues very seriously. In some areas, including air and water quality, airports often have to comply with environmental legislation. Airports have recognised, though, that sound environmental practice can also bring financial benefits through the effective management of resources including energy, waste and water. As a result, most major airports now have well established environmental strategies and relatively sophisticated policies that typically seek to reduce noise and emissions, control pollution, reduce waste and energy use, and encourage the use of renewables and public transport. Increased technology and new mitigation methods are constantly enabling improvements in the efficiencies of such policies. Smaller airports and airports in the developing world have somewhat less sophisticated approaches, but few have managed to escape the whole issue of environmental management entirely. Since airport operators themselves produce relative few of the direct environmental impacts, a key to any successful environmental strategy is a partnership approach between all the different interests on the airport site.

As every airport is different, it is difficult to gauge the popularity of the various environmental measures discussed above. However, a survey of 74 North American airports does provide some insight here, albeit that the sample is relatively small and may not be totally representative. Tracking noise complaints (58 airports), having a noise abatement runway use programme (51 airports), and having a flight tracking system (48 airports) were particularly popular initiatives, whereas less than half provided alternative fuel infrastructure (34 airports), had water-saving landscaping (23 airports), encouraged or required low emission ground access vehicles (28 airports), or had employee trip reduction programmes (21 airports). However, with the growing emphasis on environmental issues it is likely that there has been more airport involvement in some of these less popular areas in the few years since the survey was undertaken (ACI North America, 2009).

At many airports, environmental control processes have evolved into comprehensive environment management systems. These provide the framework for airport operators to develop an effective and coordinated response to all the environmental issues. Within any system, clearly defined objectives and targets are set for reducing the impacts and the most appropriate mitigation methods are identified. Through adopting such an approach, the airport operator also sends messages to the outside world that it is tackling the environmental issues in a responsible manner. In addition, when an airport is planning a major extension of its facilities, it is usually required by law to undertake an environmental impact assessment as part of the planning approval process. This will examine the potential impacts of the proposed development during the construction and operational stages. The results of this assessment are typically summarised in an environmental impact statement.

Some airports choose to formalise their environmental management system by conforming to the International Environmental Management System standard ISO 14001. This is equivalent to the ISO 9000 standard for quality management. To meet the requirements of ISO 14001, airports need to review their environmental impacts, formulate an environmental policy, ensure their practices comply with all relevance legislation, set objectives and targets to improve environmental performance, and demonstrate that appropriate measures have been introduced so that environmental practice can be monitored and targets can be reached. Dublin airport became one of the first European airports to receive ISO 14001 certification in 1999, and many other European airports have subsequently been certified (Hooper *et al.*, 2003). Toronto was the first airport in North America to achieve this standard in 1998. There are also other measures, for example within the EU there is a system called the Eco Management and Audit Scheme (EMAS) which further develops the ISO 14001 standard.

Irrespective of whether an airport uses the GRI guidelines or some other system, it needs to identify suitable environmental indicators that can be used to monitor performance and set targets. The indicators should provide a representative picture of the issue under consideration, and it must be possible to obtain relatively easily and accurately the data required for such indicators. The indicators need to be fairly simple, easy to interpret, and able to show time trends. However, there does tend to be a lack of total comparability between the indicators that makes any comparison between different airports very difficult to achieve (Upham and Mills, 2005). Table 10.4 presents the set of relevant indicators that have been suggested for US airports.

Table 10.4 *Possible performance indicators for environmental management*

Energy management	Environmental management
Airfield electricity consumption – change over prior period	Carbon footprint
Airport vehicles and ground service equipment converted to energy-efficient types (per cent)	De-icing – percentage fluid recovered
Renewable energy generated by the airport (per cent)	Leadership in Energy and Environmental Design (LEED) building projects – percentage new building projects being built to LEED standards
Renewable energy purchased by the airport (per cent)	Environmental reviews – timeliness of completion
Tenant vehicles and ground service equipment converted to energy-efficient types (per cent)	Number of environmental violations
Terminal building electricity consumption per square foot – change over prior period	Night operations – percentage using preferential runways
Utilities/energy cost, airport total – change over prior period	Noise-abatement procedures – percentage compliance
Utilities/energy cost per square foot of terminal building	Noise – number of homes within 65 dBA DNL
	Reportable discharges, number
	Stage 2 operations <75,000 lb
	Waste recycling

Source: Hazel *et al.* (2011)

A growing number of publications have been produced to help airports reduce their greenhouse emissions (ACI, 2009; CDM, 2011). One ultimate target of a growing number of airports is to become carbon-neutral. In this context, an interesting development has been ACI Europe's airport carbon accreditation scheme, a carbon management standard that was launched in May 2009. The programme is administered independently by WSP Environment and Energy, and provides airports with a common framework for active carbon management with measurable targets. It also makes a distinction between the emissions the airport operator can control and influence, compared with others. There are four levels of accreditation: mapping (which requires compilation of carbon footprint reports); reduction (which requires achieving emissions reduction targets for emissions under the airport operator's control); optimisation (which requires engaged third parties in carbon reduction); and neutrality (which requires offsetting remaining emissions to achieve carbon-neutral operations). In October 2012, 67 European airports were accredited with Sweden's national airport group Swedavia becoming the world's first national airport group to achieve carbon neutrality across its 10 airports (Table 10.5). In November 2011 the programme was expanded to the Asia-Pacific region with five airports, Bengaluru, Delhi, Mumbai, Abu Dhabi and Singapore, receiving accreditation in 2012.

This chapter identifies the major environmental impacts associated with airport operations and describes various environmental management approaches designed to reduce these effects.

Table 10.5 ACI Europe's airport carbon accreditation scheme, October 2012

Accreditation level	Number of airports	Share of European passenger traffic (per cent)	Airports
Neutrality Offset remaining emissions to achieve carbon neutral operations for all emissions over which the airport has control	14	5	Oslo Trondheim Milan-Linate Milan-Malpensa, Swedavia (Stockholm Arlanda, Göteborg-Landvetter, Bromma Stockholm, Malmö, Luleå, Umeå, Åre Östersund, Visby, Ronneby, Kiruna)
Optimisation Widen the scope of carbon footprint to include third-party emissions Engage third parties at and around the airport	10	23	CDG Paris Orly Paris Fiumicino Rome Heathrow London Geneva Antalya Manchester Munich Amsterdam Zurich
Reduction Provide evidence of effective carbon management procedures Show that reduction targets have been achieved	18	13	Madrid-Barajas Le Bourget Paris Athens Bologna Brussels Dublin Cork Eindhoven Helsinki Frankfurt Hamburg Prague Farnborough

Continued

Table 10.5 Continued

Accreditation level	Number of airports	Share of European passenger traffic (per cent)	Airports
Mapping Determine emissions sources within the operational boundary of the airport company Calculate the annual carbon emissions Compile a carbon footprint report Engage an independent third party to verify the carbon footprint report	24	12	Barcelona Lanzarote ANA (Faro, Flores, Horta, Lisbon, Oporto, Ponta Delgada Santa Maria) Budapest Dresden Dubrovnik Dusseldorf Kristiansand Leipzig Liege Nice Côte d'Azur Shannon TAV Airports Holding (Ankara, Istanbul-Ataturk, Izmir) Toulouse Warsaw Zagreb

Source: ACI Europe (2012)

Environmental issues affect most aspects of airport operations and undoubtedly will become even more important in the future. In spite of technological, operational and other mitigation measures to minimise the environmental impacts, the growth rates being predicted for air transport, if allowed to take place, will mean that the environmental impacts will increase.

This means the concept of environmental capacity will become a central issue. In a purely physical sense an airport's capacity can be defined in a variety of ways, such as the number of runway slots or the capacity of terminals, gates or apron areas. However, it is likely that increasingly in the future environmental capacity, which is set by consideration of the impacts of an airport's operation on the local environment and the lives of residents of local communities, will determine the ultimate overall capacity of an airport. Hence it may well be the environmental capacity of airports that is likely to constrain growth, rather than any physical or financial considerations. In many cases, airports will reach their environmental capacity before making full use of existing infrastructure, and they may not be able to make changes to the physical infrastructure if that involves exceeding the environmental capacity limits. In effect, airports will be able to grow only if they minimise the impact of these expanding activities on the environment and the community. Therefore the aviation industry faces a major challenge in the future. In essence, this challenge is how to maintain economic and social benefits from air transport, encourage economic development through mobility, and yet respond to the increasing environmental pressures being placed on the industry. There is still a great deal of uncertainty as to how this can be achieved.

REFERENCES

ACI (2009) *Guidance Manual: Airport Greenhouse Gas Emissions Management*, Montreal: Airports Council International.

ACI Europe (2012) 'Swedavia becomes the world's first carbon neutral national airport group', press release, 10 October, Brussels: ACI Europe.

ACI North America (2009) *Going Greener: Minimising Airport Environmental Impacts*, Washington, DC: ACI NA.

Berry, F., Gillhespy, S. and Rogers, J. (2008) *ACRP Synthesis Report 10: Airport Sustainability Practices*, Washington, DC: Transportation Research Board.

Budd, T., Ison, S. and Ryley, T. (2011) 'Airport surface access in the UK: a management perspective', *Transportation Business and Management*, 1(1): 109–17.

CAA (1998) *The Single European Aviation Market: The First Five Years*, London: Civil Aviation Authority.

CDM (2011) *ACRP Report 56: Handbook for Considering Practical Greenhouse Gas Emission Reduction Strategies for Airports*, Washington, DC: Transportation Research Board.

CE Delft (2002) *Economic Incentives to Mitigate Green House Gas Emissions from Air Transport in Europe*, Delft: CE Delft.

—— (2008) *Lower NOx at Higher Altitudes Policies to Reduce the Climate Impact of Aviation NOx Emission*, Delft: CE Delft.

Coogan, M. (2008) *ACRP Report 4: Ground Access to Major Airports by Public Transportation*, Washington, DC: Transportation Research Board.

Copenhagen Economics (2012) *Airport Competition in Europe*, Copenhagen: Copenhagen Economics.

Department for Infrastructure and Transport (2011) *Submission to Productivity Commission Inquiry into the Economic Regulation of Airport Services*, Canberra: Department for Infrastructure and Transport.

Department for Transport (2011) *Factsheet 5: Aviation Greenhouse Gas Emissions*, London: DfT.

—— (2012) *AVI0107 – Mode of Transport to Selected UK Airports: Time Series*, London: DfT.

EC (1999) *Air Transport and the Environment: Towards Meeting the Challenges of Sustainable Development*, Com (1999) 640 final, Brussels: EC,

—— (2002a) *Council Directive 02/30/EC of 26 March 2002 on the Establishment of Rules and Procedures with regard to the Introduction of Noise-Related Operating Restrictions at Community Airports*, Official Journal L85 28 March, Brussels: EC

—— (2002b) *Council Directive 02/49/EC of 25 June 2002 relating to the Assessment and Management of Environmental Noise*, Official Journal L189 18 July, Brussels: EC

—— (2008) *Noise Operation Restrictions at EU Airports*, Com (2008) 66 final, Brussels: EC.

—— (2012) *European Advanced Biofuels Flight Path Initiative*. Online. Available HTTP: http://ec.europa. eu/energy/renewables/biofuels/flight_path_en.htm (accessed 30 November 2012).

Edinburgh Airport (2012) *Edinburgh Airport Surface Access Strategy 2012*, Edinburgh: Edinburgh Airport.

MPD Group Ltd (2007) *Study of Aircraft Noise Exposure at and around Community Airports: Evaluation of the Effect of Measures to Reduce Noise*, London: MPD Group Ltd.

Fakiner, H. (2005) 'The role of intermodal transportation in airport management: the perspective of Frankfurt airport', in Delfmann, W., Baum, H., Auerbach, S. and Albers, S. (eds), *Strategic Management in the Aviation Industry*, Farnham: Ashgate.

Girvin, R. (2009) 'Aircraft noise-abatement and mitigation strategies', *Journal of Air Transport Management*, 15(1): 14–22.

Gossling, S. and Upham, P. (2009) *Climate Change and Aviation*, London: Earthscan.

Hazel, R., Blais, J., Browne, T. and Benzon, D. (2011) *Resource Guide to Airport Performance Indicators*, ACRP Report 19A, Washington, DC: Transportation Research Board.

Hooper, P., Heath, B. and Maughan, J. (2003) 'Environmental management and the aviation industry', in Upham, P., Maughan, J., Raper, D. and Thomas, C. (eds), *Towards Sustainable Aviation*, London: Earthscan.

Humphreys, I. and Ison, S. (2005) 'Changing airport employee travel behavior: the role of airport surface access strategies', *Transport Policy* 12(1): 1–5.

Humphreys, I., Ison, S., Francis, G. and Aldridge, K. (2005) 'UK airport surface access targets', *Journal of Air Transport Management*, 11(2): 117–24.

IATA (2009) *A Global Approach to Reducing Aviation Emissions*, Geneva: International Air Transport Association.

ICAO (2010) *Resolution A37–19: Consolidated Statement of Continuing ICAO Policies and Practices Related to Environmental Protection – Climate Change*, Montreal: International Civil Aviation Organization.

Intergovernmental Panel on Climate Change (1999) *Aviation and the Global Atmosphere: Summary for Policymakers*, Geneva: IPCC.

International Transport Forum (2010) *Reducing Transport Greenhouse Gas Emissions*, Paris: ITF.

Ison, S. (2008) 'UK airport car parking management', *Journal of Airport Management*, 3(2): 164–75.

Ison, S., Humphreys, I. and Rye, T. (2007) 'UK airport employee car parking: the role of a charge?', *Journal of Air Transport Management*, 13(3): 163–65.

Scheelhaase, J. (2009) 'Local emission charges – a new economic instrument at German airports', *Journal of Air Transport Management*, 16(2): 94–99.

Schiphol Group (2012) *Annual Report 2011*, Amsterdam: Schiphol Group.

Upham, P. and Mills, J. (2005) 'Environmental and operational sustainability of airports', *Benchmarking: An International Journal*, 12(2): 166–79.

11 Future prospects

A dominant theme running through this book is that airports are going through a period of unprecedented change. Enhanced competitive pressures from airline deregulation and airport privatisation, coupled with increased demands for a more sustainable and quality conscious industry, have brought many new challenges for the airports. New airline models and groupings have emerged. In addition, airports have had to face the unparalleled consequences of a number of unpredictable events, notably 9/11, SARS and swine flu, the LAGS security issue, volcanic ash and the recent global economic crisis. The price of aviation fuel has been another major uncertainty. All of this means that the sector has been operating in a much more volatile and unclear environment and all indications are that this is not going to change in the future. This is likely to lead to more flexibility and adaptability in the way airports are operated, and will result in the industry devising new coping strategies and becoming more experienced and knowledgeable in areas including crisis and recovery management.

One of the most important changes that has occurred within the airport sector is privatisation. While a number of significant airport privatisations have taken place, currently the degree of concentration and private sector involvement within the airport industry is fairly small – much less than in the airline industry. However, more privatisations are planned for the future. This may be in order to finance and develop airports in regions including Asia, Africa and South America, or it may be just to help reduce the sovereign debt problems of governments, particularly in Europe. Whatever the reason, investors are much more cautious than they were in the early days of privatisation, and particularly the number of traditional airport operators who may be interested in getting involved with other airports does not seem likely to expand dramatically. At the same time, though, new investors that were not present in these early stages of privatisation, most notably from the financial sector, are now emerging as dominant players. As the industry evolves, more secondary sales are likely. All this raises the fundamental question – are airports really any different from any other business once the technical and operations know-how has been acquired? It is probably still too early in the evolutionary stage of airport privatisation to answer this question with any degree of certainty, or to identify the factors that will determine the most successful type of airport management or that will bring the greatest value-added in the long run.

The impact of such fundamental structural changes within the airport industry cannot be assessed without considering the parallel airline developments towards deregulation and privatisation.

The post-deregulation environment in many countries has meant that airlines are trying hard to control costs to improve their operating margins, and consequently are exerting greater demands on the airports to control their costs and keep down their level of airport charges. Slower and maturing traffic in some markets, on top of the effects of the economic recession, coupled with unprecedented fuel prices increases, has resulted in such pressures becoming very much greater. The evolution of airline alliances at one extreme and the LCC sector at the other is producing new challenges for airport operators in coping with different types of customer. Such developments are irreversibly changing the traditional airline–airport roles and interactions that have existed for many years.

The creation of airline alliances has meant that airlines are no longer automatically linked to the national airport of the country, and airports can no longer, as before, be guaranteed of their custom. Even if they retain the business of such airlines, the needs and requirements of the customers will be different. Alliance members want to be able to share and achieve cost economies and brand benefits from operating joint facilities at airports. For other airports it may be the emergence of the LCC sector that has been the key driver of change. Naturally, these airlines have a very strong focus on costs which requires appropriate responses from the airport operator. In these and other cases, airports have to devise different strategies to cope with these diverse airlines, and a 'one-size-fits-all' approach is now rarely appropriate. A major consideration in the selection of such strategies must be the associated impact on the non-aeronautical revenues because of the two-sided nature of the business. In short, the challenge here is to balance the airline requirements with optimising commercial revenues while at the same time maintaining a favourable passenger experience.

Undoubtedly the airline and airport industries are operating in a more competitive environment nowadays, and this seems set to continue as more and more markets are deregulated. The actual extent of competition that each airport will face, however, will always remain variable depending on location, the nature of the airlines and their services, and other factors. A major issue within the industry that is becoming more important is consideration of whether airports possess sufficient market power to warrant economic regulation. Experience, particularly in Europe, Australia and New Zealand, has shown that different stakeholders have very contrasting views about this.

Technology developments for essential processes, including check-in, security and border control, potentially can offer considerable advantages to passengers, airlines and airports. Passengers will have simpler and quicker services, airlines will reduce their costs, and airports will be able to use their scarce terminal space more effectively and provide a better quality product. Ultimately how far these technologies can go in producing overall simplified and integrated processes rather than the cumbersome and discrete ones that exist today will depend on many factors, including the cost of the technology; the ability of the different stakeholders to work together and coordinate their efforts; and the ability of governments to reach agreements on very sensitive and important matters concerning national security and immigration. One area of certainty is that the days are long gone when everyone at the airport queued up at a traditional airline desk to check in. It seems very likely that mobile technology, combined with innovations including NFC, will play a major role both in aeronautical and non-aeronautical areas in the future. Technological improvements to airfield and airspace infrastructure, and initiatives including airport collaborative decision-making, should improve efficiency and at the same time reduce some of the undesirable environmental impacts of airports. The evolving e-economy will also continue to have a major impact on the nature of cargo operations at airports, as will industry e-procurement policies.

The more uncertain airport environment makes it increasingly difficult to produce accurate forecasts, but overall most stakeholders are of the view that demand, if accommodated, will grow significantly. Forecasting in the short term is particularly challenging, but the passenger forecasts produced by ICAO in 2012 showed that passenger-km were expected to expand by 6.0 and 6.4 per cent in 2013 and 2014, respectively. The slowest percentage growth for the two years was expected in North America (3.1; 3.5) and Europe (4.4; 4.8) – primarily due to austerity burdens and sovereign debt – with the highest growth being forecast for the Middle East (10.2; 11.0) and Asia/Pacific (8.6; 8.8) (ICAO, 2012). IATA (2012a) forecasted a lower overall tonne-km forecast of 3.7 per cent for 2013, but again with high growth rates in the Middle East (12.3 per cent) and low values in North America (0.4 per cent) and Europe (4.4 per cent).

In the medium term, IATA (2012b) predicted an annual growth rate in passenger numbers of 5.3 per cent per year between 2012 and 2016. Again, the emerging economies of Asia-Pacific, Latin America and the Middle East were forecast to experience the strongest passenger growth, and in particular China was estimated to account for nearly one in four of the additional passengers. The ten fastest-growing international passenger markets were identified as Kazakhstan, Uzbekistan, Sudan, Uruguay, Azerbaijan, Ukraine, Cambodia, Chile, Panama and the Russian Federation. The five fastest-growing international cargo markets were forecast to be Sri Lanka, Vietnam, Brazil, India and Egypt.

In the longer term, ACI is predicting that passenger numbers will increase by around 4 per cent per annum to reach 12 billion by 2031 (ACI/DKMA, 2012) (Table 11.1). ICAO and Boeing have similar forecasts of passenger volume. The manufacturers and ICAO also produce forecasts of passenger-km that are actually more relevant to airlines than airports. These tend to push up by up to 1 per cent per annum, as the average distance flown is predicted to increase and so overall these forecasts are fairly similar to those of ACI. Growth in aircraft movements is likely to be less than growth in passengers, as more larger aircraft, such as the A380, are used and as airlines continue to fly with higher load factors.

As in the past, economic growth, which affects business activity and personal wealth and the cost of travel, will continue to play a major role in shaping the growth in passenger demand. For certain markets, particularly within the United States and Europe, the responsiveness of demand to changes in income may be weakening as demand maturity sets in. Elsewhere, especially in more developing areas of the world, the relatively immature market and higher-than-average predicted economic growth will ensure high growth rates. Of the 6.8 million additional passengers being forecast by ACI for 2031, 87 per cent are associated with emerging economies and only 13 per cent with mature economies. Ongoing liberalisation and higher economic growth in these emerging economies will encourage greater competition, reduce air fares and stimulate demand among large groups of middle-income classes that are developing in a number of these countries. Overall, just 2 per cent growth rates are being predicted for North America and 2.9 per cent for Europe. This European value is actually an average of lower growth in most of the

Table 11.1 Long-term forecasts of global traffic growth

Organisation	Time period	Traffic measure	Average annual growth rate (per cent)
Passengers			
ACI	2012–31	Passengers	4.1
Airbus	2012–31	Passenger-km	4.7
Boeing	2012–31	Passenger-km	5.0
Boeing		Passengers	4.0
Rolls Royce	2012–31	Passenger-km	4.5
ICAO	2005–25	Passenger-km	4.6
ICAO	2005–25	Passengers	4.1
Cargo			
ACI	2012–31	Cargo tonnes	4.5
Airbus	2012–31	Cargo tonne-km	4.9
Boeing	2012–31	Cargo tonne-km	5.2
ICAO	2005–25	Cargo tonne-km	6.6
ICAO	2005–25	Cargo tonnes	5.5
Aircraft movements			
ICAO	2005–25	Aircraft departures	3.6

Sources: ICAO (2007); ACI/DKMA (2012); Airbus (2012); Boeing (2012); Rolls-Royce (2012)

Western European countries, with higher growth in Eastern Europe and Turkey. By contrast, the largest growth rate is for Asia (6 per cent), led by China which is forecast to account for 2.6 billion passengers by 2031, but also for other countries including India, Indonesia and Vietnam. Latin America/Caribbean, the Middle East and Africa are all also expected to see growth rates of around 5 per cent. Brazil, with events including the World Cup (2014) and the Olympics (2016), will be one of the major drivers of demand in Latin America. Meanwhile, Middle Eastern traffic will continue to grow significantly as a result of the region's convenient location, a huge guest worker population in need of air travel, predicted economic and tourism growth, and a young population with the potential to travel in the future. Some African countries are also experiencing strong economic growth and this, combined with tourism development and poor ground transport links, is likely to cause higher-than-average growth in the future (Figure 11.1). Overall, these trends will result in the Asia/Pacific market having a market share of 41 per cent in 2031, followed by Europe (23 per cent) and North America (19 per cent), which is considerably different from the global split shown in Figure 1.1 where the three regions had similar traffic volumes (Figure 11.2).

Cargo traffic is generally expected to increase at a faster rate than passenger traffic, again with Asia/Pacific markets having the highest average growth rates. Air cargo demand is also driven primarily by economic growth and travel cost, as well as international trade. Higher growth is generally expected because of globalisation trends that have led to increased reliance on global components and products that need to be transported around the world. The rapidly expanding knowledge-based industrial sectors, including computing, electronics, communications and

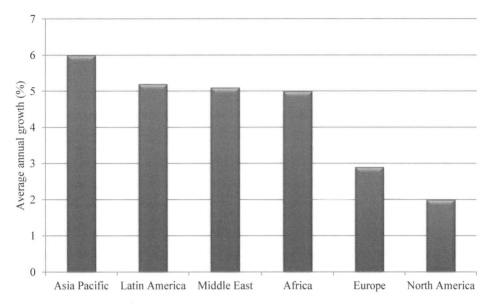

Figure 11.1 *Airport passenger growth forecasts by region, 2012–13*
Source: ACI/DKMA (2012)

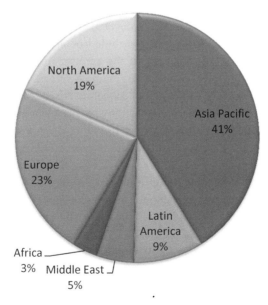

Figure 11.2 *Airport passenger forecasts by region, 2031*
Source: ACI/DKMA (2012)

pharmaceuticals, are the most international and are heavily reliant on air travel for the transportation of their high-value/low-weight products. Increasing reliance on just-in-time inventory systems favours air cargo. E-commerce has also brought substantial reductions in the distribution costs of air cargo and increased demand for the integrators and the express mail sector.

If this growth in both passenger and cargo traffic is to be accommodated, there is a need for much more airport capacity. In the United States it was estimated that 18 airports will need additional capacity by 2015 and 27 by 2025 (FAA, 2007). Elsewhere in Europe, it has been estimated that 10 per cent of the potential demand will not be accommodated by 2030 because of capacity shortfalls. There will be 19 airports operating at full capacity, with airports such as London Heathrow, London Gatwick, Paris Orly, Milan Linate and Dusseldorf being worst affected. Other airports, including Amsterdam, Madrid, Munich, Rome Fiumicino and Vienna, are also likely to have major capacity problems (EC, 2011). While the recent dampening of demand has given airports some breathing space, the problems have not gone away. In the short term a more effective slot-allocation process might alleviate some of the capacity bottlenecks. Secondary and regional airports could also take some of the growth away from major airports, as they have already done, and so could high-speed rail.

However, in the long term there will be a need to expand airport capacity if the forecast demand levels are to be realised. This is very challenging for a number of reasons. First, the finance for such development needs to be found. Many funds traditionally came from public sources, but increasingly this sector is unable or unwilling to provide such support, especially in today's economic climate. Privatisation may yield a solution in some, but not all, cases. In certain countries where there is strong political will to develop air transport, as in China for instance, airport expansion can be agreed swiftly and with little trouble. The same is true of a number of other Asian countries. The development of the aerotropolis Dubai World Central with Al Maktoum International Airport is a similar example (albeit that this project has been revised and slowed down because of the global economic crisis). Meanwhile in other regions it can take years for airports to gain approval through the planning process which can be excessively long and costly. It can often take over 10 years for the process for expanded airport facilities, and even longer if a new greenfield site airport is being considered. The London Heathrow terminal 5 inquiry in the late 1990s in the United Kingdom lasted more than 4 years and was one of the longest planning enquiries in UK history. Overall, the whole planning process took 14 years. Extra runway capacity for the London area is now also being considered, again likely to be a very long exercise. Likewise the planning process for Munich airport took 22 years. Other examples include the new parallel runway at Seattle airport which opened in 2008. This was 20 years after it had received initial approval by the local authorities, with the delays being due to environmental objections and a number of lawsuits filed by local residents. Very few new airports or fully expanded airports have been built in the United States or Europe in recent years, Denver, Munich, Oslo, Athens and Milan being the only examples (Berlin is another, but the opening has been postponed). Elsewhere, in Narita in Tokyo the second runway was opposed for over 10 years by local politicians and farmers, and eventually was approved but with a shorter length. And in Auckland it took 7 years to get the second runway approved.

Without doubt, the greatest challenge that the airport sector, and indeed the whole air transport industry, faces is coping with the expected traffic growth while at the same time living with the huge pressures to reduce global warming and achieve greater sustainability. At a local level, issues related to quality of life have to be balanced against desires for greater mobility. The more extreme environmentalists will continue to argue that there is no way the potential demand for air transport in the future should be met, and that the solution is to constrain growth. Others hold less radical views, but most agree that the industry has to focus much of its effort and resources on developing sustainable solutions if it is to be allowed to grow at all to meet increasing traffic levels.

In conclusion, airport operators face a challenging time ahead. The volatile operating conditions of the past decade or so show no signs of disappearing, with economic downturns, political instability and natural adverse events likely to continue to play a major role. Increasingly airport operators are being confronted with conflicting demands from their different stakeholders. Different airline groupings and types of airline are favouring more differentiated facilities and services, and putting increasing pressures on airports to reduce their costs. Airline customers are also changing more frequently, with the modern-day operating environment encouraging more airline failures. Passenger expectations in terms of service quality are rising. Regional authorities want to ensure airports generate maximum economic benefits while not harming the wellbeing of the population in the region. National governments want to ensure the environment and society are adequately protected, and may also want to guarantee, perhaps through regulation, that airports are not abusing any excessive market power and are not acting in an anti-competitive manner. Then there are the financial demands from the airport owners or shareholders, which are increasingly driven by private sector motives. Finally, everyone wants the airport to provide a secure, safe and healthy environment, which has arguably become more difficult to achieve in recent years because of the new security and health risks that now exist. This book considers all these important interrelated issues and aims to provide some insight into how airport operators might address the challenges of the future.

REFERENCES

ACI/DKMA (2012) *20 Year Outlook: Expansion lead by Economies outside Europe and North America*, Montreal: ACI/DKMA.

Airbus (2012) *Global Market Forecast 2012–2031*, Toulouse: Airbus.

Boeing (2012) *Current Market Outlook 2012–2031*, Seattle: Boeing.

EC (2011) *Communication from the Commission on Airport Policy in the European Union – Addressing Capacity and Quality to Promote Growth, Connectivity and Sustainable Mobility*, COM(2011) 823 final, Brussels: EC.

FAA (2007) *Capacity Needs in the National Airspace System 2007–25*, Washington, DC: Federal Aviation Authority.

IATA (2012a) *Industry Financial Forecast December 2012*, Geneva: International Air Transport Association.

—— (2012b) 'Airlines to welcome 3.6 billion passengers in 2016', press release, 6 December. Online. Available HTTP <http://www.iata.org/pressroom/pr/pages/2012-12-06-01.aspx (accessed 10 December 2012).

ICAO (2007) *Outlook for Air Transport to the Year 2025*, Montreal: International Civil Aviation Organization.

—— (2012) *Medium-Term Passenger Traffic Forecasts*. Online. Available HTTP <http://www.icao.int/sustainability/pages/eap_fp_forecastmed.aspx> (accessed 10 December 2012).

Rolls-Royce (2012) *Market Outlook 2012–2031*. Online. Available HTTP <http://www.rolls-royce.com/civil/customers/market_outlook.jsp> (accessed 10 December 2012).

Index

Note: Page numbers in **bold** type refer to **figures**
Page numbers in *italic* type refer to *tables*